Lucky Him
The Life of Kingsley Amis

Lucky Him

The Life of Kingsley Amis

RICHARD BRADFORD

PETER OWEN
London and Chester Springs

828.91409
B799

PETER OWEN PUBLISHERS
73 Kenway Road, London SW5 0RE

Peter Owen books are distributed in the USA by
Dufour Editions Inc., Chester Springs, PA 19425-0007

First published in Great Britain 2001
© Richard Bradford 2001

ISBN 0 7206 1117 2

A catalogue record for this book is available from
the British Library.

Printed and bound in Great Britain by
MPG Books Ltd, Bodmin, Cornwall

To Amy Burns
Lucky me

Acknowledgements

First of all, thanks are due to Martin Amis and Zachary Leader for allowing me to see the originals of Kingsley Amis's letters before publication. A number of people have kindly offered me their time, attention and memories in interviews, and in this respect I am particularly grateful to Martin Amis and Elizabeth Jane Howard for their help. Esmund Cleary, Sam Dawson and James Michie offered enlightening anecdotes and recollections. Robert Conquest was good enough to reply to my enquiries by post.

At the University of Ulster Professor Robert Welch and Beth Holmes have provided practical assistance. Peter Owen, Antonia Owen and their colleagues have done an excellent job. Thanks are due finally to Amy Burns who has put up with a lot.

All illustrations herein, except where otherwise attributed, come from the Amis collection, copyright Lady Kilmarnock. While every effort has been made to obtain permission from owners of copyright material reproduced I apologize for any omissions and will be pleased to incorporate missing acknowledgements in any future editions.

Contents

List of Illustrations

between pages 224 and 225

Introduction

A T the beginning of his authorized biography of Kingsley Amis Eric Jacobs makes it clear that this will be the life of a writer and not an interpretation of his life through his writings. The only novels and poems he will treat as autobiographical will be the very few which are transparently so. The rest, the majority, are inventions and the territory of literary critics, not biographers.

Amis himself frequently affirmed that his fiction was certainly not based upon his life. His longest and most elaborate note of denial was an essay he did for the *Times Literary Supplement* in 1973 called 'Real and Made Up People'. He states that some parallels are obvious and hardly worth comment, such as the fact that Jim Dixon of *Lucky Jim* was, like his creator, a young, poorly paid academic in a provincial university. He admits that one of his novels, but only one, was 'out of laziness or sagging imagination' based almost entirely upon actual people and events and is as a consequence 'by common consent my worst . . . *I Like It Here*'. The rest, he acknowledges, have been influenced by his experiences and temperament, but overall, invention has superseded imitation. He has no particular objection to writers who fictionalize fact, but this practice has obvious limitations. 'The writer whose direct experience gives him one satisfactory novel (as opposed to a short or very short story) in fifty years is very lucky' (*The Amis Collection*, p. 3).

One begins to suspect that he protests too much, and the example he gives of how life can rarely provide enough material for fiction is, to say the least, suggestive.

> If in life, his marriage breaks down, he takes off with somebody else, has difficulties with her and with his children and finally returns home, or stays away, he has little hope of writing about that experience and these people and coming through with a novel. (p. 3)

This is a candid summary of the life of Kingsley Amis from 1963 to 1973 from which he 'came through' not with 'a novel' but four. He worked hard and quite successfully at obscuring the autobiographical thread that runs through these books, deflecting the truffle-hunter's attention with narratives and scenarios that could only have been invented – in *The Green Man*, for instance, the main character's marital problems are sidelined by visits from God and an agent of Satan. At the same time, in each novel a particular relationship, sometimes an unsteady one, underpins the more prominent themes and plotlines, and this relationship is a version of his own with his second wife, Elizabeth Jane Howard.

In what follows I shall treat Amis's fiction as one of the most entertaining and thought-provoking autobiographies ever produced. With regard to facts, the novels disclose little more than can be found in Jacobs, in Amis's *Memoirs* and *Letters* and in the various interviews and profiles that attended his literary career. They offer a supplement to what is known, something less tangible and more intriguing. In most there is a self-portrait, sometimes accompanied by a confession, a projection of what might have been or, less frequently, an act of revenge or self-justification. He will alter experience not only to disguise it, and not quite beyond recognition for those who knew him, but also to allow himself space for conjecture, as a means of exploring his thoughts about his life.

Jacobs's career in investigative journalism is reflected in his considerable use of background research and interviews. He maintains an air of impartiality, but inevitably this would have been compromised by the fact that he talked with Amis about the work in progress. I have found no evidence to suggest that Amis censored or altered the available facts, while at the same time it is clear that Jacobs was in awe of his subject. When Amis engaged Jacobs as his authorized biographer his own *Memoirs* (1991) had just been published and in the preface to these he states bluntly that 'those who know both [the novels] and me will also know that they are firmly unautobiographical' (p. xv). Jacobs in his own preface implies that this left him with few options regarding the relationship between the life and the work. He states that they 'argued a good deal about this'. 'I thought I had found traces of him where he did not think they existed', but eventually they reached 'a compromise' which, as Jacobs half concedes, favoured Amis's opinion. If the compromise was inaccurate then 'I can only say it would have been terrifyingly more so if I had been left to interpret his novels on my own' (p. xii). In short, Amis got his way.

Obviously, given that Jacobs was soon to put together a very candid account of his life, misdeeds and imperfections included, Amis was not maintaining the fiction-is-fiction line because he wanted to protect secrets. What he did wish to protect was something more intimate than his behavioural characteristics, something that most writers try to keep to themselves – how and why they produced their work.

In a 1969 review of Roth's *Portnoy's Complaint* Amis almost accuses Roth of discrediting the profession of writing through his lazy and self-indulgent use of fiction as stylized disclosure. Amis cites Lawrence as a licensing influence. Since Lawrence,

> it has become all right to supplement the deficiencies of one's personal life as source material, not by rearranging it, editing it and

13

extrapolating from it, but merely by coating it with style and tone of voice. (*What Became of Jane Austen?*, p.108)

Intriguingly, Amis does not dismiss the use of life as fiction; rather, he implies that extravagant transparency is inimical to the essential qualities of the novel. 'Rearranging', 'editing' and 'extrapolating', effectively the confection of an elegant disguise, is the correct policy, and Amis's novels are a testament to this critical maxim.

It would be possible to raise all manner of questions about whether or not the reader should be left to come to his or her own conclusions about the relationship between the life and the work of a writer, but I will not, because in Amis's case the answers are self-evident. It will not be my intention to treat his writings as a kind of diary in code. That, inevitably, would diminish their purely literary value, compromise their deserved status as original and brilliantly crafted contributions to post-war English fiction. Paradoxically, Amis's fears regarding the disclosure of his blend of autobiography and invention are not only unfounded but counter-extensive to his reputation as a writer. As I shall show, there is a dynamic relationship between what he did, thought, experienced and what he wrote. He did not use his personal world, internal and external, as a substitute for imaginative effort; quite the contrary. His literary skills were tested and extended in their dealings with the confounding, puzzling panorama of his life. At the same time it is impossible to offer a comprehensive picture of Amis the man, as husband, philanderer, friend, father, jester, son, boozer, agnostic, pseudo-socialist and club-land Tory, without considering the relationship between what we know and that private world in which what he knew was re-examined, remodelled and written.

As the contents page indicates, I have, while following the chronology of Amis's life, subdivided much of it according to the publication dates of his novels, his disguised autobiography. Consequently the book involves some unusual synchronizations of real, fictionalized and recollected time. For example, while Part 1 deals with the basics of Amis's childhood and youth in Norbury, the more intriguing elements of his early relationship with his father, at least as he perceived them, feature in Part 3, Chapter 15, on *The Riverside Villas Murder*. This novel, written when Amis was fifty, is a candid remembrance of teenage rebellion against paternal authority disguised as a murder story. In his *Memoirs* Amis avoids potentially unsettling accounts of his relationship with Hilly, particularly during the 1940s and 1950s. Instead, these feature both in *Take a Girl Like You* (1960) and *You Can't Do Both* (1994), the latter involving the story of their early courtship, her pregnancy and their eventual decision not to have a then illegal abortion. While my version of Amis's life attends to the events as they occurred, it pays equal attention to his own revisitations of them, sometimes decades later.

PART 1

BEFORE JIM

1

Norbury

KINGSLEY Amis was born in a south London nursing home on
16 April 1922. It was Easter Sunday, an early spring day of
characteristically English temperament: torrential rain driven by
cold winds. He was an only child, and from infant to late teenage
years he lived with his parents, 'Peggy' (Rosa Anne, née Lucas) and
William Amis at 16 Buckingham Gardens, Norbury, London SW16.

Shortly after *The Old Devils* had won him the Booker Prize in
1986, the BBC commissioned Amis to do a kind of televisual autobiography, with the camera following the distinguished author
through the important sites of his previous six decades. Buckingham Gardens and indeed the whole physical environment of suburban Norbury had not changed very much, and Amis on camera
seemed to find a peculiar satisfaction in the fact that Number 16
was one of those houses that beggars architectural description – the
kind of post-First World War semi-detached that would be immediately forgettable had it not been reproduced thousands of times in
suburbs all over England. And he appeared agreeably amused that
the present resident, while pleased to have her home on television,
was obviously puzzled by why exactly its previous occupant
deserved to be accompanied by a BBC camera crew.

Amis did not say very much, but his sidelong glances at camera
invited speculation on what he was thinking. The air of timeless

boredom offered by Norbury and the lady's friendly ignorance must have struck him as a sardonic and very apposite comment on his own memories.

Comedy was an ever-present and unobtrusive feature of all of Amis's fiction. He wrote novels about age, murder, the afterlife, Christianity and totalitarianism, and he could capture the habits and moods of contemporary society with crisp veracity, but his signature, his trademark, was the thread of humour that ran through everything he produced. He came to believe that fiction that was not slightly irreverent was the equivalent of philosophy in disguise. When reading his novels, we are continuously aware of a presence which hovers behind and around the narrator, always ready to pounce and never willing to allow a piece of dialogue or a solemn proclamation of intent to get past without first puncturing whatever pretension to absolute validity it might carry with it. Nash, a psychiatrist in *Stanley and the Women*, his most depressing and least amusing book, allows us a glimpse into Amis's most essential literary precept: 'The rewards for being sane may not be very many but knowing what's funny is one of them. And that's an end of the matter.'

So when the Booker-winning author returned to his childhood home to find he had become anonymous, we witness a sardonic smile beginning to form; he could have written this himself. Moreover, the incident might also have reminded him of aspects of his time in Norbury. His experiences, before going up to St John's College, Oxford, aged nineteen, were largely unremarkable, but normality and routine were frequently attended by degrees of absurdity and farce.

He began school at St Hilda's, within walking distance of his home, and his enduring memory was the sense of shock at finding himself in the presence of so many other people who were apparently the same age and size as himself, some of a different sex. Before that, as an only child with distant cousins, he had imagined that children were single units attached only to larger groups of adults. And his new-found peers turned out to be unfathomable perversions of their elder counterparts. On the first day in the playground a boy called John Skelton bit him on the arm. And within a few weeks he was introduced to fundamentalist religion by a Roman Catholic boy who informed him that God was everywhere, under chairs, down the street and always watching him. His parents, non-practising Baptists, had never mentioned this.

Amis's parents were an intriguing couple because, when compared with the rest of their respective families, they were astonishingly normal. Amis's account in his *Memoirs* of this 'other' family, beyond the comfortable routines of Norbury, is tinged with disbelief. For the child, these figures must have unsettled any standard perception of conventional adulthood.

Kingsley's paternal grandfather was called officially Joseph James Amis but was known to the family, 'perhaps with a hint of satire', as 'Pater' or more frequently 'Dadda'. Dadda lived in Purley, about an hour from Norbury, with his wife Julia ('Mater') in an upmarket Victorian residence equipped with two maids. Amis would be taken there for meals at Christmas and for family birthdays.

Amis can never recall Dadda addressing him directly, but he can remember being obliged to kiss both of his grandparents who apparently had an almost equal preponderance of facial hair. He also remembers how Dadda would sit at the head of the table, napkin stuffed into his shirt collar, and between savage bouts of eating and drinking tell jokes which combined the vulgar with the surreal. The actual presence of Dadda would have been disturbing enough, but this was later supplemented by William's account to the teenaged Kingsley of how Dadda had effectively ruined the family business. J.J. Amis & Co. were glassware wholesalers, and Dadda had on one occasion become convinced that he had access to a brand of unbreakable plates, glasses and related domestic paraphernalia. To test his thesis, or perhaps just to entertain the family, Dadda once crept into the drawing-room and hurled one of the items at the stone fireplace, a performance he repeated for potential clients in the company office. He was on all occasions apparently both surprised and disappointed when these products disintegrated. Mater was equally peculiar but far more disagreeable. Her legendary meanness involved the leaving out of only two matches for the maids to light the gas in the morning and the substitution of grocer's bags for lavatory paper.

Amis's mother's sister, Dora, went mad, officially. Amis remembers, aged about eleven, sitting with her in his parents' kitchen. She kept asking him to move his chair away from the window so that she could 'see if there's anyone out there'. This sense of anticipating something quite dreadful, apocalyptic but never clearly specified, attended Dora's entire existence, and eventually, in 1941, she was committed to a mental hospital. Apparently she flourished in this environment, virtually taking over the running of the kitchen from the employees. On the day she heard of her mother's death her neurotic symptoms, already in abeyance, disappeared for good, and within a year she was taken on as a middle-rank administrator in the same hospital.

Amis's father's brother, Leslie, replaced Dadda as manager of the ailing J. J. Amis & Co. Glassware and after Dadda's death was responsible for the increasingly unpleasant Mater. Amis liked Leslie and was saddened by 'his horrible life'. In his late teens Amis was approached by his father with some apparently disturbing news. Leslie had told his brother that he wanted to go to bed with men, and William had advised him to 'see a doctor'. No one knew if Leslie's homosexual instincts were real or hypothetical, but in any event when Mater died everything changed. Leslie sold the business premises and invested his inherited capital in a world cruise, during which he 'fucked every female in sight'. Two years later he was dead.

Freudians would no doubt have had a field-day with all of this, but we can leave its effect upon Amis to common sense. His aunt, mother's side, and his uncle, father's side, had reconciled themselves to their own identity only after the death of their last parent. Amis, by the time he left home, would know that he had already embarked upon a very effective strategy of independence. '[A]s I came to sense the image in which my father was trying to mould my character and future I began to resist him, and we quarrelled violently at least every week or two for years' (*Memoirs*, p. 14). Amis in the *Memoirs* concedes, if only implicitly, that his father *did* play a vital role in the shaping of his tastes and character. He operated as a foil, a testing ground, for enthusiasms and inclinations that Kingsley would acquire independently.

Music was a constant source of conflict. William regarded Duke Ellington's jazz as evocative of dark-skinned savages dancing round a pot of human remains and much classical music, without the human voice, as a form of grandiose self-indulgence. Amis Senior preferred Gilbert and Sullivan. Kingsley's early encounters with Mozart, Haydn, Schubert and, particularly, American jazz were instinctive and unfocused. But after fractious exchanges with his father he took on the role of learned polemicist, which he never really abandoned.

William was once a Liberal who turned into an arch-Tory after the Great War, an affiliation strengthened by the General Strike and the emergence of the Labour Party as a serious contender for power. Amis himself, summarizing his father's view of him, became a 'bloody little fool of a leftie' and an avid supporter of Joseph Stalin. Unlike his love for music, which was transparent and unflagging, Amis's political opinions were always reactive, shifting, often self-contradictory, a condition that owed something to his early instinct to rebel against anything his father espoused.

Their arguments were on Kingsley's part rooted in a level of self-willed alienation. 'What my father wanted me to be was, of

course, a version of William Robert Amis, a more successful version
. . .' (*Memoirs*, p. 17). After war service spent tending airships in
Scotland, William Amis had joined Colman's, the mustard manu-
facturers, as a junior clerk, where he stayed, gradually acquiring
seniority, until retirement. Kingsley never regarded his father as a
failure, but he hated the idea that success involved, at least for people of his own lower-middle-class origins, a future in the higher
regions of banking or commerce.

Amis's early life was an assembly of adult narratives, stories of a
potential future, all of which he strenuously avoided and rejected.
But what was their alternative?

At St Hilda's Primary School Amis was introduced to literature
by a Miss Barr, a 'tall, Eton cropped figure of improbable elegance'.
He cannot recall the texts promoted by Miss Barr, but after moving
to Norbury College, a local state school with ambitions, he encountered Mr Ashley who employed what was in those days a radical
method of teaching English. Ashley made them read Shakespeare
and then had them contrast this with almost contemporary poetry,
mostly the verse of the Georgians. He also believed that for his
pupils to properly understand and appreciate literature they should
attempt to write it. Aged ten, Amis had written ninety-nine lines of
blank verse and a 300-word short story, published in the school
magazine, on Captain Hartly, a 'veteran hunter' of rhino.

In 1934, aged twelve, Amis went to the City of London School,
an institution of solid academic reputation which took boys of various backgrounds. His father and his uncle Leslie had been pupils.
William paid for his first year there, gambling on Kingsley's securing
of a scholarship, which he did in his next year. At the school middle-
class fee-payers mixed with a large number of scholarship boys, and
for Amis his six years there were like university and often better. He
was taught Latin and Greek poetry in a way that encouraged him to
enjoy its distant beauty and to recognize that poetry *per se* tran-
scended linguistic difference. He discovered Housman, whose verse

he would treasure, even more than his friend Larkin's, for the rest of his life. And he talked with the Reverend C.J. Ellingham, a unequivocal Christian, of how Housman's agnostic inclinations mattered little in comparison with the sheer quality of his verse: 'so I saw for ever that a poem is not a statement and the poet "affirmeth nothing"'. A Mr Marsh would lend out editions of verse by Auden and MacNeice; Eliot and Pound were talked about by masters and pupils.

With his peers Amis discussed sex, radical politics, French verse, Fats Waller, Delius, Charles Morgan and sex. Fifteen per cent of the boys were Jewish, but Amis claims to have never encountered anti-Semitism nor even its polite middle-class version.

The City of London School provided a cosmopolitan contrast to Amis's family life. His parents had little time for 'serious' literature. His mother, Peggy, enjoyed the work of contemporary novelists such as Ursula Bloom, Norah C. James and Ann Bridge, which, in Amis's view, were not 'the classics but not "slop" either'. When Kingsley seemed to have little else to do Peggy would encourage him to 'do a bit of writing', although he was never quite certain of what she imagined he would write. William read detective novels 'by such as R. Austin Freeman, Francis Greirson and John Rhode from the middle part of the spectrum'. The only member of his family whose interests corresponded with Kingsley's growing awareness of mainstream literature was his maternal grandfather, George Lucas. Lucas died before Amis was old enough to talk with him about books, but Peggy provided her son with an anecdote which must have seemed consistent with the tragi-comic mythology of the rest of his extended family. His grandfather would read out his favourite passages to his wife, who, when his head was lowered to the page, would make faces and gestures at him indicating various expressions of boredom, ridicule and contempt. This, says Amis, 'helped to make me hate her very much'. And we might recall that this was the woman whose death had caused her mad daughter to regain almost instantaneous sanity.

It would stretch credibility to cite too many direct channels of influence between Amis's early life and his writing, but some parallels are evident enough. Housman became his favourite poet and he also, at CLS, discovered the novels of G. K. Chesterton. Characteristically, Chesterton would use witty and often disturbing paradoxes to startle his readers, to disrupt the comfortable expectation of what a character was really like or what would happen next. Amis's favourites, from his early teens onwards, were *The Napoleon of Notting Hill* (1904) and *The Man Who Was Thursday* (1908). Both novels defy easy categorization. They mix the genres of fantasy and science fiction with political diagnosis and a style that reflects contemporary habits and locutions. Amis in such middle-period novels as *The Green Man* (1969) and *The Alteration* (1976) would do something similar, but his attraction to Chesterton ran much deeper than that because his childhood was in itself not unlike a mixed-genre narrative. His world seemed to be comprised of not quite compatible segments of experience, but he found that he was able to drift between them without much effort or distress.

In only two of his novels did Amis engage directly with his pre-Oxford life. The first of these, *The Riverside Villas Murder* (1973), is ostensibly a detective story set in the mid-1930s in a suburban area not unlike Norbury. At its centre, however, is the relationship between Kingsley the teenager and his father, recollected a decade after the latter's death. *You Can't Do Both* (1994), Amis's penultimate novel, is more transparently autobiographical, focusing on the significant events of his life from childhood to the early 1960s. In this he implicitly acknowledges that in his previous accounts of his relationship with his parents his mother is always in the background. This, to his regret, is how he tended to recall her, given that the hostilities between father and son would always feature as the most memorable contrast to the otherwise unremarkable routines of life in Norbury. In fact Peggy Amis, in an albeit unassertive and almost diplomatic manner, played an important part in Amis's early years. Throughout his life Amis had a fear of complete darkness, made worse when he was alone. It began when he was about eight, and Peggy, with a good deal of shrewd and tolerant understanding, would help him through what in modern parlance are called panic attacks. She would also function not exactly as a referee but more as a counterbalancing presence, a friend to both parties, in the disagreements between Amis and his father, a day-to-day activity that would prepare her for the more demanding role of negotiator. Two events, the first involving his affair with a married woman and the second the pre-marital pregnancy of his eventual wife, would cause William to ostracize his then adult son. Peggy brought them back together, and in *You Can't Do Both* Amis repays the debt.

Amis's first period away from his parents was caused by the war. Months before it was declared, the CLS had made arrangements to evacuate its central London premises in expectation of the city becoming the target for German bombers. Marlborough College in Wiltshire agreed to share its buildings and grounds with CLS, and in late August 1939 staff and pupils, the latter allowed one large suit-case each, boarded the train from Blackfriars Station to Paddington and there changed to the Taunton Express.

Amis recalls the experience as both sinister and exciting. War would not be officially declared until 3 September, but most people were aware of its inevitability. The famous 'Walls Have Ears' posters advising everyone to remain discreet about practically everything, given that Hitler's agents might be listening in, would not appear for a year, but CLS pre-empted them. Apart from the senior masters no one knew where they were going. The train made an unscheduled stop at Savernake, a few miles from Marlborough. They had arrived but, until later that day when officially informed by the masters, Amis and his friends did not know quite where they were.

Amis never made use of the actuality of these events in his

fiction, but one suspects that his remembrance of the atmosphere created by them informs the texture of his mid-period novel *The Anti-Death League* (1966). In both, the metropolis and the comfortable home counties are visited by a blend of secrecy and subdued anxiety.

Autumn 1939 to early summer 1940 at Marlborough was Amis's final year at school, and it influenced his adulthood in a number of ways.

For the first time in his life he had the opportunity, indeed the obligation, to properly get to know people outside the family home. Leonard Richenberg, then head of CLS school, shared a room with Amis in a decrepit, unheated farmworker's cottage just outside the school grounds. Richenberg, together with Peter Baldwin, George Blunden, Cyril Metliss and Saul Rose, became Amis's closest friends. He had, of course, known them before, but all were now detached from their families; they spent their days and evenings in each other's company. Marlborough was for Amis a rehearsal for Oxford. He became the figure whose intelligence was respected by his peers but who seemed intent on making everything a lot less serious, more absurd and amusing than it might appear to be. The recollections of his friends are both affectionate and accurately inconsistent. Blunden remembers him as someone who 'set the standards of cultural and intellectual activity . . . the intellectual star', Metliss as 'a great mimic and full of fun' (Jacobs, p. 60).

When interviewed by Eric Jacobs, all five of Amis's school friends stated that when they read *Lucky Jim* it was as though they had been returned to the atmosphere of Marlborough, with Amis the at once iconoclastic, hilarious and confidently clever leader of their group. Amis the man would, reinforced by Marlborough, become a puzzling combination of an intellectual and an anti-intellectual farceur, but it was fifteen years before he realized that this blending would be the essence of his early success as a writer.

Marlborough was one of England's senior public schools. Its

pupils, then all fee-paying, came from a class above Amis and his CLS pals; they were the sons of QCs, landowners, rich, socially aspirant businessmen and minor aristocrats. The CLS boys were treated by their hosts with a mixture of arrogance and condescending politeness. While Amis and his friends were from comfortably-off homes he felt that the tension between themselves and the haughtily distant pupils of Marlborough was like something out of Dickens, people who existed in the world mixing uneasily with people who thought they owned it.

It was Amis's first real encounter with the pre-war English class system. His family, Norbury and the CLS incorporated various strands of lower-middle-class London with relatively slight variations in lifestyles, speech patterns and levels of income. His own accent was inherited from his father. It was what used to be referred to as 'BBC English' involving an unflamboyant attention to 'correct' grammar and habits of pronunciation. It was neutrally middle class, suggesting a comfortable enough background but invoking no clear affiliation to a particular region nor any obvious political allegiance. As such it became the ideal foundation for Amis's talents as a mimic, a bare canvas on to which he could project all manner of caricatures and representations. He began to perfect these at Marlborough.

The evacuation of CLS had created something like a bizarre socio-linguistic experiment. The college was not attached to a town of any size, and outside it the quaint verbal mannerisms of the West Country predominated. A regiment of middle-class Londoners had suddenly created an unusual counterbalance to the stark contrast between the upper-class drawl of most of the college boys and the differently relaxed burr of the surrounding district. Amis thrived on this. It made him more aware than he had previously been of how the way people sound is as much a feature of their perceived personality as the way they look and what they actually say. He started paying closer attention to how vocal habits merged with temperamental and physical attributes, and his unnervingly accurate imitations of the CLS masters had his co-evacuees in stitches. As a means of becoming one of a crowd his talent would prove very useful in Oxford, but more significantly he would eventually recognize it as not incompatible with his intellectual astuteness, and out of this Jim Dixon would be born.

More predictably, the class divisions of Marlborough encouraged Amis's affiliation to Marxism. Despite the fact that both schools now existed in the same place, he could not remember anything resembling a conversation with one of the Marlborough boys – their choice apparently. He recalls that they behaved as though their privileged part of the world had been invaded by individuals who, simply because of their background, did not deserve to be there. The officer/other ranks structure of the army would a few years later further provoke his anger.

This was his last year at school. His masters knew that he would go to Oxbridge and that he was capable of winning an exhibition or scholarship. He had to, given that his parents could not afford to pay his fees. There were far more classics prizes available than for any other single humanities discipline, and Amis was recognized as the best classics scholar in CLS. But he chose to read English Literature. There were few English scholarships at either of the old universities, and his choice caused him to spend a year after leaving school at home with his parents. Competition was fierce, and he would not secure an Oxford exhibition until 1941.

2

Oxford and Larkin

A MIS arrived in Oxford just before his nineteenth birthday in April 1941. Freshmen would normally arrive in October, but this was wartime. The traditional academic calendar had been abandoned in favour of a shortened curriculum, with undergraduates beginning, graduating or deferring the completion of their degree for military service more or less at random.

So when Amis 'came up', the experience carried with it an air of anxious unreality, rather like joining a group of his peers in a railway station waiting-room served only by a capricious, ever-changing timetable.

Amis had won an exhibition, 'a kind of cut-price scholarship', to read English at St John's College. Without this award university for Kingsley would have been well beyond his parents' financial means, and his decision to do English was regarded by his schoolmasters with a mixture of surprise and tolerant support. There were dozens of Open Scholarships in Classics, but for English, still a relatively new university subject, there were only two at Oxford and two at Cambridge. In 1940 he had sat for one of the Cambridge prizes and failed.

Amis was given a 'nasty little pair of rooms' in the front quad. Most of his contemporaries were obliged to share, the New Quad being occupied by civil servants doing secret work that everyone knew involved the administration of the white fish and potato ration – earning St John's the nickname of Fish and Chips.

Wartime Oxford was a city in a state of suspense and disguise. St John's, like the rest of the colleges, had taken on the dreary uniform of the blitz. Fire buckets, extinguishers and sandbags decorated the staircases and quads, and the mullioned windows had tape on the glass and black-out curtains on the frames. Rumour had it that Hitler was about to supplement his saturation bombing of the major urban centres with morale-sapping raids on the glittering prizes. Oxford was never bombed, but college life reflected an atmosphere of imminent catastrophe, with every undergraduate obliged to do an all-night 'fire-watching' stint every ten days or so.

No other CLS boys had gone up to St John's, but the dozen or so in the rest of the university welcomed Amis in his first week with a sherry party, held next door in Balliol. This, he recalled, was his first experience of extreme drunkenness. He tells in his *Memoirs* of how, after staggering back to his St John's rooms, he had had his vomiting session interrupted by canvassers for the Oxford University Conservative Association. Taking account of the chamber pot on his lap, their spokesman politely acknowledged that 'perhaps we had better return at a more convenient time'. Amis began telling this unconfirmed story in the 1980s when the Conservatives had certainly returned, for himself and everyone else. But perhaps this is merely a coincidence.

In the same week Amis recognized in St John's one of his Cambridge co-failures from the previous year, Norman Iles, and forty years later he remembered him with a fair degree of loathing. Iles, according to Amis, was a cross between a *Brideshead* throwback and a self-promoting vandal. Iles, also reading English, mocked the degree course and its teachers – charlatans in his view – and advocated a general avoidance of lectures, tutorials and essays. His cynical, nihilistic programme also involved the theft of coal, jam (severely rationed) and other consumables from the rooms of his fellow undergraduates. But Iles did have a role in the better part of Amis's Oxford life. He introduced Amis to the man with whom, when Iles turned up, he shared a tutor: Philip Larkin. Their meeting is the stuff of myth and legend. According to Larkin, Iles had pointed out to him Amis's name on the Porter's Lodge list of Summer Term freshmen, noting, enigmatically, that he was a 'hell of a good man . . . who could shoot guns'. Later that afternoon, 5 May, Larkin found out what he meant. Iles pointed his right hand, pistol-style, at a 'fair-haired young man' emerging from the corner staircase of the front quad and did a passable imitation of a shot. The stranger clutched his chest and half collapsed against the piled-up laundry bags. After introductions Amis offered them his own recently practised pistol-shot performance, supplemented with ricochet and echoes. Larkin's account of this ends with the comment: 'I stood silent. For the first time in my life I felt myself in the presence of a talent greater than my own' (*Required Writing*, p. 20). There is more than a hint of sarcasm in this. Larkin wrote it twenty-three years after the event, reflecting perhaps on how the time he spent with Amis in Oxford was rather like a living parody of serious young writers honing their skills and exploring their ideas. All that Amis could recall of their first meeting was that Larkin had offered him a cigarette.

Amis's 'talent' for sound-effects and imitations is part of the mythology of these years. What is rarely mentioned is that in Oxford at the time practically everyone else was doing this, and Iles's initial recollection of Amis from the Cambridge interview as the gifted sound-effects man reflects the clubbish status of the activity. Iles himself did it, and Amis remembers another St John's freshman, Edward du Cann, later to become one of Mrs Thatcher's cabinet ministers, performing his 'set-piece' reproduction of a Soviet propaganda film 'full of small arms fire and shell noises'. Amis and Larkin traded imitations of senior English Faculty dons. Amis would offer a version of Lord David Cecil's effeminate upper-class drawl, in which 'do you mean Chaucer ... Dryden ... Shakespeare?' became 'dough mean Chauthah ... Dvyden ... Theckthypyum' (*Memoirs*, p. 101), in return for Larkin's rendition of J.R.R. Tolkien's impenetrable, semi-audible mumble. As Amis himself comments, 'it was a great time for imitations' (*Memoirs*, p. 39), and Amis was rated by everyone who met him as the best. His most famous was done as he and a couple of other undergraduates were crossing St Giles for a drink in the Eagle and Child (aka the Bird and Baby). A man had just dismounted his motor cycle and turned off the engine. As he began to walk away, and as Amis and his pals were passing the machine, the rider heard what seemed to be the sound of the engine restarting itself. They left him staring with shock and disbelief at the motor cycle with a mind of its own.

Larkin in 1963 writes of how a photograph taken on the sunny lawn of the college in 1942 seems to capture the mood of the time. Six undergraduates, including Amis, are doing imitations, all of which combine facial versions of wartime images ('Edward du Cann ... withdrawing the safety pin from an invisible hand grenade with his teeth') with various evocations of drunkenness. His comments on Amis are significant. The photograph reminds him of 'how much our daily exchanges were informed by Kingsley's pantomimes'. But, he adds, 'This is not to say that Kingsley dominated us. Indeed to some extent he suffered from the familiar humorist's fate of being unable to get anyone to take him seriously at all' (*Required Writing*, p. 21). His 'serious side', as Larkin put it, involved his membership of the Communist Party. At the time this consisted roughly of half the Oxford University Labour Club. Just before Amis's arrival a split had occurred between the hard-line, pro-Stalin Communists (who continued to support the Nazi-Soviet pact) and a more moderate group which called itself the Democratic Socialist Club. The latter included Roy Jenkins and Tony Crosland, while the Communists drew in Amis, Iris Murdoch and Denis Healey.

Amis gave a good deal of time and commitment to the Communist Party. Along with meetings, he attended study groups on Marxian ideology and life in the Soviet Union and later claimed to have spent many hours reading 'Marx, Lenin and Plekhanov'. George Blunden, a friend from CLS who was then at University College, remembers Amis asking him to come along to one of the meetings, at which he found individuals addressing each other as 'Comrade', followed by exchanges so laden with jargon as to be virtually incomprehensible. Blunden was bored, but he was also intrigued by the spectacle of Amis, a man for whom everything seemed to be touched by humour and absurdity, solemnly participating in something that was almost self-parodic.

Amis admitted in his *Memoirs* that at Oxford the effort of being a Communist was 'on balance a poor return for having, in this most banal of ways, rebelled against my father'. Before Oxford his extreme left-wing attitudes had been inspired mainly by his desire to irritate his father, and it seems odd that he should so enthusiastically commit himself to this spurious 'cause' when his audience consisted only of his friends. In an unpublished 1961 radio broadcast called 'Brave Causes' Amis was a little more honest. He confessed that he enjoyed being 'one of an embattled minority' and of how he felt 'a deep-seated need [to be] always swimming against the stream'. On the surface, this seems to be an admission that, like many other nineteen–twenty-year-olds, he simply enjoyed the romance of radical politics, but an observation by Larkin suggests that his Communist stance was rooted in a personal trait that ran much deeper than that: 'in his efforts to prove he had a serious side he became insulting in his emphasis, which made him disliked by many [who] could not appreciate the humour that he breathed like air'. In short, Amis's double role as hard-line Stalinist and clownish entertainer could be unsettling. He could even do a hilarious rendition of a comrade with a cockney accent ('Eeesa poincher see . . . essa poincher see'). His friends were unsettled because they were never quite certain of how to react. Was Amis the entertainer also engaged in a systematic assault upon the establishment, or was the Comrade Kingsley an addition to his comic repertoire?

The puzzling, contradictory nature of Amis's attachment to Communism becomes evident in his letters to John Russell Lloyd in 1941. Lloyd came up to St John's shortly after Amis and was effectively recruited by him to the Communist Party. On 5 November 1941 Amis wrote to Lloyd, who was evidently having doubts about his new affiliation, and reassured him that his 'mental equipment is more than enough to fit you for the Party'. He went on to cite an article in a party publication which reports that 260 new members joined the party at a recent meeting, adding: 'do you suppose that any, let alone many, of those 260 are expert Marxist Theoreticians? No, sir, they are not. So rejoin the Party right away.' He more than implies that Marxism is an all-embracing neo-religious commitment, a faith. In another letter (13 January 1942) he addresses Lloyd to such questions as 'What is the CP policy towards the punishing of Germany for atrocities, oppression and general war-guilt?' Does this differ from what is known of the policies of the 'CPSU' (Communist Party of the Soviet Union)? How might 'we', that is, 'we British Communists', deal with potential disagreements? The subtext here is that Soviet involvement in the war will guarantee the defeat of Germany and that Europe, post war, will inevitably be Communist-affiliated.

These letters evince genuine, involved commitment and the contrast between this version of Amis and the one who took nothing seriously is striking. The most obvious parallel is with the infamous 'Cambridge Four' (Philby, Burgess, Maclean and Blunt). They, like Amis, enjoyed being enigmas, men who were part of the Establishment but were equally committed to an ideology which guaranteed its demise, and their future lives, as spies, enabled them to sustain their addiction to split-personaeism. Amis did not enter the Civil Service or MI6. He became a writer. The Cambridge Four inhabited a fiction, while Amis, eventually, would make use of his recollected obsession in the writing of it. By the mid-1950s, specifically in a pamphlet called *Socialism and the Intellectuals*, he had made it clear that he perceived ideology as a disease, something which diminished and restricted our intellectual range. He would know; he had tried it out.

Amis at this time had not even considered becoming a novelist – he was more concerned with poetry – but Larkin's profile of the undergraduate picks out key elements of the writer that would make him both popular and controversial. His early talent for recreating people through their use of language became a unifying feature of his fiction. He tells you what they look like, what they do and where they come from, but he enables them to tell you just as much, and more, simply by making them speak. And just as his youthful tendency to allow his comic roles to undermine his serious side would trouble his peers, so a similar habit in his fiction caused many of his reviewers to dismiss him as a joker masquerading as a realist. In the middle of a novel that might seem to address the reader to complex contemporary issues the mask would slip. *I Like It Here* (1958) engages with the tensions between national identity and the cosmopolitan status of literary art, but its central character, in league with his narrator, often causes the reader to feel slightly foolish at being taken in by such a seriously intellectual agenda. Garnet Bowen, the writer abroad, recounts an episode with one of his language students, involving a discussion of 'Grim Grin' (Graham Greene), 'Ifflen Voff' (Evelyn Waugh), 'Zumzit Mum' (Somerset Maugham) and that champion of literary Europeanism, 'Shem Shoice', the author of *Ulysses*. And Bowen himself is troubled by the international version of A.J. Cronin's *The Keys of the Kingdom* which resurfaces as 'Sickies of Sickingdom' by one Edge Crown. In his 1960s' novel *I Want It Now* Amis tackles the divisive topic of Southern American racism. Amis in private and in print was resolutely anti-racist, yet in the novel he cannot help using the accent of a hard-line Confederate throwback as the filter for his own addiction to fun. 'Arcane standard Hanna More. Armagheddon pier staff' is an Amis classic: 'I can't stand it any-more. I'm a-getting pissed off.' Amis the undergraduate, who blurred the distinction between disposable humour and a commit-ment to serious thought, was the prototype for Amis the novelist. It would, however, take him another ten years to recognize that these two apparently irreconcilable elements of his character would fuel the dynamic energy of his fiction.

Amis's friendship with Larkin would not develop fully until he returned to England after the war, but in 1941 they recognized in each other an intriguing blend of similarities and differences. Ironi-cally, but appropriately, it was the inconsistent, unsettled elements of their respective personalities that drew them together; and these same features would in due course enable them to realize their liter-ary ambitions.

He and Amis helped to found a group called 'The Seven', the other five being Jimmy Willcox, Philip Brown, Nick Russel, David Williams and Norman Iles, all St John's undergraduates. No one was quite certain of the purpose or objective of the group, except that it enabled its members to meet at least once a week, tell jokes, get drunk and discuss contemporary literature. Often they would pass round a poem that one of them had written and talk honestly about its various qualities and shortcomings, at least until the drink began to take hold. This combination of high culture and disorgan-ized indulgence accurately reflects the nature of Amis's and Larkin's friendship. The two of them would spend long periods, usually in Amis's rooms, listening to jazz records, often prancing around the room in an attempt to embody the rhythms and improvisational nuances of the piece. In the Victoria Arms in Walton Street Larkin could sometimes be persuaded to do a twelve-bar blues number on the battered piano, and 'if there were no outsiders present' Amis would join in with lyrics borrowed from their records.

Larkin's recollections of his time with Amis in Oxford often carry a slight but tangible note of envy and resentment, and there was sufficient cause for this. It was as though they were two versions of the same character created by a novelist who was uncertain about which would make it to the final draft. Their backgrounds were remarkably similar. Larkin's school in Coventry was the provincial equivalent of CLS, and for each of them school was a treasured alternative to their uneasy relationships with their respective fathers. Larkin's father, Sydney, could have been William Amis rewritten as a more unsettling presence. Both were hard-working, self-made office men and both were agnostics. Larkin Senior was an accountant who eventually became Treasurer of Coventry Corporation, and like William Amis he had gradually moved to the right. He went beyond Conservatism and became a fascist, sympathizing with the Spanish, Italian and German regimes of the 1930s and 1940s. He took his son to Germany in 1936 and 1937 to impress upon him the benefits of Nazism. Larkin had no particular interest in politics, but even if he had wanted to assert his independence, as Amis did, by espousing radical causes that were antithetical to his father's this would have been made difficult by the fact that Sydney Larkin had become his mentor. He encouraged and promoted all of the activities that in the Norbury household functioned as symbols of youthful dissent. Larkin, like Amis, enjoyed jazz and Sydney, on learning of his son's new interest, paid for a subscription for the jazz magazine *Down Beat* and bought him a drum kit. He encouraged Larkin to write poems and short stories and introduced him to the works of D.H. Lawrence, James Joyce, W.H. Auden and Christopher Isherwood.

Sydney Larkin was by all accounts a dominating, sometimes frightening figure but one who combined these autocratic features with an open-minded enthusiasm for his son's interests in all types of culture; high-brow, experimental and popular. When Amis and Larkin talked to each other of their families, it must have seemed to the latter as if his friend had drawn the longer, more generous straw.

The literary and cultural affiliations that Amis used as a means of projecting himself into a kind of independent adulthood appeared for Larkin to have been anticipated and pre-empted by his father.

Amis also had other advantages. He remembers Larkin as some-one who dressed in a self-consciously unusual manner: 'tweed jacket, wine-coloured trousers, check shirt, bow tie . . .' Amis, in an interview with Andrew Motion, inferred that his friend's sartorial flamboyance was a compensation for his physical shortcomings. He wore thick glasses, was already going bald and was, in Amis's view, 'a little ridiculous in appearance, unlikely . . . to be attractive to girls' (Motion, p. 58). Conversation with strangers worsened his tendency to stammer. Amis's unassertive mode of dress shrewdly enhanced his handsome, youthful appearance, and he was earning himself a reputation as one of the wittiest men in Oxford.

They talked a lot about literature, and Amis later claimed that Larkin 'was always the senior partner . . . the stronger personality, always much better read'. This was true in that Larkin knew a lot more about contemporary writing than his friend. He encouraged Amis's slight interest in Auden and introduced him to the idiosyn-cratic fiction of Flann O' Brien and Henry Green. He also recom-mended to him Julian Hall's *The Senior Commoner*, a humourless exploration of class difference, isolation and repressed sexuality. This would influence Amis's first novel, *The Legacy*, completed after the war and unpublished. *The Legacy* was like none of the works that would sustain his career as a novelist. It was introspective, lacked narrative energy, contained nothing resembling wit, and in an intriguing, rather paradoxical way it reflected the nature of Amis's early friendship with Larkin. Amis's presence encouraged, even licensed Larkin's taste for visiting upon respectable culture a blend of the satirical and the obscene, as a valve for his frustrations and uncertainties regarding his serious literary ambitions. At the same time Larkin's learning and sophistication offered Amis a stabilizing counterbalance for his own addiction to irresponsible humour.

Eventually the experience of *The Legacy* would show him that as a writer it is counterproductive to model yourself upon someone you admire.

According to Amis, Larkin would write obscene clerihews about the college dons, and they collaborated on a record cover involving 'Bill Wordsworth and his Hot Six': 'Wordsworth (tmb) with "Lord" Byron (tpt), Percy Shelley (sop), Johnny Keats (alto and clt), Sam "Tea" Coleridge (pno), Jimmy Hogg (bs), Bob Southey (ds) . . .' During their discussion of other people's poems, including those of friends from 'The Seven', they considered having two rubber stamps made, reading 'What does this mean?' and 'What makes you think I care?' Larkin later commented, enigmatically, that there would be 'one for each of us', and we will never know which question best reflects the attitude of either himself or his friend. They even evolved a private, ritualistic habit of speech in which, to save time, any idea or person they regarded as pompous, boring or pretentious would be attached without connectives to an obscenity: Spenser bum, piss William Empson, Robert Graves shag. This mildly juvenile practice survived in their letters until Larkin's death. Despite being much more shy than Amis and less inclined to turn his taste for mockery and caricature into a public performance, Larkin could be far more cynical. He wrote a parody of Keats's 'La Belle Dame Sans Merci', which included the sensitive Romantic's confession that

> And this is why I shag alone
> Ere half my creeping days are done
> The wind coughs sharply in the stone
> . . . There is no sun. (Motion, p. 58)

Amis's copy of Keats's *Poems* contained a comment by Larkin on that famous moment of ethereal unification and transcendence in *The Eve of St Agnes*: 'YOU MEAN HE FUCKED HER.'

It was as though both were in private able to enjoy breaking down the institutionalized borders between comic irreverence and high culture, while in their attempts to produce proper literature they deferred to the humourless conventions of the latter.

Around the same time as this Amis had taken on, for a term in 1942, the editorship of the University Labour Club *Bulletin* and in the Spring issue he included two of Larkin's poems called 'Observation' and 'Disintegration', the titles of which bespeak their intense, self-focused moods. During this period Amis himself wrote practically nothing. He produced a few self-conscious, introspective poems for 'The Seven' and for Larkin, but none were published and none survive. His first poems to appear in print would do so in his collection *Bright November* (1947) and were written mainly during his army years. These, like Larkin's early output, deliberately exclude the farcical, sardonic, indeed the more entertaining features of their author's character.

In early 1942 they collaborated in what Amis later called a series of 'obscene and soft-porn fairy stories'. One was entitled 'The Jolly Prince and the Distempered Ghost' and was a parody of the sometimes dreary medieval narratives that were a compulsory element of the Oxford curriculum. It involved a ghostly presence whose insubstantiality is belied by his constant habit of farting. Another, called 'I Would Do Anything for You', was about two beautiful lesbians who discover in their Oxford flat a collection of jazz records left there by the previous, male, occupant. Scrupulously these records are listed, and they are the ones which both Amis and Larkin had read about but never heard. This is an intriguing evocation of circumstantial and psychological pessimism. If the man had returned to the flat to reclaim his property he would have found women to whom he was attracted but who would never feel anything similar for him. The records, similarly observed but not experienced by the authors, testify to their own anticipation of failure – although for Larkin, much less attractive and confident than his co-author, the symbolism would have been more cutting. The story, combining in one figure characteristics of each of them, would remain a token of their early friendship: Amis refers to 'IWDAFY' on at least six occasions in his letters to Larkin during the 1940s and 1950s.

The sense of stoical gloom that underpins the story would re-emerge in Larkin's first published novel, *Jill*, four years later. It is a novel that is addressed to his own ever-present sense of vulnerability. The element of mildly pornographic irresponsibility and the sheer fun that had attended his collaboration with Amis had disappeared. It was only when he began to write his 1950s' poems that an assertive, sardonic spark of the latter began to show itself.

Although Amis described Larkin as the 'senior partner' in their friendship, this is more a tribute to the latter's learning than an accurate reflection of their conventions of exchange. For Larkin their co-authored stories involved a degree of self-mockery. He had become a devotee of the psychologist John Layard whose theories of sexuality, identity and socio-cultural enclosure found parallels in the fiction of D.H. Lawrence, whose work Larkin also admired. Amis summed up his own view of Layard and Larkin's pre-occupation with his ideas as 'all that piss about liar's quinsy', and he loathed D.H. Lawrence. Lawrence, in Amis's opinion, was a psycho-sexual evangelist masquerading as a literary writer. Amis always believed that whatever else literature might be it should not become the vehicle for an explanation of the human condition. Amis and Larkin did not argue about this, because Amis simply forbade from their exchanges anything which in his view was spurious, intellectually pretentious and consequently boring, and Lawrence was top of the list.

So while their stories might appear to be the product of similarly disposed *farceurs*, they grew out of the unevenness of their relationship. For Larkin they provided some relief from the harsh and unsettling world of self-examination that constituted his early writing. Amis, as Larkin has stated, did not really have another world;

he 'lived in a zone of the most perfectly refined pure humour'. The early Amis–Larkin friendship at Oxford looks forward to and is reflected back from their later work.

Amis would achieve virtually overnight fame with *Lucky Jim* (1954), and the novel carries the imprint of his first encounters with Larkin. Jim Dixon finds potential for ridicule in practically anything, but unlike his author he has to keep this aspect of his personality to himself for much of the book. It is communicated to the reader via the exchange which takes place between Jim and his quietly sardonic other half, his narrator. In Oxford, and even more so after the war, Larkin and Amis conducted a similarly exclusive dialogue. The ideas and intellectual preoccupations that Amis excised from their conversational rituals were similar to the satirical targets selected by Jim and his narrator, but they are never allowed to interfere for too long with the dialogue-driven story. Every character who wishes to discuss such matters is presented as an irritating bore. Prior to the planning and writing of *Lucky Jim* Larkin had been Amis's mentor regarding the attempted production of verse and fiction, in that Amis never seriously considered his talent for satire and anarchic farce as part of his literary potential. Then suddenly Amis had become a popular and controversial writer by drawing upon the interchanges that both had previously regarded as a private sub-literary pastime. The note of unease which informs Larkin's account of their early Oxford years in his introduction to the 1963 edition of *Jill* is never explained, but there is sufficient evidence to regard it as a reflection of his feelings about *Lucky Jim*. Soon after the novel was published Larkin wrote to his friend Patsy Strang that while *Lucky Jim* 'is miraculously and intensely funny . . . I think it is over-simple', that 'It's in the general thinness of the imagination that he falls down.' Behind these comments was surely an awareness that their exclusive world upon which Amis had imposed his own anti-intellectual preferences had been transformed into the keynote of the novel that had launched his reputation.

3

The War

IN July 1942 Amis arrived at Catterick Camp in Yorkshire for basic army training. He had completed only a year of his degree when he was called up. After two months as a private he was posted to the neighbouring Royal Corps of Signals depot as an officer cadet; and six months after that was awarded a commission as a second lieutenant.

Amis was well prepared for the shift from university to military service. At CLS, aged fourteen, he had joined the Officer Training Corps and he transferred to its adult version, the Senior Training Corps, at Oxford. In the OTC he had become a first-class rifle shot, and at CLS and Oxford he proved to be a talented practitioner of drill and marching. New, physically fit soldiers could choose their regiments and specialization, although practically all able and mentally competent men were obliged to join active service units. Amis, following the advice of his Oxford acquaintance Norman Manning, went for what seemed the safest. The Signals, as its name suggests, was the communication department of the army. They set up and maintained radio links between fighting troops and their support and they worked largely behind the front line. Amis during his period in Europe in 1944–5 witnessed the consequences of war but never quite its practice. He landed in Normandy three weeks after D-Day, and he followed the advance through France, Belgium and

Germany always at a relatively safe distance from the exchange of fire.

Amis provides four accounts of his military service. *Who Else Is Rank*, a novel, was co-authored during his time in Europe with his fellow Signals officer E. Frank Coles. It was never published, and the typescript is deposited in the Huntington Library, California. Several of the poems in his first collection, *Bright November* (1947), refer obliquely to his wartime experiences. In the 1950s and early 1960s he wrote and published three short stories based mainly upon real incidents in Europe in 1944–5, and in his *Memoirs*, written forty years after the war, he gives a chapter to 'The Army'.

All of these writings are candid, but they are also selective. Each tells us something about their author but it is only when we read them as a form of dialogue, often taking place between older and younger versions of the same person, that we encounter the real Amis.

The parts of *Who Else Is Rank* written by Amis involve Frank Archer, a young, sensitive lieutenant in the Signals, whose story is based almost exclusively upon Amis's experiences in 1943–5. Archer undergoes basic training in Catterick, and one evening he meets a young woman in the King's Arms, Richmond, a market town a few miles from Catterick Camp. The woman is attractive, has 'dark brown hair and rather peculiar eyes a long way apart and rather long from corner to corner'. Her name is Betty Russell, and she is an exact reproduction of Elisabeth Simpson whom Amis did meet in Richmond, in the King's Arms. Her fictional name reflects Amis's continued attachment to Larkin. In their letters in 1943–4 he always refers to her as Betty, and the other name that occurs most frequently in these letters is Pee Wee Russell, one of Amis's favourite jazz players.

Coles and Amis wrote the novel over several months in the winter of 1944–5 when their Signals Company was stalled a few miles from Brussels. As Amis put it in his *Memoirs*, 'Ennui had time to set in.' Their temporary officers' mess was a well-furnished bourgeois house, and after dinner they would compose and read to each other their respective chapters. Amis's Archer and Coles's Stephen Lewis were first-person narrators whose experiences and observations would often intersect. Significantly, however, Coles/Lewis tells us a great deal about Amis/Archer, while the latter is more preoccupied with his own activities.

Amis's chapters are, as one would expect of first attempts at fiction, uncertain exercises in how to blend the message with the resources of the medium. The two chapters entitled 'Rhapsody' and 'Ecstasy' concentrate on his relationship with Elisabeth Simpson and are as much a means of exploring his own feelings and recollections as an attempt at publishable fiction. In one episode in 'Rhapsody' he describes in about 160 words several days in the lives of Betty and Archer, but the phrase 'A few days later in the waiting room at Catterick Bridge Station' is the only specific reference to place and time. The rest of the passage is concerned with 'kissing' (three references), Betty's 'breasts' and Archer's contact with them (twice), her 'legs' and 'thighs' and, predominantly, her response to his attentions: 'her heart . . . beating as fast as mine', 'she seemed very tense and quivering', 'still didn't say anything', 'She writhed in my arms', 'She was breathing very deeply' (Kingsley Amis Collection, Huntington Library, California).

'Ecstasy' tells us of a weekend they spend in York in a hotel, of how Archer feels something more than desire for Betty and eventually of Betty's declaration that their relationship must end. Her husband is on active service in the Middle East. She does not love him, but she feels she must return to him for the sake of her daughter. When Amis wrote this in 1944–5 it was an accurate account of the state of his relationship with Elisabeth Simpson. He concludes the chapter with Archer saying, 'I'm seeing you again', as Betty boards her train. After the war they kept in occasional contact by letter, but their relationship was effectively over before Amis left for Europe. Amis even includes in 'Ecstasy' a version of his father's discovery of his affair with Elisabeth. Archer tells Betty that his father is 'a bit suspicious' and that he thinks of her as 'a designing woman', which, in the light of William Amis's actual reaction, is a trifle generous. In truth, William ostracized Kingsley who was home on leave. Only Peggy's shrewd, diplomatic policy of persuasion caused him to resume communication with his son.

In the letters exchanged between Amis and Larkin in 1942–3, when Amis was in Catterick, we can recognize parts of the narrative of *Who Else Is Rank*. In practically every letter Amis mentions Elisabeth, or 'Betty'. On 20 August 1943 Larkin replies to a letter of the week before in which Amis had told him of how Elisabeth effectively dominated their relationship, referring to him as a 'funny, silly creature'. Larkin writes that a woman who had said this to him 'would find herself on her back before she knew where she was' and he was not referring to sex. He adds that Elisabeth 'sounds delightful, honest she does. I know she isn't really.' It is clear that Amis has presented Elisabeth to Larkin as someone who both excites and, to an extent, intimidates him, and in his letters he includes examples of fictional dialogue based upon his own exchanges with her. In a reply to him on 16 September 1943 Larkin writes that 'these "pattern conversations" are the last word'. Amis provided Anthony Thwaite, Larkin's letters editor, with an explanation: 'a pattern conversation was a typical conversation between young man and young woman showing how she could twist y.m. round her little finger – "What's wrong?" [asks y.m.] – "Nothing" – "If there's something wrong I wish you'd tell me" – "If you like me as you say you do you wouldn't need telling", etc.' (p. 70).

Amis supplied Thwaite with these details in the late 1980s, but what he did not recall was the intriguing function of pattern conversations, both as a private joke between himself and Larkin and as a testing ground for his first attempts at writing fiction. Writing to

Larkin from Catterick (26 October – 6 November 1943) Amis suspends the gossipy flow of the letter and offers his friend an example of pattern conversation.

> 'It was awfully nice of you to come and see me tonight, darling, when you've got all that work to do.'
>
> 'Don't say that. I wanted to.' (Liar.)
>
> 'It's been awful this week. I've missed you so much.'
>
> 'It hasn't been nice for me either. I've missed you too.' (Liar.)
>
> 'You know, Bill . . . it's just like having . . . pins and needles . . .'
>
> 'You'll have to get used to being without me, you know.' (Bastard.)
>
> 'Yes, I know.'
>
> 'Never mind, May. I shall never forget you.' Yes, I really did say that.

The 'May' referred to was an ATS soldier based at Catterick with whom Amis (Bill) was having an affair alongside his one with Elisabeth, and one assumes that this is a transcribed recollection of an actual exchange. A very similar conversation appears in *Who Else Is Rank* following the 160-word description of Archer fondling Betty.

> 'Are you all right?' I said.
>
> 'Yes, I'm all right,' she said. 'You mustn't do that,' she said. 'I felt like crying.'
>
> 'But I like you very much,' I said.
>
> 'You wouldn't have done that if you really liked me.'

One wonders if Amis adapted a transcription of his exchange with May for the one between Archer (himself) and Betty (Elisabeth). The only significant difference is that the former includes, for Larkin's benefit, disclosures of Amis's blatant insincerity

('Bastard', etc.). *Who Else Is Rank* bears practically no resemblance to the fiction that Amis would eventually publish, with the exception of the pattern conversations. These resurface in a more accomplished, merciless form in the exchanges in *Lucky Jim* between Dixon and his horrible girlfriend Margaret Peel. And again we encounter a connection between the closed, confessional exchanges between Amis and Larkin and the former's writing, first in *Who Else Is Rank* and more significantly in *Lucky Jim* where Margaret Peel, the pushy woman attempting to 'twist the y.m. round her finger', is based upon Larkin's girlfriend, Monica Jones, whom Amis openly disliked. It is also worth noting a close resemblance between Amis's pattern conversations and the dialogues between the nervous, hesitant John Kemp and practically everyone else, particularly the women, in Larkin's first novel *Jill*, which he first mentions to Amis in a letter written three weeks before he congratulates his friend on this misogynistic contribution to the novelist's task.

In the first chapter of *Who Else Is Rank* we find Archer leading a convoy of lorries through Oxford, losing contact with his command and almost running over an undergraduate in his attempt to rejoin them. Nothing like this happened, but one suspects that the contrast between his military role and his previous world reflects his irritation, made clear in his *Memoirs*, at the large number of his undergraduate friends, including Larkin, who had escaped conscription for 'medical' reasons. He would probably have enjoyed offering one of them a close encounter with a three-tonner.

At one point Archer obtains an evening pass for a few drinks with some of his Oxford friends – he, like Amis, has had to interrupt his degree for war service. One of his friends is wearing purple corduroys, very thick glasses and an orange bow-tie, and his manner drifts between the anxious and the affected. His name is Bruno Coleman. One of the mildly surreal and unpublished short stories that Larkin wrote, without Amis's cooperation, although he read it, was about a dominant lesbian figure called Brunette Coleman, who,

Andrew Motion suggests, was a fictional projection of Larkin's own thoughts on the possibility of his own homosexual inclinations. Was this simply an affectionate jibe at his friend's sartorial and imaginative excesses, or did it also carry a note of bitterness, evidenced by Amis's presentation of him as a pretentious, effeminate aesthete? Another character, John Reith-Hobbs, is equally arty and attempts to focus on people through glasses even thicker than Coleman's. The poet John Heath-Stubbs was a contemporary of Amis's at Oxford and he, like Larkin, avoided war service because of poor eyesight. He would soon go blind. Amis did not enjoy the army, partly because it appeared to have selected only him from his Oxford network of friends with literary ambitions. He was doubtful that *Who Else Is Rank* would make it into print, but it certainly enabled him to exercise his frustrations through fiction, a tendency that would eventually become more practised and sophisticated.

Archer operates as a channel for a number of Amis's states of mind, and as a character in his own right he is little more than a projection of ruminations and ideas. Seen, however, from Coles's perspective in the chapters dominated by his character Lewis we get a clearer, more objective impression of Amis during his army years. He was, in effect, the Oxford Amis in a more hostile environment. In Coles's half of the story we are told that Archer's/Amis's 'talent for impersonation' could amuse his fellow officers but that it 'won him short-lived popularity'. Coles/Lewis likes him: 'There was no meal that was not duller if Archer was on duty, no incident that was not livelier if [he] had witnessed it too.' But Coles/Lewis was the exception. Amis was from a decent enough school, an Oxford man, and his accent was acceptably middle class, but he behaved in a way that was certain to unsettle the conservative habits and inclinations of most of his fellow officers. Archer/Amis 'played no games . . . he philandered in public; he talked freely of his homosexual friends in Oxford; he spoke of intercourse between the sexes much as the rest spoke of football, eating or drinking; he wrote poetry in the Signals

Office and used a typewriter for it; . . . he mooched along like a student and when he saluted he compelled you to observe how badly he did it'. 'It was', observes Coles/Lewis, 'as though his only pleasure derived from being outrageously provoking.'

Amis's Communist sympathies had in Oxford at least provided him with a serious counterpart to his farcical persona. In the army they made him the target for the hostility of his peers and, more painfully, his senior officers. In one of Coles's/Lewis's pieces we find Archer/Amis in a bar in Belgium being encouraged by his officer friends to speak his mind on politics and the Britain that would emerge out of the war. Archer/Amis tells them that the Officer/Other Ranks structure of the army reflects the unjust class system of Britain, that the NCOs, corporals and signalmen of their regiment had done as much as them, often much more, in the war effort and that peacetime Britain would eventually recognize the unacknowledged contribution of ordinary people to the general good. And he concludes:

> We must see to it after we're demobilized that these common men, from whom we're separated only by a traditional barrier – we're no more than common men ourselves – benefit from the work that has been done, and if the system won't let that happen, well, we shall just have to change the system.

Amis might not have delivered such a lengthy diatribe, but it is an accurate assembly of the opinions he professed to hold (and, one might add, a shrewd prediction of the 1945 Labour victory). It was not that the promotion of socialism was forbidden in the officers' mess but the manner in which Amis asserted his views annoyed many of his fellow officers. As Coles/Lewis puts it, his attitude 'might not have been so bad if he had used any tact; but his superior knowledge was always deployed recklessly and the advantage quickly lost'. Amis behaved as if he were still in Oxford, and the army involved conventions that were less flexible and individuals less tolerant than at the university.

In 1956 a short story by Amis called 'Court of Inquiry' was published in the *Spectator*. In it he appears as Frank Archer, a lieutenant in the Signals. The company is in Belgium, it is 1944 and Archer has managed to mislay a vehicle battery charger. The charger is obsolete and no great loss, but Major Raleigh has 'had just about enough of young Archer' and decides to convene a disciplinary hearing, the court of inquiry of the title. Archer is reprimanded and it is clear that the court is an exercise in humiliation. The story is based entirely upon fact. Amis did lose a charger and went through an identical dressing-down in Belgium in late 1944.

The story is narrated by Captain Jock Watson, and there is enough evidence to show that Watson is Amis's version of Coles/Lewis. There are a number of almost verbatim borrowings from the Coles/Lewis account of *Who Else Is Rank*, then still in Amis's possession. When Archer faces the court he salutes and, according to Watson, 'the effort forced you to notice how badly he did it'. According to Coles/Lewis, 'when [Archer] saluted he compelled you to observe how badly he did it'. Watson tells of how Archer often unsettled his fellow officers by treating the other ranks as equals and of his 'undeviating politeness to them on all occasions'; and Coles/Lewis informs us that he was always 'polite and considerate to his inferiors and was therefore unable to exercise command'.

In 1956 no one except its two authors knew of *Who Else Is Rank* – it was unfinished and had never been sent to a publisher – and the question of why Amis was conducting this private exercise in role reversal, merging his own narrative voice with Coles's, can be answered when we consider in the short story Archer's performance before the court. He confesses embarrassingly and expresses his shame at having let down the company. Later when talking to Watson – they are, like Coles and Amis, close friends – Archer tells him that his confession was one of his well-known pieces of play-acting. But Watson has his doubts.

> Archer was a good mimic . . . but it was questionable whether any amount of ordinary acting talent could have produced the blushes I had seen. On the other hand I had no way of knowing how deeply he had thrown himself into the part. (*Collected Short Stories*, p. 41)

In the original, Coles/Lewis made much of Archer's/Amis's prodigious capacity for role-playing, but he was always able to distinguish the real character from the performance. Watson, it seems, is not, and in a way Amis is using his updated version of his army friend as an index to how he himself had changed over the previous decade.

By 1956 Amis's ability to switch personae had become a fundamental element of his life. He had published two well-received novels which involved a good deal of calculated evasiveness, and in his personal life he was playing a similarly chameleonesque game. He could slip between the roles of dutiful family man and prolific adulterer with impressive ease. When he wrote the story and compared his own version of Archer with Coles's, the sense of a presence which was an even more unnerving composite of different perspectives than its 1944 version must have seemed appropriate, and he offers his old comrade an oblique note of thanks and perhaps confession. The story involves three references to a general whose 'lines of communication' are constantly endangered by Archer's reckless behaviour. The general's name is Coles, and the message seems to be that while in 1944 E. Frank Coles had offered a shrewd and incisive portrait of Amis, by 1956 this picture had become much more blurred. Perhaps the title 'Court of Inquiry' refers as much to Amis's investigation of himself over the previous decade as it does to the committee of senior officers he faced in 1944.

In 1962 Amis published a story called 'I Spy Strangers', and again Lt Archer is the central character. The Signals Company is now in Germany. The war has just ended, and much time is spent discussing the likely result of the forthcoming General Election, to the extent that the officers and men convene a mock House of Commons, with the soldiers becoming cabinet ministers and voicing their own political opinions. Signalman Hargreaves is the very left-wing foreign secretary and Sergeant Doll the ultra-conservative opposition spokesman on defence. The mock Parliament is pure invention, but there is a close similarity between the 'system must change' speech delivered by Archer in the bar in Coles/Lewis part of *Who Else Is Rank* and Hargreaves's parliamentary performances in 'I Spy Strangers'. Significantly, Amis in the later story makes Archer Speaker of the House, someone who mediates between the opposing ministers but who can express no political opinions of his own. 'I Spy Strangers', like 'Court of Inquiry', is Amis revisiting his past and taking with him many of the changes that had occurred in the interim. Hargreaves is a private soldier: articulate, committed, informed, a socialist and a homosexual. He is not Amis, but he is an embodiment of the views on class, sexuality and politics that Amis claimed to have held and with which in Coles's/Lewis's story he provoked his fellow officers. Hargreaves's is Amis's past and Doll is in some ways his future.

In 1962 Amis had not exchanged socialism for Doll's neo-fascism, but Doll's prediction that the West would face a new totalitarian threat from the Communist Bloc is an accurate reflection of his author's political drift rightward during the 1950s, particularly after the Soviet invasion of Hungary. More significantly, Doll functions as the figure who secretly controls the narrative. His manner is superficially respectful to his seniors but with an underpinning of shrewd sarcasm. He knows the system. Major Raleigh, who had convened the court of inquiry in the earlier story in order to humiliate the rebellious Archer, contrives in this one to have Archer and Hargreaves, in his view 'tarred with the same brush', posted to the

Far East. Doll rewrites the orders with the result that Hargreaves goes East with his alleged homosexual partner Hammond, and Archer returns to Britain to complete his Oxford degree. Doll is a strange combination of beneficent fate and considered recollection. His real-life equivalent did not exist, but Amis himself managed to avoid a posting to the Far East and was back in Oxford a few months after the election. There is something final and symbolic in the fact that Hargreaves is sent so far away. It is as though Amis is officially removing himself from his radical past but in a humane and sympathetic manner. Hargreaves the revolutionary has gone, and Doll makes sure that he takes with him his homosexual partner, an act that seems to be inconsistent with Doll's right-wing, reactionary persona. In 1962 Amis had lost faith in socialism as a solution to all social ills and inequities, but he maintained a commitment to a number of causes that at the time were regarded as left-wing, among them the legalization of homosexuality.

Most of the army chapter of Amis's *Memoirs* is written in the first-person style of Isherwood's *Goodbye to Berlin*. He leaves as much out as he includes, and he manages to combine immediacy with misanthropic distance. Everything he encounters and experiences appears to be a mildly surreal distortion of what, outside the army, one might expect. He tells of how in Normandy in July 1944 he and two non-commissioned officers set off on a bartering expedition, encounter a genial old farmer, and are introduced to Calvados. Some time later Corporal Beavis is observed running through the orchard, jumping over fallen branches and shouting, 'Look at me! Look at me! I'm a horse! I'm a horse! Whee-ee-ee-ee-ee-ee.' Two weeks later his company follow the front-line troops through the Falaise Gap and Amis has his first experience of mass slaughter. The bodies of German soldiers lie unburied alongside those of cows and horses. 'The horses . . . seemed almost more painful, rigid in the shafts with their upper lips drawn above their teeth as if in continuing pain', unlike Corporal Beavis's happy imitation.

The dreary months in Belgium involve similar, if less distressing, juxtapositions of normality and unreality. Amis's duties involve the supervision of '"traffic" (messages in transit)' via teleprinter, wireless and dispatch rider, and his signals room 'command' comprises two corporals who do most of the work. The potentially distressing fact that most of the messages relate to death and killing has long since become a feature of their monotonous regularity and is hardly worth mention. More interesting are the 'urgently needed military objects', demanded via special dispatch rider by Colonel the Lord Glenarthur, which consist of new shirts, clean bed linen and crates of cognac. Amis had provided an account of these incidents in his 1955 short story 'My Enemy's Enemy' in which he changed the greedy, authoritarian Glenarthur's name to Fawcett, pronounced, of course, Force-it.

Amis in the *Memoirs* is intrigued by the way in which the army both emphasizes and refashions the class structure of pre-war Britain. His fellow officers are drawn from the middle-England stratum of estate agents, accountants and junior bank managers, but once in uniform they assume the attitudes and mannerisms of the gentry. And even though he was writing it about forty years later, long after abandoning all affiliations to the left, Amis's account is still informed by a mood of resentment, of how for three years of his life he was obliged to be part of a conservative institution that was almost beyond parody.

The other officers shared none of his literary interests and did not respond well to the combination of radical bombast and comic dexterity that had been a key element of his Oxford life. He encountered a version of the latter in the obtuse, mildly satirical discourse of the other ranks, but being an officer he could not join in. 'Lucky fucking saddle,' comments Driver Thompson, as a local Belgian girl cycles past, and company Sergeant Major Hadlett adds, 'I'd rather sleep with her with no clothes on than you in your best suit, sir.' Amis suggests that this continuously inventive linguistic culture was rather like literature, or at least his notion of literature; a commentary on 'every moment of a soldier's day, concocting it, ironizing it. "Are you waiting to see me, sergeant major?" – "No, sir, I'm just standing here for a bet"' (*Memoirs*, p. 95). What he does not say is that the linguistic texture of the signalman's and NCO's world bears a close relation to an Amis novel, in which language, spoken or written, is never allowed to remain transparent, is always twisted into something close to a sardonic ambiguity or an unspoken attitude.

In the *Memoirs* Amis tells of a 48-hour leave spent in Brussels, where he gets drunk, has sex with an agreeable prostitute and, several hours later, with an attractive waitress called Joanne, and from one, although he's not certain which, he acquires a mild, curable form of venereal disease. He consults the Medical Officer, and when their paths cross again a year later it is in the front squad of St John's. The MO is now the college doctor and he does not recognize his former patient. Amis is not surprised by this. The man had seen many faces during the war, and in any event it was not his patient's face that had previously required his attention.

In an account that builds anecdote and candour upon a convincing foundation of detail, it is odd that the two people who meant a great deal to Amis in this period, Elisabeth Simpson and E. Frank Coles, are never mentioned. His sexual adventures in Brussels with the prostitute and Joanne are followed by feelings of 'pleasure and satisfaction mixed in with bits of guilt and shame'. Perhaps this is an oblique reference to the woman back in England to whom he had declared his undying love. Perhaps.

His account in the *Memoirs* of the long, boring periods spent off-duty in the drawing-room requisitioned as the mess with men who would not talk about culture is equally puzzling, given that at the same time in the same place he had spent many evenings preparing a 60,000-word novel with his friend and fellow officer. When the medical orderly Corporal Clough is anointing his genitalia with 'some pleasant cooling white stuff' prescribed by the MO, Amis finds that Clough had worked on the books page of a northern newspaper – as had Coles – and they talk about literature, 'almost my first [conversation] on such subjects since donning uniform'. This 'almost' is a poor acknowledgement of his regular, lengthy exchanges with Coles.

There is no easy explanation for Amis's ruthless editing of his army experience, except that it is consistent with his long-practised habit of selecting from and redistributing elements of his life in his writing. The Amis who wrote the *Memoirs* adopts the skilfully paced, sardonic manner that had become the stylistic signature of much of his fiction. This presence would not have been comfortable with the love-lorn, self-obsessed writer of *Who Else Is Rank*, nor with the figure who in Belgium and Germany wrote his first publishable poems. The seven or eight that contain references to the war years make up about a quarter of *Bright November*, published in 1947. The most explicit is 'Letter to Elisabeth' drafted in Belgium little more than six months after his uncertain, last encounter with Elisabeth Simpson. It is, in effect, a poetic version of the 'Ecstasy' chapter of *Who Else Is Rank*. The Amis/Archer narrator who tells the departing Betty that their relationship will not end, despite her insistence that it must, becomes Amis the Poet, a presence far better suited to transforming the harsh realities of the world into the charitable ambiguities of the text. Practically every trope returns us to a single theme: I suspect that our relationship is over but I'll do my best to convince myself that it is not. They 'discussed the end of what has had no end', his 'scene has shifted but / still flows your northern river like a pulse, / carrying blood to bodies at their poles', and 'Nothing exists now that can go away. / The eyes that looked goodbye will look at love / As from this sleep we know ourselves alive.' Amis has a number of problems with this poem. He uses ambitious, mildly surreal metaphors, and here the influence of Auden is persistently evident, with particular echoes of the famous 'Lullaby'. Auden evolved a style that reflected his intellectual and temperamental state. Amis borrowed it for the single purpose of altering reality. He is both uncomfortable with a manner that is not his own and too extravagant in his use of it.

> A time for feeling,
> Uniting lovers in the spring, fulfilling
> The fumbling gesture and the hoarded pain
> The static hand of love wrenching the pen,
> Shall come to us in our new year, shall come
> As certainly as separation came . . .

The Amis of the 1950s, the common-sense defender of accessibility, would have pointed out that this is figurative language gone mad. How can a 'gesture' and a 'hoarded pain' be 'fulfilled'? And how can a 'pen' be 'wrenched' by a 'static hand'?

Amis's wartime poems combine a self-conscious desire to disclose his emotional condition with an uncertain engagement with other poetic voices. 'Radar' revisits the 1930s' idiom of Auden and Lewis and mixes peculiar metaphors with scientific diction, the latter acquired by Amis when doing his Signals training in radio and, peripherally, radar. 'Belgian Winter' was probably one of the pieces first drafted by Amis on the typewriter in the Signals Room, perhaps, as Coles/Lewis suggests, as a self-conscious rebuke to his unpoetic fellow officers. It adopts a detached, slightly superior attitude to the recently liberated Belgium and its allied liberators. Wrecked tanks and lorries, 'splintered houses', are juxtaposed with a town of impersonal pubs and whores. Its style mixes a few Audenesque borrowings with echoes of T.S. Eliot, and it is intriguing to compare this poem with the 'Army' chapter of the *Memoirs*. The latter was, of course, a remembrance of the same place and time from four decades later and is not a poem, but in it we hear the voice of the public Amis, as much concerned with turning the truth into a good read as with disclosing its imponderable nature, as much aware of the absurdities of the place as its tragic complexities. He would not successfully combine his personal idiosyncrasies and idioms with his respect for the craft of verse until the 1950s, and one of the few poems of *Bright November* that anticipates this is 'Bed and Breakfast'. Its focus is a particular room in a B&B, not unlike the one in which he and Elisabeth Simpson spent their final night together. The poem was drafted in late 1945, after Amis's discharge from the army and two years beyond his break-up with Elisabeth. Its point of inspiration was the same as 'Letter to Elisabeth', but while the earlier poem was a confusing struggle with extravagant style and disappointment 'Bed and Breakfast' balances emotion against a retinue of subtle stylistic devices. He writes that 'love, once broken off, builds a response / In the final turning pause that sees nothing / Is left, and grieves though nothing has happened.'

When writing these lines he was clearly as much concerned with their structure as their personal resonances. The 'turning pause' might carry a memory of his last encounter with Elisabeth, but Amis is now thinking also about his reader, who will be intrigued by the interplay between the phrase and the self-consciously clever 'turning pause', otherwise known as enjambment, which separates the potential finality of 'that sees nothing' from the syntactic continuity of the next line, 'Is left'. The Audenesque influence is disappearing, to be replaced by something more individual, a control of the mechanisms of verse which acknowledges also the presence of the person writing the poem.

4

Oxford Again

Amis returned to Oxford in October 1945 and was given comfortable rooms in the New Quad, the part of college previously occupied by the Ministry of Food and Fisheries. He felt relieved that his army experience had introduced him more to institutionalized boredom than warfare, yet resentful that he had lost two and a half years of his normal life. Most of his friends and acquaintances from 1941–2 had avoided military service, finished their degrees and gone on to other things. Larkin had got his first in English in 1944, published more poems and his first novel, *Jill*. His second, *A Girl in Winter*, was finished and would be accepted by Faber and Faber a year later. Bruce Montgomery, another friend from the pre-army year, had published a detective novel, *A Gilded Fly*, in 1944 and had one more in press.

Amis had almost two years of his degree course left. He would work hard at this, but he decided also to give much of his available time to writing. In Catterick, before D-Day, he had begun to plan a novel involving half-formed ideas on marriage, sexuality and the influence of the family upon the individual. A number of these found their way into *Who Else Is Rank*, but the original project had been sidelined by Amis's years of active service in Europe. Back in Oxford he decided that these early drafts and sketches would form the basis for his first serious attempt at prose fiction. He would finish *The Legacy* in 1948, and it would never be published. (The type-script is in the Amis Collection, Huntington Library, California.)

Alongside this new commitment to fiction Amis wanted to make something of what was still his preferred affiliation – poetry. Larkin had become a librarian and found a job in the public library in Wellington, Shropshire. He and Amis had returned to regular correspondence. They met in Oxford in November, and Amis confessed to feeling uneasy about his lack of material in print. Over the previous two years Amis had written about forty poems and published none. Larkin advised him to send this collection to Reginald Caton, the proprietor of the Fortune Press and the publisher of *Jill*. Two weeks later Amis forwarded thirty-one of these pieces to Caton, and they were accepted for publication in May 1946. Larkin later wrote to his parents that 'If one can't get out of a mess oneself, the best thing is to drag someone else into it.' The mess referred to was Caton's unreliable, careless treatment of Larkin's first novel.

Caton was an enigma. The Fortune Press made him money principally through its steady output of pornography, including novels entitled *Boys in Ruin* and *A Brute of a Boy* and monographs such as *Chastisement Across the Ages*, a detailed study of corporal punishment in German women's prisons. It was rumoured that Caton's interest in proper literature was a means of providing his pornography list with a shroud of respectability and, given that it made him little money, as a tax dodge for his other role as landlord of a large number of low-rent, barely habitable properties in Brighton. Alun Lewis, one of his serious authors, accused him of publishing poetry without having read it, and Amis suspected that his own volume spent the six months between submission and acceptance gathering dust in Caton's office. But Caton's apparent status as a low-life charlatan is belied by the impressive list of authors that he did choose to publish, including Larkin, Amis, Alun Lewis, Julian Symons, Dylan Thomas, Roy Fuller and C. Day Lewis. During the war years the Fortune Press provided a valuable outlet for new writers who experienced more difficulties than usual with the established presses, cash-strapped and paper-rationed as they were. In 1944 it published *Poetry from Oxford in Wartime*, including verse by Larkin and John Heath-Stubbs and a similar collection from Cambridge.

Caton certainly left an impression on Amis. He met him once at his dingy basement office in central London, and he reproduces the episode in *The Legacy*. Caton's fictional counterpart, L.S. (Lazy Sod) Caton, appears, albeit briefly, in each of Amis's published novels from *Lucky Jim* to *The Anti-Death League* (1966). In *Lucky Jim* he features as a suspect academic who promises and fails to publish Jim's article on medieval shipbuilding in his new journal, and in the rest he resurfaces as a similar figure whom we never actually meet. He communicates with the characters only by post, telephone or rumour, a shadowy, distant presence who makes promises that he never keeps and disappears when his fraudulent activities become known.

Caton features in Amis's novels far more frequently than any other life-based character, apart from the author himself, and there are several reasons for this curious obsession. For the episode in *The Legacy* in which the narrator, called Kingsley Amis, meets the potential publisher of his volume of poems, Amis did not have to change many details. The real Caton was almost beyond parody, dressed in a greasy suit and collarless shirt and equipped with a linguistic strategy of substituting digressive diatribes for answers to questions. Most of his statements would conclude with the phatic verbal question mark of 'what?' The office itself carried an air of dissolute impermanence. On the office door Fortune Press announced itself with a cardboard notice in red ink; the phone was disconnected, and most of its flat surfaces were covered in dust-laden volumes and typescripts, 'little of any literary interest', that Caton seemed either to have forgotten about or abandoned.

In the novel Caton demands £20 to cover initial publicity costs, and in life Caton required Amis to buy, wholesale, and resell the first fifty copies of *Bright November*. Many of these would be purchased in Berkhamsted by friends and acquaintances of Amis's proud mother.

When he was writing *The Legacy* Amis's meeting with Caton provided him with very usable copy. His own fictional counterpart was a struggling unpublished poet, aged nineteen, who inherits £30,000 from his father, Lionel. In order to qualify for this legacy on his twenty-first birthday, Kingsley must marry Stephanie Roche, a 'suitable wife' chosen by his family, and join his father's wholesale grocery firm. Otherwise the money will go to a bizarre religious sect called the League of the New Tabernacle. Kingsley wants to marry Jane Taylor, a 'respectable' Yorkshire girl (with echoes of Elisabeth Simpson) and spend his time writing poetry. In the end Kingsley surrenders to the family, gives up Jane and poetry, agrees to marry Stephanie, join the business and consequently collect the cash. The novel was unlike anything that Amis would eventually publish, yet in a curious, unintended way it was prescient. It is, in the worst sense, autobiographical; an exploration of Amis's doubts, anxieties, fears and uncertainties, written by Amis, about Amis and to Amis, with scant regard for the reader who might wish to be entertained by a good story. Amis's use of dialogue as an indicator both of context and character, his continuous interweaving of sardonic humour and brittle commentary became the trademark of his published fiction. In *The Legacy* these are largely absent. Instead we encounter the narrator, Kingsley Amis, a mixture of objectivity, aloofness and lurking pessimism and not unlike the narrative voice of Larkin's *Jill*. Larkin's narrator is a successful literary presence because, temperamentally and verbally, he reflects the mood and condition of the central character, John Kemp, and his author. The novel is about Larkin, and its style is well matched with its subject. It is a novel written by a man who, in truth, was a lyric poet. *The Legacy* is a novel written by a man whose desire to be a poet effec-

tively strangled his natural inclinations towards mimicry and representation. He would eventually make use of these talents in *Lucky
Jim* as a means of reworking central thematic elements of *The
Legacy*. In the latter the fictional Kingsley is constantly attempting
to reconcile his emotional and aesthetic ideals with the demands of
the real world. This tension resurfaces in *Lucky Jim*, but while the
Kingsley of the first novel is defeated by circumstances Jim Dixon's
abandonment of arty academia for crude prosperity is presented as
a victory.

When writing his popular 1950s' novels Amis's mind must have
gone back to *The Legacy* and to a particular part of the typescript
where, several days after meeting Caton, the fictional Kingsley telephones his reconnected publisher and tells him that he wants nothing more to do with his 'miserable, dishonest, rotten little concern,
what, what, what, what, what, what?' He abandons his poetic
ambitions and heads for the security of a marriage to Stephanie and
a management career in grocery. Amis himself continued to write
poetry, but he must eventually have come to recognize ironic parallels between the decision made by the struggling poet to give up
verse for the real world and his own recognition that poetic, introspective fictions such as *The Legacy* were a poor reflection of the real
Kingsley Amis.

Amis's encounter with Caton in life and in fiction became a kind
of private talisman, a Swiftian footnote. As his own literary career
proceeded, the incident collected further echoes and resonances.
Based as it was upon fact, it stands out as the only comic episode of
The Legacy and therefore as a slight but tangible connection
between Amis's abandoned novel and the very different type of fiction that would make him famous. During the 1950s Amis's most
hostile critics presented him as a talented hoodlum who would drag
serious writing into a moral cesspit, and he must have noted an
ironic similarity between this public image of himself and the constantly blurred distinction between Caton as an authentic, if slightly

bizarre, patron of the arts and a low-life charlatan for whom literature was a front. It is interesting that Amis told Clive James that had
he 'bumped [Caton] off' in *The Anti-Death League* because this was
the first of his novels that he wanted his readers to 'take seriously'.

Amis first saw Hilary Bardwell in a café in High Street, Oxford,
one morning in January 1946. She was pretty and blonde, and he
arranged for a girl he knew to pass on his name to her, along with a
polite enquiry as to whether she might like to go for a drink some
time. A few days later he found a note in the porter's lodge with her
name and telephone number.

Hilly was a popular date with undergraduates, and Amis's
request was one of many. She did not, initially, find him particularly
attractive or charming, but the more they discovered of each
other's personalities the more they began to find unlikely points of
attraction. Hilly, despite looking and behaving like a woman in her
twenties, was seventeen, and for a female teenager in the 1940s she
displayed an unusual, almost rebellious, tendency towards eccentricity. She had left her decent middle-class boarding-school,
Bedales in Hampshire, aged fifteen, having run away from the institution on several previous occasions. After that she had become a
trainee kennel maid in a dogs' home in Surrey run by two lesbians,
enrolled as an art student at Ruskin College in Oxford, abandoned
her course and, when Amis met her, was earning a small amount of
money as a model at Ruskin. Superficially, Amis and Hilly were ill-
matched. She was clever, but she had no real interest in literature or
politics. She was articulate and certainly not shy, but she regarded
lengthy conversations as a waste of time and effort.

In August 1946 Amis, Hilly and Amis's friend Christopher Tosswill spent a three-week holiday in the Vosges, close to the
France–Germany border. Amis had first persuaded Hilly to have
sex in May, an event he triumphantly announced in a letter to
Larkin, but the holiday was their first attempt at living together, and
it did not go well. He wrote to Larkin complaining that, while he

enjoyed her company, she was too quiet, and he compared his time with her, unfavourably, with the dynamic exchanges that took place between himself and Larkin. But by the end of the trip they had made things up. Something kept them together, something more than the sexual attraction which each could easily have found elsewhere. Almost half a century later, in his *Memoirs*, Amis tells us what it was. He states that apart from a few facts and dates he will say very little about Hilly, 'after just one mention of the word love'. This word tends to mean what we want it to mean, and I would venture that for Amis and Hilly it meant finding that you felt something exceptional for someone with whom you had practically nothing in common.

Socially they became a double act. Amis would play his by then established role as raconteur, mimic and polemicist, while Hilly would appear interested in something else and complement his verbal energy with distracted behavioural gestures. She would drink beer and swear – most unladylike habits – and sit on the floor. Anne Cleary, the wife of Amis's Swansea colleague Esmond Cleary, had first met Amis and Hilly in the late 1940s. Her family lived in Berkhamsted, near Amis's parents, and she recalls that even before *Lucky Jim* Amis had developed an almost charismatic reputation. He and Hilly were, in Oxford, the couple to know. They were unusual, slightly anarchic in a manner that would not become fashionable until the 1950s, and in a peculiar, indefinable way they seemed to belong together.

In December 1947 Hilly discovered that she was pregnant. First, they planned to have an abortion, then illegal. They consulted a number of doctors in London, and one of them was honest about the dangers to Hilly of the operation. Amis wrote to Larkin that for both of them marriage and a baby seemed a far better prospect 'than such a disaster as might happen' (12 January 1948). (Amis would recollect these events almost fifty years later in his penultimate novel, *You Can't Do Both*.) The wedding took place on 21

January 1948 in the Oxford registry office, then conveniently situated next door to St John's and above the Lamb and Flag public house. Neither family was happy with the arrangement, but both eventually conceded that there was no alternative. In February they found a cramped, expensive flat in north Oxford, which by June they had exchanged for a more spacious farmworker's cottage in the village of Eynsham, twenty minutes by bus from Oxford. Hilly gave birth to Philip (named after Larkin) Nicol on 15 August 1948.

The immediate effects of Amis's relationship with Hilly upon his literary ambitions were negligible. He did not get on with her family, and her father Leonard and brother Bill would eventually provide models for the horrible Welch clan of *Lucky Jim*. Throughout the 1950s and finally in *You Can't Do Both* Amis would involve versions of Hilly in his fiction principally as a long-suffering, tolerant counterpart to his own selfish, unfaithful inclinations. During their courtship and the early years of their marriage he managed to draw a line between his actual life as husband and father and his potential life as a scholar, poet and novelist.

Soon after Hilly became pregnant Amis gained a first in English, and shortly before their marriage he enrolled as a BLitt postgraduate student. He won a small grant, and the remainder of the costs of supporting a wife and child was provided by his and Hilly's parents. In 1947 decent although modestly paid jobs for graduate ex-servicemen were easy enough to find, and his decision to spend the next few years in relative poverty was inspired partly by advice from John Wain, with whom he had become friendly in 1945. Wain was three years younger than Amis but had avoided military service and secured for himself academic posts in English both in Oxford and the nearby University of Reading. Wain assured Amis that with his first and a postgraduate degree he would find a lectureship in one of the expanding provincial universities, rather than 'the suburban schoolmasters job I had vaguely envisaged' (*Memoirs*, p. 42). Hilly, to her credit, did not complain about having to spend the first year of her married life largely on her own in a dull Oxfordshire village with little to spend or do, while her husband travelled every day to the Bodleian and St John's to research his thesis, finish his novel and draft a few poems.

Amis's B.Litt. thesis (deposited in the Harry Ransom Humanities Research Center, University of Texas) is an intriguing commentary upon the tensions and uncertainties that beset his own attempts at literary writing. Its title is an accurate description of its contents. 'English Non-Dramatic Poetry, 1850–1900, and the Victorian Reading Public' is about the relationship between poetry and its audience. He deals with most of the major poets of the period – Christina and Dante Gabriel Rossetti, Morris, Thomson, Swinburne, Hopkins, Wilde, Fitzgerald, Browning, Arnold and Tennyson – and his method pre-empts Richard Hoggart's radical *The Uses of Literacy*. Amis did an immense amount of contextual research, quoting and summarizing reviews from the popular press and literary journals, citing sales of volumes and reprints and generally attempting a balance between his own view of a poet's work and a more objective picture of its status as variously popular, marginal, obscure or accessible. Out of this emerges an academically respectable thesis on the nature of Victorian literary culture and its contribution to the modern status of poetry as a slight, elitist art form. Amis uses a formula which divides the late Victorian poet's audience into three categories. The 'inner audience' involves the poet, his friends and family who will talk with him or her about the unfinished work and contribute to its final published state. The 'intermediate audience' consists of an assembly of commentators; people in the press, in publishing and solidly established in the broader cultural fabric who will promote or ruin the reputation of the writer. The 'outer audience' are the people who respond to good reviews in the popular press or to cultural trends and who buy and read the poems.

Amis attempts to maintain a level of scholarly objectivity, but very frequently he allows his opinions to inform his observations. He likes D.G. Rossetti because he brings the reader into the poem. Rossetti does not surrender elegance to populism, but he is clearly writing to someone and not only about something or himself. Hopkins, on the other hand, seems to communicate only with his inner audience, principally himself and the slightly bemused Robert Bridges. Tennyson he approved of as someone who maintained an egalitarian balance between the expectations of the three types of audience; except in his later, popular verse where in Amis's view he attends too much to low-cultural instincts and expectations. This notion of good literature as something that is accessible but not simplistic, sophisticated but not self-indulgent, would permeate Amis's later critical writing but is at odds with the kind of literature that he produced during the period in which he wrote the thesis.

Judged according to his own criteria, much of the verse of *Bright November* confines itself to an inner audience, principally himself and Larkin, and borrows continually from the stylistic habits of others and, contra Rossetti, often frustrates the reader who might want to know what it actually means. His explanations of why some Victorian poets deserve less respect than others often sound like a self-critical commentary on *The Legacy*. Meredith was, in Amis's view, far too concerned with his own social and moral inclinations ever to appeal to an outer audience of any size. Wilde and other *fin-de-siècle* aesthetes were equally self-obsessed, their 'faded' poems embodying the conviction that 'communication is not a necessary part of the literary process'. William Morris 'sacrificed the task of communication . . . to the easier pleasure of putting words down'. *The Legacy* involves exactly such a self-fixated lack of concern for an outer audience. Its subject, a man whose aesthetic, emotional and social predispositions alienate him from his family, could have been woven into an engaging narrative, but, instead, Amis used it to explore his own feelings of resentment and failure. *The Legacy* was rejected by Longmans and Gollancz in 1949, and a year later

Doreen Marston, a reader for Collins, sent Amis a report involving numerous and grimly ironic echoes of his own evaluations of a number of the Victorians. It suffers from 'redundancy and lack of conflict', meaning that the main character's problems and uncertainties are turned inward rather than used as the vehicle for a narrative in which things actually happen. 'There is no suspense; there is, in its place, a good deal of boredom' (Jacobs, p. 127). Amis's one successful publishing project in post-war Oxford was as co-editor, with his friend James Michie, of *Oxford Poetry 1949*.

Amis's view that Hopkins failed as a poet partly because his inner audience, Robert Bridges, misunderstood him and indulged his stylistic idiosyncrasies carries an echo of Amis's dependency upon Larkin. In January 1950 Amis wrote Larkin a peculiar, very long letter of thanks. He asks if his friend recalls the weekend in late 1945 when Larkin visited him in Oxford, read his poems, 'liked them on the whole, thought they were good' and advised him to send them to Caton. He actually calls Larkin his '"inner audience", my watcher in Spanish, the reader over my shoulder . . .', adding that *The Legacy* 'only got written in response to your suggestions'. The suggestions and the encouragement were well meant, but during the five years following the war they sustained the division between Amis's actual character and temperament and his adopted literary persona. For example, during their first year in Oxford Larkin had introduced Amis to Julian Hall's *The Senior Commoner* (1933). In a 1982 essay on the novel Larkin writes of the 'brittle plangency of the style' and an odder quality he calls 'circumstantial irrelevancy', the use of diversified detail for no apparent purpose. Larkin's *Jill* shows a slight acknowledgement of this effect, and Amis in *The Legacy* attempts his own version. Doreen Marston describes its disastrous consequences. 'If I tried to count the number of times your characters repeated themselves, the number of times they light a cigarette, pour out tea, pass plates of food, etc. this letter would be an essay in statistics.'

Amis submitted his B.Litt. thesis in May 1950, and when he wrote the letter to Larkin he would have been completing the final draft. The letter is a thank-you note, but for what exactly Amis is expressing his gratitude remains affectionately ambiguous. He states that without Larkin's encouragement he would have given up attempting to write anything, and he refers continuously to the way in which, in their letters and in each other's company, they could make each other laugh. Doreen Marston notes that in *The Legacy* there is a 'total lack of humour', and Amis in the thesis quotes Rossetti's statement that 'good poetry is bound to be amusing' and adds approvingly that this is an 'insistence on entertainment as an essential quality of poetry'; if we substitute 'literature' for 'poetry' this looks forward to Amis's own creative trademark.

The thesis and the letter are to Larkin, respectively, moments of recognition and transformation. In the thesis he sides with writers such as Rossetti who can be simultaneously humorous and serious and Tennyson who combines philosophical insight with writing that can be enjoyed and understood by everyone. In the letter he says goodbye to the type of writer he had tried to be, more concerned with himself than with his outer audience, and introduces Larkin to the writer he would soon become. Comedy had previously been an element only of their social milieu but would now be part of his writing. At the end of the letter he states that he will soon show Larkin parts of his new novel, 'D and C', Dixon and Christine. This would become *Lucky Jim*. Thirty-five years later, in another letter to Larkin, he reflects on the pre-Jim years, again without accusing his friend of leading him in the wrong direction but inferring much. 'I wasn't creatively inactive in those years between Jill and Jim, no, no, I was writing callow bullshit. All those terrible poems. *The Legacy*. You "matured" long before I did. It just happened like that. You see, some of us (pause) have a harder time growing up than others . . . But really I was bloody lucky almost none of it got into print' (25 April 1985). Lucky him.

PART 2

SWANSEA

5

Lucky Jim

*L*UCKY *Jim* piloted Kingsley Amis from relative obscurity to nationwide fame. It went through ten impressions in 1954 and has never gone out of print. It became the benchmark of 1950s' iconoclasm and its targets were numerous.

Jim Dixon is a young, untenured history lecturer in a provincial university and he becomes the agent for a fast-moving, almost random sequence of satirical attacks. His boss, Professor Neddy Welch, is a semi-articulate buffoon with a taste for folk dancing and madrigal music and a commitment to the organic simplicities of medieval England. He is the archetype of head-in-the-sand academia. Bertrand, his son, is an artist of loud pretensions and limitless social ambitions. Jim's colleague and occasional girlfriend, Margaret Peel, is theatrically neurotic, sometimes simulating the kind of nervous breakdown favoured by intellectuals but only when this is tactically propitious.

Lucky Jim became a bestseller partly because it pre-empted *Private Eye* in its swipe at establishment posturing and self-regard, but its principal source of popularity was its hero Jim Dixon. Evelyn Waugh's early heroes – Pennyfeather and Boot particularly – find themselves bounced from one set of absurd circumstances to another and respond with an almost complicit degree of tragi-comic stoicism. But Jim refuses to play the hapless victim. For much of the story he has to put up with the irritations and absurdities of his life, but eventually his 'luck' enables him to escape the mundane hypocrisies of provincial academia for a well-paid job in industry, and he takes with him Christine, Bertrand's stunningly attractive and unpretentious girlfriend. But Jim's triumphant departure is not his only act of revenge, because throughout the book he has continually undermined and ridiculed both the world in which he finds himself and its worst cohabitants. He has done this through his alliance with the anonymous narrator.

David Lodge (1966) has noted a comic tension between Jim's 'inner and outer worlds': the outer consisting of mainly deferential relations with a circle of characters, including the Welches and Margaret, whose opinions will affect his future life; the inner of Jim's actual feelings and thoughts, including a desire to ram a necklace bead up Margaret's nose and plant his head of department in a lavatory basin. But the narrator does not simply show us the comic interplay between Jim's inner and outer worlds; he functions also as Jim's superhuman alter ego. He times and structures the narrative with the same deft, sardonic irony that Jim would have used if he had told his own story. It is as though there are two Jims: one inside the narrative, struggling with his own impatience, frustration and rage; the other controlling and orchestrating the narrative, ensuring that the reader will share Jim's perspective on the idiocies of Welch and the pretentions of Bertrand and Margaret. Jim the character is 'lucky'; he gets the girl, he gets the job and he gets out, and the other Jim has all the time been exacting a kind of revenge on the characters and the world that seemed intent on denying him these prizes.

Lucky Jim was Amis's first piece of published fiction. It is completely unlike anything he had planned or attempted to write before. The idea for it came to him in 1948; he began work on it the following year, and the completed typescript was accepted by Gollancz in 1953. Given Amis's other commitments at the time, it was finished with remarkable speed. He and Hilly had a one-year-old son, Philip, with a second on the way (Martin, born August 1949). His government grant was about to run out, and in the summer of 1949 the Amises were obliged to leave their cottage in Eynsham and move in with Hilly's parents in Harwell. Throughout the summer of 1949 Amis had been applying for lectureships in provincial universities and had been interviewed and rejected by Liverpool, Birmingham, Durham and Manchester. His last hope was a late-advertised post in the University College of Swansea. The telegram inviting him for interview arrived just before they left their cottage. Despite the fact that he was suffering from a particularly unpleasant form of influenza, he impressed the panel and was offered the job. A demanding schedule began immediately. He had to deliver about six lectures a week on everything from Chaucer to Browning, take Oxbridge-style two-to-one tutorials and mark weekly essays. Amis knew his material, but he had never delivered lectures before. His performances were scrupulously researched, comprehensive and, by all accounts, opinionated and amusing. On top of this he had to find accommodation and support for his wife and family, all on a starting salary of £300 (the equivalent of about £8,000 today). For three years the Amises lived in cramped, poorly furnished flats in the run-down Mumbles area of Swansea, and one can appreciate his wry quotation of the old song that gave the novel its title: 'Oh Lucky Jim, how I envy him.'

Things improved in 1951 when Hilly received a legacy of £2,400; enough to buy a house, a washing machine and a fridge. No. 24 The Grove was a three-storey terraced Edwardian building of agreeable aspect. It had a small front garden and looked out on to a mature, tree-lined square. More significantly, it had a spare room, where Amis completed and rewrote the typescript of *Lucky Jim*. Swansea Council has not so far erected a plaque.

There is an obvious connection between Amis's new life and the setting that provided *Lucky Jim* with much of its irreverent energy, but it would be wrong to regard the novel as simply a satirical attack on Swansea, its environs and university. Many of the characters of the book were drawn from Amis's pre-Swansea experiences, and the more absurd events and circumstances of Jim's world were largely invented. Despite being poorly paid and overworked, Amis enjoyed teaching English literature and he quickly made friends in Swansea, both inside and outside the university. What university life did was to provide Amis with a fictional environment, a catalyst for an immense variety of inclinations, opinions and instincts that had previously only been part of his personality and completely unrelated to his endeavours as a literary writer.

The Legacy was a mixture of social commentary and contemporary existential crisis. More significantly, it contained no trace of humour. *Lucky Jim* brought together Amis the writer and Amis the man. The latter was addicted to practical jokes; he was the person at the night out in the pub or the dinner party who tried, usually successfully, to be funnier than everyone else. Academia as a fictional setting enabled Amis to combine his undoubted writerly talents with his less respectable tastes for ribaldry, wit and shameless ridicule. It did so because it both reflected elements of the real world yet was peculiarly detached from it.

The idea for *Lucky Jim* came to Amis a year before he went to Swansea, during a visit to Philip Larkin at Leicester University, to which Larkin had moved from Wellington and become assistant librarian. (At the time of Amis's visits Larkin lived in 12 Dixon Drive.) They spent half an hour in the senior common room, and Amis was fascinated by the unreality of the setting and its characters.

> I looked around and said to myself, 'Christ, somebody ought to do something about this.' Not that it was awful – well, only a bit; it was strange and sort of *developed*, a whole mode of existence no one had got on to from the outside, like the SS in 1940, say. I would do something with it. (*Memoirs*, p. 56)

Within a year he would be part of it and would start to do something with it. More specifically, he would employ it as the backdrop for a variety of his own characteristics, attitudes and talents.

Swansea offered Amis a setting for his novel, but the book's energy and edge were inspired by another source; his friendship with Philip Larkin. The most telling record of their relationship exists in their letters. The style of these exchanges is self-consciously farcical. Both were men in their mid-twenties; they had writerly and academic aspirations, firsts from Oxford and serious interests in serious literature. But their letters belied these public personae; they might have been written by over-talented, sex-crazed six-formers. They played with words; practically every other line contains a *double entendre* or typographical pun. In February 1947, for example, Larkin informs Amis that his 'buck' (*A Girl in Winter*) is coming out and that he is annoyed by the 'dos't jack it'. A year earlier Larkin had first thanked him for 'Yoor letar' and gone on to offer an opinion on 'Emily Prick-in-son', a 'tidy wordlocker'. Significantly, Amis was the only person to whom Larkin wrote in this way, and Amis responded in kind, although less extravagantly. They had evolved a kind of private, neo-Joycean discourse (although neither had much of a taste for Joyce's writing) which they often used to exchange the most personal and potentially embarrassing details regarding their sex lives, anxieties, distastes and ambitions.

The letters between Amis and Larkin, supplemented by their occasional, booze-fuelled meetings, were the originators of the dynamic relationship between Jim's public and private personae and between Jim and his alter ego narrator. In 1950 Amis wrote to Larkin and thanked him for 'encouraging me to be funny'. He did not mean that Larkin had encouraged his social propensities and talents – they had always been there. He meant that Larkin, more by accident than design, had prompted Amis to recognize a productive alliance between his taste for irreverent humour and his literary ambitions. He also tells Larkin that 'you are my "inner audience", my watcher in Spanish, the reader over my shoulder'; not unlike the relationship between Jim and his narrator. And we should note that the term 'inner audience' is borrowed from Amis's B.Litt. thesis, where it refers to those people who are close enough to an author to almost be an extension of his own personality. Their letters and meetings had provided each of them with an outlet for their respective encounters with anger and frustration. They had made fun of everything, and Amis, through those exchanges, had discovered his literary voice. In his 1950 letter Amis promises to show Larkin an early draft of 'D and C' when they next meet. 'D and C' stands for 'Dixon and Christine', his working title for *Lucky Jim*.

The idea for a novel about a young academic in a provincial university might first have occurred to Amis during his visit to Leicester, but until he went to Swansea its inspirational focus lay elsewhere. On 16 January 1949 he informed Larkin that 'I have jotted down a few notes for my next book about Daddy B; I don't see how I can avoid doing him in fiction if I am to refrain from stabbing him under the fifth rib in fact.' Daddy B was Amis's father-in-law, Leonard Bardwell, who would eventually become the model for Professor Neddy Welch, Jim's boss. The notes, which Amis continued to make during 1949, no longer exist, but a version of them can be found in the letters to Larkin. Throughout the year, with the move from Eynsham imminent and job prospects uncertain, Amis became more and more aware of the dreadful notion of actually having to live with the Bardwells. Since meeting and marrying Hilly he had been variously bored, enraged and frustrated by her father's obsessive interests in cultural arcana: Bardwell was keen on English 'folk culture', particularly Morris dancing, and was fluent in three languages – Welsh, Swedish and Romanish – whose common feature was that they were spoken by practically no one he was likely to meet.

Amis in 1949 reports incidents to Larkin that would also go into his notes, be reformulated a couple of years later and fitted into the plotlines of the novel. In the January 1949 letter he writes of how, following an evening of being bored by Bardwell's accounts of Sweden, folk dancing and folk cultures, and the language of the Romaneschi, he is next morning lying in a half-filled bath 'with him [Bardwell] in the room underneath accompanying on the piano, his foot regularly tapping, folk tunes which he was playing on the gramophone . . . As one vapid, uniformly predictable tune ended and another began I found that the hot tap was now dispensing cold water, and, getting out of the bath, began drying myself.' The notes-inspired memory of this weekend at the Bardwells' would become the foundation for Jim's enforced weekend at the Welch house with an evening of compulsory participation in madrigal singing. Jim escapes to the pub and wakes up next morning, hung over. This time Welch is in the bath, singing a piece 'recognizable to Dixon as some skein of untiring facetiousness by filthy Mozart'. The tune might have become up-market and classical, but Jim, like Amis, is still obliged to 'marvel at its matchless predictability, its austere, unswerving devotion to tedium' (Chapter 6).

In the same letter Amis writes that 'I have been thinking of a kind of me-and-the-Bardwells theme for it all, ending with me poking Hilly's brother's wife as a revenge on them all' (he didn't). This instinct was surely still present when he used the horrible weekend-with-the-Welches as the occasion for Jim's and Christine's tentative indications of mutual attraction. Christine is almost engaged to Bertrand and she is, for the Welches, a socio-cultural trophy, upper class and well connected with the London-based arts establishment. Her preference for Jim certainly registers as an 'act of revenge'.

The 'me and the Bardwells theme' emerges again in Amis's report to Larkin on his Whitsun weekend at the in-laws' house (9 June 1949). Bardwell is as usual 'a proper scream' with his accounts of 'folk dancing'. This is supplemented by music from Hilly's composer brother William ('conchertoes and sympathies', 'a talentless flavourless sonata played me gratuitously'), which might explain the eventual upgrading of Bardwell's folk playing to an equally unpleasant rendition of a classical piece by Welch in the novel: the Bardwells' badness transcends musical boundaries. William Bardwell, 'Bill B', causes Amis more irritation with his arty obsession with French cuisine, culture and lifestyle, 'his I'm-more-at-home-in-France-than-England-balls'. The Welches are similarly obeisant to Frenchness, giving all of their children French Christian names (Bertrand is Bertro*nd*, with the second syllable predominant and pronounced 'ornd'). In the letter Amis writes that 'Two things only pleased me. Bill B has *given himself the shits* by his own *filthy French cooking*' (transposed perhaps to 'filthy Mozart' in the novel). The other agreeable incident involves Marion, the three-year-old child of the Bardwells' daughter Marion. As Bill picked her up, 'She instantly shat over his trousers'; 'amn't I telling you we had the big laugh there the two of us, me and myself'. There are no defecating children in the novel, but one wonders if the incident was in Amis's mind when, in a confidential moment, he has Jim ask the Welches' cat to 'pee on the carpet'.

Amis kept carbons of his letters to Larkin and these, with his notes, would have been with him as he wrote *Lucky Jim*. A few particular incidents were recycled as set pieces for the book, but equally intriguing are the more oblique, peripheral connections. On 9 May 1949, for example, Amis reports that the 'best news from here for a long time is that old Bardwell was taking part in some lunatic folk-fandango [morris dancing] in which the men swung the steves about and ducked and jumped over them'.

> Well, old B's opposite number swung his stick at the wrong time, or old B mistimed it or something: anyways, the upshot is that old B takes *one hell of a crack on the brain box*, and is laid out for some time, and *suffers a lot of pain*, and has to be treated for shock. NOW THAT'S FUCKING GOOD EH?

Throughout *Lucky Jim* Dixon wants something like this to happen to Welch. He wants to hit him, dump him in a lavatory basin or whirl him around the swing doors of the library. Jim cannot tell Welch that he really thinks him an idiot almost beyond parody because his job is at stake, just as Amis is prevented by decency and convention from saying the same to Bardwell. But, for both, moderate violence, actual, accidental or imagined, is a fair compensation.

Two months later (12 July) Amis writes to Larkin of how an otherwise agreeable weekend in Eynsham was spoilt by the arrival of Bardwell. A village carnival was taking place, and Hilly, Amis and some friends from Oxford were enjoying themselves 'until old apeman turned up – he had "come to see the county dancing"'. Bardwell as 'ape man' is the keynote of the letter: 'WITHOUT THE APE we should have been a merry party, but THE APE WENT ON SITTING ABOUT AND GRINNING and *spoiling* everything by his presence and *not realizing it* . . .' The joke, with Larkin, is that Bardwell's obsessive concern with folk culture, medieval England as an artistic reviver, is about as useful and relevant as the case for a return to the instinctive prelinguistic communities of our simian ancestors: apes. Again Amis states that he wants to take revenge by putting Bardwell in a novel: 'I shall swing for the old cockchafer unless I put him in a book *recognisably* so that he will feel *hurt* and *bewildered* at being so *hated*.'

The letter is echoed in *Lucky Jim* on several occasions. Jim, via the narrator, offers the reader a private account of what he really wants to say to Welch, much as Amis had in his letter about Bardwell: 'Look here, you old cockchafer, what makes you think you can run a history department, even at a place like this, eh, you old cockchafer. I know what you'd be good at, you old cockchafer.' Jim has been coerced by Welch into researching and delivering a public lecture on 'Merrie England', and Chapter 20 opens with what appears to be Jim's performance, an endorsement of 'the instinctive culture of the integrated village-type community . . . our common

heritage . . . what we once had and may, some day, have again –
Merrie England'. He is not in fact delivering the lecture but writing
it, transcribing Welch's thesis on the lost idyll of medieval life and
culture. His own opinions on this are disclosed by the narrator. He
stops writing and,

> With a long jabbering belch, Dixon got up from the chair where
> he'd been writing and did his ape imitation all around the room.
> With one arm bent at the elbow so that the fingers brushed the
> armpit . . . he wove with bent knees and hunched rocking shoulders
> across to the bed, upon which he jumped up and down a few times,
> jibbering to himself.

The ape-man joke with Larkin on his father-in-law's revivalist
medievalism becomes in the novel a craftily orchestrated set piece.
Welch's, and Bardwell's, ideas are too absurd to merit verbal criticism; the ape-man performance is enough.

Throughout his early planning stage Amis hardly ever refers to
Jim Dixon. He is there, in the sense that the blend of needle-sharp
satire, anti-cultural ribaldry and cautiously framed disclosure that
characterizes the letters would become the key element of Jim's
relationship with his alter ego narrator, but before Swansea the idea
of Jim as an academic was engaging but unfocused. Amis always
claimed that Swansea, town and university, was not the setting for
Lucky Jim, which was true in the sense that none of his new friends
and colleagues were remodelled as characters. However, the protocols and mechanisms of a provincial university would become the
framework for the novel. Amis did not satirize academia *per se* –
indeed he found his new job stimulating and often enjoyable – but
the university setting provided him with the opportunity to better
expose the intellectual pretensions of the likes of Welch/Bardwell,
Bertrand and Margaret Peel because it licensed them.

After October 1949, when Amis started his new job, the me-

and-the-Bardwells novel is not mentioned in the letters for the best part of a year – he was busy with other things – but on 21 August 1950 he informed Larkin that he is about to start typing the first couple of chapters of '*Dixon and Xtine*'. This would involve an exercise in selecting material from his notes and letters, adding to it and framing it within the mundane ordinariness of Swansea life.

Wales and Welshness would feature in Amis's second novel, *That Uncertain Feeling*, and in the letters to Larkin during his first two years in Swansea Amis has a great deal of politically incorrect fun with the locality, particularly the accent and mannerisms of its people. The place is mentioned once in *Lucky Jim*, seemingly as a harmless, peripheral gesture but in fact as a private joke. Academia had provided Amis with the perfect setting for his fictionalized Bardwell – his absurd interests could become a professional commitment – and the fact that Amis's own introduction to the profession took place in Wales involved an irony he just could not ignore. When Bardwell heard that his son-in-law might be moving to Wales, his enthusiasm for the country and its culture went into overdrive. 'Won't it be *marvellous* if Kingsley gets the job!!! Professor Dai ap Faeces is there, who wrote the first really Scholarly Welch grammar, I'll get it and show you . . . So handy for the National Scheissbedsodd, too' (letter to Larkin, 6 October 1949). The carbon of this letter would have been on Amis's desk as he had Neddy Welch offer a piece of characteristically irrelevant advice to Jim about his article on medieval shipbuilding.

> I was having a chat the other day with an old friend of mine from South Wales. The Professor at the University College of Abertawe, he is now. Athro Haines; I expect you know his book on medieval Cwmrhydy ceirw.' (Chapter 8)

Abertawe is Swansea in Welsh and Athro Haines is Welsh for Department of History. Would Bardwell have recognized the link?

Amis would certainly have revelled in the almost fatalistic ironies that underpinned it. When summoned for interview, Amis was still suffering the after-effects of a debilitating bout of flu, and Bardwell had offered to go with him. 'He would enjoy the trip so! To his beloved Wales!!' (6 October 1949). Amis politely declined the offer, but of course Bardwell would go with him, in his notes, and become part of his novel. But what would he call him? In all of the letters Amis wrote to Larkin during 1949–50 telling him about his new home in Wales 'Welsh' becomes 'Welch'.

The private exchanges between Amis and Larkin provide the former with a kind of scurrilous rehearsal for the cautiously framed exercises of the novel. Larkin participated willingly in his role as foil to Amis's angry projections. Indeed, he sometimes unwittingly provided Amis with ideas. In a letter to Amis in July 1946 Larkin responds to Amis's early reports on Hilly's relatives: 'an awful price to pay for Hilary,' writes Larkin, and he goes on to declare that

> I HATE anybody who does anything UNUSUAL at ALL, whether it's make a lot of MONEY or dress in silly CLOTHES or read books of foreign WORDS or know a lot about anything or play any musical INSTRUMENT (menstruin) or pretend that they believe anything out of the ordinary that requires a lot of courage, or a lot of generosity, or a lot of self-cunt-roll, to believe it – BECAUSE THEY ARE USUALLY SUCH SODDING NASTY PEOPLE THAT I KNOW IT IS 1000–1 THAT THEY ARE SHOWING OFF – *and they don't know it* but *I know it.*

This is Larkin's general response to Amis's opinions on the sham hypocrisies of the Bardwell family, and it closely resembles Jim's first public disclosure of his inner world. In Chapter 20, when Bertrand bursts into his room to warn him against flirting with Christine, Jim tells him what he thinks of him. 'You think that just because you're tall and can put paint on canvas you're a sort of demigod. It wouldn't be so bad if you really were. But you're not: your sensitivity works for things that people do to you. Touchy and vain, yes, but not sensitive.'

I think that Larkin's letter was in Amis's mind when he wrote this chapter, because earlier in the letter Larkin makes fun of his then girlfriend Ruth Bowman's upper-class habits of pronunciation: 'the same (Sam) time'. It is surely not a coincidence that Amis disarms Bertrand's intellectual pretensions by giving him a similar habit, in which 'sam' features on several occasions. During the terrible evening at the Welches', Bertrand finishes a short and pompous speech on art and modern society with 'And I happen to like the arts, you sam'. Bertrand's 'sam', meaning 'see', is different from Bowman's 'sam' – same, but Amis had adapted it to take in a broader range of Bertrand's vocal indulgences, including 'do wam' (do we) and 'hostdram' (hostelry). Bertrand uses 'sam' again in their argument in Chapter 20.

> 'If you think I'm going to sit back and take this from you, you're mistaken; I don't happen to be that type, you sam.'
>
> 'I'm not Sam, you fool,' Dixon shrieked; this was the worst taunt of all . . .

Jim takes off his glasses, and they fight.

It might seem improbable that Amis would be reading Larkin's letters, some written years earlier, when writing *Lucky Jim*, but there is evidence to suggest that this is exactly what he was doing. In the 1949 letter where Amis thanks Larkin for encouraging him to be funny, for being his 'inner audience', he comments on how their friendship only really began after they had stopped seeing each other in 1942, and he states that he has 'just laughed like necrophily' at a spoof address that Larkin had used in a letter to Amis at Catterick army camp: '6477599 Fuc. P.A. Larkin, Excrement Boy, 1st BUM, Mond's Lines, Shatterick Ramp, Forks'. This letter, which was making Amis laugh in 1949, had been written to him in July 1942.

Amis's most blatant borrowing from his language game with Larkin occurs at the beginning of Chapter 16. Johns is a nasty, obsequious figure who works in the university, ministers to Welch's cultural obsessions and seems to be part of the overall conspiracy against Jim. As an act of revenge, Jim, signing himself as Joe Higgins, sends him a letter, a piece of semi-literate thuggery in which he accuses Johns of the attempted seduction of a university secretary.

He begins with 'This is just to let you no that I no what you are up to with yuong Marleen Richards, yuong Marleen is a desent girl and has got no tim for your sort, I no your sort . . .' This is not unlike Larkin's beginning of a letter to Amis where he thanks him 'for Yuor letar, yuo can certainly Spinn a yarn, I was fare peng myself at the Finnish: rekun yuo ave the nack of writting . . .'

Amis's account of Larkin's role in the conception and gestation of *Lucky Jim* is selective. He concedes that the idea for the book originated in his visit to Larkin at Leicester, that at the beginning Dixon was, in part, to be based on Larkin but that in the end 'Dixon resembles Larkin not in the smallest particular' (*Memoirs*, p. 57). Amis also states that Larkin helped him out with the book in more practical terms. In 1950 the first draft was 'sprawling', involving an enormous cast of secondary characters such as the 'loud magnate Sir George Wettling, cricket loving Philip Orchard, vivacious American visitor Teddy Wilson' (*Memoirs*, p. 57). Larkin pointed out after reading it that this retinue of satirical targets unbalanced the book, that more room should be made for the satirical agency, Jim: 'He decimated the characters . . . I had poured into the tale without care for the plot' (*Memoirs*, p. 57).

In fact Jim Dixon had featured in Amis's friendship with Larkin for a long time before Amis named and empowered him as a fictional presence. Soon after they become friends in Oxford, Amis imposed conditions on their relationship. He did not forbid exchanges on such topics as literature, culture and politics, but it soon became clear to Larkin that these were permissible only if woven into a fabric of farce, ridicule and pun-laden invective. This peculiar blend of learning and anti-cultural mannerisms would eventually become Jim Dixon, or at least the dimension of Jim which drew the attention of the book's more hostile critics. Jim is an articulate, clever graduate, but practically all of his encounters with learning are accompanied by a disclaimer indicating boredom or indifference. When Jim sees Christine at the College Ball he comments to himself on her attractiveness and adds that 'he'd read somewhere or been told that somebody like Aristotle or I. A. Richards had said that the sight of beauty makes us want to move towards it'. He can't remember which of them said this, and he does not care. At the same event he reflects on how Bertrand continually uses his status as a potential artist as though it were a guarantee of his complex and intriguing personality. 'Dixon himself had sometimes wished he wrote poetry or something as a claim to developed character', and he makes it clear that he never will. Alfred Beesley is an English lecturer with whom Jim shares digs and who has, on occasion, lent him books. One is about love by 'somebody like Plato or Rilke' and another is a modern novel involving a character who feels 'pity moving in him like a sickness' . . . 'or some such jargon'.

At the end of the novel Dixon and Christine are about to board the train to London, and they encounter the Welch family on the platform.

> He saw that not only were Welch and Bertrand both present, but Welch's fishing-hat and Bertrand's beret were there too. The beret, however, was on Welch's head, the fishing hat on Bertrand's. In these guises, and standing rigid with popping eyes, as both were, they had a look of being Gide and Lytton Strachey, represented in waxwork form by a prentice hand.

The narrator tells us that Jim 'drew in breath to denounce them both', but instead he collapses with laughter. '"You're . . ." he said. "He's . . ."' He does not complete these sentences and we will never know if the narrator's learned allusions to Gide and Strachey are shared by Jim, which is appropriate since he is about to make his triumphant departure from the world in which high-cultural coat-trailing is a measure of importance.

Jim's philistinism would become the most controversial aspect of the novel. If he had been presented as an ill-educated, working-class type, a 1950s' version of Hardy's *Jude*, or even as an English counterpart to the anti-intellectual intellectuals who had flourished in Tzarist Russia and more recently in France, fine. But Jim does not even pay culture the back-handed compliment of bothering to dislike it, let alone wanting to know more about it as a step to self-improvement. When *Lucky Jim* was published, few people had ever heard of Amis, but through 1954 and 1955, as the book became a bestseller, it was attended by interviews with and profiles of its author, and the parallels between Jim and the junior don at a provincial university who had created him raised questions, which on 17 February 1956 were addressed by J.G. Weightman in the *Times Literary Supplement*.

> Kingsley Amis's *Lucky Jim* has spread the impression that Redbrick is peopled by beer-drinking scholarship louts, who wouldn't know a napkin from a chimney-piece and whose one ideal is to end their sex starvation in the arms of a big breasted blonde . . . If the book were directly autobiographical, as many people assume it to be, Amis would presumably have long since lost his job, and rightly so.

While Weightman had never met Amis and perceived the novel as a symptom of moral degeneration, his suspicion that Jim grew out of his author's anti-cultural inclinations is obliquely accurate.

The letters Amis wrote to Larkin between 1945 and 1953 show how the unsettled, often contradictory features of Amis the private person were eventually recognized by Amis the novelist and reconstituted as Jim.

Most of the major English writers are mentioned in the letters, and most appear to cause various moods of boredom, disappointment and irritation. He regards Chaucer as comparable with 'the big pipe, that takes away, the waste matter, from a public lavatory . . .' (15 May 1946; the intrusive commas being a parody of the locutionary habits of his tutor J.B. Leishman). Dryden is 'A SECOND RATE FUCKING JOURNALIST' (8 October 1946). He agrees entirely with the *Edinburgh Magazine* reviewer who 'saw through our young romantic parvenu [Keats] from the start', and in the same letter he states that Pope and Wordsworth, while differently inclined, are equally overrated (20 March 1947). The Renaissance Sonnet, bedrock of formal discipline and stylistic exuberance, is a horrible, ridiculous exercise. 'I always thought that Eng. Lit. *ought to be good*; I still think it, but it *isn't* . . . Do not refrain from scorning the sonnet at *every available* opportunity' (2 December 1947). Milton, Cowper, Crabbe, Blake, Hardy, Dickens and Hopkins receive similar treatment. Shakespeare is spared, by omission.

More recent writers, many of whom had been introduced to him by Larkin, do not fare too well either. The verse of the Imagists and Symbolists is incomprehensible, formless; 'like what I used to write when I came in pissed in 1943. It kept PRETENDING to mean something and NOT MEANING ANYTHING' (30 January 1947). Dorothy Parker is 'TOO OBVIOUS AND ELEMENTARY' (29 March 1946). The characters of Flann O'Brien's *At Swim Two Birds* are '[not] at all funny' (8 August 1946). Joyce's *Ulysses* is unreadable (16 January 1949). D.H. Lawrence is an ideologue masquerading as a novelist (6 August 1948). Dylan Thomas writes self-indulgent nonsense (24 March 1947) and Waugh's *Brideshead Revisited* is pseudo-elitist fantasy (8 October 1948). Graham

Greene, on whom Amis in 1948 had been commissioned to write a monograph, is found humourless and tedious (9 November 1948). Even Auden, whom he once admired and whose imprint on Amis's early verse is very evident, now irritates him (9 March 1949).

Before concluding that Amis in his twenties appreciated nothing, we should recognize that he was reading not as a critic, an evaluative scrutineer, but more like someone obliged to watch a game while all the time wanting to be a player. His abusive diatribes were symptomatic of his frustrations, and it is noticeable that after 1950 these splenetic, irritable attacks on other writers almost ceased. He had begun *Lucky Jim*.

When exactly Amis discovered that a literary presence could be distilled from his most private, candid, all-inclusive persona will remain a mystery, but the parallels between the novel and the letters are remarkable. The 1952–3 letters are different from their predecessors in a number of very slight but tangible ways, evident only if we read them alongside the novel. He gives Larkin reports on the rapid progress of the final draft, and it is as though there is a dynamic relationship between the letters dispatched to Belfast (where at the time Larkin was working, at Queen's University) and the other text, in progress and destined eventually for Gollancz.

On 9 December 1952 he lists the 'vital books' on his shelf, presumably the shelf in his study in 24 The Grove. These include all of the authors vilified in his letters of the previous seven years. He does not explain why they are 'vital' (the inverted commas are his), but unless he had undergone a personality transplant we can assume that he means necessary to own and have read – he is, after all, a lecturer in English. There is a confident irony in the remark, because he does not bother to comment on their relative qualities; he's done that. Now he's more interested in something else: 'tally-ho for Dixon. I am about to start the pin-Welch-down sequence. There has been a lot of stuff about the burnt table which you might laugh at.' He might also have noted that he had decided that his 'vital books' are those that Dixon cannot be bothered to read. Obviously he has, for his fictional counterpart, transformed his literary irritations and obligations into a state of happy ignorance.

Blake Morrison has suggested that Orwell's George Bowling is the model for Jim's anti-cultural tendencies. There are similarities, but these are outnumbered by their differences. Bowling is a vehicle for Orwell's exposure of the divide between ordinary people and the posturing intellectuals who, hypocritically, espouse a commitment to a class with which they have nothing in common. Jim is from the north, but class, region and politics never feature in his exchanges with anyone, nor in the narrator's guide to Jim's character. Jim is not an Orwellian throwback. He is the initiator of a characteristic of novels by David Lodge, Malcolm Bradbury, Tom Sharpe and Howard Jacobson. In all of the 'academic' novels by these writers, the principal character has plenty of cultural and literary credentials, but these always pull against his more basic inclinations, principally a desire for a good life and the attentions of attractive women.

This tension between being an intellectual and all that this involved and being an ambitious, irreverent, lecherous man informs the exchanges between Amis and Larkin. *Lucky Jim* would not have existed without Amis's friendship with Larkin, but it also drove a wedge into their relationship. Margaret Peel, Jim's pretentious girlfriend, is an unnervingly transparent version of Monica Jones, the university lecturer in English Larkin had met in Leicester in 1946 and who remained as his regular, if not his only, partner until his death in 1985. Margaret looks like Monica, both in terms of her physical appearance and in her taste in clothes and casual jewellery. Every time Jim meets her or even thinks about her, the passage involves a precise description of what she is wearing, often supplemented by a comment on her posture or physiognomy. She wore 'a sort of arty get-up of multi-coloured shirt, skirt with fringed hem and pocket, low-heeled shoes, and wooden beads' and in the next chapter 'She was wearing her arty get-up, but had discarded the wooden beads in favour of a brooch consisting of a wooden letter "M"'. No one else in the book receives anything like the attention to physical detail given to Margaret. 'As if searching for a text he examined her face, noting the tufts of brown hair that overhung the earpieces of her glasses, the crease running up the near cheek and approaching closer than before to this eye socket (or was he imagining that?) and the faint but at this angle unmistakable downward curve of the mouth.' Jim's apparent obsession with her appearance might simply be a way of emphasizing his dissatisfaction at being attached to a woman he finds unattractive. But at the same time one suspects that Amis is suggesting a causal relationship between women who look and dress like Margaret and a propensity for pretentiousness and faked psychological complexity. Jim's close reading of her face occurs during their conversation in Chapter 2 in which she insists on describing in detail the emotional crisis that attended her attempt to commit suicide (which eventually turns out to have been faked). Her account resembles an extract from a particularly bad existentialist play. Jim, via the narrator, does not bother to comment on the gross theatricality of Margaret's speech, but he does seem to need continually to remind the reader of what this irritating person looks like. 'She leaned sideways on her barstool in laughter, her hands clasped around one knee, the quasi-velvet shoe falling away from her heel.'

Margaret's face, hair, spectacles, her taste in clothes and jewellery, would show anyone who knew Monica Jones, and knew of Larkin's friendship with Amis, that Margaret was based on her. And there were also parallels between their quasi-radical attitudes to culture and their verbal habits, so much so that Larkin was prompted to ask Amis if 'you weren't actually there taking notes [of our conversations], were you?' (Jacobs, p. 146). Margaret is selfish, potentially vicious, a liar and an emotional charlatan. Monica Jones was nothing like this, and nor was Larkin's attitude towards her anything like Jim's view of Margaret: their backgrounds, family histories and related anxieties were similar, and they shared an enthusiasm for literature, particularly in their admiration for Hardy, Yeats and Lawrence.

Amis's message must have been clear to Larkin: a woman who dresses and talks like Margaret/Monica is not worth having a relationship with. Indeed in their letters they would both be blatantly and cruelly honest about the faults, pretensions and boredom-quotient exhibited by women they had known or gone out with, but with Margaret Amis took this game too far. Larkin was uneasy about her name, which at one point was to be Margaret Jones. Amis argued for this by suggesting an in-joke, in which Larkin would tell Monica that the character was based on Margaret Aaron-Thomas, a social worker friend of the Amises' in Swansea, while Amis would persuade Aaron-Thomas that she was based on a girl in Leicester. In the end Amis persuaded Larkin to accept Margaret Peel. The rhyming association with Monica's full name of Margaret Monica Beale Jones was a slight concession to anonymity, but the echoes would have been clear enough to Monica.

And how did Monica feel about this? She knew that Larkin was helping Amis with the book, but she did not find out about her part in it until after publication. There is no record of her immediate response, but if she had read *The Times* review we can assume that it was less than ecstatic. *The Times* praises Amis's representations of the most affected, pretentious characters, particularly 'the neurotic woman lecturer' with whom Jim has 'brilliant' exchanges. When asked years later about Amis by Larkin's biographer Andrew Motion, Monica recalled that Amis would try to take charge of any exchanges that the three of them had, would attempt to exclude others from the Amis–Larkin double act. 'Kingsley wasn't just making faces all the time, he was actually trying them on. He didn't know who he was' (Motion, p. 169). When asked by Motion about Monica, Amis said that 'There was a sort of adhesive thing about her . . . Not quite predatory, but still . . .' (p. 169). It was not so much that Amis disliked Monica herself, more that he disliked her apparently close attachment to Larkin, a Larkin who was willing to talk to her about things that were forbidden from their own exchanges. This sense of Amis as resentful of women who interfered with their association is born out by Ruth Bowman with whom Larkin had an affair in the mid 1940s in Wellington. She felt that Amis 'was possessive of Philip and tried to keep me separate from him', and she tells of how she was offended by Amis's clear attempts to turn Larkin into a version of himself, particularly in his attitude to women (Motion, pp. 123, 138). In a strangely similar way, Margaret interferes with the relationship between Jim's inner and outer worlds, causing him to make continued concessions to her personality which privately he finds almost unbearable.

In the light of all this, it is possible to detect a certain amount of obfuscation in Amis's claim that Jim 'resembles Larkin not in the smallest particular'. True, he is not much like the complex, anxious, stammering, mildly neurotic fan of D.H. Lawrence, but he bears a very close resemblance to the person that Larkin was willing to turn himself into, in the letters and in Amis's company, and whom Amis tried to isolate from the adhesive, 'predatory' inclinations of women like Margaret/Monica.

Lucky Jim was published in January 1954, and apart from unfavourable pieces in the *Sunday Times* and the *News Chronicle* the early reviews were enthusiastic and full of praise. Walter Allen, who was to promote the phrase 'Angry Young Men', wrote in the *New Statesman* of a novelist of 'considerable and uncomfortable talent', with the second adjective referring to Amis's apparent ability to distil a clever and stylish novel out of an anti-cultural presence. On 24 January the *Observer*'s Sean O'Faolain took the same line: Amis had 'made the gayest of bricks with the most common straw'. John Betjeman in the *Daily Telegraph* suggested that *Lucky Jim* was the equivalent of silent film comedy in prose. During February and March Amis was bombarded with fan mail. He wrote to Larkin of this with unconcealed glee, taking particular note of how many of their mutual, often fairweather, friends and acquaintances had suddenly become devotees. He told Larkin that 'I feel in a sense "that they can't stop me now".' Six weeks after publication the novel had gone into its fifth impression: there were about 7,500 copies in print and they were disappearing as fast as they could be sent to bookshops. By the end of the year 12,000 copies had been sold. By summer the Boulting brothers had offered £200 for the film rights and foreign publishers were bidding for translation rights.

John Wain, Amis's friend from his post-war years in Oxford, played a very different role from Larkin in ensuring the success of *Lucky Jim*. Amis had sent the typescript to Gollancz at the beginning of 1953 and by March had heard nothing. Then he received a letter from Wain who had been commissioned by the BBC to edit a radio series called *First Readings* which would introduce Third Programme listeners to extracts from the work of new writers. Wain had seen parts of Amis's novel and offered to use an extract, which was daring given that Amis had yet to find a publisher. Amis sent him the passage in which Jim wakes up hung-over in the Welches' spare bedroom, has to listen to Neddy humming Mozart next door and then work out, with Christine, how to deal with the cigarette burns on the sheets, blankets and bedside table. Wain decided to use it in the opening broadcast which went out on 26 April. Amis had written to Hilary Rubinstein, the editor at Gollancz dealing with his typescript, and told him of the forthcoming reading. Rubinstein and others in the office listened in, and he sought impressions from friends. Everyone had liked what they heard and the wheels began to turn. By the end of May 1953 Amis had his contract.

A month later Wain contracted Amis to do a short volume of verse for a series he had started at the University of Reading. With wonderful timing Amis's *A Frame of Mind* went into print shortly before *Lucky Jim* in 1954 and offered interested readers another perspective on the figure behind the novel. This anti-cultural hooligan, whose hero despised books and learning, could write complex and stylish poems.

Wain's assistance in the making of what would become the mythology of Jim Dixon was initially practical and generous – but it would soon become involuntary and, for Wain, counterproductive. Wain's *Hurry On Down* was published several months before Amis's novel, and both are often cited as the initiators of the 'angry' mood of 1950s' fiction, but Wain's novel would always exist in the shadow of Amis's.

Amis's Jim Dixon and Wain's Charles Lumley are lower middle class, bored and irritated by the cultural and social pretensions of their peers; both succeed in getting the women they want and jobs that provide them at least with an alternative to their previous lives – Lumley becomes a radio gag-writer. But the similarities are superficial. Lumley embodies a political mood, a feeling of dissatisfaction with an outdated English social structure. There is humour, but it is of the submissive, stoical type which invites the reader to sympathize with the hero's sense of alienation. Jim embodies nothing in particular – for him people with 'ideas' about class and social inequality are as pretentious and boring as their privileged, disinterested counterparts. Jim, assisted by his narrator, uses comedy as a triumphant act of revenge against the people who annoy him and frustrate his ambitions. Jim's anarchic, dismissive attitude to his world seems to prefigure, even justify, his successful escape from it.

Hurry On Down belonged to a comfortably established genre of British fiction; anti-modernist and involving the ideas, conditions and idioms of contemporary life. C.P. Snow's *Strangers and Brothers* sequence of novels had since the 1940s recorded and distractedly satirized English society. Anthony Powell's *A Dance to the Music of Time* had similarly begun, and continued, as a disillusioned account of post-1930s' social arrangements. Evelyn Waugh, albeit with views which seemed to favour a return to pre-Reformation feudalism, was similarly diagnostic, assessing society and blaming it for much of his characters' feelings of rootlessness. Wain's politics were radically antithetical to Waugh's, but his fiction, like Snow's and Powell's, shared a tendency to counterpose the individual against a closely defined network of social and ideological conditions. This tendency also informed the work of new post-war writers such as William Cooper and Angus Wilson. Cooper's *Scenes from Provincial Life* (1950) involved the experiences of a schoolteacher in the humdrum environment of a Midlands town in the early 1940s (Larkin, a fan, called it with well-meant irony 'the great Leicester novel'). Wilson's *The Wrong Set* (1949) and *Such Darling Dodos* (1950) quietly ridiculed the pretensions and self-deceptions of lower-middle-class England, but again his principal figures seemed to be trapped in a world to which sceptical endurance was the only available response.

Lucky Jim at once extended and broke with this tradition. It was satirical, in the sense that it dismantled a range of social and intellectual pretensions, but its only alternative seemed to involve making fun of people and having a good time. It was realistic. The university setting, the characters' backgrounds, the way they behaved and talked, were lifted from England and Wales circa 1950, but it used this naturalistic framework as the basis for a fairy-tale, an achieved fantasy. Jim is frustrated and irritated, but he is never offered as a means of diagnosing contemporary states of angst or alienation. He wants the pretty girl and the good job in London; his 'luck' gets him both, and he is happy.

The fact that Wain's and Amis's books appeared within a few months of each other meant that reviewers would immediately recognize that Amis had done something different. Walter Allen's piece in the *New Statesman* in early 1954 dealt with both, but Allen pushed Lumley into the background and considered Dixon as a character without an obvious precedent, an assembly of paradoxes. Is he, asks Allen, 'the intellectual tough or the tough intellectual?'

Amis read *Hurry On Down* while he was waiting for *Lucky Jim* to go into print, and in a letter to Wain (6 November 1953) he offers, with some slight qualifications, an approving estimation. He 'thoroughly enjoyed' it and 'read it whenever I had a free moment till I'd finished it. It is very funny in parts and does succeed above all in getting across a grotesque and twisted view of life (which is what I try to do, though it's not the same view – this I think is where we're similar), which is the main point as far as I'm concerned.' Four decades later in the *Memoirs* he was a bit more honest about how he felt. 'It seemed to be of a certain banality of conception and style [but] this could not in the nature of things be the case, with John being so well up on everything, and that therefore the novel I had myself written must all be on some dismayingly wrong . . . track' (pp. 42–3). Amis was politely, perhaps anxiously, dishonest in 1953 because he knew that Wain, although yet to earn his credentials as a novelist, was in a number of ways part of the literary establishment – his academic posts, work for the BBC, publishing projects, along with his stylistic conservatism testified to that. If new novels like *Hurry On Down* were the benchmark for acceptance, then *Lucky Jim*, which departed radically from the mainstream, was in dangerous territory. In the end, he need not have worried because the press coverage and controversy generated by his novel effectively sidelined Wain. In the *Memoirs* he was resurrecting his triumph of 1954 when the pupil had beaten his mentor and adviser. In the early 1960s Magnus Magnusson had briefed Amis on a forthcoming radio interview and told him of how a few weeks earlier he had similarly primed Wain and suggested that he might introduce him as 'the poor man's Kingsley Amis'. Wain had threatened to leave the studio.

After 1954 the relationship between Wain and Amis became a sequence of insults and rebukes. In his *Memoirs* Amis interweaves with a grudging appreciation of Wain's help anecdotes that present him as egotistical, envious and far too confident of his own, in Amis's view questionable, literary talents.

Larkin, too, was unsettled by the immediate success of his friend's novel and not only because of the Margaret/Monica episode. Larkin's reputation as a poet was increasing, but he had not abandoned his original, more powerful ambition to become a respected novelist. *Jill* and *A Girl in Winter* belonged to the mainstream of new realism, projecting the anxieties and crises of their characters into a detailed representation of contemporary Britain. His ambivalent feelings about Amis's departure from this tradition is reflected in letters sent to his Belfast friend Patsy Strang soon after *Lucky Jim*'s publication.

He praises the novel's comic energy: 'sends me into fits of howling laughter', 'miraculously and intensely funny', 'the Kingsley humour I think quite unrivalled, quite wonderful'. He could have been writing about the Kingsley with whom he had shared private, anarchic exchanges. This world was now public property, was being taken seriously by critics, and Larkin's other comments reflect his unease. 'Apart from being funny, I think it is somewhat over simple', 'It's in the general thinness of the imagination that he falls down.' He compares it unfavourably with a story from Angus Wilson's *The Wrong Crowd* which, 'to my mind, makes the Welch family hardly satire at all' (3 February 1954).

On 23 January Amis wrote to Larkin to thank him for the poem he had written to commemorate the birth of the Amises' third child, Sally, born shortly before the publication of *Lucky Jim*: 'Sodding good and touching . . . moving me a great deal as a poem and a friendship assertion.' A week later Larkin wrote to Strang of how he had felt obliged to compose a 'fudged up' and 'mechanical' piece for his friend's new daughter (3 February 1954).

For Larkin their relationship had changed, and this is confirmed in his 1958 reply to a letter from William Van O'Connor, an American academic researching a book on the post-war British novel. Larkin writes that he has known Amis 'fairly well since 1941'.

Our affinity is difficult to explain, since I do not think we have many artistic aims in common, but we usually agree in the things we find funny or desirable. [*Lucky Jim*] is fair evidence of this and commemorates a period of intense joke swapping just after the war. (2 April 1958)

The word 'commemorates' suggests that the novel both made public and undermined this particular aspect of their friendship, a suggestion confirmed by Larkin's statement that 'we have inevitably had less time for each other over the last five years or so'. The inevitability of this would not be clear to O'Connor, who had met neither of them, and one suspects that Larkin's personal feelings here have penetrated his otherwise dry, objective account, particularly when we compare it with Amis's reply to O'Connor in which he states that 'Philip Larkin in fact I regard as my best friend' (21 January 1958).

Amis and Larkin remained friends. They continued to meet and exchange letters, and throughout the 1950s Amis continued to treat Larkin as his confessor, particularly regarding his adulterous activities. What had changed was that their intimate, interactive language game, which for Larkin had been a substitute for the shy, anxious element of his character, had now for Amis become the vehicle for literary fame.

Amis would never again show his ongoing drafts to Larkin. He would write and rewrite, but with the exception in the 1960s of his second wife, Elizabeth Jane Howard, no one would see the material until the typescript went to the publisher. Throughout his writing career Amis would tie elements of his lived experience into the fabric of an ongoing novel and then, almost arbitrarily, alter or exaggerate these or interweave them with their exact opposites – rather as if he felt uneasy about borrowing so heavily. He established this precedent in his use of Swansea, its university and academia in general in *Lucky Jim*.

Amis's job became available as a consequence of the post-war expansion of provincial universities. During his first few years he made friends with a group of similar new recruits, men largely of the same age and background, who had ended up in this remote academic encampment more by accident than design. There was Willie Smyth, a Dubliner and new lecturer in Classics, who shared Amis's taste for drink and, before the arrival of Hilly and the children, his digs in St Helen's Place. James 'Jo' Bartley was almost a decade older than Amis. He had previously held a Chair in English at the University of New Delhi and, for reasons still shrouded in mystery, felt obliged to leave India very soon after independence. He was a native of Ulster and when drunk, which was a very frequent occurrence, his most remembered line was 'Mountbatten shot my bearer'. Esmond Cleary, an Englishman, was a lecturer in Economics who Amis asked for an article title which indicated the incredibly boring contents of the piece. Cleary came up with 'The Economic Influence of the Developments in Shipbuilding, 1450 to 1485'. Jim Dixon would try to place this in a journal run by the mysterious L. S. Caton in order to maintain his employment as an untenured academic. David Sims, another new member of the English Department, came from the Welsh valleys and would play an important part in Amis's research for his second novel, *That Uncertain Feeling*. Sam Dawson, also of the English Department, was a few years younger than Amis. A devotee of F. R. Leavis, Dawson would have regular arguments with Amis on the nature of literature, high culture, university teaching and what all of these things meant.

None of these characters became subjects for the novel in the same way that Amis's in-laws Hilly and Monica Jones had done, but the experiences Amis shared with them, the sense of a slightly rebellious, collective unity against prevailing circumstances, contributed to the presence and effect of Jim Dixon. Throughout the novel there is a sense that practically everyone connected with the university is intent upon the social, sexual and professional ruination of

Jim; with the exception of his colleague Goldsmith, who shares
Jim's suspicions about the academic credibility of their seniors,
Beesley, another lecturer, who shares Jim's digs, and Bill Atkinson,
the only resident of the boarding-house who is not connected with
the university. Atkinson, a salesman, is a prototype for the intelligent, no-nonsense antiheroes that would be central to the writings
of Braine, Storey and Sillitoe. Jim's allies reflect his state of scepticism and dissatisfaction and will, we know, enjoy his successful act
of rebellion. This fictional alliance drew upon the us-against-them
mood of Amis's new colleagues and friends.

University College Swansea in 1949 was informed by the
Chapel-based morality that was still very influential in South Wales.
Until the early 1950s alcohol was not allowed on the premises. The
Senior Common Room, set up soon after Amis's arrival, could not
serve drink in the first year of its existence. Amis rejoiced in the fact
that its first barmaid was a well-known local ex-prostitute. (Her
Christian name, Betty, is passed on to a woman of the same profession who features in his 1956 Swansea-based short story 'Moral
Fibre'.) Even before *Lucky Jim* gained him public notoriety, Amis
had been noticed by the dissenting ministers and local politicians
who sat on the various boards and governing bodies of the college.
Sam Dawson tells of how, on the first Saturday after pay-day, Amis,
Hilly, a few of his colleagues and undergraduate students would
begin with drinks in the Grand Hotel, go on to the Metropole for a
cold-table lunch and back via several pubs to the Amises' house in
The Grove for further refreshments. Swansea was a small town,
most of its undergraduates were from the locality and the spectacle
of academics drinking with their pupils, for whom they were also
expected to provide moral guidance, caused whispers of imminent
social decay.

Amis treated his students as friends and equals. In his lectures he
combined informality with inspiration and raised iconoclastic questions on why and how the established names of the English canon

had achieved their status. He encouraged his students to re-evaluate sacred authors, to make use of their own developing critical skills and effectively become reviewers of works such as *The Faerie Queene* and *Paradise Lost*. And his lecturing style was, for the time, somewhat indecorous. On 9 January 1950 Amis informed Larkin that term would begin the next day.

> At 11 a.m. I deliver my first lecture. It's about the aesthetic move-
> ment (don't grin like that) . . . 'Wilde united the qualities of silliness
> and high intelligence in a degree unparalleled since Keats' – yes,
> I'm going to say that.

Amis's first head of department was the complete opposite of Neddy Welch. W. D. Thomas became his confidant and mentor, and on one occasion in 1951 he felt obliged to summon Amis to his office and ask him to consider if his approach to teaching was a little too radical for an institution which depended upon the approval of local dignitaries. Thomas had picked up ominous rumours from members of the College Council, to which he would soon have to submit a report on the still probationary new lecturer.

Amis in his first novel sought revenge against those aspects of academia that annoyed him, and one can imagine the way in which his irritations influenced the chapter in which Jim causes offence to assembled dignitaries at his public lecture on the joys of medieval England. He is drunk, he sports a black eye from the previous evening's fight with Bertrand and is cheered by his undergraduates.

For both Dixon and Amis publications were important, and Jim's desperate attempts to place 'The Economic Influence of the Develop-ments in Shipbuilding, 1450 to 1485' become a running joke of the novel. In Chapter 1 we find Jim in Welch's car being driven to the latter's house 'for tea'. He has just attempted to convince his boss of the scholarly qualities of the piece, and the narrator discloses his actual thoughts on its 'niggling mindlessness, its funereal parody of yawn-enforcing facts, the pseudo light it threw upon non-problems'. Next, Welch attempts to pass a bus on a corner, almost kills them both, and comments, 'Well, that ought to do nicely, I should say.' We are never sure if he is referring to his own suicidal motor-ballet or to the satisfactory status of Jim's article. At the time he wrote this scene Amis was experiencing professional uncertainties not unlike Jim's. In November 1950 he travelled from Swansea to Oxford for his B.Litt. viva to find that the senior examiner was his ex-supervisor, Lord David Cecil. Cecil failed the thesis, and his reasons for doing so were not academic. Cecil treated Oxford as a feudal fiefdom in which he was answerable to no one, and Amis had clearly annoyed him. When his pupil had sought advice on the direction of his thesis Cecil could hardly ever be found. Eventually Amis asked if he could change supervisors, and F.W. Bateson agreed to take him on. Cecil signed the appropriate form without comment, but his reappearance as vengeful examiner indicates that the sensitive aristocrat had been offended. Amis's tenure was not conditional upon the success of his higher degree, but its failure was a black mark. Bateson advised him to turn his thesis into an article, which he did in 1951. *Essays in Criticism*, which Bateson had founded and now edited, published it in 1952. (In *Lucky Jim* when Dixon is desperately trying to find a way of returning Christine to the Welches' party, from which they have both absconded, he spots a sign reading '*Cars for hire – Bateson's – Repairs*' (Chapter 14) – a sardonically apposite comment if ever there was one.)

The article was a distillation of the challenging and original elements of Amis's thesis, on how nineteenth-century readers responded to contemporary poetry, and was certainly nothing like Jim's 'parade of yawn-enforcing facts', but Jim's feelings about the worthlessness of academic research must surely have been influenced by Amis's experience of scholarship and its rewards as a kind of lottery. Although Leonard Bardwell was the model for Neddy Welch, Cecil played a part in the latter's construction. Like Cecil,

Welch treats his professional environment as a fiefdom and cares very little about the future prospects of his juniors. When Jim attempts to speak to his boss about his article, Welch always seems to have something else to do, not unlike the graciously indifferent attitude of Lord David to his graduate student. So, when Amis invented Jim's nightmarish car journey with an eccentric dimwit whose driving skills reflect his state of detachment from the real world, his thoughts could easily have been on his own equally nerve-racking, if not life-threatening, journey through the academic profession.

Amis's other satirical stab at academia involved an individual he would never meet, at least not to speak to, but who was known to everyone who studied or taught English: F.R. Leavis. Amis as an undergraduate had read Leavis's *Revaluation* and a number of his essays on Shakespeare. Leavis published *The Great Tradition*, his mapping out of the ideal English canon, in 1948, just as Amis was starting work on *Lucky Jim*. Amis read it and found that Leavis's first team of 'English' novelists (including an American and a Pole) consisted of Jane Austen, George Eliot, Henry James, Joseph Conrad and D.H. Lawrence. Leavis's almost religious dedication to Lawrence annoyed Amis, but his criteria for selecting the great authors irritated him most of all. The best novelists, and consequently the ones worth teaching in universities, were those who in some way preserved the moral positions that underpinned English culture. These positions advocated an 'openness' in the face of life, a commitment to the value of traditionally English folk ways, an approval of a natural, organic mode of existence and a mistrust of modern, post-industrial and metropolitan culture. Amis loathed the view that literature should be used or interpreted as a vehicle for moral, political or philosophical ideals, and he must have been particularly annoyed by Leavis's opinion that *Tom Jones* did not belong in the canon because it seemed to endorse the immoral, directionless urbanity of its eighteenth-century readers (see Leavis, 1948, p. 4).

Fielding was and remained Amis's favourite pre-twentieth-century novelist. His combination of satire, moral relativism and his tendency in fiction to reflect the world rather than attempt to improve it – all in opposition to Leavis's criteria – would, as Amis later stated, influence his own work. Neddy Welch's obsession with folk culture was partly a borrowing from Leonard Bardwell, but only partly.

Compare the following passages. The first is from Jim's Welch-inspired lecture on the joys of medieval England and the second is from one of Leavis's essays on the same topic.

Amis: What, finally, is the practical application of all this? Can anything be done to halt, or even to hinder, the process I have described? I say to you that something can be done by each of us here tonight. Each of us can resolve to do something, every day, to resist the application of manufactured standards, to protest against ugly articles of furniture and table-ware, to speak out against sham architecture, to resist the importation into more and more places of loudspeakers relaying the Light Programme, to say one word against the Yellow Press, against the best-seller, against the theatre organ, to say one word for the instinctive culture of the integrated village-type community. In that way we shall be saying a word, however small in its individual effect, for our native tradition, for our common heritage, in short, for what we once had and may, some day, have again – Merrie England. (Chapter 20)

Leavis: This strength of English belongs to the very spirit of the language – the spirit that was formed when the English people who formed it were predominantly rural . . . And how much richer the *life* was in the old, predominantly rural order than in the modern suburban world . . . When one adds that speech in the old order was a popularly cultivated art, that people talked (so making Shakespeare possible) instead of reading or listening to the wireless, it becomes plain that the promise of regeneration by American

slang, popular city idiom, or invention of *transition* cosmopolitans
is a flimsy consolation for our loss. (*Scrutiny*, 1933)

Within a year of the novel's publication the assumed parallels
between Jim and his creator were beyond Amis's control.

In Walter Allen's 1954 review article on Amis and Wain it is
clear that he regards their respective heroes, Jim in particular, as
lenses for their authors' cynical, sardonic perceptions of contemporary life. Allen was aware of a number of biographical connections
between Jim and Amis as young academics, and he asks if the new
hero is 'the intellectual tough or the tough intellectual', a question
raised by the paradoxical relation between Jim's cleverness and his
apparent loathing for academics and 'artists'. 'At the least suspicion
of the phoney he goes tough', a recollection perhaps of the set-to
with Bertrand. 'He sees through the academic racket as he sees
through all others. A racket is phoneyness organized, and in contact
with phoneyness he turns red, just as litmus paper does in contact
with acid' (*New Statesman*, 30 January 1954) – red enough to
imagine planting a necklace bead up his pretentious girlfriend's
nose and his head of department into a lavatory basin.

As Weightman's *Times Literary Supplement* article showed, the
possibility that Amis the university teacher might behave like Jim or
hold similar opinions caused some people unease. Almost a year
after publication W. Somerset Maugham contributed a piece to the
Sunday Times 'Books of the Year'. He does not use names, but it is
clear to anyone who has read the novel that, for Maugham, Dixon
is Amis.

They do not go to university to acquire culture but to get a job and
when they have got one scamp it. They have no manners and are
woefully unable to deal with any social predicament. Their idea of
a celebration is to go to a public house and drink six beers. They are
mean, malicious and envious. They will write anonymous letters to

harass a fellow undergraduate and listen to a telephone conversation that is no business of theirs. Charity, kindliness, generosity are qualities which they hold in contempt. They are scum. They will in due course leave the university. Some will doubtless sink back, perhaps with relief, into the modest class from which they emerged; some will take to drink, some to crime, and go to prison. Others will become schoolmasters and form the young, or journalists and mould public opinion. A few will go into Parliament, become Cabinet Ministers and rule the country. I look upon myself as fortunate that I shall not live to see it. (*Sunday Times*, 25 December 1954)

At the end of 1953 W.D. Thomas, Amis's boss and ally, retired, and in early 1954 the college appointed Professor James Kinsley as his replacement. Kinsley had previously worked in Aberystwyth. He was a teetotal, Methodist lay preacher, and his lifestyle obviously impressed the Nonconformist brethren of the selection committee. Few members of the English Department liked Kinsley, and Amis came to loathe him. He was an academic scholar who regarded literary writers as subjects, not potential colleagues. Within months of his appointment he found that his department had become famous. It employed a novelist who, in Allen's view, had exposed academia as a 'racket', an assembly of 'phoneys'. Within a year of the publication of *Lucky Jim* Kinsley was making enquiries about whether Amis could be sacked for bringing the institution, indeed the entire profession, into disrepute and was advised that only a criminal prosecution or insanity were grounds for dismissal, not the publication of a novel. Next he attempted to have Amis's salary stopped at the so-called 'efficiency bar', because he seemed to spend more time writing fiction than preparing academic papers. Kinsley was overruled in both strategies by the college principal, John Fulton, a pragmatist who recognized that the presence of a new, controversial novelist would do no damage to the reputation of an otherwise remote provincial institution. Kinsley disliked Amis because his junior colleague had undermined his own academic status. When Kinsley attended conferences fellow scholars were often more interested in where he came from than what he had to say about Dryden, his specialization. Did people really behave like Jim in the Swansea English Department? Were senior academics like Neddy Welch really employed by his university?

The jokes, intended and accidental, generated by the similarities between Amis's Christian name and 'Kinsley' caused the latter a good deal of bitterness against what seemed to be a comedic act of fate. In 1955, for example, the front page of the local paper *Swansea Voice* carried a large photograph of a very attractive young woman in evening dress and crown being congratulated by Amis. It shows 'Mr Kinsley Amis: the Swansea author, and the Mazda Queen of Light, Miss Shirley Corey, of Bishopston, after her selection at the Casino Ballroom, last week.' Kinsley, by all accounts, was the only person unamused by this.

In Swansea itself the rapid success of the novel generated a good deal of gossip and speculation on its origins in fact. For his students, Amis became an embodied myth. His customary informality in lectures and tutorials was always balanced against his scholarly learning, but everyone seemed to be waiting for a Dixonesque act of rebellion. Sam Dawson, his colleague, was frequently asked if he was the model for Jim. Dawson was the youngest member of the department and the only one with a northern accent, like Jim's. But he was also an advocate of the critical ideas of Leavis. Was Jim both a version of Dawson and a means by which Amis might parody the opinions of his colleague? Sam's Christian name resurfaces as a locutionary keynote of Bertrand's angry, pretentious diatribes. 'If you think I'm going to take this from you, you're mistaken; I don't happen to be that type, you sam.' But this was pure coincidence; the 'sam' joke came from Amis's farcical exchanges with Larkin.

Novels that transpose themselves with contemporary life and appear to embody the unorthodox mindset of their author always create a modest industry of speculation. Readers and critics tend to treat them as a verbalized dimension of someone they know or have come to know. This certainly happened with *Lucky Jim*.

Hilary Rubinstein, who commissioned the book, later confessed that he was unsettled on first reading by the relationship between Dixon and his imagined creator, whom he had yet to meet. 'I doubted whether Jim Dixon would have gone to the pub and drunk ten pints of beer. Ten pints seemed too much. I didn't know Kingsley very well, you see . . .' (Salwak, p. 61).

John Betjeman, whose review of the novel had introduced him to Amis, wrote to him soon afterwards and confessed that he was slightly uneasy about the 'Wodehouse-like evasion at the end', too much of a fairy-tale finish; 'better to have left him in the dark brown stuff'. Yet he qualifies this by adding that 'one begins to care about what happens to Dixon, and its nice to find he gets out . . .' At this point Amis and Betjeman had communicated only by letter, but Betjeman gives the impression that by reading the novel he has already met its author.

Respondents to *Lucky Jim* generally fell into two categories: those who felt personally affronted by Jim and those who regarded him as a new-found friend. It was not simply that Maugham and Weightman disliked Jim's advocation of anti-culturalism, more that they felt personally unsettled by his manner, at once clubbable and aggressive, affable and sharp. It was as though he had walked off the pages and begun an exchange with them. Similarly, the people who liked him felt this way not so much because they shared his opinions but because they enjoyed his presence.

Amis always denied, spuriously, that *Lucky Jim* was based on his personal experience, but fate, or its literary advocate, took a hand and made sure that Jim would become part of his life. Amis did not leave academia, he did not want to, but what Betjeman calls the book's fairy-tale finish, Jim's joyous elevation from penury to well-paid comfort along with the woman he loves, was not unlike the effect that the novel had upon Amis and Hilly. Following the enthusiastic reviews and on the official day of publication, they went out to the Grand Hotel, Swansea, and ordered a bottle of champagne. Swansea was a small place, and the contrast between this conspicuously hedonistic couple and their downbeat, still blitz-savaged environment drew local comment. Hilly's legacy had made life bearable, and soon this would be supplemented by royalties. 'We were pretty well on our uppers . . . now we got two-figure, even three-figure cheques' (Salwak, p. 63). It was not just the financial benefits and critical approbation of the novel that pleased Amis. It was, to put it bluntly, the fame. Frequently in the letters to Larkin of 1951–4 Amis complains about the mundane ordinariness of things. On 13 January 1953 he writes of how bored he is with conversations about unemployment in Llanelli or Dylan Thomas, recently deceased; with reports from Hilly about the Gower Riding Society; and, worst of all, with the prospect of examiners' meetings on this year's Finals Class. 'You know what I should like to see? Apart from two corrupt schoolgirls undressing, I should like to see *a bit of life*. Almost *any sort*. Drinking, or sex, or fine talk, especially . . .' This, of course, could have been written by Jim, stuck in the middle of nowhere in a job with no exciting prospects and with a social life that was largely an obligation. Jim is projected into a fantastic realization of his desires, and the parallels between what happened to him and what his creator wanted to happen while he was waiting for this exercise in wish fulfilment to go into print are striking. On 26 November 1953 he wishes that 'something nice would happen to me, like having a fuck or selling the film rights of *Jim*. That'd be funny, wouldn't it? Dixon, Alec Guinness; Christine, Gina Lollobrigida; Margaret, Dulcie Grey; Bertrand, Orson Welles; Welch, Boris Karloff; John, Peter Lorre; Atkinson, Trevor Howard. Music by Bruce Montgomery. Screenplay by Eric Ambler. Directed by Alfred Hitchcock. Just pipe dreaming, dear.' Pipe dreaming he might have been, but within a year the film rights had been sold to the Boulting Brothers, after Hitchcock had indeed shown more than an interest but had withdrawn his bid (letter to Larkin, 18 October 1954). On 13 November 1954 Amis imagines himself 'snogging' with whichever actress would be chosen for Christine. Throughout 1954, when bids for the film rights were coming in, and during 1955, when the Boulting Brothers were planning the project, Amis's letters to Larkin are regularly peppered with reports on who would be playing the various roles. He had heard that Norman Wisdom was interested in playing Jim (14 March 1954) and that Kenneth More was also a contender; Amis imagines coaching More for the 'face making' episodes (4 April 1954). After More dropped out, George Cole was approached as his replacement, along with Alastair Sim as Welch (22 August 1955). In the end Ian Carmichael played Jim, Terry-Thomas was Bertrand, Hugh Griffith was Welch and Christine was played by Sharon Acker.

Amis had always been a film fan, particularly of the kind of film which did not make the suspension of disbelief a great effort, and the prospect of seeing a version of himself on screen was obviously what lay behind his regular reports to Larkin on how and by whom this fantasy would be realized (briefly he actually did become part of it, when he and Terry-Thomas were publicizing the film at the 1956 Edinburgh Festival and did a short performance of the Jim–Bertrand argument). And one suspects that the experience of his first novel as almost literally a dream come true played some part in the fact that his next four would, in a variety of ways, involve a struggle with the presence of Jim. Aspects of his personality that had only been inferred or shiftily cited would become central features of his successors' states of mind – lechery, an uneasy relationship with mainstream culture, loneliness, selfishness. From *Lucky Jim* to *One Fat Englishman* (1963) Amis continually re-explored the figure who had made him famous and who was a version of himself. He uncovered different aspects of this presence and successively created an all-inclusive picture of Kingsley Amis.

6

That Uncertain Feeling

WHEN *Lucky Jim* was published, Amis had reached page 40 of his next novel, *That Uncertain Feeling*. This was finished by the end of the year and came out in July 1955. Throughout 1954 Amis was doing fortnightly book reviews and articles, mainly for the *Spectator*, travelling regularly to London for interviews and other *Lucky Jim* spin-offs and continuing to fulfil his demanding commitments at the university. Amis overshot his deadline with Gollancz by three months, but his second novel was completed with impressive speed.

Most of the reviews were tolerant but slightly disappointed. Overall, reviewers agreed that he had reinforced his first impressions as a writer of considerable comic talent but that these abilities were, at present, rather unfocused. Most found the book to be stylish and funny, but no one seemed to know what it was trying to do. In a letter to Rubinstein (2 September 1955) Amis expressed relief that four of them had regarded it as 'vulgar': 'I was afraid some of them might have praised it for being "sensitive".' One suspects that his relief at not being completely rejected as a one-book wonder hides a degree of disappointment. *That Uncertain Feeling* is far more 'sensitive' than *Lucky Jim*. It is, in many ways, a more intriguing book.

The plot is relatively simple. It involves a first-person account of a couple of months in the life of South Wales librarian John Lewis. Lewis spends the greater part of the novel considering the attractions and consequences of adultery with Elizabeth Gruffyd-Williams and the likelihood of promotion to a modestly senior post in Aberdarcy library. Both prospects are complicated by the fact that Elizabeth's husband, Vernon, is a local industrialist and council executive who will have a decisive influence on the placing of the library job. Paraphrased thus, it sounds like a typically 1950s' piece of pseudo-naturalism – sex, class and ambition in a drab provincial world. The social fabric of Lewis's world is far more vivid and plausible than Jim Dixon's, but what puzzled reviewers was the peculiar relationship between the actuality of Lewis's story and the way that he tells it. He treats his wife, Jean, with exceptionally foul expediency, and there is enough circumstantial evidence to place Elizabeth in the category of a tragically unstable victim. We know this, and Lewis seems disarmingly honest about his own moral and emotional shortcomings, but at the same time his clever, dry, sardonic presence always short-circuits our inclination to judge him properly.

Chapters 11 and 12 provide a particularly good example of how Lewis manages to split the reader's perspective. He meets Elizabeth in a pub, where they discuss the job, her husband's influence upon it and, more obliquely, their mutual attraction: they have not yet had sex. Lewis arrives home to find Jean talking with Mrs Jenkins, the wife of Ieuan, his friend, colleague and rival for the senior library post. Jean's manner is cold: she already suspects that something is happening with Elizabeth. His young daughter Eira, innocently unaware of this tension, is just happy to see him. This web of emotions is further tightened by his reading of a letter from his father whom he loves and who asks for news of the 'better job' at the library and closes with 'warmest regards' to 'my dear Jean and my little Eira and Baby'. Minutes later Mrs Jenkins tells him of how Ieuan 'is worrying himself sick' about the forthcoming interview, which, as Lewis knows, has already been decided by his forthcoming adulterous contract.

So within about half an hour of real time Lewis is visited by feelings of lust, ambition, guilt, love, betrayal, attachment, sympathy and anxiety, often simultaneously. And how does he deal with this? He discloses his state of unease and uncertainty but at the same time projects it into the more secure zone of humour and verbal craftsmanship.

After he has left Elizabeth in the pub and is walking home, he reflects upon the moral and personal implications of his forthcoming affair, but his thoughts are interrupted by 'two small dark men . . . carrying large coffee tins in which lascars are known to store their personal effects'. One asks him: 'Where is pain and bitter laugh?' Lewis feels that this is indeed an appropriate question, but before he can, as he puts it, 'strike my breast and cry "In here, friend"' the questioner's 'cousin' explains that they are actually looking for somewhere with 'a piano and a bit of life, please'. Lewis directs them to the pub he has just left and advises them to 'walk straight in and ask for Lizzie'. And Chapter 11 concludes:

'Thanks, mister, you are very good.'
'Yes, I'm very good all right.'

Lewis's reply is partly an example of self-conscious guilt and partly a reminder, as much to the reader as to himself, that he is indeed very good at turning his apparent state of unease into an entertaining read. And he continues. Throughout the episode at his home involving Jean, Mrs Jenkins, Eira and his father's letter, Lewis constantly adjusts the emotional registers of his account. He feels guilty about Mrs Jenkins. Her husband is older; he needs the job more than Lewis does, and Lewis knows, through his own forthcoming relationship with Elizabeth, that Ieuan does not stand a chance. As a means of diffusing his sense of guilt he turns Mrs Jenkins into a comic presence. The chapter begins with her greeting, 'Good evening, John', and a sidelong look, 'as if she wondered whether or how heavily I was armed'. Quite soon she becomes a 'domestic version of the Medusa and female version of Generalissimo Chiang Kai-Shek (there was a physical resemblance too)'. Her glances at him suggest that 'I might suddenly spring at her with a hatchet, or possibly not bother to fetch the hatchet and just sink my canines into her jugular'.

With Eira, Jean and his thoughts of his father Lewis shifts into very different levels of candour and sincerity. He tells of how Jean's hair 'made her look younger and more severe at the same time', of how Eira's 'enormous eyes looked into mine' and of how his affection for his widowed father was strengthened by his 'never making any appeal to that affection'.

All of this is, of course, addressed to the reader and not to the other participants in this tense domestic scenario. John Lewis is showing us the John Lewis that none of the cohabitants of his story properly appreciate or understand. This is a man who knows true feeling and affection, while being able to intersperse his transparent sincerity with recklessly dark humour. Moreover, he can draw together these apparently incompatible states into an impressively seamless discourse. It is as though Lewis's condition of being different people at different times is what enables him to tell his story with such confident verbal dexterity. He seems to feel uneasy about his inclination to fabricate and deceive, but it is evident that it is the task of sewing together these conflicting elements of his life and character that drives the narrative forward and makes him such a good storyteller. And in this respect John Lewis *is* Kingsley Amis. It is not simply that Lewis's story mirrors Amis's life in the mid-1950s – and there are many very close parallels – more that Amis the man, like his fictional creation, seemed to thrive on an existence that involved functioning as very different personae.

Amis, too, was an adulterer who loved his wife and family, but in his former role he was far more prodigious and calculating than Lewis. Amis had met Robert Conquest in 1952 at a party in Chelsea held to launch a new PEN anthology of poems in which they both featured. Conquest went on to edit the *New Lines* collection of 1956, which is credited as a yardstick for the Movement style of poetic writing, but their friendship had as much to do with a shared taste for boozing, irreverent humour and laddish self-indulgence as it did with an interest in the state of English verse. Throughout the 1950s Conquest would put up similarly inclined writers and their families in his house in Hampstead: 'Amis and his wife, Enright and his wife and daughter, Davie, Wain and Larkin stayed with me for the odd night or nights for one time or another – the Amises quite frequently' (Morrison, pp. 47–8). Just as frequently, particularly after *Lucky Jim*, Amis would visit London on his own, ostensibly to see his publisher, to promote his own writing or in connection with his regular work for the *Spectator* and the *Observer*. By the time he wrote *That Uncertain Feeling* Amis was also writing to Conquest with requests to borrow his other residence, a flat, for sex. He often used Conquest as his fellow conspirator. Conquest was on close terms with Hilly; she trusted him and Amis exploited this as a means of providing plausible alibis for his adulterous liaisons. In 1957 Amis sent Conquest a letter that resembles the plan for a chapter of a novel. It specifies, in five sections, the narrative for the afternoon of Friday 13 September – including the invention of 'a vague cousin or brother-in-law of yours – a nice circumstantial touch, I thought' (Jacobs, p. 172). Lewis plans his liaisons with Elizabeth with far less tactical precision, but the sense of life imitating art is born out in a variety of other ways.

In the previous year, 1956, marital relations between the Amises had reached crisis point. Amis went to bed with practically anyone he found attractive and willing. He could never have hoped to keep all of his affairs secret, and Hilly struck back by having a few of her own, in Swansea, and without serious attempts to keep them from Amis. This had been happening during the completion of *That Uncertain Feeling*, and the sense of irretrievable breakdown felt by

Lewis and Jean in the penultimate chapter is an accurate prediction of what would happen with the Amises in October 1956, when divorce became a very likely prospect. Amis, in the novel, has Jean attempting an act of sexual independence very similar to Hilly's, but he had no doubt comforted himself by matching her with the playwright Gareth Probert, an extreme, but not inaccurate, parody of Dylan Thomas. In a letter to Larkin, written after he had started *That Uncertain Feeling* (26 November 1953), Amis states that 'I think [Thomas] a bad poet and a bad influence [Amis was preparing a review for *Essays in Criticism* of a volume by the Thomas-influenced poet W.R. Rodgers] . . . A Bloomsburyite to his *dirty* fingernails, that was him, and only sentimentalizing ignorant horsepiss about his Welchness can conceal the fact.' Here again the boundaries between life and fiction become blurred. In the novel Lewis discloses no writerly ambitions. He does not have to, because his own narrative style is so self-consciously polished – particularly when compared with the pretentious inaccessibility of Probert's play (see Chapter 9). Hilly was not having an affair with a version of Probert. There is a sense of Amis displacing his own feelings of unease about his marriage into a confidence-building exercise: the one thing he could be certain of was that he could write good novels.

At the end Lewis and Jean are reunited, and this, too, was a remarkably accurate prediction of what would happen with the Amises by the end of 1956. In November Amis broke up with his regular girlfriend and a month later Hilly agreed to a six-month trial separation from her current lover. There would be further problems, but the Amises managed to stay together, and it is here that their parallels with the Lewises became both intriguing and revealing.

Hilly's attempt to reinstate monogamy was sincere and honest, but Amis, while desperately attempting to preserve his marriage, was telling lies. On 6 December Amis wrote to Larkin that there was an 'increased cordiality' between him and Hilly, and he also confessed that he was particularly happy because, without Hilly's knowledge, 'I have got my girlfriend back too.' A couple of weeks earlier he had written to Conquest again to ask for the flat: 'You bachelors have got to stand by us married men, you know' (Jacobs, p. 172). Apart from the fact that he was lying to Hilly, Amis also seemed able to offer slightly different personae to two of his closest friends. His letters to Larkin in this period are selectively honest. He is distressed by the likely consequences of his behaviour, and he seems to use Larkin as a confessor; less prominent is the ribald, anarchic energy that informed their exchanges before *Lucky Jim*. This is partly transferred to Conquest, to whom he is a conspiratorial jack-the-lad, full of shameless energy for the next seduction. And who knows what derivation or transformation of these he offered to his various lovers.

Amis was living several lives and the creation of a character such as Lewis who could sew a similarly varied catalogue of emotional states into a clever narrative fabric must have given him more than aesthetic satisfaction. Whatever feelings of unease we might harbour for Lewis the man are frequently displaced by our admiration for Lewis the writer; and it is not impossible that the man who constructed this evasive interchange between writing and feeling experienced a similar although more personal degree of displacement.

It can be unwise and presumptuous to regard books as symptoms of an author's state of mind, but from what we know of Amis's life the concluding chapter of *That Uncertain Feeling* invites us to do just this. Just as the Lewises' marital breakdown seems to have become irreparable, we find them back in the mining village where Lewis was born, his librarianship exchanged for an office job in the local pit. They are happy, and the inhabitants of their new world are – apart from the conspicuously Elizabeth-like Lisa from whom Lewis beats a hasty retreat – honest, candid salt-of-the-earthish individuals – particularly Lewis's father, an almost fantastic combination of working-class pragmatism, friendly wit and unpretentious intelligence. And so unlike William Amis. None of these people play out social, sexual or cultural 'roles', and Lewis is not tempted into a complicity of deception. He signals this change to the reader by completely altering his narrational style. It is as though he has walked into the stereotypical vision of South Wales mining communities of Richard Llewellyn's *How Green Was My Valley* (1939), and his language has changed appropriately.

> I took Jean's arm and we moved across the square. The shift at the pit had just emerged and colliers in their neat suits and caps were walking past us or towards the pub. I waved to an overman I knew. An ancient bus half full of more colliers chuntered by. At the pub door we had to wait for a moment until the way cleared ahead of us. To anyone watching it might have looked as if Jean and I, too, were coming off shift.

This is the closing paragraph of the novel, and Lewis has clearly shed both his role as socially ambitious lecher and his more complex persona as shiftily evasive narrator. It reflects the open, transparent mood of the entire chapter, and it is intriguing to compare it with an earlier passage, again from Chapter 12. Mrs Jenkins has left and Eira has been sent to bed. Jean accuses Lewis of having an affair with Elizabeth and he sets off to end their liaison from a phone box. He looks out over the estuary.

> Somewhere in the background were the narrow-waisted tanks of the Cambrio-Sudanese people, full, among other things, of the wherewithal for more dry Martinis, garden statuary and black cigarettes with gold tips. I trod on a loose paving stone, a hazard in which this district abounded: it tipped up and squirted dirty water in my shoe.

The crowded jerkiness of allusion is typical of Lewis. Without being told, we know that the oil tanks remind him of his unfixed, almost hypocritical, attitude to Elizabeth and her social network; and he cleverly allows the references to dry Martinis and black cigarettes – definitely Elizabeth – to roll back through the sentence and endow the 'narrow-waisted' oil tanks with a very human, sensual presence. The loose paving stone that squirts dirty water on his shoe is a convenient supplement. 'This district' is not just the working-class world detached from the life of flashy drinks, cigarettes and garden statuary; it also involves his own condition of sexual and social ambition, and deceit: the loose pavement and its messy consequence echoes his recent exchange with Jean.

The stylistic density of the passage is very different from the easy, albeit happier, mood of the last chapter. The Lewis of the substance of the novel feeds upon the continual conflicts and tensions of life, in all their social, sexual and emotional manifestations. The Lewis of the closing chapter has chosen an escapist compromise.

Despite his 1956 truce with Hilly, Amis continued to pursue his sexual ambitions with reckless enthusiasm, including a number of brief affairs with students at Swansea. In November 1957 he wrote to Conquest to report on the state of his sex life. With Hilly he has 'nothing to complain about', and he promises to tell Conquest of an amusing 'extra-marital one . . . you'll be the ideal audience for it'. He concludes: 'Oh, why isn't there *more* of that kind of thing' (Jacobs, p. 176). The kind of thing he refers to is the opportunity to sustain a happy marriage while pursuing another life of apparently limitless sexual encounters. The Lewis of the last chapter had given up that kind of thing, and he had also become the kind of writer that Amis never could be or would want to be. The deceptions and anxieties that had energized his style and emboldened his narrative presence had disappeared. In the majority of Amis's subsequent novels the central male character is caught between his attachment to or pursuit of a particular woman and an equally powerful desire to unshackle himself, temporarily, from the sense of being part of the emotional and sexual life of one person, and this effectively energizes their style.

The novel is not only about sex, and Amis's experiences of the class structure of south-west Wales was the basis for Lewis's own account. The Lewises' flat is an accurate version of several dwellings rented by the Amises from November 1949 until Hilly's legacy enabled them to buy a house in The Grove in 1951. These were primitive places with shared bathrooms and in one case an electric cooker that guaranteed shocks for the user. For a while Hilly, like Jean, found herself obliged to bathe her youngest children in an enormous kitchen sink. For the first six months of 1950 they shared a house with Amis's English Department colleague David Sims. Sims became one of Amis's closest friends in Swansea and provided him with some of the background material for Lewis. He had grown up in New Tredegar, a pit village in the valleys, and like Lewis he was a clever, university-educated man with a working-class back-ground. In the summer of 1951 Amis and Sims spent a week with the latter's widowed mother in New Tredegar marking 800 school examination papers for the Joint Welsh Board. They loathed the job, but they needed the money, and New Tredegar offered them a base removed from the distractions of Swansea. Amis liked the area, and it became the model for Forestfawr, Lewis's home town to which he retreats with Jean at the end of the novel.

During these years Amis and his new colleagues at the university were paid slightly less than many employees of the recently created National Coal Board. Hilly, like Jean, had to find part-time work, the former washing up at a fish and chip café in the Mumbles. On one occasion in early 1950 Amis wrote to Larkin with a request for £5 to keep them going until his next pay cheque. Amis, Sims, Dawson, Smyth and others drank in the same pubs, ate in the same cafés and attended the same dance halls as the builders, shipyard workers, dockers and miners of the area. Amis had never been well-off, but his background in London, the home counties, Oxford and the army had been predominantly middle class and this was his first real encounter with working-class life. Lewis was born out of it and his uneasy, guilt-ridden excursions into the other world of the Swansea bourgeoisie was also founded upon Amis's experience.

Margaret Aaron-Thomas was the social worker who, as Amis had persuaded Larkin, might be cited as the real model for Margaret Peel of *Lucky Jim*. She was a friend of Hilly's, and she provided them with the home-help/babysitter, who would become Betty in his short story 'Moral Fibre', a spin-off from *That Uncertain Feeling*. In the story Lewis, and indeed Amis, present the promiscuous, mildly criminal and irresponsible Betty with a degree of sympathy, mainly because her social worker, Mair Webster (a version of Margaret Aaron-Thomas), treats her as a symptom of capitalist injustice and a poor education system: Amis and Lewis regard her as rather like anyone else who wants a good time. Amis saw Margaret Aaron-Thomas as a living stereotype, a middle-class woman with a patronizing social conscience, but this did not prevent him from becoming part of her social circle. Her husband John owned the *Newport Argus* and a successful timber business in Swansea, and they were certainly in Amis's mind when he invented the Griffith-Williamses. Their surnames, at once Welsh and haughtily double-barrelled, cemented the association. Amis enjoyed being simultaneously involved with the different social and cultural strata of Swansea life, and his tendency to keep them in separate compartments is reflected in his writing. On one occasion the Aaron-Thomases were invited to the Amises' house in The Grove for drinks and food and arrived in full evening dress. Amis turned the incident into one of his amusing anecdotes, emphasizing their mildly farcical, mutual misreadings of different social mores and expectations. Significantly, he told the story only to his university friends who he knew would appreciate his smirking ridicule of posh locals. Lewis plays a similar game with his own experience of Swansea lifestyles, quietly mocking the habits of the Griffith-Williams set and contrasting them with the rough, but admirably transparent, manner of the ordinary people of the area. Lewis sympathizes with the latter, but until the final chapter he successfully distances himself from both: he is the storyteller who knows his material well but does not identify with any of it.

When *Lucky Jim* transformed Amis from provincial academic into nationally acclaimed novelist, his credit with the wealthy and – so they aspired – culturally sophisticated people of the region increased significantly. Jo Bartley, his colleague who had exchanged a Chair in India for a lectureship in Swansea, introduced Amis to the Swansea Yacht Club, and while Amis had no interest in sailing he certainly enjoyed being talked about and introduced to people in the club as a controversial author. Lewis, despite his protests, relishes a similar role. He is not a writer, but he is someone different, someone slightly unpredictable who enjoys existing on the margins of a comfortably exclusive social network.

In Chapter 3 we find Lewis and Jean at a Gruffyd-Williams house party surrounded by local representatives of what he calls the 'anglicized Aberdarcy bourgeoisie', a phrase he uses four times and for the reader only. For Lewis, such jargon is as pretentious as the people it purports to represent. At one point he contemplates the kind of behaviour that would establish him as 'impossible' (that is, dangerous) in 'the eyes of the Aberdarcy bourgeoisie'. Should he 'bawl a defence of the Welfare State, start undressing myself or the dentist's mistress, give the dentist a lovely piggy-back round the room, call for a toast to the North Korean Foreign Minister or Comrade Malenkov?'

For Lewis, left-wing politics has become a badge, something that is consistent with his working-class background and which operates as a subtext in his exchanges with the Aberdarcy bourgeoisie. It makes him interesting and, it is implied, increases his sexual attractiveness for Elizabeth as a radical alternative to her rich husband. Amis, too, enjoyed his status as the suddenly famous novelist with anti-establishment views.

At the Yacht Club Amis met Eve and Stuart Thomas. Stuart

Thomas and Amis soon became friends, remained so during the Swansea years and after Amis's departure Thomas was the only one of his local acquaintances with whom he remained in regular contact. It was, on the surface, a peculiar friendship. Amis had long since abandoned Communism, but he still voted Labour. At election time his house was festooned with posters, and Hilly would use the family car to ferry elderly, infirm or disinclined electors to the polling station in hope of securing a gratitude vote for Labour. Stuart was a solicitor and an active member of the Conservative Party. He had no time for the Welfare State and is remembered as a Dickensian throwback who, when dealing with clients requiring legal aid, would remove the chair from the other side of his desk to ensure a brisk disposal of business with the lower orders.

Thomas does not become a particular character in the novel, but his role as the absolute opposite of Amis is carefully distributed through its fabric. Stuart Thomas went to school with his namesake, Dylan. He became a founding member of the Dylan Thomas Society and was appointed by the late poet's family as legal executor of his estate. Amis loathed Dylan Thomas's work and between 1955 and 1989 he wrote six articles which present him as vastly overrated, a literary fraud whose reputation has been sustained by pseuds, academics and middle-class patrons of the institution of 'Welsh' literature. In *That Uncertain Feeling* Dylan Thomas becomes Probert (including a brilliant parody of Thomas's verse by Amis), a figure who further threatens Lewis's already fragile relationship with Jean. This was written during a period in which Amis had become friendly with the kind of people, the Thomases and the Aaron-Thomases particularly, who were creating a local mythology for Dylan Thomas, sanctifying the man and his work as part of the indigenous culture of the area. In the novel these people are presented as charlatans who variously avoid or patronize the ordinary people of Swansea while venerating a writer who, in Amis's view, had nothing to do with the real Wales.

Many of the characters and situations of *Lucky Jim* were drawn from Amis's experience, and he used them mainly as foils for his and Jim's satirical angst. Shortly after *Lucky Jim* had been accepted by Gollancz, Amis informed Larkin (26 May 1953) that he was having difficulty finding a subject for his next novel. He did not want to use Oxford, the Army was out of the question – 'I didn't do any fighting and I've forgotten what I did do' - and he has already done 'carledge life' in *Lucky Jim*, 'which leaves only bourgeois life in Swansea, and that's really too *boring*. . . ' 'What do you do when you've run out of backgrounds?' This is revealing, in that Amis obviously needs a background, a context with which he is intimately familiar to begin even thinking about invention. In the end he chose bourgeois Swansea as an anchor and made it less boring by looking at it from the perspective of a man who knew the real Wales, the unpretentious, working-class culture of the valleys. It was as though Amis had set himself the task of writing a novel about Kingsley Amis while continually raising questions about this character: what would I be like if I had done this and not that; if I had been part of, rather than only witnessed, a particular way of life? Lewis, like Amis, is a witty raconteur, a lecher who loves his wife and children, a man who enjoys the moneyed lifestyle of the middle classes while parodying their pretensions. This is the confessional aspect of the book, and in life Amis remained unable and indeed unwilling to resolve these conflicts. He created John Lewis as an experiment, as someone who was a version of himself but whose background and circumstances were different, differences which enabled him to become the person that Amis could never be. Amis's left-wing affiliations began essentially as a rebellion against his family background, particularly his father. Lewis was born into a family, a society and a culture where such ideals were fundamental. So, when Lewis contrasts his own albeit sceptical leftish sympathies with the world of the Griffith-Williamses, the distinction is rooted in unalterable circumstances. For Amis these contrasts were deliberately contrived and perverse. His accent, his education, his manner-isms were English and middle class: he fitted in with the Swansea Yacht Club crowd to the same degree that Lewis did not. Amis's experience of the ordinary people of south-west Wales offered him an autobiographical hypothesis: what if I, Kingsley Amis, with all of my temperamental inclinations had, like David Sims, for instance, been 'born in the valleys'?

The feature of the novel that crossed the boundary between experience and hypothesis was the evocation of the Lewises' home life which, despite John's dangerous excursions, remained, at least for his children, happy and secure. Martin Amis testifies to the fact that this was based accurately upon the Amises' family life in The Grove and Glanmor Road. 'There were rows [between Kingsley and Hilly], though as infants we didn't know what they were about, but these were far outnumbered by gestures of mutual affection, often involving very intimate embraces. "Oh, stop, kissing," we'd say. It embarrassed us, the kids, but nicely.' Martin remembers that he, Philip and Sally were treated as participants in what seemed then like an ongoing adult party. (He recalls that one Christmas his own presents included a packet of cigarettes; he was nine.) Jazz records would be played late at night and the children would stay up, and when Amis's friends visited Swansea the children would participate in the easy joviality of things; Bruce Montgomery and Larkin are recalled by Martin as comedic uncles, the first voluble and generous ('he always seemed to bring us fireworks'), the second quiet and slightly unusual. Aspects of this are transferred to the novel, in that the only element of Lewis's life which is not 'uncer-tain' is the sense of bonding he feels with his wife and family. At the same time, Amis projects his fictionalized account of his home life, accurate as it was, into an exercise in wish fulfilment.

When Lewis returns to the valleys there is no longer a conflict between his left-wing attitudes and the people he lives with. The class distinctions of Aberdarcy/Swansea no longer exist. And this sense of feeling at home where people are individuals and not graded by their accent, manner or attitude enables him to rein in his adulterous inclinations, become part of a world where monogamy is a natural condition. At the end of the closing chapter Lewis and Jean are walking to a 'do' at Edie Rhys Protheroe's, 'the premier hostess in this part of Wales', a wonderfully classless gathering where intelligent conversation is stripped of its social pretensions. On the journey Jean asks him if, by moving to Forestfawr, they are 'running away'. 'Yes,' he says. 'Our kind of running away was a stroke of bloody genius. It's always the best thing to do in that kind of situation.' He does not need to explain this enigmatic response, since the previous five pages tell us all we need to know. As they pass the pit, where he now works, we are told of how the 'wheel turned merrily in the gear, twinkling as the sun fell on it'. The coal trucks being shunted from the sidings, the coal dust rising from the screens and the spoil heap nicknamed 'Spion Kopje' are described without comment or reflection, but the description suggests a kind of natural symbiotic grace in which the people of the valley are content with their less than beautiful surroundings. A jolly man is delivering dandelion and burdock from a Corona lorry, a milkman is having a laugh with an old lady with a hearing aid, and Howell the greengrocer hails Lewis from the shop doorway for a chat about family, kids and tickets for the forthcoming Rugby International in Cardiff. Happy valley and, for Amis, fantasy land. It is the kind of social-political paradise that was promised by the 1945 Labour government, an idea, an idyll that Amis had almost but not quite abandoned. More significantly, it is a world, a background into which he imagined himself, an unreal hypothesis where the conflicts between his different aspirations and personae did not exist, where he was content with his circumstances and with the woman he had married.

7

Amis Abroad

THE typescript of *That Uncertain Feeling* had been sent to Gollancz in early 1955. Amis had no clear plans for his next novel, but at the end of March fate helped him out. He received a telegram in Swansea from Hilary Rubinstein informing him that *Lucky Jim* had won the Somerset Maugham award for fiction. Amis was gratified and amused. Three months earlier the esteemed benefactor of the prize had written of *Lucky Jim* as a symptom of widespread moral and cultural degeneration: evidently Maugham was not on the panel of judges. The award of £400 was generous, almost half of Amis's academic salary, but it was attached to a condition: that the author 'agree to spend [it] on three months travel or residence abroad'. Amis would be able to fit the three months into the Swansea summer vacation, but he had no particular interest in foreign travel and no contacts abroad. Apart from periods with family, local excursions to the Gower and a few weeks in a caravan near the Thames, the Amises had never been on a proper holiday since their marriage and Hilly was more enthusiastic about the prospect than Amis. They thought about returning to France, which they had visited briefly in 1947, but eventually they sought advice from their wealthy friends the Aaron-Thomases. John Aaron-Thomas said he would contact Signor Pintos Bassos, a businessman with whom he and his wife had stayed in Portugal. Dates and addresses were forwarded and the Amises with their three children boarded the Southampton–Lisbon ferry on 23 June.

They would not stay with Pintos Bassos but with one of his employees, a senior clerk called Billy Barley. Barley was proud equally of his Portuguese nationality and his English father, which for him recreated the sixteenth-century alliance between Portugal and England. He was honoured to play host to a writer from his paternal homeland and from whom he would ask £3 7s. a day for board and lodging, an exorbitant amount in Portugal in 1955. Barley had spent the previous month building extra interior walls into his modest single-storey house in Estoril, half an hour from Lisbon. When the Amises arrived they found a bizarre assembly of rooms the size of large cupboards which would accommodate Barley, his wife and two children and the Amises and their three. Amis did not dislike Barley – he described him to Larkin as 'very amiable in a childish way' – but he felt that the cramped quarters, the heat, the mingled smells from the kitchen and the adjacent lavatory and their attendant insects were a kind of Maughamian revenge. By the end of July the Amises had decided to move to a boarding-house in the Algarve.

In *I Like It Here* Billy Barley becomes C. J. P. Oates. Barley's wife and children, his Anglo-Portuguese background, his accent, the cramped house with its smells and discomforts, even his transport, a dangerously decrepit moped upon which Amis and Bowen are offered a lift which they politely decline, resurface with little embellishment or alteration. In the Algarve the Amises met an Ulster couple, the Tyrrells, who were renting a mountain chalet. When the Tyrrells moved on, they offered the chalet to the Amises, who gratefully accepted it. Again, all of this is reproduced in the novel with autobiographical verity. Tyrrell becomes Bannion, and Bannion like Tyrrell is prone to embarrassing imitations of foreign persons, including a Frenchwoman who seems to have acquired her native language in an Ulster grammar school, plus recitations of 'The Charge of the Light Brigade' by four individuals from different parts of Europe.

The Barleys, the Bannions and the Amises' farcical trek through Portugal had great comic potential in themselves, but this was the only occasion in his literary career when Amis borrowed so blatantly from real life. He did so as an act of convenience. The figures and events that almost wrote themselves provided Amis with a sub-plot for the book that he really wanted to write.

I Like It Here was written after Amis's return to Swansea in September 1955, but there is no evidence that he had originally planned his period abroad as the basis for a work of fiction. In May, soon before he left for Portugal, he had written a review article for the *Spectator* on Laurie Lee's *A Rose for Winter* and Peter Mayne's *The Narrow Smile*, literary travel books about their respective authors' experiences in Spain and in Pakistan and Afghanistan. Amis used the article as the occasion for a diatribe against the view that British writers could only earn their esteem by becoming part of or writing about somewhere else; that the likes of Lawrence and Greene and the Irish Joyce and Beckett had become great writers because they had detached themselves from their parochial circumstances. Amis wanted to write a non-fictional travel book that would undermine these assumptions. He abandoned the project because he realized that if it were to be taken seriously it would have to be based upon its writer's personal experience of abroad, and after three months in Portugal Amis's amounted to little more than a catalogue of incidents that veer between the farcical and the mundane. In the end the only piece of non-fictional writing to be salvaged from the summer was a brief contribution to the *Spectator*'s 1956 travel supplement, on the varieties of alcohol available in Portugal.

Instead of a travel book he wrote a novel and used these real events as an amusing backdrop to another story, completely invented, throughout which Amis, via Bowen, distributes opinions on literature and identity that would have been central to his original project.

Garnet Bowen's trip to Portugal is sponsored by his publisher, Hyman, and in return for a free holiday Bowen is asked to unravel a literary detective mystery. Hyman has recently received a manuscript from a person claiming to be the Wulfstan Strether who had published five acclaimed modernist novels in the 1930s and 1940s, has not been heard of for a decade and has since acquired cult status. Strether is an assembly of all the traits and affectations that Amis associates with the mythology of the British writer abroad, and Bowen has to find out if this is the real Strether or a talented pretender.

In Chapter 9 we find Bowen alone in the Barley house trying to divide his time between his own writing and his assessment of the alleged Strether typescript. Bowen is attempting to write a play that will satirize and parody various aspects of British life. He is happy with the dialogue, but he cannot stop himself using the stage directions as an extended commentary on the characters. The message to the reader is implied. Bowen should be writing a novel not unlike those of Amis, including the one he is in, in which the ingenious shifts between reported speech and narrational orchestration jar the expectations and hold the attention of the reader.

At the end of the chapter Bowen channels his frustration into an encounter with Strether's *One Word More*. Strether's fiction, like Bowen's drama, involves an imbalance between speech and narrative, but it exists at the opposite end of this spectrum. Strether's characters make brief, enigmatic statements and their exchanges are divided up between thousand-word excursions into their existential states of which the following is a brief example:

> and on the instant before his eyes there wheeled momentarily, duskily, the vision of black sea-flowers at a depth coiling offendedly aside at the lurching, slowed fall of a rotting and timbered prow, won from deck and keel by soft, century-long motions at the sea's floor.

There is no single target for this parody. It combines endless Jamesian sentences with a pseudo-mystical intensity reminiscent of Lawrence. Bowen later comments, via his narrator, that Strether would

fit in 'at our older universities, where he would be a valuable coun-
terblast to clever young men like F.R. Leavis'. It is surely no coincidence
that when Amis returned from Portugal he was sent a review copy of
Leavis's *D.H. Lawrence, Novelist*, in which Leavis refers to how 'honoured' he would have felt had Lawrence become a don at Cambridge.

Chapter 9 is part of a literary critical thesis which Amis weaves
into the novel. We are invited to consider the reasons for Bowen's
problem with language and its context and Strether's elaborately
turgid avoidance of speech. The most obvious connection involves the
isolation of both writers from the world in which their native language
is a constant, insistent element of everyday life. Amis's first two novels
were praised for the manner in which narrative and dialogue cooper-
ate and intersect. When his characters speak we begin to know them,
an impression that the narrator will variously confirm, embellish or
undermine. Amis's source material for this was the fabric of ordinary
day-to-day exchange, and in Portugal he felt the loss. On 10 July 1955
he wrote to Larkin of how the worst aspect of being 'abroad' is

> You haven't got any of your friends with you, you see, and you
> can't make friends with the locals because they're foreign and don't
> understand what you're saying and you're not here long enough
> . . . Now I'm funny. I like talking to chaps I like talking to and wd.
> rather not . . . talk to chaps I'd rather not talk to . . .

Bowen's struggle with the relationship between linguistic
exchange and its context is an encoded statement by Amis about
what, in his view, were the necessary conditions for writing literature which is not detached from the inclinations, preconditions
and, crucially, the linguistic habits of its readers, and Amis created
Strether as the precise opposite of this creative manifesto.

Soon after Bowen meets him, Strether suggests that they visit
Henry Fielding's tomb in Lisbon. They do so, and Bowen's suspicion that he is with the real Strether is confirmed. Only someone

who had actually written novels would have the gall to pronounce himself superior to his long dead predecessor, and Strether does just this. The episode sustains our interest in the literary detective story, but its real purpose is to provide Amis with material for the next part of his critical essay. Strether's vainglorious speech before the tomb is politely learned. He praises Fielding's comic talent but declares that the only authentic literary voice is tragic, 'that alone can speak to us of the loneliness and the dignity of man', as indeed Strether has done in his verbose, humourless disquisition on existential torment. Bowen keeps his opinions to himself, but Amis offers them to us. Fielding is his hero, someone who two centuries after his death could still be read 'with unaffected and wholehearted interest', a man who combined comic genius with an ability to delineate and distinguish between the good and the bad, the sincere and the fraudulent, 'a moral seriousness that could be made apparent without the aid of evangelical puffing and blowing'.

What he does not consider is whether Fielding has a twentieth-century counterpart. Later, talking to his publisher in London, Bowen comes close to doing this. He associates Strether with the group of 'prancing, posturing phoneys' who held sway until 'about 1930 [and] the death of Lawrence . . . or perhaps 1939', in short the modernists. And he speaks enigmatically of the 'next bunch . . . Greene, Waugh, Isherwood, Powell'. Read between these lines and you will encounter the mind of their author extending this brief essay on literary history to include a new member of this 'next bunch'. This novelist is the closest equivalent to Fielding that post-eighteenth-century literature has produced. He, too, buttonholes his readers, amuses them yet guides them through stories that capture their experience; a narrator whose honest, not quite judgemental pictures of life are accompanied by a conspiratorial smile and a wink. He is Kingsley Amis.

The episode at Fielding's tomb – which Amis did indeed visit – is Amis's first and only use of fiction as a vehicle for ideas. It was a practice that he loathed. Like Fielding, he would show his readers levels of decency and misbehaviour but he would not instruct. Amis can be excused this moment because *I Like It Here* is not about how we should live and behave. It is about himself and his writing.

The reviewers were generally united in their perception of the novel as different projects sewn together and with its seams left showing. G.S. Fraser called it 'less a novel than a series of farcical incidents loosely tied to a travel narrative' (*New Statesman*, 18 January 1958). Others found it 'ambivalent' in 'attitude' and 'careless' in construction. Twenty years later Amis himself referred to it as 'by common consent my worst novel' and explained that it failed because he had tried to 'put real people on paper', adding that 'the closer the likeness of the real interesting person, the less interesting he will be in the novel' ('Real and Made Up People', p. 3).

As usual, Amis's honest self-criticism is selective and evasive. It *is* an interesting book, at least for the person who is interested in the relationship between Amis the individual and Amis the writer. If we untie its loose threads we find a man who is simultaneously attempting to reconcile his past with his present and his undecided future. By 1955 Kingsley Amis had become different things to different people. Jim Dixon and John Lewis were interchangeable with their creator, who, for some, was an anti-cultural vandal and to others part of an intellectual new wave involving radical ideas about society and sex. Amis attempted to clarify matters in several ways. His regular review articles for the *Spectator* and the *Observer* addressed an enormous variety of fictional and non-fictional work, and he would always be waiting on the periphery to offer his own opinions on writing, culture and politics. When he began *I Like It Here* in late 1955, Gollancz had just agreed to publish *A Case of Samples*, his first volume of poems to appear under an established imprint. This came out in 1956. Many of its pieces involved oblique, unsettling pictures of contemporary experience, and they contrasted sharply with Amis's popular persona as a novelist addicted to farce. In early 1956 the Fabian Society had commissioned Amis to write a pamphlet, which the following year would be published as *Socialism and the Intellectuals*, a sceptical assessment of the British labour movement and its advocates. It could have been written by a serious-minded John Lewis.

I Like It Here became part of this broader project to build an intellectually, aesthetically respectable version of Amis into his established image as a talented entertainer. If it has a unifying feature, it is Amis's affinity with Fielding. John Aaron-Thomas's suggestion of Portugal as the site for his summer trip was unplanned, a matter of convenience, but suddenly for Amis it attained an almost fatalistic significance. Fielding's *Journal of a Voyage to Lisbon* (1755 – note the last two digits of the date) was first intended as a travel book about his experiences in Portugal. In the end it became an account only of the voyage, which Fielding finished in the last few months of his life in the Portuguese capital.

Fielding's final, posthumous work was in Amis's mind as he planned and revised his own account of abroad. (In a letter dated 10 July 1955 he refers to Larkin as 'the recipient of my Portuguese Journal'.) Fielding described it in his preface as 'a novel without a Plot', meaning that while the narrative would be based on real events these would be enriched with his talents as a fiction writer. Before Amis left for Portugal, when he was considering his own version of Fielding's project, he argued in his review of Lee and Mayne that the inherent defect of the travel book was that it relied too much on chance and circumstance, faithful descriptions of real occurrences and places that would not necessarily make them interesting. He suggested that Lee and Mayne should instead have fictionalized their material, produced works in which 'selection and emphasis' would sideline scrupulous fidelity to fact. When he returned to Swansea in the autumn of that year he set about writing such a book.

First of all, he toyed with the idea of bringing back Jim Dixon who would be sent to Portugal by his employer, Gore Urquhart, and there meet an author called Kingsley Amis. Again, Fielding was in his thoughts. He, too, had used his own name, yet been both himself and a version of himself in a work which blended fact with invention. Amis abandoned this idea because its twentieth-century manifestation would probably be viewed as a concession to modernism, a self-conscious, self-referential reflection upon the nature of fiction. Instead he produced a book that was both a tribute to Fielding's narrative technique and a use of it to interweave the largely incompatible elements of his own life.

Chapter 8, for example, consists mainly of the opinions and disclosures of a man called Gomes whom the Bowens meet in a bar in Estoril. Gomes is a Portuguese aristocrat who had been in Oxford before the war. His English is perfect, and he talks with the Bowens of the contrasts between his remembrances, his current perceptions of Britain and his view of his own country. Gomes describes Salazar's regime as a farcical and corrupt version of pre-war fascism. He explains that his own use of a cigarette lighter is an illegal act. Salazar had outlawed the use of this instrument in response to complaints from his friends in the match-making industry who felt that such devices were reducing demand for their product.

Neither Gomes nor anyone like him existed in Amis's experience of Portugal. On the one hand, Gomes discloses the restrictive, violent and often absurd features of Salazar's dictatorship. On the other, he reminds Bowen/Amis that British sympathies for the Stalinist, Eastern European socialism conveniently ignore its similarities with fascism. At the end of their conversation Bowen/Amis reflects that 'Gomes seemed to have provided yet another excuse for people like Bowen to be politically apathetic at home.' For Bowen read Amis who, in *Socialism and the Intellectuals*, would show that he, too, had chosen a form of apathy as an alternative to his previous attachment to socialism.

The Gomes chapter was written in 1956. It is an assembly of details that Amis had gathered during his period in Portugal and afterwards in England. It has nothing to do with the rest of the narrative, and Gomes never appears again. It is inserted into the story partly as an indication that Amis had indeed learned something of Portuguese politics and society and partly as a reflection of his own political scepticism. Also it carries an echo of Fielding, who would in his fiction frequently disclose his origins as a dramatist by stopping the action and allowing one of his characters to digress for a while on a topical issue.

Another part of the narrative involves an oblique commentary on Amis's private life. He had begun the novel as soon as he returned to Swansea in late 1955, but by the following summer had barely completed the first two chapters. His marriage was in a seemingly irretrievable state of decline. He and Hilly had become friendly with the journalist Henry Fairlie during their occasional visits to Conquest's house in London for weekend parties. Fairlie had been invited back to Swansea and by early 1956 had begun an affair with Hilly. In September 1956 Hilly informed Amis that her relationship with Fairlie had progressed beyond its original, tacitly agreed, status as a compensation for his own frequent and incompetently disguised bouts of infidelity. She was thinking of divorce; she would take the children and move in with Fairlie in London. Nothing was certain, but she had decided that for the next few months she and Fairlie would 'decide whether they are victims of an "infatuation" or of "something more important"' (letter to Larkin, 22 October 1956), and during this period marital relations with Amis would cease. They would live in the same house but separately. Amis informed Larkin in October that 'my marriage has a one in four chance of surviving till next summer', but by December the odds had improved: 'much increased cordiality between the partners to the matrimonial arrangement in question' (letter to Larkin, 6 December 1956). (This state of things had been helped, from Amis's point of view, by Fairlie's arraignment in November for fraud and his brief imprisonment for contempt of court.) By January 1957

Hilly had decided that her affair with Fairlie was over and had engineered a post-hostilities agreement with Amis involving restraint
and, when this was unsteady, candour. (Amis's observance of it can
be judged by his letter to Larkin of 27 January on their forthcoming
weekend in London: 'We can both stay with my girl . . .')

During all of this the Portugal novel had been shelved. 'Can't
seem to work much these days, somehow. My novel had rattled
along merrily to p. 49 when the blow fell; now remains there' (letter to Larkin, 4 November 1956). By spring 1957 he had returned
to it. The notes from Portugal provided plenty of incident and contextual detail but nothing resembling a story. Once the Strether
mystery was solved, all that was left was the Bowens' departure, so
at the twelfth of the sixteen brief chapters Amis has Barbara Bowen
summoned home by telegram to look after her seriously ill mother;
and she takes the children. The parallels between the Amises' near
break-up and the Bowens' benign separation might seem slight, and
at the time no one outside a very confined circle of friends knew
anything of the former – Amis in his 22 October letter to Larkin had
asked him to keep it all in the strictest confidence. However, Amis
uses the closing chapters as a channel for, perhaps a purgation of,
the feelings of uncertainty which attended the months after October
1956. In the letter to Larkin, Amis admits that the 'light and banter-
ing tone' of their correspondence is for once beyond him and would
in any case be 'a poor index of how I feel this evening'. Despite having behaved in a way that justified Hilly's inclination, he is still disturbed by the suddenly very real possibility of being on his own.

> . . . it means presumably that the children, about whom I feel
> strongly, will accompany their mother to her new home. I shall be
> able to see them 'often' of course. But that isn't the same as having
> them in your home all the time, you see . . . Having one's wife
> fucked is one thing; having her taken away from you, plus your chil-
> dren, is another, I find . . . Dividing the records, selling the house,

storing the furniture and all that, it seems inconceivable. Reckon I shall resign here and go to London or somewhere when the time comes. It'll be odd to be a bachelor again. (22 October 1956)

Through Chapters 13 and 14 Bowen's Portugal experience appears suddenly to have become more engaging, now incorporating a variety of enigmatic, intriguing and sinister figures of Strether's acquaintance, but he seems to find it difficult to maintain an interest. Every thousand words or so a more persistent feature of his mindset interrupts his perception of actual events. 'He was thinking about Barbara, whom he had seen off on the plane to London, together with the kids, ten days earlier . . .' (p. 139). 'Why hadn't he gone back with Barbara?' (p. 141). '. . . sitting on Buckmaster's veranda with a glass of Madeira before him, and thinking about Barbara . . .' (p. 141). 'Since his marriage he had never spent more than a few days away from Barbara' (p. 157). '. . . too sleepy to think about Buckmaster. He thought about Barbara instead' (p. 171). Why, one is prompted to ask, is Bowen so unsettled by a mutually agreed few weeks away from his wife and children?

At one point he is about to have alfresco sex with a young friend of Strether's, Emilie, but is prevented from doing so by a wasp bite on his leg. As a piece of fiction the moment is both arbitrary and unconvincing: Emilie features nowhere else and Amis's male characters generally require a more significant cause for restraint. But, like the rest of the closing chapters, it indicates that Amis has more on his mind than the scrutiny of the suspicious reader.

Amis weaves into his account the very personal hypothesis of his letter to Larkin: what would it be like if he were on his own again, a freewheeling bachelor? And he also addresses this to a particular reader. He was not attempting to convince Hilly, via Bowen and the Emilie incident, that he had become a natural monogamist by inclination – hence the wasp bite as an unconvincing act of fate. He knows and implicitly confesses that he will go on being attracted to attractive women, but he also makes it clear, through Bowen's persistent and intrusive thoughts about Barbara, that such instincts can be overruled by his attachment to his wife. In effect, he writes into the novel a version of the agreement he had reached with Hilly in January 1956; an uneven but circumspect blend of candour and restraint. The more unsettled, non-fictional counterpart of this can be gauged from a comparison between the letters he wrote to Larkin during this period and the one he sent to Fairlie (1 November 1956). In the latter he adopts the style of a distraught victim, a decent husband and father (circa 1856) who faces the loss of all that is dearest to him. 'This [separation of Amis from his wife and children, who would live with Fairlie] will be agonizing for them, but not as agonizing as it is for those who are suffering instead of merely inflicting cruelty, and if they are already selfish and ruthless by nature, as I think you are, they will be less agonized still.' Three weeks earlier he had reported to Larkin on which of his new first-year students would 'be best for a bit of ah ha ha'; the 'dreamy freckled lascivious Heather Harding' or maybe the 'high-breasted squirming Wendy Roberts' (8 October 1956). (And one wonders why Amis did not try out the epistolary novel; he could certainly reinvent himself in letters.)

When Bowen returns to London and is waiting for Barbara on the station platform, he reflects on how the likes of Emilie mean nothing to him compared with the woman he is about to meet. Barbara leaves the children with the luggage and sprints towards him. 'They kissed. Bowen had never felt so relieved in his life.' Why 'relieved'? There was absolutely no suggestion that their separation was anything more than a practical inconvenience, at least not in the novel. But in one word Amis had allowed his own feelings to undermine the pretence of fiction. There are no reasons for Bowen to feel 'relieved' at his sudden reunion with his wife, but for Amis there were many. As he wrote to Larkin (6 December 1956), 'I am less of a misery now, because I have more or less got my wife back (no Henry for 6 months; resumption of marital relations; much increased cordiality between the partners . . .) and that is sodding good-oh, believe me, sport.' However, one should not regard Bowen's feeling of relief at being united with his beloved wife as an exact version of Amis's. Later, in the same letter to Larkin, he reports that 'I have got my girlfriend back too. And that, as well, is very nice (indeed to fook) . . . yes my love-life is quite near an even keel at the moment.'

I Like It Here became a novel that Amis wanted to forget. He talks of it in his self-critical 1973 essay, but more significantly neither it nor the summer in Portugal are mentioned in his *Memoirs*. Here he states that he intends to leave out 'as much as possible of potentially hurtful topics' (p. 47), particularly those relating to Hilly. This is a creditable decision and, given that the events of 1955–7 were a prelude to their actual separation five years later, it is understandable that the novel which refers, albeit obliquely, to these events is prescribed. But perhaps there are other reasons for its omission. He speaks of it as his 'worst' novel, and it probably is in the sense that in it Amis attempted to do and say far too many things, some involving his attitudes to politics, literature and national identity, some involving his more private states of mind. Worse than this, he attempted to do so while borrowing from the techniques of his mentor. Fielding's novels had no secure structural foundation or precedents and were, in the most literal sense, experimental. They involved a constant and, to Fielding's credit, entertaining tension between the devices of fiction and the plausibility of the events described. Amis in *I Like It Here* also attempted an interweaving of reportage and invention, but he could not quite make up his mind about whether he was writing a novel which was confined and determined by real people, places and occurrences or an essay about writing a novel. Like the trip on which it was based, the book is an untidy mixture of contingency, forbearance and obligation.

8

The 1950s and the Poems

THE unifying feature of Amis's life and writing during the 1950s was his almost fanatical desire to dissociate. He came to detest intellectual positions that claimed to explain the individual as a symptom of something collective, and he progressively detached himself from institutions and groupings which might involve the sharing rather than the possession of opinions.

The two cultural phenomena most commonly associated with the 1950s are the Movement and the Angry Young Men, and Amis has been classified as an example of both. In a 1960 article he reflected on the passing decade.

> The less appealing side of the Angry Young Men business was that it embodied and encouraged a Philistine, paraphrasing, digest-compiling attitude to literature, one which was favoured not only outside the phantom 'movement' (on the daily's book pages) but inside it as well. ('Lone Voices', p.163, reprinted in *What Became of Jane Austen?*)

Amis was irritated by the critical and journalistic inclination to treat literature like politics, to subsume individual writers within a broader doctrine. But he overstates his case, because the Movement was certainly more than a 'phantom'.

The term was given its capital letter M by J.D. Scott in an anonymous leader in the *Spectator* on 1 October 1954, but it had for several years before that been attached by reviewers to a definite article. 'The' Movement referred to a group of writers, mostly poets, who had started to publish in the late 1940s. By the early 1950s reviewers began to notice common features in their work. They often counterpointed informal, contemporary locutions against traditional verse forms and maintained a prose-like coherence. They were largely anti-modernist. Donald Davie, himself deemed a Movement poet, argued that they had revived the Popean blend of accessibility, correctness and journalistic relevance; he called them 'the New Augustans'. The critic Anthony Hartly (1954) thought they had more in common with the sardonic ironies of the school of Donne.

They certainly existed. The 1953 PEN anthology contained verse by Amis, Larkin, Elizabeth Jennings and Robert Conquest, who edited the collection. The archetypal Movement collection, *New Lines* (1956), was also edited by Conquest and contained verse by himself, D.J. Enright, John Holloway, John Wain, Elizabeth Jennings, Donald Davie, Larkin and Amis. In the introduction Conquest propounded a manifesto. Poetry, he wrote, should be 'empirical in its attitude to all that comes', should 'resist the agglomeration of unconscious commands' and 'maintain a rational structure and comprehensible language'. Amis's verse of the 1950s and 1960s satisfies this definition, and Conquest's criteria inform Amis's own critical judgements. In 1953, for example, he reviewed in *Essays in Criticism* a collection by the Ulster poet W.R. Rodgers, in which he accused Rodgers of a 'partial abandonment of articulate language', of entering the sphere of 'infant language play, schizophrenic "word salads"'. Rodgers wrote verse very similar to that of the Movement's *bête noire*, Dylan Thomas, which Amis also attacked and which is the working antithesis of Conquest's ideal.

Amis's 1960 dismissal of the Movement as a myth contradicts a letter he wrote to Larkin six years earlier (14 March 1954), in which he states that 'There's no doubt, you know, we are getting to be a movement.' He qualifies this by specifying the 'we' as himself and Larkin and dismissing the other members of this new group, declaring that he couldn't 'give a pinch of shit' for the work of Donald Davie, Al Alvarez and John Wain. Amis's hostility to the Movement was not so much ideological as private and personal.

In a letter to Larkin (19 April 1956) he compares his friend's 'An Arundel Tomb', which he likes, with Wain's 'Usefulness of Light', which in Amis's view is 'frightful'. 'What I think about poetry is that ... it has got to be *instantaneously comprehensible* if anyone at all is going to read it these days. No use this "difficult simplicity" lark; no use being clear after one reading. Got to be clear *line by line*, see?' This makes Samuel Johnson sound like a woolly-headed liberal, but what lay behind Amis's intolerant maxims was a sense of anxiety that his and Larkin's writing would soon be swallowed by an encroaching, all-inclusive notion of period style. What this would involve, he feared, was the licensing of accessibility as a foundation for self-indulgent puzzle-making. Later he comments on Iris Murdoch's *The Flight of the Enchanter* (1955), which seems to him 'very unreal' despite its spurious concessions to transparency. 'I can't believe that the chaps in it are real or doing things that real people do . . . the characters all seem abnormal, somehow. Any moment I expect to come across one of them singing the only song he knows, or turning out to be a dwarf all along . . .' He hated Murdoch's implied thesis that reality was a shroud for more complex states and registers and the broader implication that literature should be a vehicle for exploring philosophical conundrums.

In 1957–8, after seeing the typescript version of Larkin's 'The Whitsun Weddings', Amis set himself the task of producing a sequence of brief poems, each reproducing the style of someone associated with the Movement and all involving the same setting as Larkin's piece, a train journey. Amis himself and Larkin are on the list, along with Conquest, Donald Davie, D.J. Enright, Thom Gunn,

Elizabeth Jennings and John Wain. Amis's parody of himself, called 'Getting Somewhere', exaggerates his tendency to interweave informal locutions with traditional metrical structures, such as:

> Before you start to blow your top,
> Look at the chaps who've brought the train
> Two hundred bloody miles non-stop . . .

With the rest Amis shrewdly mixes a particular idiosyncratic feature of the poet's literary persona with interpersonal conventions that had already become associated with Movement writing: each is cautiously precise in their use of metaphor, nods respectfully towards conventional verse form and is crisply accessible. This exercise (which first appeared in print in the appendix to Amis's *Letters* and on which Amis never commented) is revealing in that Amis is deliberately, and very subtly, causing the individuality of these poets to conform to a critical generalization. While he approved of the anti-modernist tendencies of many of his contemporaries, Amis was equally unsettled by collective, predictable elements of their work.

As I shall show, he began writing poems in the early 1950s that were very different from his wartime output of *Bright November*. In these new pieces the speaker resembled Amis's fictional personae, except that he turns his verbal resources inward, uses them to capture his own states of guilt, uncertainty, inadequacy, sometimes despair. There are indeed formal similarities between Amis's verse and that of other writers in volumes such as *New Lines* and D. J. Enright's *Poets of the 1950s*, but Amis resented having his most intimate, candid writings classified as part of something more general and collective.

Amis's view of the Angry Young Men as an invention had far more basis in fact than his dismissal of the Movement. The Angries were created by the popular press. John Osborne's *Look Back in Anger* opened at the Royal Court in London in May 1956. There were a number of enthusiastic reviews, but it was not, initially, a popular play. In an attempt to muster publicity, the theatre's press officer, George Fearon, informed a journalist that Osborne was a 'very angry young man', a phrase he had borrowed from Leslie Paul's recently published novel *Angry Young Men* which was largely concerned with the 1920s and 1930s. Fearon did not explain what exactly Osborne was angry about, but the press soon began to fill in the gaps. Dan Farson in several articles for the *Evening Standard* and the *Daily Mail* began to suggest that anger was a unifying feature of work by a number of youngish poets, novelists and play-wrights. In July 1956 he organized a launch party, somewhat belat-edly, for Colin Wilson's *The Outsider*. Present were Osborne, another playwright, Michael Hastings, and Mary Ure who played Alison in Osborne's drama, and Farson used the event in a *Daily Mail* article to claim that a British version of French existentialism had arrived; radical, leftish-leaning and very angry. Amis was not at the party, but his two novels were cited by Farson as symptomatic of this new trend. Farson had obviously not read Amis's review of Wilson's book in the *Spectator* (June 15). In this Amis associates Wilson with a tradition comprising Sartre, Camus, Kierkegaard and Nietzsche. In his view, these were lazy, self-indulgent figures who turned their particular problems into broader conceptions of the human condition: 'There is no need to erect one's boredom's into a system with oneself sitting in the middle' (*What Became of Jane Austen?*, pp. 90–1).

Farson had probably read Harold Hobson's review in the *Sunday Times* in which he claimed that '*Look Back in Anger* puts on stage the outlook of *That Uncertain Feeling*.' Hobson's comparison is fallacious. On the surface John Lewis and Jimmy Porter have things in common. Lewis's affair with Elizabeth Griffith-Williams and Porter's relationship with Alison involve a degree of excitement generated by class division and sexuality, and both men are, although for different reasons, discontented. At the same time they embody radical differences between their respective creators' outlooks and objectives. Porter is a cynical, articulate vehicle for disenchantment, and in the end he characterizes a form of powerless nihilism. He is the subject of his circumstances and his text, while Lewis, through his command of its language, is its controller. In the end, and despite his selfish, hedonistic inclinations, Lewis shows us that fidelity and the family can be the basis for happiness.

Amis in his 1960 article conceded that his unwitting recruitment to the Angries had offered him some 'free publicity', which he had enjoyed, but he maintained that this was overruled by his wish to be detached from any grouping which associated its members with a predictable view of art, society and politics. He disliked this because it would attract the person who 'would rather read a book as a purée of trends and attitudes than as a work of art having its own unique, unparaphrasable qualities' (*What Became of Jane Austen?*, p. 163). Again the keynote is individualism, and there are parallels here between Amis's public comments on culture and politics, his principal characters and the way he led his life. Dixon, Lewis and Bowen are versions of Amis in that they are exercises in declassification. Dixon is intelligent, articulate, informed, but no element of high culture is immune from his acts of ridicule. In a 1961 essay ('My Kind of Comedy', *Twentieth Century*, July 1961), another exercise in distancing himself from the alleged literary groupings of the previous decade, Amis comments on the infamous reference by Jim to 'filthy Mozart'. He explains that he wanted to 'annoy Mozart lovers, not denigrate Mozart'. Mozart should be respected for his individual genius, not displayed as a badge of cultural credibility.

Dixon likes jazz and so did Amis. In a 1955 essay ('Editor's Notes', *Spectator*, 7 October 1955) Amis attacked what he called the '"real" Philistinism of the dilettante', arguing that people who talked only of the established and usually long dead masters of classical music had stopped thinking about music *per se*, particularly the type practised by 'the sinister living figure of Mr Louis Armstrong'. He affirms that 'culture made in one's own private still is more potent than that which comes to the table in a decanter': like what you want to like, not only what is provided by your high-cultural hosts.

In *That Uncertain Feeling* Lewis attends a performance of Probert's new play, mainly because he has been invited by Elizabeth. They are bored, they leave, and Lewis comments on how 'going to the theatre' was often what people did to show that culture was one of their more respectable acquisitions. A year after the novel, in an article called 'That Certain Revulsion' (note the echo of the novel's title), Amis attacks people whose presence at plays is a complement to their other affectations, 'clothes, manner and conversation', and adds that for most people 'of my age and upbringing' film and television are just as good and usually more entertaining than the theatre. Amis loathed the kind of inclusive, hierarchical culture of the theatre-going crowd, particularly the way in which the play was treated as part of the middle-class social fabric; less a literary text, more a social gathering. Esmond Cleary and Sam Dawson, Amis's academic colleagues at Swansea during the 1950s, cannot remember him ever once attending a play (although he did act in one staff–student production). Amis's anti-theatrical stance was perhaps something of a personal eccentricity (and it re-emerges in Bowen's discomfort with the genre), but it is none the less consistent with his general aversion to the notion of culture as a collective enterprise in which the parts are subservient to the whole. One event neatly encapsulates Amis's ideas on culture and his developing and closely related political opinions.

Amis first met Anthony Powell after praising his *Music of Time* sequence in a *Spectator* article in 1953. Powell wrote him a letter, partly of thanks; they met for lunch, got on well and remained close friends until Amis's death. At first Amis felt slightly uneasy about Powell's upper-class background and lifestyle – he tells of how when the Powells stayed with them in Swansea Lady Violet, a minor aristocrat, would leave a ten-shilling note in the bedroom for 'the cleaner', which Hilly, the cleaner, much appreciated. But it soon became evident to each of them that they shared the opinion that class only really mattered to people with social ambitions or left-leaning obsessions.

In late 1955 the BBC invited Amis to interview Powell on the Third Programme, and it became clear that the producer knew nothing of their friendship. The interview had been planned as a nasty encounter between a new novelist with apparently radical ideas on society and an established figure who had more in common with the Bloomsbury Group. It would go out live, and during the rehearsal the producer became annoyed, first, because Amis seemed to respect Powell's work and, even worse, because he was talking about books as books rather than as instruments of unrest.

Amis certainly did not hold the view that literature could or should separate itself from its political, historical context; his own novels offer us commentaries on British life since the 1950s that are perceptive without being explanatory or analytical. What he did reject was the treatment of literature by its practitioners as a vehicle for political opinions and by its theorists as evidence of trends and states of mind that have little to do with the quality of the writing.

In 1956 Amis reviewed Richard Hoggart's study of working-class life and culture, *The Uses of Literacy*. He liked the book, but he qualified his praise by inferring that Hoggart had come close to sentimentalizing his own experience of northern working-class life: 'if a structure is propped up by unemployment, bad housing and an agonizing fear of debt, then we must kick the prop away' (*What Became of Jane Austen?*, p. 86). By 'structure' Amis means the culture and social fabric of working-class life, and he is uneasy with Hoggart's implied celebration of art as a compensation for poverty. Hoggart's study is rooted in the 1930s, and the 'prop' as Amis put it was now being dismantled by the legacy of the 1945 Labour government – nationalization, living wages, the National Health Service and the welfare state. The review reflects the tensions and inconsistencies of Amis's own political outlook. His enduring approval of the 1945 reforms was at odds with a more recent, more assertive, one might almost say pre-Thatcherite, inclination towards individualism. He would attempt to reconcile these oppositions in his 1957 pamphlet *Socialism and the Intellectuals*.

He begins with a candid biographical profile of himself: lower-middle-class suburban background, father a clerk, scholarship boy to a not-quite-public school and Oxford. He confesses that at Oxford he had gone through 'that callow, Marxist phase that seemed almost compulsory for my generation' (p. 1). This opening is a calculated gesture: he has confessed his own, earlier inclinations and, as the title suggests, the rest of the pamphlet will be about other people and their beliefs. Some of it is, but each point is attached to an autobiographical, self-scrutinizing subtext.

A recurrent theme is the Auden generation of the 1930s, which in Amis's view was comprised of hypocrites and charlatans: figures whose leftish leanings were partly a guilty compensation for their privileged backgrounds and, even worse, a calculatedly fashionable supplement to their writing. When writing this he would without doubt have been conscious of his own enthusiasm for Auden a decade earlier and of how *Bright November* and his two unpublished novels bear the Audenesque imprint, celebrating rebellious idealism with a pious smugness.

He goes on to claim that the hypocrisies and self-deluding inconsistencies of the 1930s have in the 1950s been refashioned by a much broader network of thinkers and political activists, some of whom now hold positions of power. He states that the 'condemnation' of the invasion of Suez by the Labour opposition was shifting and qualified and probably a concession to the nationalistic tendencies of its working-class electorate. (Decades later he would tell of how when attending an anti-Suez demonstration in Swansea he was recognized and chased down the road by an old lady who brandished a sharp umbrella and accused him of treachery.) For Amis, it was the Russian invasion of Hungary that effectively exposed the inconsistencies of British socialists, many of whom still refused to recognize that the Soviet Union was an aggressive, totalitarian inversion of the socialist idyll. He asks if there is an alternative to socialism as an all-embracing philosophical-political formula. A few, he claims, have returned to the fascism of Mosley, others find solace in religion, and some, encouraged by the likes of F. R. Leavis and J. B. Priestley, promote a brand of clubbish intellectualism. The unifying feature of these diatribes, more implied than explicitly stated, is Amis's loathing for systems, irrespective of their ideological fabric. What he is really attacking is the precondition that if you hold any opinion you must belong to a group that shares and validates it, that a particular attitude is inevitably part of a general ideology. This state of mind imposes limitations upon the straightforward, empirical evaluation of the world and very often replaces freedom of thought with pragmatic compromise. He gives examples of how important and very specific issues – racism, capital punishment, divorce law, homosexuality – have been marginalized by political opportunism. 'I cannot see myself explaining, to an audience of dockers, say, just why homosexual relations between consenting adults should be freed from legal penalty' (p. 10), by which he means that the social radicalism of Labour will provide a badge for its sophisticated middle-class adherents but will, in pragmatic terms, always attend to the illiberal bigotries of the electorate.

The pamphlet attracted a good deal of public interest. Profiles of Amis the novelist had speculated on the leftish, anti-establishment drift of his fiction as a reflection of the man, but this was the first time that Amis himself had said anything at length about his beliefs and opinions. In a review of the pamphlet in the *Daily Worker* in February 1957 the Marxist critic Arnold Kettle offered a patronizing explanation for Amis's brand of political cynicism. He was, argued Kettle, a socialist at heart, but his involvement in literature, very bourgeois, had caused his sympathies to become eclectic and disorganized. Amis, provoked, wrote a letter of reply in which the feelings that inspired the pamphlet are much less understated. 'I have . . . utterly rejected [Marxism]. No world view, it seems to me, comes within light years of being adequate to the world it professes to categorize. Each fact, each entity, each event is unique. To pretend otherwise is mere Victorian system building. Marxism, I think, does just that. It repels me also by offering certainty instead of truth.'

Kettle was wrong about Amis having being baited by the comforts of bourgeois indifference, but his notion of a causal relation between literature and belief carries a shred of truth. Amis's communist-socialist affiliations were partly a front, a lever against his father and later an affirmation of unpredictability. They caused speculation, made him more interesting. In 1957, however, Amis the novelist *was* more interesting. He had found a medium, sympathetic to his talents, that enabled him to be and do as he wished, while also allowing him to reflect upon the moral and political resonances of these activities. He could now be his own man.

Socialism had been his crutch, and by 1957 he was finding that he no longer needed it. There are parallels between *Socialism and the Intellectuals* and *I Like It Here*. The latter came out a few months later, but they were written at the same time. In the novel Amis dissociates himself from contemporary literary factions, pitches his affiliations back to the eighteenth century when no one was sure what the novel was supposed to be and do or where it was going, when the individuality of the novelist was predominant. The pamphlet was spun out of this feeling of creative independence. Throughout Amis's fiction he would address opinions and ideas, but he would never promote them. He would examine how they might influence, sometimes disfigure, the indigenous characteristics of people, but he would only observe and report. If the reader was incapable of recognizing the distinction between justice and injustice, privilege and deprivation, common sense and absurdity, then it was not the obligation of the novelist to educate this person. Such activities were non-literary, the use of literature as a channel for prefigured beliefs – Amis despised Waugh and Lawrence for this. *Socialism and the Intellectuals* was as much a reflection of how becoming a popular, respected novelist had released Amis from any kind of ideological affiliation as it was a comment on contemporary political fashions. Indeed, after promising in a letter to Larkin to send his friend an inscribed copy of the pamphlet, he cannot stop himself from making fun of the very idea of writing about politics: 'Zeece dayce we radders kennot ef*fort* to stand asite from ze clesh bit-win ze forcess off friddum ent ze blodd-stent executionerss off ze Ballshavvik empire' (2 January 1957).

Just before the pamphlet was published Tom Maschler had asked Amis to contribute to a collection of essays to be called *Declaration* in which youngish figures from the arts, mainly literature, would offer their views on society and politics. Amis declined because it seemed to him that the project was a means of providing persons recently associated with the ill-defined Angries with a vehicle for self-promotion. The eventual contributors were Doris Lessing, John Osborne, John Wain, Ken Tynan, Bill Hopkins, Lindsay Anderson and Stuart Holroyd, and the consensus was left-wing although not entirely orthodox. Lessing and Anderson addressed Amis's pamphlet with versions of Kettle's argument that its author was really a confused, irresponsible socialist; and Anderson went so far as to judge Amis's avoidance of radical ideology as the act of a 'coward'.

In a letter to Larkin (15 October 1957) Amis notes that 'John Whine' had produced an essay for 'This *Declaration* Thing' just for the publicity. 'He's not an angry young man, you sam, so he gets together with all of them to say he isn't. Ho hum. Ho, hum.'

Politics does not feature significantly in Amis's poetry of this period, but there are parallels between what happens in the verse and in *Socialism and the Intellectuals*. In the pamphlet he detaches himself from any kind of doctrine or ideology; he becomes Amis, a man with particular inclinations and opinions. In the poems he makes sure that his own voice is ever present; idiosyncratic, unapologetic and sometimes evasive, but certainly his.

Two themes recur in Amis's poetry of the 1950s and early 1960s. The first is a self-conscious awareness of Amis the poet. The episode in *I Like It Here* where Amis, via Bowen, locates himself within the history of the English novel is recalled in at least six of the poems written during this period. In these he asserts his independence from some of the most influential presences and moments of modern English verse. He does this to clear a space for the second theme, an exploration of the anxieties and complexities of Kingsley Amis.

A Case of Samples (1956) is a selection of the poems published over the previous nine years in magazines and journals, and these are radically different from the verse of *Bright November* (1947). For one thing, they no longer involve erratic borrowings from other poets' styles and techniques. Instead, the formal structure of the poem is tailored by its mood and its subject.

The title *A Case of Samples* is taken from the closing line of a poem called 'A Song of Experience'. The poet and his friends are in a pub where they meet a travelling salesman who tells them of the women he has known and seduced. The tone is informal, familiar; the conversational diction is slipped into the quatrains as easily as the traveller slips in, and out, of the lives, emotions and bodies of his women.

> He tried all colours, white and black and coffee;
>   Though quite a few were chary, more were bold;
> Some took it like the Host, some like a toffee;
>   The two or three who wept were soon consoled.

The traveller is a projection of Amis himself. True, he shares none of his interlocutor's cultural interests, but as dimensions of the same person the two figures in the poem capture with brutal honesty the Amis who could be, was, two different people; and nowhere is the real-life version of this split personality more evident than in his letters, particularly those to Larkin and Conquest. Here we encounter the literary Amis, as enthusiastically open and opinionated to his friends as he is to his readers, alongside the unrepentant and successful lecher whose job, like the traveller's, provides limitless opportunities for casual sex. They even share a taste for ribald candour. On 24 September 1956, for example, Amis wrote to Larkin of his most recent conquest, the wife of a local rugby enthusiast who has provided him with a fixture list for Swansea Rugby Football Club, 'pointing out all the Home matches, which are marked with an H. Her husband goes . . . to watch them when they play at home see. Her meaning being, that you CAN SLIP IN AND SLIP IT IN BACH.' 'Just shows you, doesn't it?' comments Amis on the astonishingly large number of home games. The next paragraph of the letter is comprised exclusively, and without a hint of irony, of his opinions on the state of contemporary poetry: the traveller is exchanged for the literary persona with seamless ease.

A couple of weeks later Amis opens a letter to Larkin (8 October) with news of the Boulting Brothers' production of *Lucky Jim* along with some comments on poetry in general, and he follows this with a detailed account of the physical characteristics of the female Honours intake for the new academic year. Of the fifteen women (only four men), '5 are bloody marvellous ooohooohooo and another couple are such as one would feel no rigid objection to sliding one's oh ho up . . .' Thomas, his head of department ('Filthy fat Scotch Burns worshipping Dryden editing . . . scheming schoolboy of hell'), has allocated the best of them to other tutors but, as Amis implies, the hunt is on.

Larkin's endlessly astonished, and sometimes quietly envious, awareness of how his friend could switch so easily between personae becomes evident a year later when he sends Amis a plan for a poem that would eventually be published posthumously as 'Letter to a Friend About Girls'. The irony of the title is clear enough in that the friend is undoubtedly Amis, while the letter is the one that Larkin never quite managed to write.

After looking at the draft/plan Amis replied to Larkin with flattered and disingenuous modesty: '. . . an absolutely fucking marvellous idea . . . But don't get me wrong (though I suppose it needn't be "me" in the poem); what I mean is I am no Don J. at all, really' (9 November 1957). Really? Larkin certainly had his friend's letters with him when he wrote the poem.

> . . . your staggering skirmishes
> In train, tutorial and telephone booth,
> The wife whose husband watched away matches
> While she behaved so badly in the bath . . .

The letters provided the poem's anecdotal substance, but its mood must have been inspired by Amis's 'Song of Experience'. In the latter Amis records the comfortable, easy co-presence of two dimensions of himself, and Larkin in 'Letter to a Friend' adds a third voice, that of someone who for a couple of decades has listened to a very real version of the poet and the traveller talking in the pub.

> After comparing lives with you for years
> I see how I've been losing : all the while
> I met a different gauge of girl from yours.
>
> . . . One day perhaps I'll know
> What makes you be so lucky in your ratio
>
> – One of those 'more things', could it be? *Horatio.*

'A Song of Experience' is not simply a means by which Amis can displace his life of lechery on to the figure of the traveller. He also projects the traveller into an exploration of the relationship between literature and sex.

> The inaccessible he laid a hand on,
>> The heated he refreshed, the cold he warmed
> What Blake presaged, what Lawrence took a stand on
>> What Yeats locked up in fable he performed.

The named writers are part of a literary tradition which turns the pure pleasure of sex into apocalyptic metaphors, in contrast with the traveller who, without apology or explanation, simply appreciates it. Amis embeds this contrast in the texture of the poem itself. Its title invokes Blake's *Songs*, and its use of the quatrain, the double rhymes and the tri-syllabic ballad metre recall their style. Again, Amis seems to be exploring complementary versions of himself. On the one hand, he shares a genre with his eminent predecessors – as he shows in his self-confident reproduction of Blake's method; on the other, he is a writer who has detached himself from their brand of moral and aesthetic elitism. They, he implies, would have treated the traveller as an intriguing specimen. For Amis, he is part of experience, his own included; something that poetry should involve and not patronize. Amis concludes:

> I saw him brisk in May, in Juliet's weather,
>> Hitch up the trousers of his long-tailed suit,
> Polish the windscreen with his chamois leather,
>> And stow his case of samples in the boot.

We know that the traveller would probably neither recognize nor care about Amis's Shakespearian allusion – he is more interested in real-life Juliets – but this is not Amis invoking his cultural superiority; quite the opposite. The traveller's case of samples enables him to enjoy a life of promiscuity, and it is significant that Amis chooses this phrase for the title of his collection. Amis's case of samples is his writing, which involves a combination of his literary talents and his less sophisticated traveller-like persona. Here, too, there is an element of confession with apology; Amis's literary reputation, his own case of samples, played an important part in his successful career as a seducer.

The use of 'Song of Experience' as a literary-critical thesis resurfaces in 'Against Romanticism' in which Amis reflects upon how, in his view, many of the literary giants, particularly the Romantics, seemed intent on turning the actuality of life into something universal, transcendent, prophetic.

> Over all, a grand meaning fills the scene
> And sets the brain raging with prophecy
> Raging to discard real time and place,
> Raging to build a better time and place.

Amis would prefer it,

> if images were plain,
> Warnings clearly said, shapes put down quite still
> Within the fingers reach, or else nowhere . . .

This is Amis's poetic manifesto: investigate the immediate, explore its effects upon what we know and feel, but do not make it a springboard for quasi-religious warnings or idealistic fantasies.

Amis's poems of the 1950s attend to this manifesto. They address a variety of topics and incidents, but throughout there is a speaking presence who interweaves the features of the self-investigating poetic craftsman with those of the unselfconscious travelling salesman.

The most famous of these pieces is 'Nothing to Fear', an account of the thoughts that run through the mind of a man in a flat 'lent by a friend, whose note says *Lucky Sod*'. He is waiting for a woman: 'the cover story pat / And quite uncheckable; her husband off / Somewhere with the kids till six o'clock.' He reflects with covetous glee on her impressive face, legs, hips and breasts, and at the end of the first stanza he dismisses feelings of guilt, compunction and 'all that cock; / It'll wear off, as usual'. But it does not, and in the second stanza the pace of the language quickens as he asks himself why he feels so uneasy: 'This slight trembling / Dry mouth, quick pulse rate, sweaty hands / As though she were the first?' The sense of unease that he had earlier dismissed becomes tangibly present in the closing lines.

> Sitting here, a bag of glands
> Tuned up to concert pitch, I seem to sense
> A different style of caller at my back,
> As cold as ice, but just as set on me.

Conventional guilt can be coped with in the manner of the traveller in the pub and Amis in his letters, but this is different: a fear of something that can only be himself, a figure who lives two lives and is rightly terrified at the thought of their intersection. The 'different style of caller' disturbs the self-contained pleasure of the illicit liaison which the rest of the poem tries so desperately to celebrate.

The poem is Amis's most blatantly autobiographical. The 'friend' whose flat he borrowed was Robert Conquest, who had control of a number of 'service flats' owned by his employers, the Foreign Office, and he personally leased a basement in Eaton Square, Chelsea. He would lend one of these to Amis whenever he needed a site for sex, which he frequently did. Amis in his *Memoirs* tells of how on one occasion, after 'Nothing to Fear' had been published, Conquest set up a tape recorder which was triggered by the main door and caused a disembodied voice, Conquest's, to recite the first few lines of the poem.

Amis no doubt includes this anecdote to indicate that his prodigious sex life and clandestine dealings with Conquest were more the basis for laddish humour than anything resembling guilt or uncertainty. If it is also intended to undermine the very convincing mood of unease generated in the poem itself it fails, because 'Nothing to Fear' is the most explicit of a series of poems in which Amis explores various states of anxiety, depression, even self-loathing, which surround the sexual act. If these were not rooted in actual feelings then Amis is the most hollow and talented liar ever to have written a poem. While preparing 'Nothing to Fear' he wrote to Larkin: 'Still haven't finished my adultery poems, but shall have a bash today before plugging on with Jenny' (15 December 1959). Jenny would become Jenny Bunn of *Take a Girl Like You*, the novel involving his first genuinely honest fictionalization of infidelity and its effects. Next in the letter he shifts from his writings on adultery to its real counterpart: 'Tackling of adultery, my activities in this direction . . .' These involve the discovery by Hilly of more letters from one of his girlfriends, the arrival next summer of a girl he had met in Princeton, his recent encounter with a 'splendid busty Redhead' and the consequent and no less frightening prospect of Hilly discovering more and leaving with the children. The letter further undermines Amis's continual claims that his writings were not autobiographical.

'Nocturne' seems to be a Movement poem *par excellence*, a very short story in verse where Amis describes the view from an upstairs window on to a dark, damp street after the pubs have closed. It is probably Swansea. Two people, apparently with nowhere else to go, fondle each other in a shop doorway, watched by a drunken sailor with an empty beer flagon 'looking for something good to smash it on'. Amis wonders what the local guardians of decency, the Watch Committee, would make of this. They would probably describe them as '*mere animals*', and Amis agrees. They are animals, but of the human variety whose bestial instincts are altered by their ability, need, to keep in their mind 'the image of another creature'. It is a poem about sex, loneliness, even envy – Amis implies that the drunken sailor's anger is partly the result of the couple's reminder that he is alone. And it is also about Amis. He knows nothing of what these people feel, but their image of drab desperation causes him to speculate on its emotional underpinnings; it is as much a moment of awareness as observation.

In 'A Point of Logic' two verse stanzas describe the same act. In the first, a couple climb a staircase 'of marble / Or decently scrubbed boards', the uncertainty perhaps an indication of the many different staircases that Amis had used on his way to Conquest's flats. In the second he advises them to 'put out the light':

> Lurch to the bare attic
> Over buckets of waste
> And labouring bodies;
> Leave the door open
> And fall on each other . . .

Throughout the poem Amis causes us to wonder if the couple are involved in a random, illicit liaison in an unfamiliar building or whether the location is their new home. Do the 'labouring bodies' and 'buckets of waste' indicate builders at work on the house, or are they part of some degenerate fantasy? At the end he advises them to 'Stay only a minute / Depart separately / And use no names.' This could be an echo of Amis's brief, almost anonymous encounters, or it could be a description of the impersonality of all sexual acts, even those with a regular partner, in which satisfaction is selfish, physical. The bizarre, almost surreal uncertainties of the account are a distillation of Amis's experiences in the 1950s. He enjoyed his life with Hilly and feared its loss, but it was not enough. In his 1957 letter to Conquest on how he had made peace with Hilly and resumed his other encounters he concludes, 'Oh, why isn't there *more* of that kind of thing?'

'Alternatives' is even more disturbing. The first three stanzas offer a brief cinematic narrative. A woman is alone in a dark house playing the piano. A man moves from the pavement and up the stairs. He enters her room and strangles her. In the fourth stanza Amis stops the film and asks if the reader would like to alter its conclusion. Perhaps the house should be empty; or maybe the woman knows and is expecting the man, whose hands will move not to her throat but to her 'eager breasts'. Amis is not suggesting that sex is the equivalent of murder, but the fine distinction between killer and lover recalls the 'different style of caller' that he senses in 'Nothing to Fear'. This time a woman is waiting for a man. At the beginning of the last stanza Amis considers the choice between the two stories, 'Neither or both for you', and against this is an echo of his own life. In his letters to Conquest there is a sense that the conditions of secrecy, the sheer badness of adultery, provide Amis with an extra, perhaps necessary, level of excitement. In the poem the man's movement towards the women carries sexual overtones. He is about to commit either a terrible act or meet his lover. For Amis, in life and in the poem, the distinction had become both blurred and addictive: 'Neither or both'. In a 1959 letter to Larkin when he tells of his 'Yank girl', a legacy of the Princeton visit, and of a 'most splendid busty redhead' acquired more recently he also reflects that while it's all 'bloody good fun' the consequences of being found out and the prospect of losing Hilly make serial adultery a more than stressful activity. 'You can't have it both ways, you see.' The two phrases from the poem and the letter would eventually provide the title for a novel which Amis would write when he was in his early seventies. Published in 1994, it would record his earlier life and be partly a note of apology to Hilly – *You Can't Do Both*.

9

Take a Girl Like You

Amis returned to Swansea from the United States in September
1959. He had spent the previous academic year as Visiting
Fellow in Creative Writing at Princeton, given lectures in other universities in the Northeastern states and on one occasion shared the
stage with Jack Kerouac. The notebook of his American experiences would provide him with adaptable anecdotes for *One Fat
Englishman* (1963), but for the moment he needed to complete a
project that had been at the planning stage for over four years.

By the late 1950s some critics were beginning to wonder if
Amis, having discovered a successful formula, was willing or able to
change it; one suggested that *That Uncertain Feeling* and *I Like It
Here* might be retitled *Lucky Jim Married* and *Lucky Jim Abroad*.
Dixon, Lewis and Bowen were indeed very similar characters;
youngish, ambitious, intelligent men of lower-middle/working-
class background, committed to one woman but with the potential
to stray. They were versions of their author, but, more significantly,
they provided Amis with a focal point for an attitude, a perspective
that permeated the texture of his novels. The books themselves
were distillations of his personality, involving an eye for the absurd
and the pretentious and combining egotistical cleverness with a
modest hint of self-parody. They did not endorse any particular
ideology or world view, and this, too, was a reflection of Amis who

in private believed in nothing much and in print continually berated the likes of Waugh and Lawrence for using novels as sermons.

Every hypothetical change from his established method seemed to involve a potentially catastrophic domino effect. If he broke the alliance between his personality and the dominant mood of the novel, he would inevitably have to temper his habit of counter-pointing serious issues and events with deftly orchestrated farce; he had, before *Lucky Jim*, tried to write fiction without comedy, all of which was unpublishable. Moreover, virtually every incident in his first three novels was connected in some way with his personal experience: Amis did not invent his fictions; he fictionalized what he knew. If he were to produce a more objective, broadly focused picture of late 1950s' Britain, and this was his aim, he needed to expand his fictional world beyond the activities of one character. In the end he made the best of a compromise. In *Take a Girl Like You* the principal male figure, Patrick Standish, is, like his predecessors, autobiographical, but while they variously improved upon their creator Patrick is the first uncensored version of Amis. The 1950s' men all had at least the potential for serial philandering, but, with the exception of Lewis's single act of infidelity, they restrained themselves. Patrick is a prodigious libertine. He inherits their pene-trating, sardonic view of the world and, like them, shares an extended version of this with his narrator, but while Amis in his 1950s' writing had chosen targets who largely deserved ridicule Patrick seems to enjoy the crueller aspects of making fun of people, irrespective of their hapless vulnerability. Sam Dawson, a colleague at Swansea, recalls that while Amis was celebrated as an entertainer these same talents often hurt and offended his more sensitive vic-tims. 'He would exaggerate the potentially absurd in people. He could make people very uncomfortable by playing upon their absurdities. But his mimicry was done so well that he made it diffi-cult for people to take exception to it.' Patrick, too, exploits his acquaintances' fears of appearing to spoil the fun. Of the 1950s' men Lewis is the most candid regarding his own uncertainties and vulnerabilities, but in general Amis presents them as tough, transparent pragmatists. Patrick carries us into private states of disillusionment, weakness, almost depression, which were honest reflections of Amis's occasional states of mind.

By drawing upon aspects of himself which had not previously featured in his published work, Amis had gone some way towards a new mode of writing but not far enough. He needed another character, and he invented Jenny Bunn. Amis had, of course, written about women before, but only Elizabeth Gruffyd-Williams and Jean Lewis came close to being three-dimensional figures, and they existed exclusively within Lewis's perceptions and presentations of them. Jenny, like her male counterparts, dominates her sections of the narrative and maintains an interplay with her third-person alter ego. She involved Amis for the first time in the creation of a mindset which was not his own and one that evinced the experiences of a woman. In a 1974 interview Amis reflected on how difficult the novel had been, how he was 'so nervous' that he had 'made at least twelve drafts of the first chapter' (Salwak, p. 109). In general, Amis's first drafts were, after corrections, his last and, significantly, the first chapter of this novel is Jenny's. What he did not disclose was the exact nature of his difficulties and how he overcame them. Jenny is based essentially upon the one person whom Amis knew almost as well as himself: Hilly. This raised problems, the most straightforward being the prospect of a journalist suggesting that his new departure was actually a reworking of his earlier autobiographical enterprises, this time including his wife. The London media and literati had a basic knowledge of Amis's personal history, and if he were to retain his and Hilly's story at the core of the novel he would need enough camouflage to make comparisons tortuously difficult. Moreover, his original plan had been for a radical alternative to his monocular, post-*Lucky Jim* formula, and the addition of one more perspective was not much of a change.

These tactical difficulties had kept the novel at the planning stage for a long time. Before leaving for Portugal in 1955 he had started compiling a notebook that would, as he put it, become 'the longest and most elaborate' he had ever kept. He began preparing drafts in 1958, a process further delayed by his year in Princeton. On his return in 1959 he abandoned all other projects and finished *Take a Girl Like You*, his longest novel so far, in record time; it was published little more than a year later. Apart from will-power, the most important factor in this rapid shift from blind-alley planning to work in progress was another novel, Samuel Richardson's *Clarissa* (1748).

Richardson's eponymous heroine is a woman for whom sexuality is coterminous with commitment and fidelity. Lovelace, a ruthless lecher and Clarissa's pursuer, exists at the opposing end of the moral spectrum. Richardson's outstanding achievement was to make them believable inhabitants of his novel's closely observed mid-eighteenth-century social fabric, yet resonant of such otherworldly conflicts as the one between the Lady and the lascivious demon in Milton's *Comus*. The narrative is concerned almost exclusively with Lovelace's attempts to seduce Clarissa and her strategies of resistance, which Richardson offered as an enactment of the moral tensions that informed his society. In the end Lovelace succeeds, but his victory presents moral decadence as at once irresistible and destructive. He rapes her.

Patrick and Jenny become mid-twentieth-century versions of Lovelace and Clarissa. Richardson's narrative is replayed but subtly altered so that it could be interposed with Amis's account of himself and Hilly. *Clarissa* is an epistolary novel, but precedence is given to letters from Clarissa and Lovelace written respectively to their closest acquaintances, Anna Howe and John Belford. Amis employed third-person narrative, but the personalities of Jenny and Patrick, like those of their eighteenth-century predecessors, dominate the fabric of the book; their respective chapters read not unlike letters.

Richardson involved more than twenty other correspondents, who represented a cross-section of English society. Their presence is felt, with many of them featuring as a consensual endorsement of Lovelace's state of mind and activities, but overall they represent the background, presences who are carried along by the tension between the two central figures. Amis does something very similar by involving a cast of secondary characters which is much larger and who are more closely observed than in his previous books. These were drawn from his record-sized notebook and had originally been models for his projected kaleidoscope of perspectives and identities, but now he had found a means of involving them without offering them narrative voices. They are all, however peripherally, in some way involved in the story of Jenny and Patrick, some as figures who offer advice, a few as attempted participants and most providing implicit points of comparison with the two main characters.

There is McClintoch who shares a flat with Patrick and would, we know, abandon his self-conscious espousal of decency if only he had Patrick's wit and good looks. Julian Ormerod, Patrick's other friend, is an ex-RAF pilot, with an unearned income, a country house and servants. He, too, is a practised seducer, but unlike Patrick he goes about this business with an air of deferential *insouciance*. He asks Jenny if she would like to be his mistress with no commitments and no offence taken if she refuses, which she does. The Thompsons, from whom Jenny rents a room, are a sad reflection of the marital institution. Dick Thompson is a grotesque, and his attempt to seduce Jenny contributes to her growing suspicion that, for men, lust will always overrule reality, let alone fidelity. Elsie Carter, Jenny's colleague, further dispels her idealistic perception of marriage by explaining, from experience, that once the kids are born the devoted husband will attempt to return to his previous role as sexual predator. One night from her bedroom window Jenny overhears a supplement to Elsie's account in the drunken monologue of a neighbour, Able Seaman Jackson. Marriage in his view is 'legalized bloody prostitution'. And on the belief that monogamous sex strengthens the 'foundation of married life?': 'Don't make me laugh.'

These figures and more are intended by Amis to reflect a social fabric in which indulgence and ethical indifference had undermined the official doctrine of morality, largely unchanged since the nineteenth century and now absurdly redundant. Amis's picture of contemporary England is a version of Richardson's presentation of its mid-eighteenth-century counterpart; decadent, directionless and unfocused. Jenny, like Clarissa, seems to be the only person in the land who espouses and maintains a life based on principle, and her demise, although regrettable and almost tragic, is inevitable. With hindsight, his view seems remarkably shrewd and perceptive in that the decade which followed the novel's year of publication, 1960, involved among other things the licensing of promiscuity as part of a new code of radical individualism: the prevailing undercurrents of his book would become a tide and conventional morality its Canute.

However, Amis's sociological divinings were founded more upon personal inclination and experience than upon external observation. His perceptions of society were a distillation of the way he lived. More significantly, the novel's transplantation of Richardson to the present day provided him with both a justification and an excuse for his lifestyle. For the general reader it was a provocative, unsettling disclosure of the real world, but for a much smaller audience, himself and Hilly, it involved a more specific combination of confession and self-exculpation.

Jenny Bunn is twenty years old and a virgin, a state she intends to maintain until she marries. She has just moved to and begun work as a primary school teacher in the home-counties town where Patrick exercises his ego and libido. She is working class and this is her first time away from her parents' home somewhere in the north.

Amis assembled these details with his customary blend of tactical care and self-generating irony.

The northern working-class hero was a very recent arrival on the literary scene. John Braine's *Room at the Top* had appeared in 1957, and a year after that Alan Sillitoe produced *Saturday Night and Sunday Morning*. David Storey's *This Sporting Life* and Stan Barstow's *A Kind of Loving* came out several months before *Take a Girl Like You*. The men of these novels were rebellious, and their sexual misdemeanours debunked the popular image of Nonconformist rectitude which had, as much in film as in print, frequently attended presentations of the north. When Amis created Jenny he found himself with a satisfying agenda of possibilities, provocative yet convenient. John Lewis had already been cited by some critics as a Welsh prototype for the later men of the north. Amis welcomed the free publicity but hated the enclosure of his work as part of yet another trend, a class-conscious extension of the Angries. (Interestingly, he wrote the essay in which he dismissed the Angries and the Movement as myths when he was finishing *Take a Girl Like You*.) Jenny's background, described at the beginning of the novel, would obviously raise expectations, but instead of becoming a female counterpart to the likes of Barstow's Vic Brown Amis causes her to unsettle both the stereotypes that Barstow *et al.* had undermined and the ones they had created as replacements. Amis makes it clear that her idealism is individualistic and self-contained. She is not a practising Christian, and it is evident that neither her family nor her environment have played any significant part in the way she has chosen to live. She never invokes nor alludes to any figure or doctrine as a foundation for her moral stance, and she does not chide her new companions for their lifestyles. It is their choice. Hers has been made not in observance of an abstract code but because she believes that it will cause her to have a happier life than them. Ironically, Patrick becomes the ideologue, the amoral preacher. He is shown to be the representative of a new, unofficial but insidious state of mind. Through a subtle inversion of stereotypes Amis represents her as the most radical, independent figure of the book. Her personal rejection of promiscuity is her act of rebellion. By 1960 the very notion of revolt, of a character who showed dissatisfaction with prevailing mores, had become, paradoxically, an established literary convention. Such figures were virtually obliged to react against conventional institutions and behaviour; Kenneth Allsop's *The Angry Decade*, published in 1958, was a monograph that might easily have been mistaken for a rule-book. Jenny, inspired by Richardson's similarly self-willed heroine, is Amis's own act of rebellion against a new orthodoxy of revolt.

His use of Jenny as a means of dismantling literary stereotypes and expectations enabled him to make her, for most readers, unrecognizable as Hilly while encoding parallels that were privately resonant. Hilly was neither working class nor from the north. She was certainly not a moralist, but nor is Jenny. Jenny might appear to embody outdated moral principles, yet she is as much a realist as an idealist; other people's lives are not her business. Her determination to preserve her virginity until marriage is pragmatic, a means of realizing a personal objective. Hilly had sex with Amis before they married, but their married relationship became an extended version of the state of conflict that exists between Patrick and Jenny. For Hilly, like Jenny, marriage should involve monogamy, not because the institution enshrined religious or abstract doctrine but for the straightforward, practical reason that extra-marital sex caused distress and unhappiness.

Martin Amis read the novel when he was about fourteen and, without discussing it with his father, he recognized his mother in Jenny. 'She [Hilly] was a paradox – yes, she was odd, rebellious, but she was also principled. She would never judge, but nor would she *fake* anything, *invent* anything. She was, is, an individual. Yes, Jenny was certainly a version of her.'

Patrick, following Lovelace's example, rapes Jenny. It is a hollow victory in that by implication he concedes that his strategies of persuasion have failed. It is a brutal admission of defeat. The act is pure fiction, but it carries a message to Hilly. Amis in 1960 knew that what he was doing, had been doing continuously, with other women was wrong, that her perception of fidelity as the only means of preserving a relationship was valid, but also that he could not stop himself.

Throughout the novel there are events and references that are peripheral, provisionally related to the story of Patrick and Jenny. For the general reader they are simply part of the representational fabric, but for Amis and Hilly they are tokens of its autobiographical core. Patrick and Jenny are immediately attracted to each other, physically and for other reasons. She is amused and impressed by his verbal panache and cleverness, and so was Hilly when she met Amis in 1946. Gradually, Jenny becomes aware that behind his public persona, confident and arrogant, is a more vulnerable, less secure individual, and something very similar occurred when Hilly got to know Amis. Since his childhood Amis had been frightened of being alone in the dark. At the end of Chapter 20 Patrick excuses himself from the company of his male friends and goes outside. The house is in the country and there are no streetlights. Suddenly he finds that his thoughts are racing from one random, half-comprehended image to another, and he searches desperately for a point of stability. 'Nearby there was a strip of illumination from an upper window. Shivering he went and stood by this, so that he could see parts of himself.' Patrick's experience of terror at being detached from things that enable him to orient himself visually, including parts of his body, is a recreation by Amis of a recurrent condition of his own which, thirty years later, he would describe as 'fears of depersonalization. I would cease to seem real to myself' (*Memoirs*, p. 114). He was particularly distressed by the prospect of waking up in complete darkness; he always slept with a sidelight on and he would never spend the night in a house on his own. These fears varied in severity and frequency, and on a number of occasions after nights out with Hilly early in their relationship she would find herself walking him home to St John's before returning alone to her digs in St Aldate's; even after the wartime black-out had been lifted the lanes and side-streets of central Oxford remained for him horribly dark places.

Two chapters after Patrick's night-time panic attack we find him alone in his room listening to jazz. It is midday, nothing in particular has happened, but suddenly 'a sharp uneasiness started up somewhere inside him. His breathing quickened and deepened as at the onset of sexual excitement, but this was not his condition.' He loses control of his breathing, his heartbeat accelerates and his immediate, very ordinary circumstances are transformed into a vision of imminent death. Amis's own experiences of these daytime seizures were less frequent than his reactions to darkness but, because of their unprompted, unpredictable nature, more worrying. He had several during his first few months with Hilly and, on her advice, consulted a psychiatrist at the Littlemore Mental Hospital near Oxford. Dr Armstrong assured him that he was not, as he feared, going mad; mad people were not self-consciously aware of their unusual states of mind, and he was.

Jenny does not become Patrick's helper, as Hilly had with Amis, but there are parallels between the two stories in that she is the only person in the novel who gets to know him well enough to see behind his brash, confident persona. At one point she reflects on how he 'was just weak and had mad impulses and was unsure of himself in spite of seeming so sure'. She suspects, shrewdly, that his public performances are to some extent a compensation for private anxieties and fears.

There are other references to their pre-marital years which only Hilly would have been able to recognize. In 1946 Amis wrote to Larkin of the fortnight he had spent in northern France with Hilly and his Oxford friend Christopher Tosswill. He reported that he and Hilly had sometimes argued and that in less tangible ways she seemed unhappy with their relationship.

The one element of the trip that did draw them together was provided, unwittingly, by Tosswill. When speaking of even the most mundane matters Tosswill was given to the kind of prolix formality usually associated with nineteenth-century prose. Hilly and Amis agreed that the mildly endearing aspect of his habit was worn down by two weeks of having to listen to him. On the return Channel crossing Tosswill had felt sick and announced that 'I always have to lie down when the water is disturbed', causing Hilly to tell Amis that he talked 'too much like a BADLY WRITTEN BOOK'; why couldn't he just say 'if it's rough' (16 December 1946). Reporting this to Larkin, Amis was obviously pleased at finding something about which he and Hilly could exchange jokes. He recreates this memory in *Take a Girl Like You* and transfers Tosswill's verbal style to Graham McClintoch, Patrick's friend and flatmate. Patrick likes McClintoch but makes fun of him behind his back, and Jenny, despite being more tolerant than Patrick of people's idiosyncrasies, is amused. In Chapter 6 she is watching Patrick bat in his school's pupil–teacher cricket match, and sitting next to her is McClintoch who is obsessively engaged in a disquisition on opera.

'Quite an interesting piece,' Graham said. 'Slight, but cleverly orchestrated.'

Jenny nodded again. That remark, and the watchful look that went with it, had in it what she now saw as the thing that ruined his chances far more than any amount of face could: a heaviness that would make *Alice in Wonderland* sound like something by Sir Walter Scott or one of those, a way of talking about everything so as to make it as important as everything else and fit in with everything else. Did it come with the face or because of it or just by chance?

Even Tosswill, if he had read the novel, would not necessarily have connected this passage with a fortnight in 1946, but Amis makes sure that one other person would. Jenny's boredom is relieved when Patrick is bowled, joins them and asks her if she would like to go on holiday with him later that summer, to France. During the first months of their relationship Amis kept Larkin informed by letter of his attempts to persuade Hilly to have sex with him. On 13 May 1946 he wrote that 'We have been arguing for the past week about sleeping in the same bed as each other . . . am trying to make her say yes, and there for the moment the matter rests', but at the end of the month he was able to report that 'Hilary had yielded' (22 May 1946). By the time they went to France in September the sexual aspect of their relationship was well established, but in the novel the projected trip becomes a feature of Patrick's strategy of seduction, with Jenny specifying terms and conditions: 'Separate rooms, Patrick.' Amis had not forgotten the order of events, and he changed it for a number of reasons.

The novel draws upon 1946–7, but it interposes these years with the effects of the subsequent thirteen. Among Hilly's many doubts about their pre-marital relationship infidelity did not feature too prominently. She knew that he was attractive to women, but she had no reason to suspect him of serial philandering. She would not have to wait very long. Following the discovery of her pregnancy, the rushed marriage and the birth of Philip a routine was established in which Amis spent much of the day in the Bodleian working on his B.Litt. thesis while Hilly was left with the baby in their rented cottage in Eynsham, north of Oxford. It was here that she discovered a notebook in which he gave accounts of what he also did when absent from the family home, including affairs with at least two undergraduates. The notebooks no longer exist, but their contents are indicated in a letter that Amis sent to his private confessor, Larkin, shortly before Hilly found them (12 July 1949). In this he reports that Hilly, then pregnant with their second child, 'hasn't gone into the life-box yet', but this would be soon, and that their first, Philip, is 'almost walking, certainly crawling and stand-ing for brief periods without aid'. With this idyll of newly married contentment dutifully evoked, Amis also reports that the previous weekend he had gone to the Eynsham village carnival, with 'Nick [Russel] and his girl and my wife and my girl (ssh!)!'. That particu-lar girl was one of the undergraduates, and along with this he keeps Larkin up to date on another of his extra-marital strategies, his regular exchanges with a schoolgirl on the morning bus to Oxford. 'When I asked her if, if I asked her, she would come out with me, I was favourably answered. But I haven't asked her yet. She is just fif-teen, very pretty and amusing . . .'

Finding out that her husband and the father of her one-year-old son was sleeping with another woman was bad enough, but the manner of the discovery, the fact that Amis had written about it, twisted the knife. The notebooks were private, but it became evi-dent to Hilly through the 1950s that Amis's letters to Larkin and Conquest involved aspects of his other life. For example, in Decem-ber 1960 – ironically, shortly after *Take a Girl Like You* was pub-lished – Amis wrote to Conquest and asked him to reply to the Swansea English Department and not their home in Glanmor Road; 'a fault in my security system has led Hilly to connect a Conquest letter with an impending Amis screw' (Jacobs, p. 173). For Hilly in 1960 there was a fine distinction between the hurt caused by her knowledge of Amis's further acts of infidelity and the less tractable sense of a verbal infidelity. Acts of adultery involved physical betrayal, but alongside this Amis was, to his friends, disclosing attendant features of his character and temperament that he kept from his wife.

Amis kept carbons of most of his letters to Larkin, and one is caused to wonder if these played some part in the structuring of *Take a Girl Like You*. In the chapters dominated by Patrick, includ-ing those involving his exchanges with Jenny, we are often aware of an edgy distinction between what he says and what he thinks. He does not tell too many blatant lies, but the third-person disclosures of his mindset offer a sometimes painfully candid counterpart to the cautiously edited public performance. And when we read some of Amis's letters to Larkin there is a similar sense of seeing beneath the surface. For example, Chapters 17 to 20 are Patrick's and involve his trip with Ormerod to London, where he has sex with Joan, a woman to whom his friend has introduced him in a Soho nightclub. Apart from being told of what actually occurs, we become aware of Patrick's reflections upon it all.

> You could not have beauty that had a look of sourness and stupidity; we didn't call that beauty. Beauty without *real* sweetness or *real* mind was as beautiful as beauty with. It was only when dealing with the two sorts that you saw the difference. Did you? Did he? In two or three years would there be much to choose between his relations with Joan if he were Mr Joan and with Jenny if he were Mr Jenny?
> (Chapter 19)

Jenny never learns of what happens in London. In fact, at the end of Chapter 16 – just as Patrick sets off – we find her musing on whether she should commit herself to their uncertain relationship, and on his return at the beginning of Chapter 21 he declares his love for her and she replies in kind. Certainly Jenny's thoughts about the future would have been altered if she had known of Joan, but she would not necessarily have been shocked – she is shrewd and perceptive enough. What would have stunned her was a knowledge of the unsettled, cynical, almost nihilistic attitude which underpinned Patrick's lechery. Compare the above passage with the following extracts from letters that Amis wrote to Larkin in 1953:

> Marriage in the abstract, as you've heard me say many a time, either doesn't exist or is sheer unmoving, dumbfounding, non-plussing buggery; but since its firmly grounded in the whole

business of getting along with, or on top of, women, it seems as mistaken to rule it out in the abstract . . . as to want to do it in the abstract . . . (21 January 1953)

I have sex all weighed up now; the only reason I like girls is that I want to fuck them, which is adolescent, cheap, irresponsible, not worth doing, a waste of time, not much fun anyway really, a needless distraction from my real vocation . . . something I shouldn't be at my age and as a married man . . . (26 November 1953)

Patrick's chapters in *Take a Girl Like You* are littered with third-person passages very similar in tone and attitude to these. We as readers know him better than anyone in the novel, and it is as though Amis is transferring the secret world of disclosure that he shared almost exclusively with Larkin to the fabric of the book. The effects of this upon the reader are unsettling, because while we are functioning as Patrick's confidant we are also witnessing Jenny's attempts to cut through Patrick's dissembling sincerity to what he is really like. When, before *Lucky Jim*, Amis referred to Larkin as his 'inner audience', he was as much commending his friend's critical acumen as acknowledging his other role as the addressee who knew more than others did. With *Take a Girl Like You* the manner in which Amis had orchestrated his life over the past fifteen years with a network of selective positionings of partners, friends and acquaintances as recipients of different versions of himself becomes the activating centre of the writing.

In a 1974 interview with Melvyn Bragg Amis described Jenny as 'a useful camera, let's say, through whom suburban life as it was at the end of the 1950s could be seen . . . [by] making her come from a distant environment, she could convey a kind of perspective that somebody inside that world couldn't do'. This was a half-truth. He speaks of the novel as an exercise in documentary realism, the corrupt south seen through the eyes of a decent, northern working-class girl, but the terms 'distant environment' and 'that world' could also refer to the relationship between Amis's lives outside and inside his novels. When Amis transported Hilly, via Jenny, into this novel he was also setting up a peculiar interplay between the dynamics of the text and those of the worlds upon which it was based. Patrick is a more candid version of Amis than his predecessors had been, and as a consequence he inherits a less comfortable version of their fictional worlds. The 1950s' novels had enabled Amis to recycle and improve his own life of deception and infidelity, but the invention of Jenny as the other half of Patrick's environment interferes with his arrangement. Her very presence seems to prompt Amis to uncover, via Patrick, his states of vulnerability, uncertainty and, most significantly, deception.

There is an intriguing moment, early in the novel, when we are offered Jenny's thoughts about a poster in the room of her arty and self-consciously French acquaintance, Anna.

> On it was a picture of a man on a blinkered horse pushing a lance into a bull's neck. There was lettering that said GRAN CORRIDA DE TOROS Y MAGNIFICAS NOVELLADAS, and a lady down in one corner with a man and a fan and a mantilla. She looked a very jolly lady, but foreign. Well, there was nothing wrong with that (though the bull part was horrid); foreigners were colourful and good luck to them. (Chapter 7)

In 1960 the poster itself would have been recognized by many readers as a frequently exhibited token of cultural sophistication – it would probably have featured in the rooms of Amis's students – and it is as though Amis is inviting us to compare Jenny's reaction with what Patrick or any of his predecessors would have made of it. It would, no doubt, have served Amis well as a prompter for an exercise in cynical mockery. But Jenny is different, perhaps more naïve and less sophisticated but at the same time more tolerant of other people's affectations; and, again, there are echoes of the young Hilly and her relationship with the brash, self-confident Amis. The moment testifies to Amis's objective in his creation of Jenny. It is as though he has allowed her, and indeed Hilly, to trespass upon the private territory of his fictional world, as if he is inferring some strange correlation between the fictions he created for his readers and the ones he created for his wife, the outside and the inside of his novels. As this novel develops, Jenny becomes, like Hilly, the witness and in the end the victim.

As well as being a slightly bizarre act of confession, the novel also enables Amis to rewrite his past as a sequence of events of which he is the principal agency but for which he is not entirely responsible. He recreates their relationship as something that involves a kind of fatalistic inevitability. The external forces favour his lifestyle and are marshalled against Hilly.

Before she really gets to know Patrick, Jenny encounters a version of him aged about ten. Michael, one of her primary-school pupils, strikes her as precociously handsome and witty, a charmer but dangerous. 'He would be a terrible one for the women when he grew up, Jenny thought, being not only lively and able to show he was wicked, but also simply incapable of noticing opposition. There seemed to be nothing to be done about it.' This is Chapter 2, but her phrases prefigure her forthcoming experiences with Michael's adult counterpart. In the middle of the novel, when Patrick is feeling particularly frustrated by her moral stance, he tells her that her ideal man 'died in 1914 or thereabouts. He isn't ever going to turn up, Jenny, that bloke with the honour and the bunches of flowers *and* the attraction.' She tells him to shut up and that he reminds her of 'someone I used to know, except that he never had the use of the gab like you've got'. The term 'used to' might, for Patrick, seem to refer to a previous relationship, but the reader knows that she is thinking about Michael. She could deal with

Patrick aged ten, but his grown-up manifestation, now with the gift of the gab, is a more difficult prospect. Her use of the past tense indicates her impossible wish to be as 'charmed by his looks and smile' as she is by Michael's yet not having to encounter the terrible adult he would become. But she does, and when Patrick finally succeeds in having sex with her, when they are both drunk at Ormerod's party, it is rape.

This of course did not happen with Amis and Hilly, yet Amis makes sure that the rape is part of the novel's hall of mirrors in which the events of their lives are reflected back to them in a disturbed but recognizable form. Soon after her enforced deflowering Jenny's feeling of distress is supplemented as she overhears an exchange between Patrick and Ormerod from the next room.

> 'Had to get it done somehow.'
> 'And it didn't much matter how, eh?'
> 'Life was becoming absolutely impossible as it was.'

Amis describes the entire party in a way that is slightly disjointed, discontinuous, evoking the effects of a noisy crowd, drunkenness and collective disorder. Throughout the novel he has shown that mass immorality, irresponsibility and selfish misbehaviour is only just kept in check by the worn-out conventions of society. Now they seem to have become licensed Patrick does his worst, and for Jenny his answers to Ormerod would carry a significance beyond their apparent admission that force is inevitable when persuasion fails. He, like Lovelace, embodies the worst aspects of the world which Jenny and Clarissa had set themselves against. So, when he declares that 'he had to get it done' because 'life was being impossible', he takes on a role as the agent of the inevitable, the immoral arbiter.

The passage also carries private echoes. Jenny, like Hilly, has become suddenly and fully aware of the distressing actuality of her man. Worse still, the overheard conversation discloses to her another level of deception, and its effect on her would not be unlike Hilly's experience on discovering Amis's notebook in 1948; not only was he an adulterer but he felt comfortable enough with this state to commit it to language. Also, the conversation carries disturbing echoes of the letters that Amis wrote to Larkin during his attempts to seduce Hilly, particularly the triumphant sense of relief when he informed his pal that 'Hilary had yielded!'

After the rape the parallels between fiction and life become even more concentrated. Next morning Patrick drives Jenny home, and she tells him that because of what he has done they are finished. Hilly in 1946, although for very different reasons, had thought seriously about ending things with Amis. He persuaded her to continue and within a year her doubts were sidelined by events beyond their control – her pregnancy. Something similar happens in the novel.

When she arrives at the Thompsons, she finds waiting for her Miss Sinclair, her headmistress, and Mr Whitaker, the father of one of her pupils, John. John had been playing in an old cottage with a friend, had fallen and broken his ankle. His friend had left him, promising to return with help but had not. They had intended to take Jenny to the hospital to visit John, which she gladly offers to do, but the mood changes. Miss Sinclair 'look[ed] her up and down from thatchy hair to muddy shoes, with wine splashed dress playing an important part in between'. She is evidently hungover and besmeared with the debris of indulgence. There is a silent exchange of signals, and Miss Sinclair states, 'There's no need to put yourself out, Miss Bunn. I'm sure you have lots of things to do.' She gives Jenny the up-and-down treatment in shortened form, then finishes: 'Goodbye.' The immense significance of her closing word is evident to Jenny and the reader. She is now deemed to be part of the world she had tried so honourably to resist. And who was the friend who had left John in the cottage, caused him distress, worsened his injury and, unwittingly, engineered the chain of events that had led to this moment? Michael, of course.

Amis does not comment on the roles of Michael and Patrick as co-agents in Jenny's inevitable defeat, but it is clear that she is aware that the forces marshalled against her are beyond her control. Soon after Miss Sinclair has left, there is a knock on the door, and it is Patrick. He had been sitting in his car round the corner, waiting. Suddenly and without explanation, she knows she must return to him.

'She knew more or less what the future would be like, and how different it would be from what she had hoped', recalling perhaps that Hilly's first discovery of Amis's infidelities would be repeated many times over the next thirteen years. But Jenny resigns herself to the inevitable: 'but she felt now that there had been something selfish in that hope, that a lot of time she had been pursuing not what was right but what she wanted. And she could hardly pretend that what she had got was not worth having at all. She must learn to take the rough with the smooth, just like everybody else.' In other words, Jenny surrenders. She realizes that her battle had not just been against Patrick but against the collective amoral consensus that he embodies.

It will remain a matter of opinion as to whether Amis's prodigious sexual career of the 1940s and 1950s was in some way endorsed by a general trend. For him, when writing the novel, this perception of things provided at least a means of rewriting his life in a way that assuaged feelings of guilt. On the one hand, he is able to present Jenny, and Hilly, as innocent victims, while at the same time, via Patrick, present himself as an agent of fate or at least its post-war sociological manifestation. All of the secondary characters of the novel, the ones that comprise the social fabric in which Patrick and Jenny play out their roles, seem suddenly to be lined up behind Patrick in these closing pages, nodding in agreement and contributing to Jenny's acceptance that she was swimming hopelessly against the tide: Elsie Carter with her stoical yet bitter diagnoses of men; the drunken seaman with his apocalyptic vision of moral decay; Ormerod and his autocratic indifference to ideals; the Thompsons with their co-performed mockery of marital bliss. She, like Richardson's Clarissa, is outnumbered.

In the final paragraph Jenny speaks to Patrick.

> 'You know, Patrick Standish, I should really never have met you. Or I should have got rid of you while I still had the chance. But I couldn't think how to. And it's a bit late for that now, isn't it?'

Yes it is, or it was for Hilly in 1960, with three young children, married to a man she loves but whose activities she abhors and knows she cannot change.

Amis's reviewers hardly ever reached a consensus, but with *Take a Girl Like You* it sometimes appeared as though they had been reading different books. For *The Times* it was 'to put it mildly, a sad disappointment'. The anonymous reviewer was reminded by Patrick of Jim Dixon, but this novel lacked the verve and energy of its famous predecessor, seemed unsure of what it wanted to say about morality and was, in the end, 'dull'. The *Times Literary Supplement* chipped in with the view that Amis did know what he was doing. It might have been about class and the north–south divide, but 'this plan is soon abandoned'. It sometimes drifts towards comedy, but 'the satirical eye is less sharp than usual, the fun much less hilarious'. Worst of all, it seemed to promote in the final victory of Patrick a brand of shameless, crass immorality, with the result that 'this is a very nasty book . . . the worst novel ever written by a man who can write a novel as well as Mr Amis'.

Search through the two reviewers' attempts to pick out its worst features and you will find an albeit unintended reflection of Amis's often conflicting objectives: to write an honest novel about himself and Hilly and provide an objective survey of the gradations and transitional mood of British society. Neither reviewer knew anything of the autobiographical element and nor did Norman Shrapnel of the *Guardian*, yet Shrapnel offers a sympathetic reading of Patrick, as a less certain, more vulnerable figure than his predecessors. Amis's 'austere slant on contemporary aspects of truth has made him play down his comic urges and deny attractiveness to his leading character' (23 September). Two years later, in a longer article on Amis's career (*New Statesman*, 21 September 1962), John Gross, without citing evidence, begins to suspect that the peculiarities of the novel are symptomatic 'of a private nightmare slithering out of control' and that its conclusion is a hollow victory for Patrick, 'possibly the last anguished cry of someone falling down a bottomless well'. A year after that, again in the *New Statesman*, Christopher Ricks opens his piece by addressing the question of whether Amis is 'in collusion' with Patrick. In Ricks's view, the question should never have been raised. 'Where do we find our evidence that Standish is a bad man except in Mr Amis's novel?' Patrick, he implies, will for ever be an invention, and to treat him as a 'bad man' involves a judgemental leapfrog from reading fiction to ungrounded moralizing. Ricks seems to be aware that many of his own readers knew or thought they knew more about the book than what they had found on its pages. He was writing in November 1963, several months after the tabloids had reported the final breakdown of Amis's marriage and caused the literary in-crowd to wonder if his novel of two years earlier had combined a belated act of confession with a prediction of imminent catastrophe.

10

One Fat Englishman

ROGER Micheldene, the eponymous *One Fat Englishman* (1963), inherits all of Patrick Standish's lecherous proclivities, supplemented by a limitless desire for drink, food, money and the comfortable observation of other people's distress. He is ugly, balding, massively overweight and candidly unpleasant to all people with whom he is not attempting to effect sexual intercourse or professional advancement. He is a snob; Englishness at its worst. His card offers his full nomenclature as Roger H. St John W. Micheldene MA (Cantab). Amis's paperback illustrators faced grave problems with Micheldene, because it was difficult to offer a visual exaggeration of someone so loathsome and excessive as the man between the covers.

Amis's initial reason for the creation of so horrible an individual was that Micheldene and the novel were intended as a ceremony of expulsion that would be irreversible. His attempts in *Take a Girl Like You* to unshackle himself from his 1950s' legacy had been only partially successful. Like its predecessors, the book was partly autobiographical. Patrick was his most honest, least agreeable self-fictionalization so far, but he involved an act of confession that did not extend to self-loathing. His readers were not asked to approve of him, but nor were they quite caused to dislike him. Amis was aware that in order to initiate a new phase in his writing he would in some way have to break the habit of reinventing himself as the axis between the texture of the novel and its controlling presence, so he considered a ruthless hypothesis. Bring together all of the faults, indulgences and shameful excesses which his previous male characters, Patrick included, had managed to marginalize or humanely subdue; exaggerate, magnify and add to these. Turn him into the sort of individual who, if encountered in real life, would thereafter be avoided. Micheldene would effectively dispose of himself; and one reviewer shrewdly referred to him as 'Lucky Jim turned curiously sour'.

Micheldene was planned as a transitional figure. He would draw a line under the self-generating habits and mutations of the 1950s' books, but by the time the novel went to press events that Amis had caused but which had acquired a momentum far beyond his control had become uneasily transposed with their fictional counterparts.

By the end of the 1950s Swansea had become the fulcrum of Amis's personal, professional and creative life. It had provided him with his first full-time job, his and Hilly's first permanent home; their children had grown up there, *Lucky Jim* had been born there and without it Lewis and Bowen would not have existed. It enfolded and bespoke the tensions of his marriage, which had on several occasions almost ended there but had survived, precariously. Leaving it would not, he knew, miraculously transform his personality, habits and inclinations, but at the same time he suspected that a complete change of place and environment, a detachment from ever-present memories, would be at least a gesture towards optimism, alteration. He began to think seriously about leaving Wales during his academic year in the United States in 1958–9. Princeton had offered him a two-year extension of his contract, and he was tempted.

One Fat Englishman would be based on many of his experiences in the United States, but perversely. A more economical and honest account of the visit is provided in a letter to Larkin written shortly after his return to Swansea (30 July 1959). He had met and listened to a number of jazz players who had featured in his letters to Larkin over the previous fifteen years; the imagined presences behind the records had become real. Buster Bailey (clt) 'played far hotter and better than I've ever heard him on records, [and] yelled out during a [Speedy] Jones drum solo: "Ain't he the most, Kingsley?"' Along with the jazz Amis was impressed by the energy of the place; 'for the first half of my time there I was boozing and working harder than I have ever done since the Army . . . for the second half I was boozing and fucking harder than at any time at all. On the second count I found myself at it practically full time.' (A year earlier, just before setting out for America, he had informed Larkin (30 July 1958) of how, apart from Hilly not wanting him to 'make with the old prok swrod [pork sword] very much', he had felt for the first time in his life generally unenthused by the prospect of sex in general: obviously the United States had changed things.) But in the 1959 letter to Larkin he is ambivalently resigned to not going back, despite the attractions. 'They have more energy than we have, and they are better at enjoying themselves.' '[We] both want to go there again . . . though not, I feel definitely at the moment, to stay.' In fact Hilly had provided the common-sense argument that financially he still needed tenure and that three years abroad would disrupt their children's lives and education. He knew that his best option was another academic job in England. Along with its potentially beneficial effects upon his family life, a move would, Amis hoped, help him in his attempt to evolve a different method of writing novels. The dynamic, dialogic interplay between the narrative and the characters of his books, always with a comedic, satirical edge, had become his trademark. The technique had begun with *Lucky Jim*, and the new experience of Wales had serviced it. Amis, lower middle class and most certainly English, found himself shifting between different roles – and environments – university and town, middle and working classes, Welsh and English, breadwinner and intellectual. It was all very different from the largely predictable uniformities of his past in London, the army and Oxford. Its multi-dimensional nature energized his prose, but that had begun more than a decade earlier and something new was required.

The journalist George Gale had become one of Amis's London friends in the early 1950s. Gale had contacts in Peterhouse, Cambridge, and when in early 1961 a new post of fellow and tutor in English was created by the college he orchestrated contacts between Amis and Peterhouse's Master, Herbert Butterfield. Butterfield was fully aware of Peterhouse's reputation as the most conservative, anachronistic of the Cambridge colleges – Tom Sharpe's *Porterhouse Blue* was comprised partly of stories, many accurate, of the bizarre, ritualistic archaisms of the place. Amis was interviewed for the fellowship in March 1961. Some fellows had never previously heard of him, and others were unsettled by the prospect of bringing in someone who was as much a celebrity as a scholar. But Butterfield wanted to modernize the college, and his preference for Amis held sway. He was elected and would take up the appointment of official fellow and tutor in English in October 1961, Peterhouse's first. Amis resigned from Swansea and Peterhouse provided the family with a spacious, mid-Victorian house in Madingley Road, Cambridge. Soon he and Hilly would turn this into a version of Glanmor Road, Swansea, with regular, now more convenient visits from friends in London.

For Amis the attractions of Cambridge were various and speculative. He later disclosed in his *Memoirs* that he hoped for 'a kind of displaced return to Oxford, an echo of the romantic view of it which intervening time had enhanced' (p. 217). Within his first year at Peterhouse he had begun to regret the move. Along with teaching, Oxbridge fellows effectively owned and ran their colleges, and Amis found that even less time was available for writing than in Swansea. In 1961 the vast majority of Cambridge undergraduates, particularly at Peterhouse, were upper middle class and public-school educated, and the college was all male. Undergraduates late with essays or absent from tutorials would offer excuses that were variously insouciant, pretentious or arrogant, and Amis would recall those of their Swansea counterparts with nostalgic affection. 'Sorry Mr Amis, but I left my essay on *King Lear* on the bus, see, coming down from Fforestfach' (*Memoirs*, p. 224). Frequent attendance at high table was expected, followed by port in the Common Room. Amis loathed having to talk about academic and intellectual matters outside working hours, but his new colleagues seemed unwilling or incapable of doing anything else. After an evening during which a fellow whose universe seemed to be comprised exclusively of nineteenth-century French painting had refused to leave him alone, he found himself wishing 'for perhaps the hundredth time since arriving in Cambridge, that I were back in the Bryn-y-Mor with David, Jo and Willie Smyth' (p. 219). In a *Daily Mail* interview in 1962 he spoke of how 'arrogance' and pseudo-aristocratic 'bad manners' seemed almost compulsory in the university, and in a *Times* piece of the same year he wrote of his loathing for the 'excessive formality' of college life, of how there was 'far too much dressing up and respectability' and gratuitous 'protocol'.

Significantly, the sentence from his *Memoirs* where he wished he had been back in Bryn-y-Mor with his boozing pals was borrowed from a 1963 essay called 'No More Parades' and altered. In the original he had written that he had 'wished that I were Jim Dixon'. Amis had found himself in an environment that was the complete antithesis of his recollections of the free-wheeling, mildly rebellious Oxford years and a terrible alternative to the easy informalities of Swansea. Dixon, reborn, would have had a field day with the anachronistic, unendearingly eccentric and class-conscious denizens of Cambridge, but, ironically, the move there had been part of Amis's disposal of his past, which included the excising of the Dixonesque method from his writing. Fate seemed to be taking a darkly comic revenge on Amis; causing him to exist in a place and with people who seemed even worse than his fictional parodies and against which he had forbidden himself from retaliation.

Out of these tensions and frustrations emerged Roger Micheldene. Micheldene's snobbish mannerisms and persona, his obsessive, class-based Englishness, were a distillation of Amis's Cambridge experiences. He had started planning the novel early in 1961, but it was completed during his two years at Peterhouse. Characters like Micheldene had featured before in Amis's novels, beginning with Bertrand Welch, but never as the central figure. Cambridge itself did not play any part in the book because one element of his technique that would be maintained was the narrative energy generated by the tension between character and circumstances; a person like Micheldene and a place like Cambridge would get on too well. Moreover, for the first time Amis had decided to invent a main character who was entirely unpleasant and who would cause his readers to feel more sympathy with the people he met and knew than with him. To achieve this effect, he decided to set the novel in the United States and make use of the notebooks he had kept during his academic year in Princeton in 1958–9. Amis had enjoyed the year immensely, yet it caused his general attitude towards American life and culture to become even more ambivalent and paradoxical than it had been before the trip.

In 1957 Amis had applied for the post of Visiting Fellow in Creative Writing at Princeton University, was accepted and arranged with Swansea to give up his lectureship for the forthcoming academic year.

His reasons for wanting to spend another year abroad, given the disasters of Portugal, were complex and numerous. He certainly had no taste for American literature. It had not been taught at Oxford, and when he had written to Larkin in 1952 and listed the 'vital books' on his shelves every author was British, even to the exclusion of such Euro-Americans as Henry James, Ezra Pound and

T.S. Eliot. For Amis, the American tradition was characterized by the three worst features of any kind of writing: it was obsessively concerned by its own national identity, it was too frequently experimental and self-indulgent and, worst of all, it was hardly ever funny. '"American literature" no doubt helps to boost morale on the home front. When it goes for export, when the fashionable view here is that people write better over there, rude noises are in order. Our own lot are bad enough; *they* are a bloody sight worse' (*The Amis Collection*, pp. 17–19).

Amis was, however, attracted to the less highbrow features of American culture. In his *Memoirs* he stated that 'Americans, those of the greater part of this century anyway, are not much good at art, light art, fine art, but they are unequalled at art merged or hybridized with entertainment, as science fiction, jazz (until it became high art or nothing at all, according to taste) and films, especially the Western and the animated cartoon' (p. 199). Significantly his year in the United States produced his first book-length piece of literary criticism, *New Maps of Hell*, a study of science fiction based on a series of lectures Amis had given at Princeton. Also, for several months of his stay, he worked as film critic for the New York magazine *Esquire*.

His ostensible reason for the year away, to teach a course in creative writing, offers another perspective on Amis. At the time such courses did not exist in British universities. They were eventually introduced by the newer institutions in the 1960s and 1970s and were widely perceived as part of the radical culture of higher education of that period, a culture that Amis would attack in the so-called Black Papers. But Amis's application to Princeton reflected a genuine enthusiasm for the nature of the job. In a 1956 review of a collection of essays on contemporary literature, he took a number of the authors to task for their 'suspicious even hostile' perception of universities as environments in which imaginative writing was stifled by academicism; universities were, in Amis's experience,

197

places in which 'a good number of both staff and students' not only studied but also produced literature ('Art and Craft', *Spectator*, 13 July 1956). In a letter to Larkin (30 July 1958) he confessed that, while he approved of the idea, he was 'afraid of not being able to teach Creadive Wriding properly, or indeed at all'.

In the end, his course went well and, albeit briefly, caused him to revise his general opinion that Americans could not write. He recalled in his *Memoirs* that his four students had offered him perceptive, entertaining accounts of the United States, including stories on the subculture of hunting, working-class life on the freight river boats of the South, father–son relationships and in one case a fictionalized account of the aircrew who dropped the Bomb. Two of the students eventually made it into print, but none became famous. Amis admired their elevation of subject matter above the self-conscious preoccupation with style that often marked the work of new writers, 'such as to make any comparable Oxford example, say, look bloodless beside [their work]' (*Memoirs*, p. 196). Perhaps the Princeton course reminded him of a particular 'Oxford example' who had, a decade earlier, published a volume of poems which involved a constant battle between his stylistic borrowings and what he had to say.

Micheldene is a publisher's agent who is visiting the United States on the look-out for new writers. Much of the novel occurs in a place called Budweisser College, a somewhat downmarket version of Amis's Ivy League location, and many of its incidents are based upon things that happened to Amis. Apart from being much more unpleasant than any of Amis's previous creations, Micheldene is the first without a sense of humour. A thread of comedy runs through the novel, but it is not the type that would provoke laughter and much of it is directed against Micheldene himself. Again, this seems to have been part of Amis's attempt to exorcize the ghost of Jim.

For example, Chapter 11 begins with a silent recitation of Latin poetry, including brief comments on how difficult it is to recognize line-endings in time-based classical metres. It becomes apparent that this rehearsal of Micheldene's high-cultural reference points – extending to a survey of Evelyn Waugh's celebration of Pre-Raphaelite aesthetics – has a single functional purpose: it is his only reliable method of preventing premature ejaculation. The playful device of reader-orientation had become Amis's authorial signature, beginning with Jim Dixon apparently delivering his Merrie England lecture before doing an ape impression in what turns out to be his empty bedroom. With Micheldene, however, the method is not designed to disclose his taste for self-parody; more to extend his range of shallow, mechanical responses to events which we might expect to be attended by emotion.

Appropriately, it opens a chapter in which his state of pragmatic, guiltless hypocrisy is fully explored. He is in bed with Helene Bang, the wife of a Budweisser College academic. Helene is fascinated by Micheldene's apparently limitless nastiness, and after they have had sex she tries to see if there is anything beneath the surface. She asks him is he feels the need to have sex with every attractive woman he meets. 'That's who you really want, isn't it? Everybody?' He wishes to maintain Helene's interest in him, and his answer is an ingenious lie. He calculatedly becomes uncertain, even vulnerable, and responds to her question with a self-directed enquiry. Sex: 'A way of getting to know someone better than you can in any other way? That sort of thing?' But the narrator discloses to the reader what is actually going through his mind. Sex: 'To convert a creature who is cool, dry, calm, articulate, independent, purposeful into a creature which is the opposite of these; to demonstrate to an animal that is pretending not to be an animal that it is an animal.' Apart from the satisfaction of lust, his desire for sex seems to involve the proof-positive confirmation that all human beings share his brutal, nihilistic state of mind, despite their frequent claims to be better than that.

In the mid-1950s Amis had written a poem called 'Nocturne', and it is almost certain that this was before him as he described Micheldene's repulsive mindset. In the poem Amis from an upstairs window has been watching two people writhe and fondle each other in a shop doorway. He does not know them, and the scene appears to exemplify the notion of pure sexuality as anonymous and bestial. He asks himself the question, 'Is that *animal*?' and concludes that, no, it is something more than that, something that reflects a very human desire 'towards being understood'. The poem and the exchange between Micheldene and Helene address the same agenda but reach different conclusions. It was not that Amis himself had become more cynical than he was when he wrote the poem, rather, that the latter was a means of exploring his uncertainties while Micheldene was an extrapolation of their worst dimensions.

When Amis began writing *One Fat Englishman* Micheldene had been his goodbye note to the 1950s, an extension and an irredeemably nasty version of his previous decade of characters, a purging of his creative system. He would become a person whom even his creator would dislike, and Micheldene's anti-Americanism is a key element of this objective. The people who irritated Amis most during his trip to the United States were English, individuals who automatically treated all aspects of American life as culturally and intellectually inferior to those of the Old Country. Amis himself had some prejudices, particularly regarding the American taste for artistic experiment, but these were not nationalistic; he just disliked modernism. In an article for the *Observer* in January 1960 he described his experiences of Americaphobia and singled out, without naming, a particularly disagreeable embodiment of this who on one occasion publicly ridiculed a classics undergraduate simply because of who he was and what he claimed to be doing: a 'TEXAN studying Virgil, simply GROTESQUE'. The Englishman was the Labour politician Anthony Crosland, whom Amis had known since

Oxford and who was in the United States at the same time. Features of Crosland are borrowed for Micheldene, particularly the contrast between his assumed intellectual superiority and his asinine prejudices; and also his imposing physical presence. Amis, when he wrote the book, was experiencing middle-aged spread, but he wasn't as big as Micheldene or Crosland.

Micheldene's anti-Americanism was antithetical to Amis's opinions and experience, but at the same time he seemed intent on interposing elements of himself with his loathsome creation; perhaps as a way of finally dispatching another of the habits which had become part of his 1950s' method – the use of private, interpersonal tokens of affinity between character and author. A number of references are made to Micheldene's snuff-taking, which is partly a compensation for his having given up smoking. Amis, too, in the late 1950s was trying to cut down on cigarettes and had begun using snuff. Micheldene likes jazz but much prefers its pre-war practitioners to more recent trends, and so, too, with Amis. There was an intriguing incident during Amis's year in the United States which he adopted for the entirety of the brief Chapter 13. Amis, partly because of his film critic job with *Esquire*, made frequent trips from Princeton to New York. On one of these, to attend an *Esquire* office party, he ended up at a jazz club listening to the saxophonist Sonny Rollins – not one of his favourites, but he enjoyed the experience. It was too late to get a train back to Princeton, so a journalist at *Esquire*, Gene Lichtenstein, offered him a room in his flat, a place used by Lichtenstein when not needed by its owner, W. H. Auden. Wandering around the place in the early hours Amis started looking through the bookshelves and found an edition of Crabbe. Inscribed on the flyleaf was 'To Wystan. We must love one another AND die. Cyril'. In 1958 Auden's homosexuality was well known in literary circles but could only be referred to euphemistically in print; homosexuality was still illegal both in the United States and the United Kingdom. Apparent proof that Auden had also had an affair with

Cyril Connolly would have been usable material for a gossip colum-
nist. Amis only ever mentioned his discovery to his friends.

In Chapter 13 Micheldene, too, visits New York – not for an
office party but as part of his pursuit of Helene Bang. But
Micheldene spends the evening in a jazz club listening to players he
can tolerate and borrows the flat of another Budweisser academic,
Strode Atkins. There he discovers a notebook comprising the private reflections and remembrances of the poet Swinburne, most of
which involve precise documentation of his taste for flagellation, a
list of his similarly inclined contemporaries and further details of
sexual degeneracy. Micheldene steals the notebook, partly because
he feels it should be 'removed from American hands', but mainly
because he can use it and make money from it.

When writing this chapter Amis was not exactly praising his own
discretion and honesty – attempting to go public with the Auden
material would, in any event, have earned him more contempt than
cash. His rewritten and very private remembrance of the moment in
Lichtenstein's flat was another element of his strategy of distancing
himself from Micheldene, his vile *confrère*. Micheldene knows much
about literature, is indeed professionally involved with it, but he has
no affection or respect for it. Amis admired Auden's verse, and his
own early poetry bears its imprint. When he wrote to the Powells of
his discovery he disclosed a mixture of excitement and guilt. He
knew that the original line from Auden had been 'We must love one
another or die', that Connolly's revision of it involved a moment of
intimacy and that he was intruding upon private worlds. Micheldene
is fully aware that the Swinburne material will make him money,
because whoever publishes it will be catering for prurience disguised
as scholarship, and he does not care.

Amis's substitution of Swinburne for Auden adds to the sense of
his rewriting of his own life as that of his vicious alter ego. Swinburne's verse had been one of the subjects of his Oxford B.Litt.
thesis; he valued and enjoyed it.

The final draft of *One Fat Englishman* is all that is available for public scrutiny. We can never be sure exactly of what alterations took place between its genesis and its completion, but we know of the events that occurred during the writing of it. First, there was the move from Wales, a hoped-for detachment from and improvement upon the worst aspects of his private life. Micheldene, as part of Amis, but a part which he made so much worse that dissociation was guaranteed, was closely connected with this broader process of removal.

But after Amis had been in Cambridge for a year and was about half-way through the novel, something else occurred that was far more apocalyptic than his change of place and job and which would have much more influence upon his writing. In late summer 1962 Amis met the writer Elizabeth Jane Howard at the Cheltenham Arts Festival, and soon afterwards they began an affair. This was not an unusual occurrence for Amis, but its consequences were. In the summer of 1963 Hilly took the children and left him for good. He finished the novel in the flat he had moved into with Elizabeth Jane Howard in London.

The concluding chapters of the book were written there, and rarely can a work of literature have been so, as it were, completed by events outside it.

Micheldene is, by a combination of inclination and circumstance, on his own. He is the first of Amis's principal characters to be and remain in this state. He has been married twice, and we are caused to suspect that his relationship with his second wife, who remains in England, is entirely over. Amis had always dreaded being left by Hilly, and *One Fat Englishman* began partly as a projection, a hypothetical exploration of his worst fears. Detached from Hilly and his family, Amis suspected that he might become more like his loathsome creation than he cared to imagine. He had tempted fate, and fate with apposite swiftness had responded. He did not, like Micheldene, end up on his own; he moved in with Elizabeth Jane

Howard and began a long-term relationship with her about a week after Hilly's departure. At the same time, a sense of shock and disorientation attended these events. When Hilly left him he had not been planning anything permanent with Elizabeth Jane Howard. Indeed, he had resigned from Cambridge and was intending to move with Hilly and family to Majorca and to live there entirely from his writing. But circumstances which he had created had altered his life in a manner that was far beyond his control, and something similar happens to Micheldene.

The penultimate and final chapters were influenced significantly by the break-up of Amis's marriage. In them we encounter a version of Micheldene rather different from the figure who has raged and bullied his way through the substance of the novel. He declares his love for Helene and asks her to come away with and eventually to marry him. She explains that while his notion of love might involve all of the intensity, even the sincerity, traditionally associated with the emotion it lacks a vital ingredient. He loves her, but he does not really like her, has never treated her with the respect that betokens genuine affection. The parallels between Helene's shrewd assessment of his character and the feelings which eventually caused Hilly to leave Amis are evident. Both men had lived and behaved in ways that satisfied their own inclinations, irrespective of the effects of this upon the women they claimed were special to them. Helene tells him that even his philandering would have been a little more tolerable were it not so blatantly unemotional. 'It's all for you, all that, isn't it? You think of it and you do it. Like a lot of men.' Shortly before their break-up Hilly and Amis had spent a week in what was then Yugoslavia. There is a photograph which could well have been in Amis's thoughts as he wrote Helene's lines. It shows him asleep, possibly drunk, on a beach, and on his back Hilly has written in lipstick, '1 FAT ENGLISHMAN. I FUCK ANYTHING.'

There is a moment in the last chapter which, if not entirely disproving Helene's assessment of Micheldene, at least shows him to possess an element of vulnerability. He has boarded the liner for England. Helene has seen him off on the quay and insisted that further encounters are unlikely and unwanted, and soon afterwards,

> He looked out of his porthole and saw the quay sliding slowly past. Then he wanted very much to cry and started to do so. This was unusual for him when sober and he tried to work out why he was doing it. It was obviously a lot to do with Helene, but he had said good-bye to her and to plenty of other girls in the past without even considering crying. What was so special?

When he wrote this Amis had already begun another relationship, but one suspects that it involves some recollection of the experience of becoming detached from the woman with whom he had lived for fifteen years, albeit turbulent ones. The transposition of other memories with this one added to its poignancy. Four years earlier he and Hilly had left the United States together on a liner like the one on which Micheldene finds himself alone and distressed. Helene's closing words had been brief and unambiguous – 'Goodbye, Roger' – and he had watched as she 'reached the customs shed and disappeared from sight'.

Amis had always been aware of the curious relationship between the way in which he orchestrated the experiences of his characters and the way he ran his life, and to a large extent the former had often been an improvement upon the latter. With *One Fat Englishman* it must have seemed as though fiction had taken control of reality. Half finished, the novel of departure and change had born witness to an experience of this that its author had certainly not envisaged. His completion of it was also a penitential exercise.

Most of Amis's satirical targets had involved a blend of the cultural, intellectual and behavioural states that he found most irritating, and they frequently drew material from people he knew. In

One Fat Englishman he invented a figure called Irving Macher, an American version of Gareth Probert but much worse. Macher is a student at Budweisser and has written a novel called *Blinkie Heaven* which Micheldene suspects that his employers will want him to commission. It is concerned exclusively with the lives and experiences of blind people, which Macher presents as more sophisticated, better, than those of the sighted. For the blind, sexuality transcends the harsh discrimination of appearance; language involves a purity which vision pollutes. It is implied that Macher is a second-generation beat movement writer, whose principal objective is to unsettle established conventions, to offend and provoke the ire of conservative opinion. Macher carries echoes of Amis's own experience of the beat movement, specifically an evening of readings and questions he had reluctantly agreed to share with Jack Kerouac in New York.

Journalists had suggested parallels between the American beat movement writers and the British 'Angry Young Men'. Amis had publicly dissociated himself from the latter, and his opinions on the former were made evident in an article called 'Who Needs No Introduction' written shortly after his return from the United States. In this he gives an account of the evening with Kerouac who apparently was drunk, semi-articulate and given to haranguing and insulting members of the audience. His performance, Amis implies, was an accurate reflection of his writing.

Macher as a younger, perhaps even worse, manifestation of Kerouac and his ilk could have provided Amis with a means of revenging himself upon ideas and characters he did not respect – as with Probert and Dylan Thomas – but instead, after his break-up with Hilly, he rewrote Macher as Micheldene's nemesis.

At the beginning of the book Micheldene is obliged to take part in a game of charades and is asked to become the embodiment of 'Englishness'. The joke is beautifully engineered, because Micheldene's day-to-day presence is in itself an exaggeration of

his nationality. He is being asked to be himself; no performance required. Macher had planned this. Later Macher steals
Micheldene's notes for the lecture he is due to give on nineteenth-
century literature. Something similar happened to Amis at Princeton. His lecture was lost, not stolen, but the rewriting of the event
provides Amis with a means both of disclosing Micheldene's self-
obsession and nastiness and further dismantling his ambitions.
When he learns in Chapter 9 that Macher is the thief, he is with
Helene, who has been attempting to uncover his perhaps more
agreeable and sensitive features; she is not yet quite convinced that
he is as bad as he appears to be. He interrupts their exchange and
immediately telephones the head of the college to seek punishment
for Macher. This convinces Helene that his malice and egotism will
always overrule everything else. His wish for revenge is clearly
more important, for the time being, than their potential moment of
intimacy, and in the penultimate chapter, when Helene gives him an
account of what she really thinks of him, she refers to the pivotal
moment 'when you insisted on trying to call Maynard Parrish that
afternoon when you could have been with me a little longer . . .'
Appropriately, when Micheldene finally catches up with Helene,
declares his love for her and is rejected he also discovers that
Macher has replaced him as her lover.

At one point earlier in the novel Micheldene asks Macher if he
sees himself as his 'divinely appointed scourge'. Macher explains
that his role is more complex than that; he is rather like the author
of an existentialist drama in which Micheldene is obliged to take
part. For Amis, Macher is a self-appointed scourge. His writing, his
lifestyle, his combination of beat movement anarchy and Sartrean
pretensions, all of these would in the 1950s' novels have become
targets for satire and Macher himself rescheduled as either absurd
or ineffectual. Now, however, Macher virtually takes control of the
narrative and Micheldene's destiny, and again this is part of Amis's
strategy of self-reproach. In the 1950s' novels, despite their main

characters' failings, there was always an enduring theme of commitment to a particular woman – Amis and Hilly. It was not so much that Amis was lying about his feelings, more that his fictional presences lived up to them better than he did. It was thus appropriate that someone like Macher who previously would have featured as a victim alongside Amis's improvements upon himself should return in this novel as the agent of retribution.

In this respect the parallels with *Take a Girl Like You* become intriguing. There it was Patrick who became the irresistible controller of Jenny's destiny, much as Amis had with Hilly, and the pattern is re-enacted with Micheldene and Macher. Amis sews in a number of clues which allude to the relationship between the two novels. *Blinkie Heaven* is compared by Micheldene, unfavourably of course, with *Clarissa*. Richardson's other major eponymous woman character had been *Pamela* (1740–1). Unlike Clarissa, Pamela effectively reforms and subdues her partner's baser instincts, which Micheldene's wife has evidently failed to do with him. She does not appear in the novel, has effectively left him and is referred to only once by her Christian name, Pamela.

PART 3

ENGLAND AND JANE

11

The New Amis

Amis knew within a year that he would not be happy in Cambridge, but the mood which had prompted his departure from Swansea, a desire completely to alter his environment and working conditions and consequently his creative frame of reference, prevailed.

During the 1962 summer vacation Amis took the family on holiday to Majorca, a trip funded by a commission from the US magazine *Show* to do an interview with Robert Graves who had lived on the island since before the war. Amis admired Graves's poetry and fiction and had been in occasional contact with him by letter since 1954. Graves, although generally suspicious of prying journalists, welcomed this exchange with a fellow writer and put up the Amis family for ten days in August on his property in Deya, a fishing village then, like the rest of the island, unmolested by the tourist boom of a decade later. Amis and Graves got on well. Amis liked the area, and when he returned to Cambridge in late August he made a decision. He would resign from Peterhouse and follow Graves's example. He tendered his resignation to Herbert Butterfield in September. The terms of his Fellowship obliged him to give three months' notice, and he decided to stay for the rest of the forthcoming year. This would allow him and Hilly to arrange the rental of a property in Majorca and deal in advance with potential problems of residence there, particularly the education of the children, all now in their early teens. He planned to stay for at least a year, beginning in the summer of 1963. The budget would be tight, but he calculated that his accumulated royalties, his regular payments for articles and reviews and the island's low cost of living would enable them to exist comfortably enough.

Financially the plan might have been feasible, but in other respects it seemed slightly bizarre. As a novelist Amis had always thrived upon an interaction between the process of writing and the day-to-day environment upon which it drew, and a key feature of this was his talent for making his characters' use of language an index to their personalities and predispositions. The Portugal experience had shown him the potential drawbacks of removing himself from his active linguistic fabric. Why did he want to repeat the exercise on a long-term basis?

He was clutching at straws. He was half-way through *One Fat Englishman*, the self-evident conclusion of his 1950s' method, and he did not know where he would go next. Perhaps, despite his previous inclinations, he thought that relative isolation would oblige him to rethink his creative dependencies, might even enable him to transform his pleasures as a reader into work of his own. As a teenager he had discovered G.K. Chesterton and had continued to admire and enjoy Chesterton's ability to blend reflections of the contemporary world with fantastic projections. He had written a book about and edited volumes of science fiction, a genre whose unusual perspectives upon the human condition fed a similar taste. Graves himself had begun to produce his most popular fiction after his move to Majorca, novels which interweave the intrigues and idiosyncrasies of ancient Rome with the state of mind of the modern reader. Maybe Graves had found an appropriate inspirational mood in a world that had become familiar yet was still very different from that of his past. Graves had gone to Majorca aged thirty-five, and Amis was only five years older than that. Butterfield, on being informed of Amis's decision, was astonished. 'Romanticism, that's what they used to call it in my day.' It was indeed Romanticism on Amis's part, but it would soon be overtaken by a sequence of unplanned events that bore a closer relation to a sister genre, the gothic. In the end Amis would never move to Majorca.

In early October 1962, a month after tendering his resignation, Amis attended the Cheltenham Literature Festival. He had been invited to take part in a panel discussion on the subject of 'Sex in Literature'. The other panellists were Joseph Heller, who had recently published *Catch 22*, a surreal and candid picture of the lives of US airmen during the last war, not least their enthusiastic pursuit of sex; Carson McCullers, author of *The Heart Is a Lonely Hunter*, whom Amis had met in New York; and Romain Gary, writer and diplomat, who had presumably been brought in to offer a stereotypically exciting French perspective. Leavis's description of Amis as a 'pornographer' had already reached the broadsheet gossip columns and *Take a Girl Like You*, published eighteen months earlier, was his most explicit examination of sexuality.

In his presentation at the festival Amis argued that sex, being part of life, had to be part of fiction but that descriptions of physical minutiae betrayed the author's down-market inclinations and their readers' less-than-literary interests. Amis always believed that the immediately enjoyable aspects of sex were something that should be had rather than represented and, living up to his axiom, his concern with the debate was exceeded by his interest in the festival's director, Elizabeth Jane Howard. Hilly had gone with him to Cheltenham and his exchanges with Elizabeth, known to her friends as Jane, amounted only to flirtation, with the potential for more. The attraction was mutual. Jane Howard recalls that they had met before, briefly, on a couple of occasions. They had appeared together on two television arts programmes. She remembered one, he the other. Amis offered an amusing comment on this, and she sensed that something else was happening. Nothing specific was agreed at Cheltenham, but they exchanged telephone numbers and she suspected that he would phone 'quite soon'. He did. They arranged to meet in London and she remembers that they 'sat up and talked nearly all night'.

Elizabeth Jane Howard was a successful novelist. Her first book, *The Beautiful Visit*, published four years before *Lucky Jim* in 1950, was set during the First World War and its aftermath and had won her the prestigious John Llewelyn Rhys Memorial Prize. It combined well-crafted and evocative prose with a strong absorption in time and place. Her later novels of the 1950s, *The Long View* (1956) and *The Sea Change* (1959), brought her fictional settings closer to the present day. Amis at Cheltenham had not read any of her work, but he knew that she, like him, was regarded as a serious writer with popular appeal. Moreover, they shared the image of figures who had walked out of their own fictions; eight years after the novel Amis was still represented in the popular press as a version of Jim Dixon and Jane's chronicles of the Cazalet family were regarded as semi-autobiographical. Jane Howard's fictional world was a class above Amis's; it reflected her background and indeed her presence. Her family had, since the mid nineteenth century, owned a successful timber firm and were a classic, very English combination of unobtrusive wealth, sophistication and business acumen. She had received no formal education in school or university but had been taught philosophy, mathematics, Greek and Latin by her slightly eccentric governess, a Miss Cobhan. *The Beautiful Visit* evokes a world in which personal crisis is borne with quiet dignity, involves individuals who seem capable of transcending matters such as moneyed privilege, and Jane's own life had offered her plenty of material for the project.

Aged nineteen, she had married Peter Scott, son of the Antarctic explorer, and he had spent most of their first three years on destroyers protecting the Atlantic convoys against U-boats. In 1945 he returned as a hero, having twice won the DSC, and their marriage lasted less than two years after that. They were, they found, incompatible. During the mid-1940s Jane had, in any event, established her own sense of independence, working variously as a model, a publisher's copy editor, a minor civil servant and a BBC newsreader. When she met Amis she had recently ended her second marriage to James Douglas-Henry, an Australian journalist and broadcaster. She was also, by anyone's standards, a very attractive woman. She looked like a model, with long blonde hair and high cheekbones, but she combined this glamorous physical presence with an unshowy command of language and an equally restrained intellectual adroitness. She was a year younger than Amis.

During the next six months Amis's life progressed much as it had done for the previous fifteen years. He taught, got on with *One Fat Englishman*, did reviews and articles and existed, on the face of things, as a family man. As usual, he made regular trips to London, where he would meet Jane. A number of his male friends knew of this and, viewed from the outside, there seemed to be few differences between this particular extra-marital excursion and its predecessors. Obviously he planned to stay with Hilly. Why else would he continue, as he did, to make arrangements for their move to Majorca? Indeed, Jane recalls that Amis had stated, regarding Majorca, that he '*might* be able to get back to England, perhaps twice a year', indication enough that his affair with her, while serious, was likely to remain an affair.

However, Amis's still very new relationship with Jane was affecting him in ways that were unprecedented. The figure of the traveller in 'Song of Experience' had been a candid exploration of his tendency to report to his male friends, Larkin and Conquest particularly, on his sex life: the states of play with Hilly had been covered with the same laddish incaution as his adulterous triumphs. Now he only ever wrote of his experiences with and feelings for Jane in letters to her, and these – always in longhand, given that the home-based typewriter might involve disclosure – reveal a dimension of Amis that few would ever encounter. Some extracts: 'Never been so knocked over by love' (22 January 1963); 'I love you, everything about you, especially everything' (23 January 1963); 'You're on the edge of my thoughts all the time . . . I don't really see how you could give me more pleasure than you do already . . .' (10 February 1963); 'I do enjoy life more because of you . . . And I have nothing to bear except not being with you when I want to, which is all the time' (25 February 1963); 'I miss your mouth and your breath and your skin and your left eyelid and your right breast and right collarbone . . . And your voice. And eyes' (4 April 1963); 'I worship you' (26 May 1963). Hyperbole? Or the discovery by a 41/42-year-old cynic that love is not an abstraction? Also in these letters he tells Jane, confesses to her, of how he is fully aware of a peculiar, almost ironic, change in his personality. He states, on several occasions, that she has dispelled his previous certainty that monogamy is part-myth, part-imposition. Now, for the first time in his life, he has no interest in other women as potential sexual conquests. 'My lack of interest in other women is beginning to get me down rather. The *real* reason is, I think . . . that I know it wouldn't be nearly as good . . . I love you all the time' (29 April 1963). He writes to Jane of how simply thinking of her presence causes him to be more polite, less brittle, with people who would previously have made him angry and impatient.

Jane altered Amis the man, and her effect upon Amis the writer was equally significant. He distilled the emotional energy of the letters into two poems, 'Waking Beauty' and 'An Attempt at Time Travel'. In the latter he imagines both of them, she aged nine, he ten, on a horse-drawn buggy with her father and grandfather. She had, as she told him, done this with her family – who had residences outside London – in the 1930s: she had shown him a photograph. Amis had come from a family that was a little further down the social order, but he imagines himself there. Why, one might ask? Because she is the woman he has been waiting for; he has always been there.

'Waking Beauty' is a compressed version of Keats's 'Eve of St Agnes'. He, Amis the speaker, gets to her by cutting through thick briers 'neatly tagged by Freud the gardener', implying that Freudian notions of love and sexuality are just obfuscations, unnecessary barriers. They leave, with her 'eyes cleared and steadied' : 'Side by side we advanced'; the 'briers' that had previously kept him from her have now 'all withered'. (And one hopes that when writing this he had not consulted his undergraduate edition of Keats's poems, where twenty years earlier Larkin had inserted a marginal note at the corresponding moment in 'The Eve of St Agnes': 'You mean he fucked her.')

In August 1963 Amis finally tested Hilly's endurance of their semi-open marriage beyond its acceptable limits. Despite his attempts to keep things secret she had become aware by early summer that he was having an affair and who with. Jane recalls Amis telling her later that Hilly first confronted him with her knowledge on the train back from their visit to Yugoslavia and that they had 'the most frightful row which lasted till they got home'. (This was the holiday during which Hilly had written on Amis's back in lipstick.) At the beginning of August Amis and Jane went to Sitges in Spain for a two-week holiday. Hilly was aware that they were together and by various means found out where they were. One day, on answering their hotel room doorbell, they were confronted by a journalist from the *Daily Express*. They fielded such questions as 'Are you in love?' with standard 'no comments' and then suggested that since he had blown their cover he might want to do a full story, with photographs. They would, they promised, do a full interview after he returned to the hotel with a professional photographer, the best available being in the next town. They then fled, leaving a trail of false clues which eventually took the hack to Barcelona – they, meanwhile, had gone in the other direction.

Had Hilly informed the *Express*? It is probable, given that she had also been making other plans. When Amis returned to Cambridge the Madingley Road house was empty. A note from Hilly informed him that she had gone with the children to Majorca and that he should not follow them. Their marriage was, it seemed, finally over. The next day Amis packed what he could carry, caught the train to London and moved into Jane's flat in Maida Vale. Hilly and the children stayed in Majorca. Amis next saw his children, or at least two of them, the boys, when Hilly sent them back to London to see their father in late November. He was still living with Jane, and it was evident to all concerned that this situation was not going to change. Soon after this Amis and Hilly contacted their solicitors to arrange a divorce. It was finalized in 1965, and in the same year Amis and Jane were married.

Amis and Jane spent their first month in the maisonette which she shared with her brother Colin, known to friends and family as Monkey, in Blomfield Road, Maida Vale, and then decided that if they were starting a proper relationship they should do so on their own. They moved to a more prestigious location, a flat in Knightsbridge, Basil Street, near Harrods. Amis's calculation that Majorca would have allowed him to live solely from his earnings as a writer was not irrelevant. He now had to both provide for his own needs and support his distant family, and for the first few years Jane took care of their major expenses. She paid for the Knightsbridge flat, which itself proved to be too expensive, and before Christmas 1963 after six weeks in Majorca they moved back to Maida Vale and Monkey, who would continue to live with them in various residences until shortly before their relationship ended. The flat was small, and eventually they acquired a ten-year lease for a house, 108 Maida Vale, paid for by Jane, and moved into it in 1965.

The Anti-Death League was the first of Amis's novels to be planned and completed after the beginning of his relationship with Jane, and these years had a major influence upon it. It would be radically different from anything he had written before, but first he had to complete a number of projects that were transitional yet reflected his lack of certainty regarding his new direction. In 1960, when Amis and Conquest started to edit *Spectrum: A Science Fiction Anthology*, five volumes of which would appear over the next six years, they were also making plans to co-author a novel. *The Egyptologists* would eventually be published in 1965, and like many shared works of fiction it is suspended somewhere between the original idea and the completed project. The Egyptologists are a group of middle-class, married professional men who lease a building in West London for the pursuit of their amateur but fiercely enthusiastic interests in ancient Egypt. They hold regular meetings and seminars, invite esteemed scholars to give lectures and use the building at other times for individual study. It is also equipped with private suites of rooms which serve the society's actual function, as an ongoing, reliable alibi for regular acts of adultery. The plot clearly originated in its creators' own experiences together in London during the 1950s, particularly Conquest's provision of excuses and locations for Amis's infidelities.

The novel was successful to the extent that its plot attracted the attention of Richard Attenborough, then in the early years of his transformation from actor to director. It seemed to catch the atmosphere of the mid-1960s with a group of apparently conventional individuals desperately battling against the public exposure of a promiscuous, hedonistic reality. In the year of its publication Attenborough raised and paid them £25,000 for the film rights, an amount which by today's standards would be multiplied by about ten. The film was never made.

Amis wrote the closing chapters in late 1964. In these the general mood of lechery, deceit, cynicism and polite misogyny lifts briefly. The Treasurer has an affair with Lee Elliot Swarz, an American research student and real Egyptologist, who has become aware of what the society actually involves. He tells her that he will leave his wife and marry her and that, for once, his commitment is genuine. She declines his offer, explaining that the state of mind which first caused him to abandon monogamy is probably irreversible. As usual, this episode involves a blurred reconfiguration of various aspects of Amis's life. He wrote it when he was on holiday with Jane in Majorca. Their relationship was little more than a year old, and Jane was aware that his new, and on his part genuine, state of commitment to one woman was at odds with his past. It is thus appropriate that the Treasurer should become the only member of the society to revoke its code of infidelity and, for no apparent reason, unsettle the prevailing tone of the earlier chapters. Lee's scepticism could well be an acceptance on Amis's part that Jane herself would have occasional doubts.

The Egyptologists, like *One Fat Englishman*, was part of Amis's long goodbye to the atmosphere which dominated his 1950s' fiction. The book that tells us more about what he planned to do next was *The James Bond Dossier*, also published in 1965. This was his second critical monograph and, like its predecessor, *New Maps of Hell*, it reflects Amis's provocative, unorthodox views on what serious writing involves. Significantly it was written alongside *The Anti-Death League*, and there are overlaps.

Amis had always enjoyed Fleming's fiction, and in 1964 he sent him a first draft of the study and asked for comments. They met in L'Etoile, an elegant Bond-style restaurant in Charlotte Street. Fleming generally approved of the book and he colluded in its mild parody of academicism by correcting Amis on the precise details of how Oddjob had died and where exactly Bond had met one or the other of his stunningly beautiful conquests.

Amis in the preface is clear enough about his intentions. This would not be a patronizing, tolerant survey of low-cultural populism. In Amis's view, Fleming's novels are 'just as complex and have just as much in them as more ambitious kinds of fiction' (p. 9). The book offered Amis the opportunity to explore *ex libris* his own ideas about the type of fiction which combined states of fantasy, wish fulfilment and harsh naturalism, and it also enabled him to thumb his nose at the high-art snobbishness of the profession he had recently left. He did a lot of research and in each chapter he cites critics who had cast Fleming in the role of servant to the baser instincts of the ordinary reader. A 'female' reviewer had dismissed *Thunderball* as a combination of *Boy's Own* heroics and mild pornography, a compensation for 'adolescent inferiority feelings'. Amis finds it strange that Fleming's novel should be singled out for condemnation when similar tastes are catered for by more revered works of fiction, such as Homer's *Odyssey*. In this, Amis reminds us, we encounter embodiments of bravery, toughness, nobility and cunning in, respectively, Achilles, Ajax, Hector and Odysseus, which could be cited as antecedents for Fleming's creations. Moreover, we (that is, we male readers) do not complain about Odysseus being woken and 'cared for' by Nausicaa and her attendant maidens, so what is wrong with Fleming's granting of similar ministrations to Bond (pp. 44–5)?

The use of Fleming as a cultural battering ram becomes the keynote of the *Dossier*. On the question of whether Bond's lifestyle is a mandate for hedonism Amis further asks us to compare his taste for good food and drink, meticulously documented by Fleming, with the gigantic feasts that Dickens describes so regularly and with such attention to detail. Amis berates Eliot's *Waste Land* as hypocrisy in action. Eliot presents the low-order tastes and habits of ordinary people as a symptom of our cultural decline, while Fleming, via Bond, offers the ordinary reader a lesson in consumer sophistication (pp. 102–3). And, with tongue firmly in cheek, Amis asks if Bond's celebration of Cliquot Rosé with Belgian caviar is not as movingly epiphanous as Keats's moment with his nightingale (p. 113).

One characteristic shared by *The Egyptologists* and *The Dossier* is their satirical treatment of straight-faced academic discourse, and this to an extent showed that Amis was drawing a line beneath his previous persona as a professional academic who also produced fiction. He would go on writing about literature, but his later works subtly detached themselves from the self-enclosed university-based element of criticism. The most hilarious indication of this change in his profile occurred in an article carrying Robert Conquest's name but which in truth was written by Conquest and Amis himself. 'Christian Symbolism in *Lucky Jim*' was published in the new, radical academic journal *Critical Quarterly* in 1965 (Spring, I, pp. 87–92) and involved an interpretation of Jim's drunken awakening in the Welch house as a re-enactment of the crucifixion, along with references to such earlier theses as Mrs Joyce Hackensmith's *The Phallus Theme in Early Amis* (Concord, 1957). Later, members of the editorial board of *Critical Quarterly* claimed to know that the article was a spoof, while Conquest maintained that they did not.

Amis's accumulation of background material for the *Dossier* was so vast that he made use of the leftovers in a self-parodic piece published in the same year under the pseudonym of William James, Bond's senior in the Secret Service. *The Book of Bond* tells us in meticulous detail of how we, too, might follow Bond's example as a refined hedonist. Two years later Amis (as Robert Markham) followed James's advice and turned his fictional alter ego into Bond in *Colonel Sun*, a respectful imitation of Fleming's method. Leaving aside Amis's almost obsessive concern with Fleming himself, there was a more significant parallel between this work and his plans for *The Anti-Death League*. In the appendices of the *Dossier* Amis writes of how 'fantasy' can have 'solidly attested counterparts in the world of fact' (p. 147), and in an appendix entitled 'Literature and Escape' he argues that escapism in writing is as important as the Arnoldian tenet of self-enlightenment and that it offers us an 'implicit assurance that life is coherent and meaningful' (p. 149). Amis is arguing that a blending of the world we know with a self-evidently hoped-for or imagined version is in itself a kind of realism, a testament to the fact that we always exist at the intersection between what the world is and what we want it to be. *The Anti-Death League* is in many ways a creative execution of these literary-critical pronouncements.

The novel explores in detail themes that Amis had only touched upon in his 1950s' writing: death, absolute commitment to other human beings, our role in a world upon whose future we seem to have no influence. Its inspiration was his relationship with Jane.

The novel begins in what seem to be the grounds of a country house. Two women, unnamed, are watching an exercise in animal intrigue. A black cat is crouched in a shadow, while a bird, aware of the cat's presence, wheels in the air in an attempt to protect her nest from the hostile carnivore. Another group, 'three men in uniform', arrive and one comments: 'Look at this,' he said. 'Did you ever see anything like it?' He is referring not to the cat and the bird but to a water tower built in the same sinister, gothic style as the house. A low-flying aircraft draws the attention of both groups. It also startles the cat, whose flight across the grass causes one of the women and one of the men to glance at each other. 'Just when the girl turned and looked at the tall young man it was as if the sun went out for an instant. He flinched and drew in his breath almost with a cry.'

Throughout the passage there is a subtle and uncertain interplay between the reader's perception of the events and what we assume is felt by the participants. For the reader, the passage is crowded with ominous symbols: the cat and the bird, the aircraft and the gothic tower all carry resonances of looming and imminent terror. These events register for the participants ambiguously. The young man's brief sensation of shock is immediately absorbed by routine currencies of comment and conversation. Is he taken in by the gloomy presence of the water tower, the shock of the aircraft or the girl?

'I never took our James for a student of architecture, did you, Moti?' asked the senior of the three officers . . . 'He was really

admiring something far more worth a young man's while than cold
stones, am I right, James?'

'Well, yes. I thought she was wonderful, didn't you? Extraordinary eyes. But sort of blank and frightened.'

Is she frightened? She never explicitly betrays anxiety or fear to
her companion, but we are invited to regard the young man and the
girl as particularly sensitive to the ominous symbols and the eerie
atmosphere. The narrator is playing a game with the reader. The
events disclosed to us are portentous, loaded with premonitory
signs; or at least they would be if the reader were disposed to interpret them in this way.

The young officer and the girl are eventually disclosed as James
Churchill and Catherine Casement, whose love affair is a central
feature of the narrative. James is an officer involved with Operation
Apollo, and Catherine is recovering from a nervous breakdown. As
a means of reintroducing herself to normal life, she takes a part-time job at the village pub, where, eighty pages later, they meet
again.

'I knew you straight away.'

She could not stop herself saying, 'And I knew you straight
away.'

'I know.'

Their encounter seems to both of them inevitable, predetermined, and their relationship begins almost immediately. Amis had
never written anything like this before. The exchanges between the
men sometimes involve the banter of kinship, but apart from this
there is no comedy. Humour in all of Amis's previous fiction had
operated partly as a support mechanism against the more unwelcome aspects of harsh reality, a tendency that reached its peak with
John Lewis and its nadir in Roger Micheldene. This episode,

The garden of St John's College, Oxford, summer 1942, just before Kingsley Amis's undergraduate career was interrupted by army service. Amis is kneeling in centre front, pulling a face. Standing, left to right, are Mervyn Brown, J.B. Widdawson, Edward du Cann, Michael MacNaughton-Smith, Nick Russel, Philip Brown, David Williams, Norman Iles, Graham Parkes and David West

Photograph taken in Germany in May 1945 on the day the Germans surrendered. Amis is in the middle row, second from left. On his right is E. Frank Coles, co-author of *Who Else Is Rank*

Hilly Bardwell around the time she met Amis

Amis and Hilly with Christopher Tosswill and Philip Larkin at Cambridge, 1946–7

Hilly, Amis, Terry Scarfe and Nick Russel in Oxford, 1947

Amis in post-war Oxford

Hilly, pregnant with Martin, Amis and Mandy the dog at Marriner's
Cottage, 1948

Amis, Hilly and the children in Portugal, 1955

Philip, Sally, Hilly, Amis and Martin outside 24 The Grove, Swansea, where
Lucky Jim was written, in the mid-1950s

Amis and Ian Carmichael during the filming of *Lucky Jim* in the mid-1950s

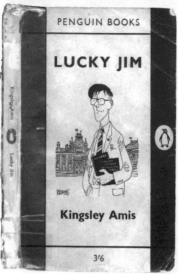

Lucky Jim in paperback. This is the earliest Penguin cover of the book (1961), with Jim bearing a distinct resemblance to Ian Carmichael

Amis and Hilly in the United States, 1959

Amis in London, late 1950s

Anthony Powell, Amis, Philip Larkin
and Hilly in London, 1958

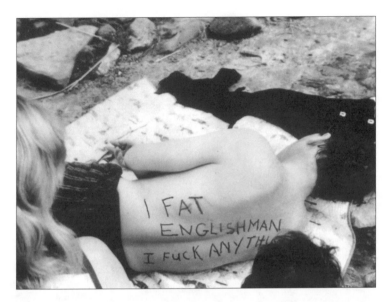

Yugoslavia, 1963, with comments by Hilly

Amis in 1963, the year Hilly left him

Above: Amis and Jane
Howard at 108 Maida
Vale, 1965

Left: Amis and Jane
outside Lemmons, early
1970s

Right: Martin Amis, Jane
and Kingsley Amis, late
1970s

Amis at Lemmons, 1973, the year of *The Riverside Villas Murder*

Amis in 1980, the year Jane
left him

Amis leaving the Garrick Club,
London, mid-1980s

Touring Wales, 1986. Amis is second from the left. Also present (from left) are Stuart and Eve Thomas (third and eighth), Paul and Mrs Fussell (fifth and ninth) and Michael and Virginia Rush (first and seventh)

Hilly and Amis, early 1990s

Martin and Kingsley Amis, 1991

involving the first encounters between James and Catherine, was based entirely on the opening months of the relationship between Amis and Jane. The brief moment of eye contact in the grounds of the house is intended to capture the resonances of the Cheltenham Festival. In the novel James and Catherine seem briefly to stand outside the fabric of their respective worlds, and their companions remain largely unaware of the feeling of recognition which they share. So it was at Cheltenham, in an albeit more mundane way, that Amis and Jane secretly made each other aware of the mutual attraction. Their subsequent meetings, unlike those of their fictional counterparts, were planned, but fate seemed to have taken a hand when Hilly and the family disappeared without explanation and Amis found himself back in London with Jane, apparently for good. Amis imbues these events with echoes of the supernatural, but he integrates this with parallels drawn from actual experience.

Also there are intriguing clues which, privately for Amis and Jane, enshrine the episode as a version of their recent, shared past. When he and Jane were conducting their secret, extra-marital affair he always in his letters addressed her as 'bird'. Both knew that the word's use as a demotic term for a young, potentially seducible and unsophisticated woman was the antithesis of their exclusive understanding of it. As Amis explained in the letters his 'bird' was a creature of beauty, perceived from a distance as invulnerable and mysterious but known to him as something more. The bird of the novel threatened by the cat is wonderfully symbolic of their first encounters. Jane was fully aware of Amis's predatory, cat-like, reputation as a successful seducer. Conscious of this, Amis frequently signed his letters to Jane as Major Hunter, another name that would resurface in the book. In the novel the cat–bird encounter is brief and delicately ambiguous. It is the beginning of a series of accidents that bring James and Catherine together; it causes them to look at each other, yet its more ominous significance becomes part of the past.

He told Jane that the central relationship of the novel would be based on theirs, he read extracts to her and invited her to name the fictional character who was, in effect, herself. She chose Catherine Casement, he James Churchill. Catherine, like Jane, was first married at the age of nineteen. Both discovered that their husbands, while decent and affectionate enough, had married them because this was what men of their age and class were expected to do. Sex was more a part of the established ritual than a reflection of intense and mutual attraction. Both married again, and disappointment was replaced by distress. Catherine's second husband became a self-obsessed bully and would beat her when she refused to conform to his expectations of what a wife should be and do. Jane's experiences with James Douglas Henry were not quite so unpleasant, but he did turn out to be a man whose thoughtless, selfish habits became unendurable. Catherine's second marriage has caused the nervous breakdown for which she is receiving treatment in the house that provides the setting for the opening episode, and here we begin to wonder about the motivation for Amis's distortions of actuality. James becomes the man who Catherine has always been looking for, the resolution of her previous experiences of discontent and maltreatment. Jane had far more strength and confidence than her fictional counterpart; she and Amis came together on equal terms, and it is evident that in his recreation of their relationship Amis was involved both in the massaging of his ego and a sincere reflection of his commitment. Jane, generously, takes the latter view. In these early years he was, as she says, genuinely in love with her.

The only similarity between *The Anti-Death League* and Amis's earlier fiction exists in the way he uses borrowings from his own experience. On the one hand, the James/Catherine–Amis/Jane parallels are private, but they also form the basis for the novel's public dimension, as a complete departure from the well-established conventions of his writing.

The book's theme is the relationship between choice, chance

and something resembling fate, and each of the main characters falls prey to this uneasy, unpredictable assembly. Operation Apollo is never really explained. It might be a secret weapon or a more complex strategic response to global events which remain equally obscure. As usual, Amis makes sure that the dialogue and the narrator's orchestration of it embeds the text in the familiar routines of the here and now. The pub in which Catherine begins her reintroduction to normal life carries echoes of the dull home-counties world of *Take a Girl Like You*, with the landlord engaging customers in characteristically boring chats about 'modernizing' the premises and how trade picks up at the weekend, with more people 'down from London'. At the same time this evocation of the comfortably mundane is shot through with sinister overtones. The characters allude to Operation Apollo and the sense of imminent crisis that seems to have prompted it, but little is specified. This is shrewd realism. A recording of actual conversations between people in England from a couple of years earlier would carry traces of anxiety, with occasional references to names, places and events. From it we would know that something frightening was in the air, but we would also need a separate knowledge of history to connect this atmosphere with the Cuban missile crisis. The texture of Amis's novel creates a similar feeling of uncertainty and subdued panic but without any clear explanation of its cause.

The book makes concessions to the kind of novel-of-ideas which Huxley produced in the 1930s and 1940s, and there are slight echoes of Orwell, but the reader should not be misled by such promptings. Its atmosphere is used as a background for an exploration of states of mind and ways of life that return us to the particular experiences of Kingsley Amis.

The name Max Hunter, borrowed by Amis from his letters to Jane, is appended in the novel to a friend of James, another officer involved in Operation Apollo, and the first of Amis's principal characters who is homosexual. He reflects Amis's liberal but not condescending opinions on homosexuality, and he catches the mood of the period. Roy Jenkins's Act which decriminalized same-sex relationships would be carried in an open vote in the House of Commons three years after the novel's publication. But Hunter's orientation is less a concession by Amis to civil rights than an oblique and intriguing perspective on male sexuality *per se*. For Hunter, promiscuity is an obligation. Anything resembling permanent commitment is impossible because it is also illegal, but commitment is what Hunter wants. At one point James suggests to him that while his enforced lifestyle denies him even the option of continued emotional involvement with one person, it also licenses uncommitted sexual activity, a state that many heterosexual men would, if they were honest, envy. Hunter answers that 'Yes it ought' and adds, enigmatically, that 'it didn't work like that. I was still finding my way in those days. I'm in no such danger now.' Hunter seems to be saying that age and endurance have immunized him from the need for emotional commitment, but the reader knows that he is lying, that James has reminded him of the cruel irony of their respective roles. James has fallen in love and has chosen fidelity, and Hunter envies James. Consider the parallels between this exchange and a not dissimilar network of reflections and decisions that would have confronted Amis during the period in which he planned the novel.

As he prepared the exchange between James and Hunter, he would have been transcribing and rewriting conversations with himself. His own libidinous career was not, like Hunter's, a legal necessity, but there were many similarities. His habit of having sex with practically every attractive woman who was similarly inclined was, as he often conceded to the likes of Larkin and Conquest, as much a condition as an option. Moreover, he shared with Hunter an ongoing mixture of fear, conspiratorial excitement and clubbish deception (and there are echoes here of *The Egyptologists*). Hunter's colleagues, like Amis's male friends, knew what he was and what he did and knew also of the dire consequences of discovery. For Amis this situation was brought to an end more by accident than design. First, he met Jane, then Hilly's sudden departure prompted their affair to become a relationship. James's relationship with Catherine is a close copy of this, and the moment at which he speculates on Hunter's existence involves Amis, via James, in looking back on what much of his own life had been like. The most intriguing element of this exercise in personality splicing is the question raised by Hunter's knowledge that although he wants to be like James he cannot be. Amis's commitment to Jane was genuine and sincere, and she was fully aware of his history, but he must have wondered if his feelings for her were powerful enough for him to displace effectively that aspect of himself that had governed much of his adult existence.

Amis's exchange of his relationship with Hilly for his new one with Jane had an immensely significant effect upon his writing. All of his pre-*Anti-Death League* novels had drawn upon and made use of the divided, multi-faceted nature of his world. The Swansea location with its interweaving of middle- and working-class lifestyles provided the background both for his ambivalent relationship with socialism and for the blend of hard-nosed experience and linguistic sophistication which many of his characters embodied. The energy of his fiction derived from his tendency to create tensions between what people did and how they felt, the way they behaved and what they thought, all orchestrated by a narrative presence that stirred the mixture without suggesting that it was a recipe for anything cohesive. The most productive parallel between his world and his writing was his life of deception with Hilly, and suddenly all of this had changed completely and apparently irreversibly.

Hilly had admired, read and enjoyed his work, but she was not a conscious participant in it. Jane was a writer. She joined in with what had now become Amis's only professional activity. Assisted by Monkey, she tried the experiment of imitating his style, and parts of *One Fat Englishman* were written by her, although to this day she refuses to identify them. In effect, the Amis who had previously been the private point of intersection between his various personae had become part of an open exchange with someone else. His keeping of secrets from Hilly, which involved the interspersing of displaced guilt with the pleasures of calculated invention, was the perfect foundation for a fictional mode that was at once candid and evasive. *The Anti-Death League* obliged him to try something different.

What happens in *The Anti-Death League* is that secrecy and truth becomes part of the book's fabric, something that its characters have to confront and not just enact. For the first time Amis obliges us to wonder if there are forces at work in the narrative and, by implication, in the real world that are not grounded only in choice and circumstance.

Soon after James and Catherine begin their relationship we find them strolling through the countryside. James

> looked at her and past her together, so that girl, trees and stream formed a unity. She turned her head and looked at him. He knew for certain that in some way this moment had become inevitable ever since that other moment the afternoon he first saw her when he had looked at a patch of country similar to this one and thought of her. He felt his heart lift. This had never happened to him before, and he was surprised at how physical the sensation was.

The style of this passage and its implied message are so different from anything that Amis had written before as to beggar belief. For James, the world appears to be both reflecting his experience and operating as its beneficent arbiter. Amis invites us to recognize echoes of the opening of the novel. They sit down in the 'deep shadow' of the trees, not unlike the 'deep shadow' in which the cat was crouched. They undress, and he watches as her expression grows 'wilder', 'less human', and in making love they seem to have become a realization of the gothic symbolism of their first encounter. However, during their post-coital embrace James discovers a lump in her breast that will soon be diagnosed as cancer. Nothing like this happened with Jane and Amis, but as the novel progresses he begins to supplement its autobiographical strand with speculations on how good fortune can be unsettled by its antithesis. Obviously the parallels between the two episodes invite us to compare them and to consider also their respective conclusions, the first magical and the second potentially tragic. It is as though Amis feels the need to qualify the mood of pseudo-mystical optimism with which the novel began, and this sense of him playing with the relation between fate and chance becomes a keynote of the book.

The narrator achieves a fine balance between the world perceived from the inside by its characters and from the outside by the reader. We are told nothing that the characters would not know, and we share the question of whether these events and conditions carry any significance beyond their status as cold empirical detail. By the end of the novel the question remains open, for all of us. It concludes with its characters in a state of temporary remission: the development of Catherine's cancer seems to have been arrested; James, who had gone into a coma, is revived; Operation Apollo is deferred but not forgotten. But to remind us that nightmares rarely have comforting conclusions the closing pages offer an unnerving sequence of twists upon a narrative sub-plot.

Along with James and Hunter, there is a third character whose thoughts and experiences draw heavily upon his author's. Major Ayscue is the regimental padre whose public persona is that of the liberal Christian. Privately he has become almost an atheist. He has substituted an orthodox perception of God for a faith based upon aesthetics. His favourite composer, one Thomas Roughhead, appears to have created patterns of symmetry and resonance that bespeak, perhaps, evidence of beneficent cosmic design. The only reason why Ayscue does not completely and irreversibly abandon his belief in some kind of God is the possibility that if man can make beautiful order from the plentiful chaos of sound then perhaps some larger hand has been at work in the world, capable perhaps of restoring his friends Catherine and James to their promised idyll. If James and Hunter carry echoes of Amis's emotional life, then Ayscue is a version of Amis the thinker. Ayscue's fragile system of belief, based as it is upon man's ability to create as a reflection of something beyond man's control, is surely not accidentally related to Amis's writing of a novel in which elements of his own life are deployed to raise the question of whether human existence is random, rooted in nothing more than circumstance, or whether some other influence is at work. Moreover, Ayscue's struggle with religious faith is only a slight distortion of Amis's own rather unusual notion of God.

His only extended discussion of religion is an essay called 'God-forsaken', which appeared in the *Spectator* in 1987 but which takes us into his past, and some of it might have been written by Ayscue. Amis tells of how his Nonconformist parents were also non-practising, of how religion was rarely a feature of family life but of how at school he was introduced to the elements of Christianity that he has always respected and enjoyed, its writings and its music. In his view, orthodox atheism and secularism also involve a degree of philistinism. It is impossible, he argues, to properly appreciate the quality of poems by, say, George Herbert without respecting and taking seriously the faith that inspired them. Of his own unbelief he states that he has often sensed the presence of an omniscient being who knows his thoughts, and sometimes of 'his own ability to reach him through prayer', but that he cannot quite bring himself to accept that such a presence exists. Towards the end of the novel Ayscue stages a performance of a Roughhead piece, and afterwards he suddenly feels the need to pray, principally for the health of Catherine. Amis describes Ayscue's thoughts in a way that prefigures his own essay of two decades later.

Whenever he prayed before it had been like talking into an empty room, into a telephone with nobody at the other end. But this time . . . somebody was at the end of the telephone, not saying anything, nowhere near that, but listening.

Outside, Ayscue's dog, his closest companion, has been disturbed by the same music whose beautiful symmetries have restored a degree of Ayscue's faith. She panics, slips her collar and is run over by a lorry.

With Jane he did talk of matters slightly beyond the empirical. She recalls that he would sometimes alternate between an intense anxiety about death and a more dismissive view of it as both inevitable and meaningless. He would never discuss in any detail the notion of God or the afterlife, but he would admit to an intense fear of the unknown. Clearly he was saving the detail for his fiction.

In an interview, some time before *The Anti-Death League* was published and while he was still revising the drafts, he stated that the novel had begun as 'the result of realizing that one isn't going to be young for ever and noting more and more that there is pain and sorrow in the world' (*Sun*, 17 December 1964). He was, he confesses, not sure where to begin. He was juggling with not obviously compatible ideas: 'thoughts about God and Death' seemed to take in the 'post-war army, with modern weapons', a 'sympathetic treatment of homosexuality' and 'a girl who had been badly treated by men and how difficult it is for her to agree to be treated nicely by a man', the last of course being an oblique and certainly not public allusion to his own thoughts about Jane. Later, after publication, he wrote in the *Daily Mail* of how he dealt with these problems of composition, of how he would go for walks from his and Jane's flat in Maida Vale and how suddenly the disparate elements of his plan would come together. 'Only a quarter of an hour's walk and I'd have the whole thing clear before I got back.' This was very different from his routine method of turning ideas into prose, which had previously involved only himself, his study, his typewriter and a large dose of self-discipline. One wonders if this new inspirational practice, more sudden in its transformations of random prognosis into coherent fiction, had in itself some influence upon the novel's self-referential yet aberrant exploration of the relationship between writing and fate.

Amis's life had certainly changed, and his novels reflected his awareness of this. After *The Anti-Death League* Amis alternated between one novel which maintained the style and contemporary focus of the 1950s' fiction and one which was, if not quite experimental, then at least unusual. This backward-forward exercise concluded with *Russian Hide and Seek* in 1980, significantly the year he separated from Jane Howard.

12

I Want It Now

H ILLY, variously camouflaged, had featured as Amis's permanent and tolerant companion in the novels of the 1950s. In
the two novels written during the early years of his relationship
with Jane she, too, is given prominence, but while the Hilly recon-
structions carried an air of guilt-ridden authenticity his accounts of
his attachment to Jane drifted towards fantasy. He began *I Want It
Now* almost immediately after the typescript of *The Anti-Death
League* had been sent to Gollancz. It would, like its predecessor,
focus upon a man and a woman who are versions of himself and
Jane, and it would also reflect the progress of Amis's at once deeply
felt and ambivalent views on politics, race, class and the state of
contemporary society. The experience that would play the most significant part in its construction was the period he and Jane spent in
the United States from October 1967 until March 1968.

Despite his being frequently presented as a xenophobe, Amis
from the late 1950s to the 1980s indulged a genuine taste for foreign
travel. In spring 1966 he accepted an invitation, delivered in person
by an embassy official, to give a lecture at Prague University on 'The
Literature of Protest in Great Britain'. Apart from the attractions of
an expenses-paid, week-long visit to one of Europe's most engaging
cities, Amis was intrigued by the prospect of seeing the place that
might have become his home. In 1948, a few months before his

appointment in Swansea, he had, as one of his desperate attempts to find an academic job somewhere, applied for a lectureship in Prague and been turned down. Then his Eastern Bloc sympathies had caused him to sideline the possibility that the real Czechoslovakia would not be as tolerable as his half-formed image of it.

Amis made full use of the generalized, slightly ambiguous title of the lecture. His principal point, that literature as a vehicle for 'protest' was all too frequently employed by Western writers as a self-indulgent reinvention of themselves as oppressed radicals, is a restatement of his late 1950s' rejection of the leftish collective of 'Angries'. He suggested that the democratic, liberal societies of Western Europe and the United States involved very little that writers could protest against. They could write anything that they wanted to – *Lady Chatterley's Lover* had been unbanned six years earlier – and any political affiliation, disguised as fiction or verse, was usable. Without limitations. He implied, of course, that Communist regimes such as Czechoslovakia's were more in need of a 'Literature of Protest' than their British counterpart. To his surprise, his audience generally agreed with him, and one should remember that his lecture was delivered at a time when Czechoslovakia was shifting towards a form of liberal, quasi-dramatic socialism, a movement that would be quelled in two years' time by the Soviet Union.

The Czech experience reinforced Amis's right-leaning, anti-socialist tendencies and also played a part in his construction of Ronnie Appleyard, the principal male character of *I Want It Now*. He has a background in journalism and, as the novel begins, is enjoying the high salary, fame and hedonistic lifestyle of a TV current-affairs programme presenter. He secures his own popularity by exposing politicians as self-serving hypocrites and by comparison presenting himself as a caring radical whose leftish opinions none the less transcend the careerist motives of politics. Amis starts the novel with Ronnie at work on screen and invites us to compare his public persona with his private reflections.

'Well, what do you think? I'll tell you what I think. I think we as a
nation have got our values all back to front. What sane and responsible society would pour its money away on useless, unproductive
things like our overseas military presences or the H-bomb – a bit
worse than useless that – while we're keeping our old people on or
around subsistence level? . . .'

To be fair to Ronnie Appleyard, he had no feelings for old
people as such beyond mild distaste, never wasted his time sweat-
ing about the H-bomb and would not have cared a curse if the
British army were to set about reoccupying the Indian sub-conti-
nent, provided they did so without calling on him for assistance.
He even wondered momentarily whether his show of concern for
the old might not tell slightly against him with the group he would
have said he spoke to and for: the intelligent and independent-
minded young. Then he cheered up again at the reflection that it
was their parents the little bastards were against, rather than their
grandparents. (Chapter 1)

A decade before this Amis had made similar use of his own even
then rather flimsy attachment to political causes in the creation of
John Lewis, who dances to a Labourite tune but does not care very
much about matters beyond his own world. With Ronnie he takes
this a stage further. Ronnie, at least at the beginning of the novel, is
symptomatic of what in Amis's view is the almost obligatory attachment to fashionable left-wing causes by writers, journalists and all
persons associated with the arts and the media. In the year the novel
came out Amis wrote a pamphlet called *Lucky Jim's Politics*, which
was published by the Conservative Political Centre. As he had done
in its predecessor, *Socialism and the Intellectuals*, he made provocative use of his opinion that political allegiance by its very nature
involves simplifications and falsifications of the contemporary

world. For Amis the Conservative Party was now the only political grouping without an all-inclusive ideology, and in Jane's view even this grudging attachment was disingenuous – his apparent interest in any kind of politics was, according to her, 'a complete façade'.

Ronnie is partly a throwback, an exaggeration of John Lewis who reflects his author's drift further rightward over the intervening decade, but this model is qualified by another intention and a particular experience. The novel would supplement the Catherine/James creation as an evocation of the uniqueness of Amis's still new relationship with Jane, and their trip to America would provide him with useful material for this enterprise.

Amis had made and maintained a large number of friends and contacts during his year in Princeton. One, Russell Fraser, had become head of the English Department at Vanderbilt University, Nashville, an Ivy League-style institution as old as the Confederacy. Fraser contacted Amis at the end of 1966 and suggested that he spend the first part of the following academic year there partly as Writer-in-Residence and partly as a replacement for an academic on sabbatical, the latter providing him with a decent salary plus expenses. Amis in his *Memoirs* wrote that he had enjoyed his first American experience so much that he accepted the invitation almost immediately and 'failed to do what I soon discovered I should have done and drop it like a hot potato'. He knew about the American South, but until he arrived in Nashville he was not aware that most of it had hardly changed at all since before the Civil War. The Amises boarded the Queen Mary in October 1967 for what would be her final transatlantic voyage. They went on their own, leaving his children, now all in their mid to late teens, with various relatives, Hilly included.

There is a joke about a man being shown the various rooms available in Hell. The best seems to involve a group of condemned souls chatting agreeably and drinking cocktails, albeit while standing knee deep in something resembling faeces. The man chooses this one only to be told that the weekly break is now over: 'Back on your heads.' An experience not unlike this was visited upon the Amises when they arrived in the United States. They first spent a week with his old friends in Princeton, where the people were much as he remembered them from a decade before, while the place had become victim to the ongoing state of 'modernization' that characterized American town planning and architecture. Things got much worse. During his previous trip Amis had visited only the Northeastern states, but during this one, as the train rolled south, he began to notice not just a change in the climate and scenery but a feeling that he was, in some less than quantifiable way, going back in time. This suspicion was confirmed by a number of his experiences in Nashville. Despite attempts by Washington governments from the Kennedy years onwards to drag the South out of its racist practices, still frequently enshrined in state legislation, racism was in 1967 very much the uncontested state of mind of the majority of its white population. Worse than that, Amis found that the university itself, which he expected to be an enlightened retreat from a world involving the Klan and the legendary 'separate-seats' policy of public transport and bars, contained a large number of educated people who regarded 'nigras' as sub-humans. Walter Sullivan, the academic and novelist on sabbatical, was an unashamed proponent of the maxim that black students could never receive 'A grades' since they were, in his view, mentally deficient. His thesis was hypothetical, because he had never had to mark the work of black students. Amis, soon after his arrival, asked a colleague if Vanderbilt had started to admit blacks. 'Yes, of course,' he was told. 'His name is Moore. But I think he has dropped out.' Amis treated the 'Moore' pun as a case of unintended and ominous irony.

For Amis, Nashville was a distorted mirror image of Czechoslovakia. In Prague people had to endure an ideology that was forced upon them and which, in their own best interests, they reluctantly endorsed. In Nashville one half of the population imposed upon the other an evil ideology that the former regarded as fact and the latter as something they could do little about.

The Nashville experience presented Amis with a problem that went beyond his loathing for the place. He had now become an eccentric Tory. He had publicly announced his support for the US policy in Vietnam – against virtually all other writers in Britain – even suggesting that Britain should join in. As he saw it, the totalitarian and overtly Maoist regime of the North would be much worse than the alleged corruption of the South.

In America in 1967 the anti-war movement was finding a voice, particularly among students and younger academics. Although Vanderbilt was in general more conservative than its northern counterparts, it was not immune from the growing mood of protest, and Amis faced, had indeed become, an example of his thesis that all-inclusive political doctrines involved innate contradictions. He frequently found himself having to explain how someone who supported the war could at the same time feel so disturbed and unsettled by the time-honoured version of apartheid still practised in the American South and publicly defended by the kind of politicians who were also enthusiastic cold warriors. This would eventually become an irritating chore, but it would also play an important part in the reinvention of himself as Ronnie Appleyard.

Ronnie is a successful and comfortably uncommitted seducer, at least until he meets Simona Quick at a London party. The event is another reworking of Amis's and Jane's meeting at the Cheltenham Festival, with the initial mood of mutual attraction and sexual potential being gradually replaced by something more unique and enduring. Amis changes a large number of things, partly to hide the personal element from reviewers and journalists and partly to mount an assault upon what he regarded as the more disagreeable aspects of late-1960s' society. Simona is nineteen, much younger than Catherine, and has personal characteristics so completely different from Jane's as to virtually announce themselves as covering devices. Her verbal habits involve the use of main clauses rather than sentences or, if she is feeling particularly bored or indifferent, monosyllables, a feature of contemporary 'youth culture' offered to Amis by his children and their friends. She is spoilt and selfish, she takes drugs and she began her sexual career aged fourteen. She has, she tells Ronnie, since then had sex with forty-two men, none of which she has enjoyed and none of whom she has even liked. The title of the novel is her response to Ronnie's unnecessarily sophisticated opening chat-up. These characteristics are, however, interweaved with a love story that is an indulgently romanticized version of the one Amis was in, so much so as to suggest parallels between himself and Ronnie as the Prince and Jane/Simona as the Sleeping Beauty.

Simona belongs to a very wealthy family. Her mother, Lady Baldock, is a successful social climber, whose first marriage to an hereditary peer, resulting in Simona, has piloted her into a career involving even richer partners. Lady Baldock and her minions profess concern with Simona's unhealthy, self-destructive lifestyle, but Amis makes it clear that their own state of indifferent greed is actually its cause. The story involves Ronnie becoming aware for the first time in his life that he cares enough about someone to risk his professional reputation and rescue her. As a consequence, Simona emerges as an individual with intelligence, self-esteem and a genuine capacity to fall in love. In between the fictional refashionings of their situation Amis's perception of himself as a class below Jane and as someone who can transcend the privileged features of her lifestyle shines through.

Jane was aware of what Amis was doing. As with *The Anti-Death League*, she would read his drafts of *I Want It Now* and offer suggestions. The model for the hideous Lady Baldock was provided by Jane, who on one occasion commented that it was fortunate for a putative human being not to have become the son or daughter of her childless friend Dolly Burns, a wealthy self-indulgent socialite and daughter of the hereditary peer Lord Duveen. Apart from his friendship with Violet and Anthony Powell, Amis's life with Hilly and before that had involved a social network that was comprised largely of the professional middle classes, alongside his experience of working-class South Wales. Jane had friends who were a little further up the social scale, including Dolly, and Amis made use of these in his scathing representation of the Baldock set, with Jane's approval.

The novel involves four lengthy chapters. It begins and ends in London and in between we find Ronnie pursuing Simona first to Greece and then to Fort Charles, Tennessee, the sites being impressive properties in which Lady Baldock holds court. Fort Charles is based on Nashville.

Racism operated in Nashville and the surrounding area as a remarkably classless doctrine, unaffected by matters such as wealth, position or intellectual acumen. Amis was introduced to the director of the Jack Daniel's distillery in neighbouring Lynchburg, who told of how they all still revered the memory of old Jack whose statue stood prominently in the town square. The director recalled an incident in which a group of blacks, who had been trimming trees around the statue, had carelessly allowed a falling branch to take a chip out of Jack's hat. The director's predecessor, a Mr Motlow, felt they should be disciplined and he shot them. When was this? enquired Amis. Back in 1890; 1910? No; 1952. Then there was the wife of the Professor of Iberian Languages who was appalled at how 'Surr Lawrence Oh-livayay' had to endure during the filming of '*Oh-thello*' the humiliating experience of being forced to 'look', 'woke' and 'toke' 'like a black mayon'.

Amis compared his own experience to that of a victim of the then popular TV series *Candid Camera* whose world suddenly begins to take on an almost surreal, nightmarish quality. At the dinner party hosted by the 'no A grades for nigras' Professor Walter Sullivan, Amis was appalled by how all of the other guests, most of them connected with the university, had either nodded assent or treated Sullivan's opinions as not at all unusual, and he had asked himself a question. What should he do? Say what he felt? Resign? In the end he decided on something else. He had his 'notebook at the ready', and many of the Nashville exchanges re-emerge almost verbatim in Chapter 3 of *I Want It Now*. Once again he draws upon his talent for cruelly incisive verbal impersonation, this time to make the Southern drawl of Ronnie's acquaintances sound as imbecilic as their views.

He also turned his delayed, vicarious response to the Sullivan phenomenon into a means of reaffirming his feelings for Jane. Ronnie has always been a man for whom hypocrisy is a professional resource. He will manufacture opinions or keep his mouth shut according to the calculated effect upon his career in the media. In Fort Charles he changes and, although it is not directly stated, this sudden shift to dangerous sincerity is obviously the result of his first experience of being in love. At one of Lady Baldock's dinner parties her friend Student Mansfield emerges as a rabid compendium of many of the racist attitudes that Amis had encountered:

> '*and* . . . we've solved the Negro problem. By realizing there is no problem, except keeping 'em down. That's what I said, keeping 'em down. They're inferior, they always will be inferior, and we in the South have the honest-to-God common sense to realize it. There's your so-called Negro problem solved. Simple . . . The only way to keep the Negro in his place is by *fear*. The only argument he understands is the *lash*.' (Chapter 3)

One can imagine Amis as he prepared this episode, back in London with his notebook, reflecting upon the choices he had offered himself at the Sullivan party. Ronnie responds with 'Balls' and follows up by informing Mansfield in some detail of his condition as 'barbaric, inhumane, foolish, ignorant, outmoded'. He is, of course, expelled from the house by Lady Baldock, whose Christian

name is Juliette. By no coincidence a beautiful Nashville undergraduate called Julie Smith had told Amis, again at a party, that the
northern states 'don't know how to keep 'em [Nigras] down'.

Ronnie knows that what he has done will cause a severe setback
in his pursuit of Simona: although he loathes Lady Baldock's circle
he needs to sustain their tolerance just to stay in contact. Here there
are echoes of *The Anti-Death League*, because, again, fate takes a
hand. After his expulsion Ronnie sets off by taxi to the airport,
aware that it will be difficult for him to see Simona again. Suddenly
she appears in front of the car, gets in, tells him that she too has left
and they will now be together.

At the time of the Nashville trip Amis and Jane were already
committed to each other, but Amis uses its fictional counterpart as a
version of their earlier coming together: unpremeditated, against
the odds, a shock to everyone but themselves. He might when writing this have recalled the night when Julie Smith had announced
herself as a racist. She had actually done so to Jane, who had accompanied Amis to a women students' sorority evening. Jane, soon
after, reported the exchange to Amis, and they had, as he implies in
his *Memoirs*, felt suddenly distant from, united against, their environment – not unlike the experience of Ronnie and Simona as they
make their escape and drive to Old Boulder Park, a national park in
an adjacent state and make it clear to one another that their relationship transcends circumstances.

Amis and Jane did indeed spend a few days in a 'pseudo-log-
cabin experience' at Standing Stone State Park as a break from the
Nashville experience, which Amis ranks as 'second only to my army
service as the one . . . I would least soon relive'. In the novel the park
provides the first real opportunity for Ronnie and Simona to be
alone together, and Simona is almost magically transformed from a
self-obsessed adolescent into an articulate, intelligent young woman.
She has already exchanged her mid-Atlantic 'drone' for her 'real'
English accent. Amis is again shifting the story back to his relation-

ship with Jane. They tell one another that when they first met each of them knew that something different was about to happen; they talk of their previous relationships and of how meaningless they have been compared with the way they feel now. In *The Anti-Death League* Amis balanced the magic against the less beneficent potential of reality, and he does so again by having the state police arrive at the holiday cabin. They cite the 1920s' Mann Act which forbids the transportation of females across county borders 'for fornicating purposes'. The police have, of course, been paid by Lady Baldock. Ronnie has to choose between allowing them to take Simona home without protest or having his public image tarnished by Lady Baldock's contacts in the media, who would present him as a cross between a kidnapper and a child molester. He gives in, enabling Amis to present himself as a man in love but still, *mea culpa*, imperfect. Ronnie and Simona are, however, reunited in London and the novel ends with, in effect, an exchange between Amis and Jane. He confesses that 'I was a shit when I met you. I still am in lots of ways. But because of you I've had to give up trying to be a dedicated full-time shit.' She, too, admits that she has often 'been a terrible fool' and that 'we'll have to work on each other'. The closing image is of them leaving the novel: 'they went out and in a diagonal shuffle, arms about shoulders, made their ways across the road'.

Amis's idyllic presentations of his new life with Jane are authentic enough. Despite his previous avoidance of monogamy, he wanted this one to work. His only other thoughts about Julie Smith, the beautiful racist, involved what he would have attempted to do a few years before – but now he was with Jane. She, too, felt that this relationship would be different from all that had happened before.

In some ways, however, the recreation of himself as James and Ronnie, figures who become both better men and points of stability for their more vulnerable partners, carried traces of egotism. Amis and Jane were both well-known novelists and their relationship was a public event. After their marriage in 1965 and their brief honeymoon in Brighton they gave an interview for the *Daily Mail*. In this Amis becomes James and Ronnie or at least his projection of himself into them. 'I remember you were very timid when I met you . . . shy and uncertain . . . She was full of doubts . . . Now she's sure . . . Women get sureness and confidence from being happy.' Jane did not counter Amis's view of things, but her responses were brief and diplomatic. 'I agree,' she says, but 'You're more relaxed too.'

Thirty-five years later Jane Howard recalls the early years of their relationship with something resembling sardonic reflection. For one thing, Amis was broke. The house in Maida Vale to which they moved with Monkey in early 1965 involved a £20,000 ten-year lease, which Jane paid. The decision to stay in London was hers. At first Amis still wanted to move to Majorca and live like Graves, and she had to persuade him that this was both impractical and selfish. Her novels sold well enough, but she had not produced one for five years and her income came mainly from her work for the BBC and newspapers. Going abroad would disrupt both the creative and financial elements of her life. And what about Monkey, who would be either left on his own or obliged to go with them to the Mediterranean? Amis abandoned the idea, but it was more difficult for him to abandon the long-established routine of him doing the writing, and previously the teaching, and his wife taking care of everything else, including the children, the food, social arrangements and the house. Jane, to her credit, took on Hilly's role while attempting to maintain her separate life as a writer, and the latter suffered considerably.

Philip and Martin had moved in with them, while Sally lived with Hilly, who after the break-up rented a property in Fulham and supported herself with a job at the Battersea Park Zoo. Eventually she would marry and move to a more secure existence in Essex and then the United States with David Roy Shackleton Bailey, a fellow of Gonville and Caius whom she had met when she lived in Cambridge with Amis.

The two boys, aged respectively fifteen and fourteen in 1963, made the most of the rebellious, narcissistic teen culture of 1960s' London. During their first years with Amis and Jane they attended Sir Walter St Johns School in Battersea, a somewhat ill-disciplined, state-run institution. They attended it infrequently and spent the rest of the time in the houses of friends, listening to music and experimenting with alcohol and occasionally soft drugs. Despite Amis's hardening right-wing attitudes, which included a general loathing for everything that we now associate with the generic terms 'youth' and 'sixties', he was somewhat indulgent with regard to his own sons' behaviour. Martin: 'Philip and I had routinely smoked joints in front of our father. He lurked back from it slightly, with a superstitious air about him, but the disapproval he expressed was also routine' (*Experience*, p. 98).

Initially Jane was resented and blamed by the boys as the principal cause of their parents' break-up. This situation was not improved when she voluntarily took on the role of responsible stepparent. Before their departure for Nashville, Philip had already left home and found a flat of his own. He and Martin had, inevitably, failed most of their O levels, and Jane persuaded Martin to try again. In 1967 she arranged for him to spend a year in Brighton and attend a crammer called Sussex Tutors, run by a friend of hers. In one year he gained five O levels, three A levels and success in the Oxford entrance examination, securing a place at Exeter College for October 1968. Some of this features in Martin's *Experience*, but a more intriguing account of the period, updated to the 1970s, can be found in his first novel, *The Rachel Papers*. Many things are changed, but the unsettled home life, the tolerant if slightly distant, indifferent father, the conflict between Martin's taste for a good time and a desire to succeed, the crammer – moved from Brighton to London – and the Oxford interview are all there. The novel was a success, and its interweaving of autobiographical detail with comic invention reminds one of his father. It was the novel by Martin that Amis liked the most.

During these years, with the exception of *After Julius* (1965), Jane virtually gave up producing fiction. There was no time. She recalls that it took her eight years to introduce Amis to the washing-machine and, unless public transport was found convenient, she was the family chauffeur. In the light of this, Amis's idyllic presentation of their life in his two mid-1960s' novels must be regarded as both an accurate reflection of their relationship and a very selective account of its practical conditions.

13

The Green Man

W HEN exactly the relationship began to turn sour is difficult to specify, but his next two novels, *The Green Man* (1969) and *Girl, 20* (1971), suggest that, at least for Amis, the fairy-tale was beginning to take on less agreeable features.

The Green Man is without doubt his most peculiar, unsettling work of fiction. It could also be regarded as one of his most auto-biographical, not because it is founded upon particular events from his life – far from it – but because it tells us a lot more than anything else he has written about the way in which his state of mind and his capacity to create were interwoven.

It was part of his strategy of alternating novels involving realist pictures of contemporary life with more idiosyncratic, experi-mental pieces. It was the second of the latter and was far more bizarre and disturbing than *The Anti-Death League*. He began writ-ing it soon after he finished *I Want It Now*. Its first-person narrator, Maurice Allington, is obliged to confront all of the opposites, the apparently irreconcilable antitheses of his, and Amis's, life, includ-ing monogamy and infidelity, God and atheism, sincerity and fabri-cation, verifiable truth and palpable fiction.

Maurice Allington owns a hotel and restaurant called the Green Man, forty miles from London and within easy reach for the culi-nary sophisticates of Cambridge. We know the location of the

Green Man, the price of its eel soup and the unsound quality of its white Burgundies before we encounter Maurice: an excerpt from *The Good Food Guide* precedes the narrative. Maurice begins:

> The point about white Burgundies is that I hate them myself. I take whatever my wine supplier will let me have at a good price (which I would never dream of doing with any other drinkable). I enjoyed seeing those glasses of Chablis or Pouilly Fuissé, so closely resembling a blend of cold chalk soup and alum cordial with an additive or two to bring it to the colour of children's pee, being peered and sniffed at, rolled around the shrinking tongue and forced down somehow by parties of young technology dons from Cambridge or junior television producers and their girls. Minor, harmless compensations of this sort are all too rare in a modern innkeeper's day.

This mixture of candour and detail sets the standard for Maurice's account. In the next five pages he tells of his family: his wife Joyce; Amy, his thirteen-year-old daughter from his first marriage; his eighty-year-old father. He confides in the reader: he drinks a bottle of whisky a day and he intends to have sex with 'tall, blonde and full-breasted Diana', the wife of his closest friend. All of this is shot through with asides on the varying qualities of his pork and salmon dishes, the gullish philistinism of his clientele and the 'hypocrisy' of having *sauce vinaigrette* with avocado pears. We might not like Maurice Allington, but he is disarmingly real.

Why, we wonder, does Maurice feel the need to confess, albeit unapologetically, while embedding these confidences in meticulous detail? He leaves nothing out of his account, partly because he needs to reassure himself that his story is true. Maurice is given to entertaining his guests, particularly Americans, with the tale of Thomas Underhill, who owned the inn in the seventeenth century, made a pact with the devil, sacrificed his wife and monitored the

murderous activities of a wood creature from whom the inn takes
its name. Maurice's tale to the reader involves his discovery that the
legend is true and that Underhill has returned.

For the first half of the narrative Maurice allows us to share his
initial scepticism. He has seen figures, shapes, oddly coloured birds.
But he is in a peculiar condition. His father has just died, his domestic life is a mess and he drinks too much. Soon after he has seduced
Diana she, too, sees a terrifying, not-quite-human figure in the lane;
but so what? This is an exciting element of their shared deception:
'she had demonstrated a fresh superiority by seeing a ghost when I
had not. Did she now think she had really seen a ghost?'

In Chapter 4 any ambiguities are removed. From his sitting-
room Maurice witnesses the freezing of time and space. 'Down to
the left, forty or fifty yards away across the grass, a couple of wax-
works cast their shadows, the seated one with a hand stuck out in
the direction of something, probably a cup of tea, that the standing
one was offering it, and were Lucy and Nick', his daughter-in-law
and son. In his sitting-room is a young man, whom Maurice
describes with customary attention to detail: about twenty-eight,
clean-shaven, good teeth, silver-grey suit, black knitted tie, humorous but not very trustworthy face. The young man is God.

> 'Are you a messenger?' I asked.
>
> 'No. I decided to come uh . . . in person.'
>
> 'I see. Can I offer you a drink?'
>
> 'Yes thank you. I'm fully corporeal. I was going to warn you
> against making the mistake of supposing that I came from inside
> your mind, but you've saved me that trouble. I'll join you in a little
> Scotch, if I may.'

Maurice achieves a remarkable balance between the cool
verisimilitude of his account and its totally implausible subject. He
passes God a glass of Scotch.

The hand that came up and took it, and the wrist and lower fore-arm that disappeared into the silver-grey shirt cuff were by no means complete, so that the fingers clicked against the glass, and at the same time I caught a whiff of that worst odour in the world, which I had not smelt since accompanying a party of Free French through the Falaise Gap in 1944. In a moment it was gone, and fingers, hand and everything else were as they had been before.

'That was unnecessary', I said, sitting down again.

'Don't believe it, old boy. Puts things on the right footing between us. This isn't just a social call, you know. Cheers.'

The quality of this passage exists in its combination of empirical detail and something that Maurice cannot describe. The hand and arm are 'by no means complete', but the precise nature of this phenomenon is registered only in allusions that Maurice can share with the reader: the fingers click against the glass as if Christ's nails are still there, and the 'worst odour' recalls equally indescribable events from the last war. Amis's signals unit passed through the so-called Falaise Gap a day or so after allied artillery had virtually wiped our several German regiments. The remains, cattle, horses and human beings, were mixed together, and the smell made it difficult to breathe. God, it seems, is quite capable of incorporating the most distressing aspects of the human condition.

The question raised by Maurice's narrative is double-edged. One wonders how Amis expected contemporary readers to respond to it and also how it reflected his state of mind. With regard to the latter, there are a number of parallels between Maurice and his creator. In an interview with Clive James five years later (*New Review*, July 1974, pp. 21–8), Amis told of how when planning the book he had speculated on ways of transforming the ghost story from a tolerated sub-genre into something that readers would have to take as seriously as mainstream fiction. His solution was to pose a question: 'What happens when the man who sees ghosts is an alcoholic?' In the interview this figure is treated as an invention, a hypothesis, but in fact Amis was talking about himself. By the end of the 1960s his drinking habits were beginning to endanger his health and, on occasions, his sanity. Jane Howard testifies to the fact that he would often match the bottle-a-day intake of Maurice. The bouts of anxiety attacks that in the late 1940s he had feared were symptoms of mental disorder returned with a vengeance. Maurice suffers from 'jactitations', an uncontrollable twitching of limbs frequently accompanied by 'hypnogogic hallucinations', and so did Amis. For both, the condition was exacerbated by excessive boozing. Jane remembers that Amis would sometimes hallucinate. On several occasions he became incapable of distinguishing between actual and imagined events. Once he spent a day arguing with her on who exactly had attended the previous evening's dinner party, when no such gathering had actually taken place.

Clearly then, Amis is making use of his own experience when he raises the question of whether Maurice's other-worldly encounters are real or imagined, and at least one reviewer responded appropriately. Michael Radcliffe in *The Times* argued that 'In relating supernatural hallucinations to the psychology of a selfish and unhappy man [Amis] has moved towards the tough metaphor of disintegration.' But Radcliffe's is obviously a misreading, because at least one other person in the narrative can authenticate Maurice's visions; his daughter Amy is pursued by the Satanic beast. Radcliffe evidently regards the novel as a contribution to that respectable vein of modern fiction in which religion and the supernatural are contrasted with the rational, secular mood of the twentieth century, recalling perhaps Waugh's *The Ordeal of Gilbert Pinfold* or more recent work by Iris Murdoch such as *The Bell* (1958) and *The Time of Angels* (1966). In short, Maurice, throughout his account, is mad. Amis in a 1975 interview disagreed. 'It all really happens . . . none of what is recounted happens only in the hero's mind' (*Contemporary Literature*, 16 January 1975). The cautiously ambiguous phrasing of this raises two possibilities: it happened also in *my* mind or it might actually have happened.

What precisely was going through Amis's mind when he wrote *The Green Man* will remain a matter for speculation, and the novel and its circumstances invite us to speculate. Unlike his two previous books, it is not a tribute to his relationship with Jane, and although he kept her aware of what he was doing he did not invite her to participate. It resembles in some ways his 1950s' habit of both involving and reinventing himself, but it is much more bizarre and unsettling. Maurice's pub-restaurant is a fashionable spot, mentioned in *The Good Food Guide*, but Maurice himself has no interest in or taste for the continental concoctions that secure his reputation. He prefers a cheese and onion sandwich and occasionally a very hot curry. So did Amis. Twenty years later, when he became restaurant critic for the *Illustrated London News* and *Harpers and Queen*, he made full use of his talents for fiction and privately looked back on *The Green Man* as amusingly prescient. On the one hand, the topic of food is part of the fabric of real life which underpins Maurice's fantastic experiences, but at the same time it introduces Maurice as a person who is playing roles.

He first has sex with his friend's wife Diana on the day after his father's death. It is surely not a coincidence that when his own father died in April 1963 Amis was living with Hilly and having an affair with Jane. The circumstances differed in that William Amis had left the Kingsley household three years earlier and was living in London, but the differences are equalled by parallels. When Amis Senior lived with his son's family the situation was endurable, yet for father and son uneasy. Maurice, like his author, is decent and tolerant enough with his father, but his description of him as 'somebody whose life I did not understand' is a fair description of Amis's relationship with William. When William died Amis was absent, which seemed to him painfully appropriate, because even when they lived together there seemed always to be an impassible distance between them. And so it is with Maurice. He is perplexed by the fact that when his father dies his thoughts attend as much to the continuance of his affair with Diana as to any real sense of loss; he is perplexed but not particularly saddened.

Maurice's son Nick and his wife visit him for a while and at one point Nick tells him that

> You're just too lazy and arrogant and equal to everything (you think) to take the trouble to notice people like your son, and your wife, and deem them bloody well worthy of being let into the great secret of how you feel and what you think about everything, in fact what you're like.

This could be a description of Amis both during his marriage to Hilly and eventually during his time with Jane. Martin, like Nick, did not dislike his father, but he was frequently angered by the way in which he regarded his own world as more important than the one he was supposed to share with his closest family. And one might recall here Jane's selfless intervention in the chaotic lives of Amis's sons, particularly Martin. Jane had effectively returned Martin to the schedule of study and examinations, and when he triumphantly announced to his father that he had got a place at Exeter Amis asked, 'Exeter University?' 'No, Exeter College, Oxford.' The fact that his son was sitting the Oxford entrance examination had slipped his mind.

Maurice's daughter Amy is thirteen, Sally Amis's age when he began to plan the novel (and one cannot help but notice the redistribution of vowels and consonants from Sally Amis to Amy Allington). Amy is really the only of Maurice's friends and family to cause him a genuine feeling of guilt. He says at one point that he has failed to 'give her a life', by which he means that while he cares for her he has never seriously attempted to help her through the loss of her mother or shown much concern about what she thinks and feels.

Sally was the only of Amis's children to stay with Hilly. She visited her father's house once a week, but in 1968 Hilly's husband accepted an academic post in the United States, and Sally went with them. While he was writing about a man who is experiencing a distressing sense of distance between himself and his daughter, Amis had to deal with the fact that the weekly encounters with his own would now cease.

Maurice Allington is certainly a representation of Kingsley Amis. Amis wrote in 1972 ('Who or What Was It?') that 'I'm more like [him] than I'm like most of the others', and he raises the question of why he chose to fictionalize so many of his more disagreeable features. Contemporary journalists and reviewers remained unaware of the direct parallels between the events and figures of the novel and Amis's private life. For his family and for Jane in particular, the resemblances would be clear, but the book can hardly be regarded as a penitential, self-reproachful exercise. At the end Maurice feels slightly chastened, but he has not changed, and Joyce leaves him. Moreover, Amis's decision to interweave the harsh reality of his own existence with a resurrected seventeenth-century Satanist, a murderous wood creature and a conversation with God might easily be regarded by the participants in the former as further evidence of his solipsistic, self-indulgent predispositions. They might well have questioned the sincerity of a private act of confession which involves itself quite so much with the unreal and the fantastic.

The Green Man was the closest that Amis ever came to the kind of self-referential 'writing about writing' exercise that we associate with modernism. He did this not as a purely aesthetic gesture but as a means of considering the extent to which his fiction had for him become as significant as the material upon which it drew. In Chapter 1, before Maurice discovers that the stories about Underhill are true and that he has become part of them, he reflects upon the tangible elements of his life – his father's death, his acts of sexual betrayal, his distance from those closest to him – and considers what a writer would do with them. 'A man has only to feel some emotion, any emotion, anything differentiated at all, and spend a minute speculating on how this would be rendered in a novel . . . to grasp the pitiful inadequacy of all prose fiction to the task it sets itself.' This is Amis speaking through Maurice, and he is saying that however well we transmute life into fiction there will always be a falsification of genuine emotion and feeling. Amis had, during the 1950s, effectively reinvented and sanitized his commitment to Hilly, and in his two novels prior to *The Green Man* he had projected his new relationship with Jane into a similarly uncontaminated idyll. When Maurice first has sex with Diana he chooses to do so in a wooded vale, a peculiar choice given that the Green Man is a hotel with plenty of empty rooms and beds. Diana comments on this, and asks him if he has visited this location before for the same purpose. He admits that he has, and so had Amis in *The Anti-Death League* when he used an almost identical situation to cement the relationship between Catherine and James, Jane and himself. In the earlier novel he had qualified the blissful optimism of the moment with the discovery of Catherine's cancer. In *The Green Man* Maurice has chosen the site for adultery not because he has used it before – he lies about this – but because it is close to the churchyard in which Underhill the Satanist is buried.

Jane Howard states that during their marriage Amis had 'at least two' brief affairs and that by the end of the 1960s his previous commitment to monogamy and fidelity was beginning to disintegrate. It thus seems appropriate that Maurice should have decided to indulge his lustful impulses in a place that is adjacent to the grave of the most horrible fictional presence that he has ever created. When he first meets the resurrected Satanist Maurice asks Underhill why exactly he has been selected as his contact in the mortal world. Underhill answers, 'How have I chosen you, when it is you that have each time come in search of me?' In the light of this, we should perhaps reconsider Amis's own claim that the implausible events of the novel 'all really happened'. Amis in *The Green Man* had, as Underhill puts it, gone in search of a figure, a state of mind, that seemed to resist all attempts at reform or redemption. Underhill, the creature and God did indeed exist, because Amis had created them, just as he had spent most of his adult life involved in a world where invention had become a version of experience.

In Chapter 2, when Maurice has discovered that his supernatural visitations are real, he returns to his earlier question of how literature can alter actuality. 'Father, Joyce, Underhill, Margaret, the wood creature, Amy, Diana: a novelist would represent all these as somehow related, somehow all parts of some single puzzle which some one key would somehow unlock.' Amis has not exactly unlocked the puzzle, but he has, in creating Maurice, made clear that he understands its nature. Underhill, via Maurice, is Amis's private demon, an exaggeration of all the apparently innate and irreversible characteristics that make him who he is.

It is an intriguing experience to read *The Green Man* alongside the article 'Godforsaken' which was written almost two decades afterwards. In the latter he again becomes a version of Maurice, a man whose rational atheistic state of mind is continuously challenged by the knowledge that 'human beings without faith are the poorer for it in every part of their lives'. Particularly intriguing is Amis's assertion that it is impossible to properly appreciate, say, seventeenth-century devotional verse without in some way sharing the poet's vision of the presence to whom it is addressed. Maurice, despite the fact that he does not believe in God, is visited by Him and God himself picks up on Maurice's earlier reflections on making literature and understanding existence.

> 'The whole thing's a game, is it?' I had returned with the drinks.
> 'In the sense that it's not a particularly, uh . . . edifying or significant business, it is, yes. In other ways it's not unlike an art and a work of art rolled into one . . . '

'Your friend Milton, for instance.' The young man nodded over
at my bookshelves. 'He caught onto the idea of the work of art and
the game and the rules and so forth.'

Amis had studied *Paradise Lost* at Oxford and taught it in
Swansea and Cambridge and he was aware of how its apparent
meaning had altered with history. Post-enlightenment Romantics
such as Blake and Shelley had found in it a radical questioning of
Christianity, and modern critics such as Empson had argued that
Milton had actually pre-empted twentieth-century rational scepticism. *Paradise Lost* is a particularly apt point of comparison with
Amis's own novel, in the sense that readers of the former have never
been able to agree on whether its author believed that the story was
true.

Neither God nor Maurice comments further on the enigmatic
reference to Milton, and one can only assume that Amis's God is a
reflection of his own eccentric brand of unbelief, that if we take
seriously the parallel between the universe and a work of art then it
is possible that the former too might also have been created by
someone or something. God even talks like an artist, responding to
Maurice's question as to whether there is an afterlife with 'I don't
know. I'll have to see.'

Despite the fact that Amis seems intent on testing the reader's
credulity, Maurice Allington is by far the most comprehensive and
unsympathetic version of himself that he had so far created. Maurice's existence is comprised of two complementary states of mind.
One involves the people that make up his world and with whom he
deals through subterfuge, diplomacy and the selective disclosure of
facts and feelings. The other involves him telling his story to the
reader with unapologetic candour and attention to detail. This is
very different from the technique of Amis's only previous first-
person narrator, John Lewis, who protected himself from the
reader's judgemental inclinations with the dispersal of hard facts

into guileless self-mockery. Moreover, Lewis's story was a sanitized, reformed version of the truths on which it was based, a tactical move that Amis hoped would reinforce his spurious claims of commitment to Hilly. Maurice's almost obsessive concern with truth is, for the reader, an intriguing vehicle for the more implausible elements of his tale. For Jane, it was her husband's perception of himself and her, and it sometimes involved grotesque refashionings of both.

The most significant of these was Amis's recreation of Jane as two women, Joyce and Diana. Joyce embodies Jane's combination of love, tolerance and endurance. Both worry about their husband's state of mind, health and self-destructive habits, take care of the mundane day-to-day chores that existed outside his selfish solipsistic lifestyle, and both do their best, with some success, as replacement mother figures for his children. Diana is Maurice's exciting excursion from monogamy and domesticity, much as Jane had been five years before, and there are more ingrained similarities. Joyce is offered Jane's more endearing qualities, while Diana is provided with those that had begun to irritate Amis. Diana is egotistical, her linguistic mannerisms are at once intrusive and theatrical, and she is intrigued by Maurice's inner turmoil in a way which, for Amis, seemed pretentious and hypocritical. Four years after their final break-up, Amis openly based Nowell Hutchinson of *Stanley and the Women* (1984) on Jane, and Nowell is Diana reborn. Significantly he confided to his official biographer, Eric Jacobs, that they should have broken up earlier than they did; 'about 1970 would be right', a year after *The Green Man* was published. Maurice attempts to persuade Joyce and Diana that a sexual threesome would for each of them be exciting and, in a perverse way, honest. This happens, with the result that the two women are far more attracted to and interested in each other than in Maurice, and soon afterwards he loses both of them.

Roughly summarized, the short story 'Who or What Was It?'

involves Amis, as Amis, telling of how he and Jane had discovered and stayed overnight in an inn-restaurant called the Green Man, run by a man called Allington (John, not Maurice), whom they never meet, managed by a person called Palmer (George rather than the David of the novel) and with a barman named Fred.

Amis asks Jane if they have crossed into some kind of parallel universe in which fiction becomes fact, and she suggests that he checks if the copy of the *Daily Telegraph* in the reception is the same as the one he has read that morning. Its provenance is confirmed by an article on trade unions by Peregrine Worsthorne which Amis had indeed read earlier that day. Worsthorne is referred to in the story as Perry, without explanation. He was in fact a friend of Amis's and Jane's who had stayed with them for a few months four years earlier when his own marriage was breaking up. Amis remains intrigued. He rings 'Bob Conquest . . . an old chum of mine' to ask him to drive up and confirm that all of this is real. Bob is out. He phones home in an attempt to reach Monkey, Jane's brother, and is answered by his son Philip who is looking after the house while Monkey is off for the night at a party. Neither can help him out. For no apparent reason Amis also tells of how Jane does all the driving, of how he will never travel by aeroplane, of how he is of a nervous disposition and can never be left alone at night in a house. All of this is true, but for whom? Most readers of the story would know nothing of Amis's private life – he certainly did not refer to this in any of his interviews or articles – and would probably regard these details simply as part of the naturalistic fabric of the tale.

What happens next is, to say the least, bizarre. Amis is convinced that the inn is a real version of his invention, and he goes outside to wait for a visitation from the murderous wood creature from whom it takes its name. The creature arrives and is seen off by Amis, in the manner of Maurice.

In the novel Maurice is told by Underhill that his only means of protection from the encircling Satanic forces is a silver cross that has been buried with him in the village churchyard. In the middle of the night, Maurice, accompanied by Diana, reopens Underhill's grave and takes out the cross, which does indeed protect him from the beast. Maurice does not fully explain why he chooses Diana as his assistant, but the implication is that she is attuned to, even complicit in, the element of Maurice's character that has drawn Underhill to him. In the short story the parallel between Jane and Diana is reinforced, when Amis borrows from her a gold cross, bequeathed by her mother, which she always wears. This, too, causes the beast to dematerialize.

Back in their room Amis tells Jane what has happened, and she informs him that he has obviously imagined it, given that at the time he was supposed to be dealing with the wood creature he was in fact with her. The cross which Amis claimed had disappeared along with the beast is back on its chain around her neck. Their argument over whether the event was real or imagined is, as Jane can confirm, based upon the actual exchange which took place after Amis had recollected the dinner party which had never happened. The only element that is purely fictional is the cross, which resembled nothing that Jane had inherited from her mother.

At the end of the story Amis asks, 'Who or what was it that had taken on my shape to enter that bedroom, talk to Jane with my voice, and share her bed for at any rate a few minutes?', because who or whatever it was had done more than sleep, and Jane has been to see their GP.

It was negative then, I said. Yes, Jane said.

Well, that's it. A relief of course. But in one way rather disappointing.

14

Girl, 20

Dᴜʀɪɴɢ the 1940s and 1950s Amis was a prodigious role-player. His talents as an imitator and his private world of dissembling and fabrication fed his fiction. With Jane, things began to change. He believed, or rather he made himself believe, that he could distil his conflicts and polarities into the essential Amis, particularly in his commitment to her, and his 1960s' novels testify to this valiant struggle. In the end he failed, and his writings offer an intriguing commentary on his realization that he was facing an impossible task.

The Anti-Death League, I Want It Now and *The Green Man* record the early years; optimism and actuality are in hand-to-hand combat. *Girl, 20* is an acknowledgement of defeat.

The novel involves two principal male characters, both of whom reflect features of Amis. Sir Roy Vandervane is a 53-year-old composer and conductor, and his friend and confidant Douglas Yandell, who tells the story, is a music critic and twenty years younger. Their age difference functions as an autobiographical trick of the light, because Amis carries forward to Vandervane many of the temperamental and behavioural features of himself from his early thirties: he is an irresponsible, egotistical lecher. Yandell embodies elements of the more detached, phlegmatic presence of his author, circa 1971, then only a few years younger than Vandervane. This recycling of the past and the present involves no particular resolutions of the personal crises that underpin it. The book is a meditation upon ineluctable moods and conditions.

Its settings and locations are its most explicit autobiographical component. It begins with Yandell receiving a phone message asking him to visit his old friend, Vandervane, with whom he has been out of touch for several years, at his manorial residence on the outskirts of London. Yandell has not been there before, and his account of the place is an almost exact representation of the house in which Jane and Amis lived from 1967 to 1975.

When they returned from the United States in 1968 they began looking for a larger house. The one in Maida Vale was not big enough to accommodate its expanding number of permanent and occasional residents. Monkey, like Amis, worked from home, and his friend the jazz musician Sargy Mann had moved in while the Amises were away. Martin would soon go up to Oxford, but he would continue to live with Amis and Jane during vacations, and Jane's mother, Katherine Howard, then in her seventies, had joined them permanently. On top of this, Amis and Jane enjoyed having guests for the weekend or longer.

Gladsmuir in Barnet was a detached, Georgian country house. To its front were the semi-rural vistas of Hertfordshire; at its back was London, and a twenty-minute walk would take you to a tube station. At £47,000 it was a bargain. Hilly's recent marriage had provided her with financial independence from Amis, Jane's sale of the lease of Maida Vale raised £10,000, and Amis's share of the film rights for *The Egyptologists*, plus his move from Gollancz to the more lucrative Cape, made the purchase feasible.

The eight years in Barnet were pivotal in a number of ways. When they arrived, the fun and optimism of Amis's first three years with Jane were still the predominant features of their relationship, but by the time they moved to Hampstead in 1975 they were both trying to preserve something that had virtually disappeared. *The*

Green Man records the early signs of disintegration and *Girl, 20* casts an even more pessimistic shadow which would continue to fall across his fiction until the mid-1980s.

For a while Barnet seemed to indicate new beginnings. The setting and atmosphere of the house bespoke a lifestyle that Amis had witnessed and written about (Julian Ormerod of *Take a Girl Like You*) but never experienced. It was set in nine acres of landscaped gardens, and an attached cottage would be occupied by a resident housekeeper. In the main house there was a library, a drawing-room, dining-room, six bedrooms and three bathrooms. Amis had a study on the first floor and Jane had one upstairs. The building dated from the late eighteenth century, and Jane discovered from the deeds that it had once been owned by Frances Trollope, mother of the more famous Anthony and herself a prodigious writer and literary hostess. Then the house had been called Lemmons, and the Amises officially renamed it as such. Its past association with two literary figures, one male and one female, seemed a good omen. Amis's feeling of optimism is reflected in a letter to Larkin (11 May 1969). 'This is a bloody great mansion, in the depths of the country though only 15 miles from the centre, with lots of room for you to come and spend the night.'

In 1967, just before the move, Cape published a collection of Amis's poems of the previous decade, and the more significant of these dated from his time with Hilly. The title of the new volume, *A Look Round the Estate*, in one sense indicated that Amis regarded these pieces and their background as something he could now reflect upon from a safe distance, but it also echoed an oft-repeated joke. Lemmons and its grounds were so vast that he would sometimes announce, usually when going to the bathroom, that he was taking 'a look round the estate'. For Amis mild self-parody usually signalled a state of optimistic contentment. Four years later Vandervane, too, seems to be enjoying his role as lord of the manor – like Amis his background is lower middle class – but in reality Vandervane's opulent home life, his version of Lemmons, is a rapidly disintegrating bulwark against a more powerful feeling of impatient discontentment.

The Girl, 20 of the title is actually seventeen, and Sylvia Meers is an awful combination of the anarchy, narcissism and hostile self-indulgence that, in Amis's view, were the predominant features of contemporary youth culture. She is also Vandervane's mistress. Amis in 1971 was not having an affair with a seventeen-year-old nymphet, but his creation of Sylvia was one element of the novel's private investigation of a state of mind that involved hopelessness transmogrified into self-loathing. Vandervane is a middle-aged version of the Amis of the 1950s, and he is also a nightmarish embodiment of how age can be destructive in a way that is worse than physical. Vandervane, fifty-three, seems to be facing a world that is a malicious parody of his past. His son, aged six, frequently tells members of the family and visitors to fuck off, refuses to go to school if he is so disinclined and urinates regularly on the bathroom floor. Ashley, too, is part of the reshuffled time frame in which Amis's remembrance of past irresponsibility becomes Vandervane's present. Penny, Vandervane's daughter, finds solace from her disjointed world in heroin. He also has a grown-up son, Christopher, who features briefly and states that 'He's always let us do exactly as we like, and we liked that until we realized that it was all just less trouble for him' (an exact paraphrase of the comment made by Allington's son, Nick). This picture of two sons and one daughter variously damaged, unsettled and angered by their father's self-obsessed indifference can hardly be a coincidence. Amis's own tendencies towards hedonistic irresponsibility had been fuelled partly by his rebellious attitude to his own father's rectitude, but at the same time William Amis had, through his careful encouragement of Amis's intellectual talents, inculcated a sense of balance. Amis, although he rarely acknowledged this, had benefited from his father's sponsorship of his school and university career. He had learned that careless indulgence had to be bought by an equal commitment to hard work. Amis had not created the same productive tension in the early lives of his own children. They had been allowed to do more or less as they liked and, particularly with Philip and Sally, drugs and drink had become a detrimental feature of their personal and professional lives. Hilly and Jane, like Vandervane's wife Kitty, tried their best, but without the assistance of Amis. Martin, the successful one, is almost certainly Christopher, who, despite his father, has made a life for himself and feels confident enough to rebuke him.

Vandervane's reputation, indeed his knighthood, have been secured by his involvement with classical music. Now he has put together a piece called 'Elevations 9', a horrible interweaving of classical allusions and rock music. Its performance is Vandervane's denouement. Afterwards he is beaten up by drunken, disappointed rock fans and his much-loved Stradivarius is smashed. Amis projects himself into Vandervane in a manner that is candid and hypothetical, guilt-ridden and unreal. Vandervane's lifestyle, involving fame, sex with whoever is willing and insidious, addictive deception, mirrors Amis's during the 1950s, but society appears to have caught up with him and seems intent on reaping a kind of nastily appropriate vengeance. In 1970–1 irresponsible selfishness had for many people become a licensed, almost obligatory condition. It is as though, through Vandervane, Amis is confronting a bizarre state of retribution. His self-indulgent past has become a present that is shared by many others much younger than himself. As a payment for rejoining, officially, this network he must renounce all of his more enduring, stable elements.

Amis, unlike Vandervane, did not in any way defer to the popular culture of the 1960s and early 1970s. He treated it with a mixture of indifference and loathing, and he was particularly angered by the growing tendency to regard disposable entertainment as art or political commentary. He wrote to Larkin, 'Oh fuck the Beatles.

I'd like to push my bum into John L's face for forty-eight hours or so, as a protest against all the war and violence in the world' (19 April 1969). His views are succinctly stated in a poem called 'Shitty', written at the same time as the novel, in which he lists the worst conflations of mass culture and artistic pretension.

> ... soccer stars
> Soccer crowds, bedizened bushheads
> Jerking over their guitars,
>
> German tourists, plastic roses,
> Face of Mao and face of Che,
> Women wearing curtains, blankets,
> Beckett at the ICA.
>
> High rise blocks and action paintings,
> Sculptures made from wire and lead ...

Vandervane's study involves similar juxtapositions, but with a particular emphasis upon how the dreadful present has entered a hungry relationship with the more creditable past. On his desk a bust of Mao faces one of Beethoven, and on the wall a poster announcing a Nikisch concert of 1913 is next to one promoting an anti-Vietnam war demonstration of 1969.

When tackled by Yandell, Vandervane half concedes that his energetic espousal of contemporary trends is a façade and by implication that fame and self-gratification are more important to him than artistic principles.

Yandell operates rather like Dante in his tour of Purgatory, distressed by what he witnesses while maintaining a self-serving detachment from it all. He is at once saddened and fascinated by Vandervane, and the damage he causes to those closest to him, but they share a characteristic that unites them with their creator.

Yandell's girlfriend, after splitting up with him, tells him that his apparent concern with other people's problems is a disguise for solipsistic disengagement. Another character informs him of 'what an extraordinary number of things you don't think about and haven't got time for . . . I suspect that you must find a great deal to occupy you in other ways. Your music and all that.' For 'music' we might substitute 'novels'.

Enough clues and oblique allusions are sewn into this novel to prompt anyone close to Amis to look at Yandell and Vandervane as a complex double-image of the man himself. Yandell, when not doing newspaper reviews, is writing a book on the composer Weber. This might seem a random, peripheral citation, except that Jane during their early years had persuaded Amis to move beyond his private canon of favourite composers. One figure whose work he had never listened to before, and who with her encouragement he grew to enjoy and respect, was Weber. Yandell reports on the chaotic Vandervane household as someone seeing it for the first time, and his description of his initial encounter with the building itself carries more than an echo of someone being shown the place by an estate agent. And were does Yandell live? Maida Vale, the Amises' home before Lemmons.

Vandervane is indifferent to the distress he has caused his wife and family, and Yandell reports this from the outside, as if Amis is making himself revisit Lemmons as a more objective witness. For Yandell the place seems to speak of imminent catastrophe. He finds 'used crockery, brimming ashtrays, vases of decaying flowers', 'naked gramophone records' on the floor and all around 'a lot of empty whisky and wine bottles'. The house and its inhabitants appear to him as a project begun with enthusiasm but gone into reverse, 'a tiny elementary universe of despair and hatred'. Yandell's picture of the Vandervane household corresponds closely with Amis's growing sense of disillusionment, but it is a selective, partial reflection of Lemmons. It was generally agreed that since

Amis earned more money than the others he should be allowed more time and space to get on with his writing and spared the routine domestic chores. There was a resident housekeeper, Mrs Uniacke, but much of her time was spent helping out with Jane's ailing mother. Jane, assisted by Monkey, Sargy and, when at home, Martin, was responsible for the upkeep of the main house. Yandell's account of shambolic degeneracy is accurate enough, except that Amis was its principal cause and focus. He would leave his clothes all over the floor and expect replacements to be available as if by magic. (This habit is distilled into Vandervane's obsession with clean underwear, which intensifies with the likely prospect of adultery and provides a warning signal for his wife Kitty.) Amis's study was often a concentrated version of Yandell's general description of the house, with empty bottles, used ashtrays, discarded drafts and books randomly distributed across the desk and the carpet. Jane cleaned up.

Amis's recreation of himself in Yandell and Vandervane resembles his use of Joyce and Diana in *The Green Man* as distant but complementary versions of Jane. Yandell, Vandervane and Vandervane's wife Kitty form a triangle in which Kitty is Jane and the two men represent increasingly discordant elements of her relationship with Amis. Kitty continuously seeks Yandell's assistance in her attempts to save the marriage, while at the same time Vandervane uses his old friend to provide alibis for his meetings with Sylvia. Amis was becoming aware that his attempts to reinvent himself as an archetype of responsible monogamous commitment were failing and would fail. He and Jane were almost fifty, both had experienced disastrous marriages, and they knew that this one was effectively their last chance. Yandell's alliance with Kitty is an acknowledgement by Amis that they would go on trying, despite the odds.

15

The Riverside Villas Murder

H IS previous four novels had charted the progress of his relationship with Jane, but after *Girl, 20* there seemed little more
to be said. The situation had neither improved nor deteriorated. So
for the first time Amis chose to set a novel in the past, his own.

Before this his father had featured only twice in his writing,
obliquely in *The Green Man* and more candidly in the poem 'In
Memoriam W.R.A.' In the closing lines of the latter Amis had been
honest enough about how his father's death had caused him to feel
a retrospective sense of loss and failure, a missed opportunity.

> I'm sorry you had to die
> To make me sorry
> You're not here now.

The Riverside Villas Murder supplements regret and belated
affection with reinvention.

The setting is autobiographical. The central character, Peter
Furneaux, is fourteen, and in 1936, the year of the story, so was
Amis. The family home in Riverside Villas is an exact reproduction
of the post-First World War two-up-two-down semi in which the
Amises lived in Norbury, and Peter's school, Blackfriar's Grammar,
is a version of Amis's City of London alma mater. His father,

always referred to as Captain Furneaux (ex-RFC), is William Amis. Peter has difficult exchanges with him on everything from cricket to correct English, in much the same way that Kingsley and William had engaged in regular bouts of verbal warfare. Yet between the fictional father and son there is a first unspoken and eventually acknowledged feeling of warmth and closeness which Amis later admitted, in his *Memoirs*, that he only really felt with hindsight.

Amis's mother's name, Peggy, features, but as that of his pregnant aunt. Mrs Furneaux is never given a Christian name and is absent for much of the story, looking after her sister. In a sense Amis is making space for a one-to-one with his recreated father, but he is also juggling with memories of how he felt about his parents and hypotheses on how he might have felt had things been different. Early in the book Peter reflects upon his experience as an only child, on having 'the whole of your parents reserved for you instead of divided up into three, say'. He tries to imagine how a brother or sister might have altered his life and his relationship with his parents, but since he has never had either he can't. Peter 'liked his father', but 'would have preferred on the whole to have him as an uncle, even one living in the same house. His mother he quite loved but there again she talked to him about a lot of things he could not remember afterwards, even the next minute.'

Peter's reflections are as poignant an evocation of Amis's childhood as the later recollections of the *Memoirs*. Peter's anonymous, slightly spectral mother, whom he 'quite loved', embodies, or rather disembodies, Amis's ambivalent feelings about his own. Amis appreciated his mother's almost obsessive concern for his health and welfare, but he also felt that as a person he did not really know her. The notion of Peter's father as an uncle, of the close, affectionate type, is a convenient summary of the feelings of retrospective affection and distance that attended his memories of William.

Before this novel Amis had said practically nothing in print about his childhood. When the book was published, and indeed afterwards, he cautiously avoided any reference to its autobiographical parallels.

Amis had first written to John Betjeman after the latter's enthusiastic review of *Lucky Jim*. They became friends and communicated regularly by letter. Amis had sent Betjeman an early review copy of *The Riverside Villas Murder* and asked for his impressions, partly because Betjeman had as an adult known the period that Amis was so meticulously attempting to recreate from a combination of childhood memories and research. Betjeman wrote back, twice, praising Amis's 'vigorous style', 'narrative power' and the 'poetry of your acute observation'. Amis replied, thanking Betjeman for 'getting it *right*, seeing what I was trying to do' (Amis Collection, Huntington Library). In fact Betjeman saw very little of what his friend was trying to do.

In an interview soon after publication Amis made much of how the novel was a new departure, a murder mystery whose plotlines would be far more significant than those of mainstream fiction. The specifics of who committed the crime, how and what clues were left, would effectively determine the behaviour, the future and the emotional condition of the characters involved. In no other type of fiction, he suggested, is the disclosure of verifiable fact so closely intertwined with the disclosure of personality. He also spoke of how the nature of the project had involved him in more research than ever before. He had chosen a date, 1 June 1936, and read through that month's back numbers of *The Times*, *Punch* and *Radio Times*. He wanted his invention of the narrative of the crime to be accompanied by the actualities of its setting – other crimes reported in the papers, sport, weather, what people would be listening to on the radio.

All of this, the exchanges with Betjeman and the detailed description in the interview of his method, is true, but it is the truth carefully marshalled as camouflage for what really lay at the heart of the project: Amis's exploration of his own past and a search for some explanation of his present.

The murder of the title is committed by the Furneaux's neighbour, Mrs Trevelyan, who kills herself before she is charged. The victim is her lover, Inman, and a few days before the crime she introduces Peter to sex. Mrs Trevelyan is presented as a woman whose intelligence along with her emotional and sexual unorthodoxies are at odds with the world in which she lives. This is suburban, lower-middle-class London of the 1930s, in which sex occurs but is never spoken of. Amis in the *Memoirs* recalls an incident in which he is in the kitchen with his mother and a neighbour who, apparently, is about to say something about her friend's honeymoon. His mother 'gave a fierce (and absurdly visible) shake of the head . . . I must have been fourteen' (p. 12). Peter, also aged fourteen, has adulterous sex with a woman who turns out to be a murderess, but, because of her fortuitous suicide, no one ever knows.

Amis is doing two things. He is projecting his late adolescence into his early adulthood, and he is recalling an event that reinforced the irreconcilable differences between him and his father. In the summer of 1943 Amis was at home on leave from Catterick when his father, searching his greatcoat for cigarettes, found a packet of condoms. William was shocked and, with what turned out to be disastrous candour, Amis informed him that not only was he having sex, he was doing so regularly with a married woman, Elisabeth Simpson. The reader of the novel knows what would have happened if Captain Furneaux had found out about Peter's brief affair with Mrs Trevelyan, and Amis himself had experienced the very real counterpart of this when he told his father of Elisabeth. William accused him of unspeakable depravity and alienated him for several months.

In 1943 Amis was a 21-year-old subaltern, soon to confront the distinct possibility of violent death, and his father treated him as though he were still fourteen. Elisabeth Simpson had killed no one, but for William Amis she was guilty of an equally appalling crime in which his son had connived.

The Riverside Villas Murder is an intriguing piece of work because it reinforces the much-denied truth that Amis's fiction was his autobiography. The only major figure in the novel who seems not to be based upon Amis's recollections is Colonel Manton, the detective in charge of the case, but he is in fact a version of Amis himself or, more accurately, an adult foil for Peter.

Throughout the novel Peter's perceptions hold centre-ground, but Manton, in a Holmesian manner, engineers events so that secrets are disclosed that would in normal circumstances have remained unknown to an adolescent. Manton could indeed have co-authored the book. Apart from Peter he is the only character whose exact age is given. He is fifty, as was Amis when he wrote the novel.

Peter spends an afternoon in Manton's house and finds that they have interests in common which separate them from the rest of the cast, particularly Peter's father. Manton peppers their exchange with Latin quotations and literary allusions in a way that is neither patronizing nor pretentious. He seems to suspect that Peter has a genuine interest in these topics, which his family does not share, and Amis begins the process by which Manton becomes a channel between his recreated adolescence and his mid-life reflections. William Amis was pleased by his son's academic abilities, but for him literature and classical learning were hurdles on the route to success, and he did not appreciate the fact that his son actually enjoyed them. 'Art', Amis later recalled, was 'not a word or a concept my father had much truck with'.

In Chapter 3 Peter asks his father if he can listen to jazz on the wireless, and his father dismisses such music as 'that nigger row'. In Chapter 8 after a similar request to tune into London Regional and listen to the BBC Orchestra performing Mozart – always Amis's favourite composer – he is told that he cannot, because it is time for bed. Twenty years after the novel Amis remembers his father's comment on how Duke Ellington's music put him in mind of 'a lot of savages dancing round a pot of human remains' and of how, too often, when he wanted to listen to classical music on the wireless his father 'after a day at the office and getting on for an hour's journey home, would very much not. And there we were' (*Memoirs*, p. 17). During their afternoon together Manton and Peter discover that they share an enjoyment and respect for contemporary jazz – Manton has a signed photograph of Duke Ellington – and classical music; and again Manton provides some relief from the 'isolation' felt by Peter/Amis, the only child, and embodies the rift between them and their respective fathers.

Amis sews into the narrative a rumour which is never confirmed that Manton is a homosexual. This provides his suspects, including for a while Peter's father, with a private, revengeful slur, and it also involves oblique recollections on Amis's part: William Amis regarded homosexuality as a clinical, indeed criminal, disorder, evidenced by his horrified reaction to his brother Leslie's 'confession' of potential homosexual inclinations. In a broader sense, this enables Amis to present Manton as someone who is mysteriously 'different' from the other characters. Along with Mrs Trevelyan, he carries into the novel a degree of rebellious sexuality, and both characters reflect Amis's retrospective feelings of being chronologically and temperamentally isolated from the world in which he grew up.

Manton's affinities with Peter, the implied notion that each is in some way superior to the suburban banalities of Norbury, develop at the end of the novel into a rewriting of the past that is at once unsettling and intriguing. In the last two pages Furneaux confesses to his son that his disfigured arm is not, as he has always maintained, the result of an air crash during his war service with the RFC. He was in the RFC but as ground staff, not as a pilot. The injury was caused in a car accident. Peter tells him that he does not care, that he respects him all the more for his honesty, 'not because anyone's making you, but because you want me to know you. I think that makes you a good father.' The implausibility of a fourteen-year-old responding to his father with such poised and generous authority testifies to the fact that Peter involves for Amis both a revisitation and a reinvention of his past. Furneaux's confession to Peter and Peter's response is of course a reversal of the exchange between Amis and William regarding Elisabeth Simpson, and in a curious way Amis is both saying goodbye to and sustaining the conflict. Peter Furneaux, aka Kingsley Amis, is evidently a more tolerant individual than his father, someone for whom commitment and affection transcend such local difficulties as the keeping and disclosure of secrets. Amis is rewriting his past, wishing his father had responded, had been capable of responding, in the way that Peter does, but he almost rebukes himself for doing this. At the end of Peter's litany of praise Captain Furneaux seems to reciprocate. He begins, 'And you're the best son . . . ', but Peter interrupts him with 'Well . . . I think I'll go out for a minute, Dad.' He goes out in pursuit of Daphne Hodgson, a neighbour's daughter. She is a couple of years older than him, precocious and previously dismissive of his coy advances, but he now feels confident enough to try his hand. The adolescent has become the apprentice adult, and in one page Amis has concentrated a still unsettling catalogue of memories. After he joined the army he never again lived permanently with his parents. He visited them regularly, particularly after he had begun a family of his own, and this arrangement involving a combination of distance and diplomatic good terms suited him. In 1957 his mother died suddenly of a stroke and while William, then retired and in reasonably good health, could look after himself he was on his own and for the next three years he lived with Kingsley and Hilly in Swansea. In his *Memoirs* Amis deals with this period cautiously, telling of how on an average day, after the *Telegraph* crossword, a light ale in the pub and lunch at home, William was 'glaringly at a loose end' (p. 22). All of this suggests that the age gap between his father and most of the Amises' friends was the principal cause for the feeling of unease, which would lead in 1960 to William's decision to move back to London. In truth, Amis regarded his father as an intruder, an inconvenience. To Larkin (24 May 1958) he wrote that he was

> browned off by the continuous presence of my male relative. Why doesn't he go away for good? Failing that, why can't he go away for a very long time and go away again almost as soon as he has come back? I can't look for anything . . . or he says *Qu'est-ce que tu cherches?* When my friends call . . . he *talks to them.* When Hilly and Mavis and Mary Morgen were having a girls' chat he *sat with them* for 2 *hrs.* He doesn't like old people, you see. He likes young people.

Read between the lines of this account and the William who emerges provides something of an explanation, if not an excuse, for his son's bitterness. The jovial repartee, the fun with language, the preferred company of young people, women particularly, involves for Amis a somewhat grotesque, elderly version of himself: the jokes are not funny any more and, embarrassingly, he cannot accept that he is old. According to Sam Dawson, Amis's English Department colleague, William actually enjoyed life in Swansea and got on well with Amis's friends, without imposing himself upon them.

Whatever the exact reason for his resentment at his father's presence, the fact was that when William left in 1960 Amis was relieved. William died on 18 April 1963, when the Amises were in Spain, and 'In Memoriam W.R.A.', written shortly afterwards, is apologetic, slightly guilty, regretful. It involves Amis and his father at a cricket match, one enthusiasm they shared, but more significantly the poem spirals around a particular moment when Amis detaches himself from his father's attempt to talk with him.

The on-and-on of your talk,

My gradually formal response

That I could never defend

But never would soften enough,

  Leading to silence,

  And separate ways.

The moment is returned to in *The Riverside Villa's Murder* as Peter curtails Furneaux's sentence and goes outside; in the novel Peter never speaks to Furneaux again. In *The Green Man* Maurice's father, too, has seen the ghost, but Maurice is always too busy to listen to him and he dies, desperately trying and failing to speak to his son about an experience he knows they have shared. And in Amis's penultimate novel, *You Can't Do Both*, we encounter Robin outside his terminally ill father's hospital room knowing that it is too late to talk to him about their previous arguments, their mutually felt but obdurately avoided feelings of affection. No other sequence was returned to, recycled so frequently in Amis's writing, which testifies to its enduring resonance as a token of his mixed feelings of guilt and sadness at an opportunity missed. The years in Swansea with his father could have been different if Amis had been more tolerant and thoughtful. But, like Peter, he went outside.

The *Riverside Villas Murder* is, like much of Amis's fiction, two novels in one. For most contemporary and subsequent readers Amis's role in it is simply that of author, the maker of a story about how intrigue, crime and passion can enliven the dullness of English suburbia – and Orwell's essay 'The Decline of the English Murder' on how killing can be made more macabre and exciting by the blandness of its context is brought to mind. But he is also writing to himself. He inserts private clues, autobiographical talismans, partly perhaps to secure within his writing a second life, something which might be discovered later by outsiders.

Just prior to Peter's final exchange with his father he has been driven home by Manton and they have said goodbye. Curiously, the precise location of Riverside Villas has never previously been mentioned, except that it is on the outskirts of London, but here, as the story is about to close, Manton's and Peter's journey is described with a meticulous attention to detail that seems unrelated to the content of the novel. Norbury, the real site of Amis's memories, is named for no other reason than to inform us that they drive through it and go further west: 'this was Surrey now, not London. Nearly home.' The journey is Amis's in life and through the novel. The brief visit to his childhood is over, and he will soon be back in the present, through Surrey to Hertfordshire, Barnet, Lemmons, his wife Jane and their respective families; all so different from the past returned to in the book.

Peter's parting exchange with Manton is deliciously resonant of the two-novels-in-one exercise. Peter begins with 'I don't suppose we . . . ', and while 'will meet again' is the assumed conclusion of his sentence he seems unable or unwilling to include it. Manton helps him out.

> No. How sound your instincts are. I now know you know what I am, or what I used to be: a small enough part of my life at any time, but the smallest part is too much. That – thing in me enabled me to understand her and to predict how she would behave, with a result I expect could be called socially useful. But friendship between us has become impossible, I'm afraid. It's the sort of penalty one pays for – well, for existing, really. Still, there's always youth. Isn't there? We'll see each other again and perhaps talk these matters over. But not yet . . .

If read as part of the invented fabric of the book the passage seems to allude to Manton's alleged homosexuality, but its autobiographical thread is equally persistent. They will not meet again, at least for the duration of the novel, because Manton is no longer needed as Peter's contact beyond the claustrophobic world of the Riverside Villas: within a page Peter will assert his independence and make his symbolic departure. Peter does indeed know what Manton is, that 'thing', that small enough part of his life, because Peter and Manton are dimensions of the same presence, projections of Amis. Continued friendship is impossible, because the fiction which has created and sustained it is about to end. It is what enabled Manton to 'understand her', Mrs Trevelyan, since she too was part of this temporary recreation of Amis's past life. He and Peter must part – 'It's the sort of penalty one pays for – well, for existing, really' – and here the apparent allusion to homosexuality becomes a little more ambiguous. Perhaps 'for existing' means for being made to exist; existing in a fictional world. The enigmatic drift of Manton's speech continues with his statement that 'there's always youth. Isn't there?' and his vague promise that they will see each other again and talk: 'But not yet.' Amis is conducting a dialogue with himself. Its subjects, the past and the present, are the themes of the novel. The date is 1936, Amis's remembered 'youth'. Peter and Manton will indeed meet again, in 1973, and 'talk these matters over'.

16

Ending Up

IN a 1974 interview with Clive James, Amis told of how the idea for the recently published *Ending Up* had come from his own experience of 'relations and people living in', with the added hypothesis of 'what would this sort of arrangement be like if one had a pack of characters who were all about twenty years older?' What he did not mention was quite the extent to which these characters would be modelled upon the permanent and temporary residents of Lemmons.

The novel takes us through the last three months in the lives of five septuagenarians who find themselves thrown together, by grim financial necessity, in a place called Tuppeny-Happeny Cottage. Muriel Spark's *Memento Mori* (1959), William Trevor's *The Old Boys* (1971) and John Bailey's *At the Jerusalem* (1967) constitute a sub-genre of the elderly confinement novel, and each injects an appropriate degree of compassionate good humour into its largely conventional narrative. Amis constructs a narrative which a sympathetic reader might construe as an enactment of the black comedy of ageing but which, in truth, is far more black than comic. In the interview he spoke of how he had tried to imagine 'a situation where everybody was old, everybody had got to the end of their lives, and everybody had been there for a good long time so that all knew how boring one another was, and exactly the areas where one another was most vulnerable'. In fact his imagining and representation of age was also a means of specifying, by exaggeration, his own state of mind and his perceptions of the people with whom he spent most of his days. His governing premise was that age involved an inevitable decline in those aspects of personality which variously improved upon and compensated for their less agreeable counterparts. This, while being debatable, was convenient in that it enabled him to offer a vision of life in Lemmons comprised only of its worst aspects. By 1973–4 his gradually diminishing enthusiasm for the continuation of his marriage was equalled by a growing, fatalistic awareness that the longer they kept it going the more they became aware that they would have to keep it going. Ageing meant that, incrementally, there were fewer alternatives to the state you were in. Amis, when he wrote the novel, was not particularly happy with the place in which he lived and the people whose day-to-day existence he shared, but what else could he do? His idyllic, romantic perceptions of his life and future with Jane had been replaced by a feeling of begrudged dependency.

In 1972 he had been revisited by the combination of panic attacks and mild hysteria that had been part of his experience in Oxford after the war. One day he had found himself on a tube train waiting in a station near Barnet, and there was no one else in the carriage. He felt at once entrapped and terrified. Again, he was reminded that the presence of other people was a necessary part of his daily existence. Jane advised him to visit a psychologist, which he did, but the effects were not beneficial. He knew that his life at Lemmons, while now a debasement of its earlier, optimistic prospects, was all he had. He was, for various reasons, frightened of being alone.

The creation of the inhabitants of Tuppeny-Happeny Cottage, in a state of obligated togetherness, was a projection of Amis's feelings about Lemmons. The permanent residents were himself, Jane, Monkey and Sargy. For three years, until 1971 when she died,

Katherine Howard, Jane's mother, had lived with them. Soon after that her suite of rooms had been reoccupied by the then poet laureate Cecil Day Lewis, an old friend of Jane's, who was terminally ill and who died there in May 1972.

In his notebook Amis sketched out the five elderly characters (Amis Collection, Huntington Library). Each is a blending and a redistribution of real people, but most of the material drew upon the tensions between himself and Jane. There is 'Bernard', Bernard Bastable, 'being deaf . . . angry at simple questions . . . lying about what has happened . . . whose side he was on in an argument'. Amis's hearing difficulties would not cause serious problems with communication for about another decade, but when he wrote this novel he was aware of their onset. Bernard is angry, dispirited by this situation and so, more and more, was Amis, and it showed. There is 'Shorty', Derrick Shortell, 'repeating the wrong bit . . . punning dud spoonerisms – polysyllabic facetiousness . . . lots of accents and dialects . . . leaving possessions about'. Amis throughout the 1970s was still willing to play the role of entertainer in residence, doing the imitations and anecdotes, with sound-effects, that had guaranteed his popularity since Oxford. Shorty is a hapless parody of this. His imitations of foreign accents are banal, clichéd and no one finds them funny. Amis, like Shorty and much to Jane's irritation, left possessions about.

Bernard is an ex-army officer, and Shorty had been his batman. The reason for their 'ending up' together in the cottage was their homosexual relationship. Homosexuality in this novel is a device employed by Amis to divide features of himself between two separate male characters. Their army background is a private token of their status as projections of their author. Amis during the war had frequently ridiculed and attempted to break down the class-based division between officers and squaddies. The pompous brigadier and the low-life mess sergeant ending up as partners was an ironic remembrance of this.

In the notebook plan the two women characters, 'Adela' and 'Marigold', share a tendency to speak in a manner that variously obscures and delays the point of their statements. Adela: 'interrupting with a) with fresh matter b) provoking "I was coming to do that" . . . explaining the obvious or irrelevant and not explaining the obscure and relevant . . .' Marigold: 'annoying answers . . . reacting wrongly . . . taking a long time to decide on what drink or whether drink, then changing mind . . .' Amis confided in his official biographer, Eric Jacobs, that for him Jane's most annoying characteristics were verbal. 'Amis would ask Jane a question and instead of answering she would ask why he'd asked it, as if nothing could be straightforward, not even a simple question' (Jacobs, p. 318).

Amis also told Jacobs of how Jane had complained that Victor Gollancz, whom she had met socially, could never remember who she was and kept mistaking her for an actress. Amis reflected, privately, that Victor's error was understandable, given that she was so 'affected'. Marigold is selfish, vain and an ex-actress. The dividing up and reassembling of features of himself and Jane within the four most prominent residents of Tuppeny-Happeny Cottage was a not inaccurate reflection of the Lemmons' hierarchy. Regarding practical matters, she ran the place while Amis regarded himself as the chief breadwinner and monarchical head of state. At the same time Amis provides the characters with enough temperamental and ingrained, habitual differences to create a network of subtle tensions similar to that generated by the four permanent residents of Lemmons. Significantly, two of them, Adela and Bernard, are sister and brother, as of course were Jane and Monkey.

The fifth member of the household is George Zeyer, an incapacitated ex-academic. George has had a stroke, has to spend much of his time in bed and suffers from aphasia. Again, there are echoes of Lemmons, which for two consecutive periods was home first for Jane's ailing mother and then for the terminally ill C. Day Lewis.

George is a refugee from Czechoslovakia who carries the title of Emeritus Professor of Central European History from Northampton University. When Amis began planning the novel one of his closest friends, Tibor Szamuely, had recently died of cancer. Szamuely had fled from Hungary not Czechoslovakia, but since the two uprisings were roughly a decade apart, and the novel is set twenty years hence, the parallels are clear enough. Szamuely, too, was a historian whose most respected work, *The Russian Tradition*, was published posthumously in the same year as *Ending Up*. Amis created George Zeyer as a tribute to his late friend. He becomes the least pretentious, perhaps the most endearing resident of the cottage.

As Amis's notebook shows, the novel at planning stage drew heavily upon his life at Lemmons. From the nature of this material one might have suspected that the completed work would become a vehicle for its author's prejudices regarding his co-residents, an act of vengeance upon unhappy circumstances, but quite the opposite occurred. Bernard emerges as the most prominent of the five characters, in the sense that his acts have more effect upon the eventual direction of the narrative than anything else. Each of the other four involves a blend of personal flaws and more endearing elements of decency and kindness, combinations which age has cemented. Bernard appears to be the only one who is still subject to change. He is the most bitter and the only comprehensively unpleasant member of the cast, and as the story progresses he gets even worse.

The structure of the narrative is innovative, fascinating and ingeniously appropriate to the subject of the novel. Each chapter is rarely more than 1,500 words in length, and within these brief units there is an almost manic, kaleidoscopic blending of different foci. Through this strategy Amis achieves a multiplicity of effects. The narrative moves with alarming speed. Within about four minutes of reading time we will encounter George Zeyer, alone in his bedroom and trying to remember the right word, shift to Marigold and Adela in the woods near the cottage discussing Bernard's foul mannerisms, and then to Shorty enjoying a glass of beer and a Players Number 6 in the kitchen. In practical terms their worlds have been slowed down: the physical consequences of old age have caused a deceleration of all the things they want or have to do. But in an ironic, paradoxical way their mental activities have been speeded up. All suffer from an age-induced, shortened attention span. Everyone seems incapable of talking or thinking about a particular topic for more than a couple of minutes, and their collective experience is conveyed to the reader through a narrative which seems to be accelerating, introducing topics and personal characteristics and quickly leaving them behind.

Out of this blending of claustrophobic proximity and introspective brevity emerges the loathsome presence of Bernard Bastable. Bernard hates his co-residents.

> There was still a little satisfaction to be had out of scoring off them in talk, but it did seem to be on the decrease. He must see if he could not come up with some less subtle means of venting on the four of them his lack of respect and affection. What had happened, what was the change in his circumstances that had led him to this decision? Well, anyhow, such a project would help to pass the time.

Bernard sidesteps the self-addressed question of why he feels and acts in the way that he does, but the answer is there for the reader. Bernard, when younger, had thrived upon the interconnected tensions and deceptions that had made up his life. On the one hand, he was a respectable officer with a wife, Vera, and a son, while, on the other, he was engaged in a long-term homosexual relationship which was all the more satisfyingly degenerate because it was with a man regarded as inferior in rank, class and intellect. Along with this double life, Bernard enjoyed all activities that allowed him to practice hypocrisy. Now his wife is dead, his active relationship with Shorty is over, and all he is left with is the necessity of survival. Malevolence is the only thing which seems to hold the promise of pleasure and satisfaction.

Everyone dies in the concluding chapter. They do so alone, in a variety of sordid and uncomfortable ways, with many of their heart attacks, broken bones and internal haemorrhages in some way connected with Bernard's residue of practical jokes. None of them has the opportunity to reflect upon the death of anyone else, and their bodies are discovered by Bernard's son with whom he has not communicated for thirty years. The end has the grim textual symmetry of a Shakespearian fifth act. The overcrowded cottage is like the stage. The characters carry the entirety of their lives into this compressed textual space, and as we leave it so do they, alone.

As a vision of life at Lemmons, albeit twenty years hence, it is depressing, but it is clear also that Amis has based Bernard, effectively the cause of the collective distress, upon the very worst aspects of himself. The other characters are, by comparison, blameless victims. Jane recalls that alongside their marital problems Amis by the 1970s had begun to think that 'life was passing him by', in that the complexities and excitements of pre-middle age – the affairs, the ambition, the juggling between job and writing, the periodic desire to start again somewhere else – were what had made his life worth while, and they were all now largely in the past. She says that he constantly seemed to be looking for replacements and that even the purchase of and move to Lemmons was partly a means by which he could get involved in something new and unusual, but that once they were established there the excitement wore off. He enjoyed the idea of a country residence – hence his 'look round the estate' joke – but he had not thought about its practical consequences, such as travelling between Barnet and central London. And in 1976, mostly at Amis's instigation, the family exchanged Lemmons for a house in Hampstead, closer to the centre of things. All of which takes us back to Bernard's question regarding his malevolent state. His life, or at least those aspects of it that he enjoyed, had completely passed him by. In Lemmons and later in Hampstead Amis did not turn his frustrations into a vicious campaign against his co-residents, but he clearly wondered whether if he were still in the same place with the same people in twenty years' time – with everything that had once engaged him just a memory – would he become as evil as Bernard?

The novel won him the Book of the Year award from the *Yorkshire Post* and was shortlisted for the Booker McConnell Fiction Prize which was, in the mid-1970s, not quite the media circus that it would become a decade or so later but was even then the most prestigious and lucrative British literary prize. The judges were impressed by Amis's blending of subject and technique as an innovative representation of age. They were not, of course, aware that both were projections of his life.

17

The Alteration

*T*HE *Alteration* (1976) invites comparisons with Huxley's *Brave New World* and Orwell's *Nineteen Eighty-Four*, with an echo of Swift's *A Modest Proposal*. Ostensibly its subjects are religion and sex – the dictatorship of the former and the consequent near-criminalization of the latter – but at its core was the personal experience of its author. During the mid-1970s Amis began to lose his desire for sex. Hubert, the hero of the novel, is too young to have shared such desires with his creator and faces the prospect of never being able to do so.

The Alteration is set in England in 1976, but this is 1976 as it would have been if Henry VIII's elder brother Arthur had lived on to become king, married Catherine of Aragon and sired a line of alternative Tudors. England and the parts of Europe uncolonized by the Islamic enemy have remained Catholic, and the religious institution has effectively replaced secular power. It tells the story of Hubert Anvil, ten years old and the best boy soprano in living memory. The alteration of the title is the planned surgical castration of Hubert, which will preserve his magnificent voice and secure for him respect and position in a world where the arts are the esteemed preserve of the Vatican hierarchy. The vaguely liberal alternative to Catholic Europe is New England, an independent settlement on the American continent populated by Red Indians and descendants of European exiles

291

and dissidents, including, some time earlier, William Shakespeare. The narrative focuses upon Hubert's attempt to avoid the alteration. He eventually finds brief sanctuary in the New England embassy, but before that his status and his escape attempt provide us with an insight into a society that is at once surreal, horrific and unnervingly familiar.

The chilling question of whether the alteration will take place is punctuated by Hubert's growing awareness of the world in which the arguments for and against have been formed. We see this world partly, but only partly, through Hubert's eyes. He is a precocious ten-year-old and intellectually he can hold his own with most of the adults he meets, but at the same time Amis uses the combination of his inexperience and prepubescence to provide the reader with a double perspective. As he becomes more puzzled and perplexed by what he finds, we experience a parallel process of recognition.

In Chapter 3 his mother and Father Lyall engage with him in a debate on the different kinds of love. Hubert:

> 'He talked of love, Mama. He said there were many kinds of love: love of friends, love of brothers and sisters, love of parents, love of children – I shall be able to love children, the children of others. And there's the love of virtue and the love of God, the highest kind. And of course the love of men and women, which is not the highest kind, Papa said. He was right, wasn't he?'
>
> 'He was quite right, Hubert.'
>
> 'Forgive me, Father, but I must know what Mama thinks.'
>
> 'Papa was right,' said Margaret, and looked down at her hands, which were clasped in her lap.
>
> Hubert gazed at her. 'Tell the truth, Mama.'
>
> 'It is the truth . . .'
>
> 'Then why do you say it as if it's a lie?' (Chapter 3)

Hubert is shrewd enough to suspect something from his mother's tone of voice, but what he does not know is that the priest's influence on her is due to the fact that they are having an affair. Even if he were aware of this, it has already been made clear that his knowledge of the 'many kinds of love' has been acquired via a grounding in abstract moral and theological tenets. He knows the meanings of the words he uses, but he has no sense of how these can be variously altered and shaped by adult experience. Hubert's elder brother comments that in trying to explain to him the relationship between human love, involving sex, and love for God, 'they might as easily explain the colour red to a blind man'.

In the next chapter Hubert, still seeking some understanding of these matters, addresses a more basic enquiry to the stable boy Ned. 'What happens when you fuck?'

> 'Here it is, now. I grapples her and I near kiss her bloody mouth off the face of her and I gropes the cunt of her till her's all stewed and ready, see? Then I haves the clouts of her and lays the fusby on her back and I shove my pen all the way up her fanny artful and I bang and bang, see?' For a moment longer, he appeared to Hubert angrier than ever, the corners of his mouth drawn tightly back as he puffed out the words. 'I goes on at her cruel till my knob starts to whack her tripes and her cry me mercy, see? Then I feel a start to . . . Christ I could . . .'

The contrast between the priest's idealistic notion of 'the love of men and women' and Ned's account of things brings to mind a similar one between the 1956 letter that Amis wrote to Henry Fairlie celebrating the idyll of married life (which Fairlie was threatening) and the letter he wrote to Larkin shortly afterwards exalting the joys of an illicit shag (see p. 000). For poor Hubert, however, such adult contraries remain as abstractions.

This far into the novel the focus has been chiefly upon Hubert's own puzzled perceptions of what the alteration means, but the perspective broadens and we begin to find disturbing parallels between the society that has created his dilemma and aspects of our own. Art is regarded by the Roman Catholic dictatorship as a key element of man's obeisant duty to God, and Amis makes it clear that once art becomes part of ideology its relationship with the individual imagination is terminated.

The scholar Abbot Thynne has recently ordered 'a new commentary on the *De Existentiae Natura* of Monsignor Jean-Paul Sartre, the French Jesuit'. Hubert sings Mozart's Second Requiem (K878), 'the crown of his middle age', to the congregation in Coverley (based on Cowley, outside Oxford) Cathedral, whose walls carry 'Blake's still brilliant frescoes depicting St Augustine's progress through England', 'Holman Hunt's oil painting of the martyrdom of St George' and the 'excessively traditionalist almost archaizing' Ecce Homo mosaic by David Hockney.

A.J. Ayer is Professor of Dogmatic Theology at New College, Oxford – so much for logical positivism. The only unbanned books recommended for young readers are *The Wind in the Cloisters*, *Lord of the Chalices* and *St Lemuel's Travels*. Shakespeare had been charged with heresy and forced to flee to New England. All of his works were burned. Since there was no enlightenment and no age of revolution, the Romantic movement had never existed. An obscure, frustrated poet called Shelley had lived in a state of despair until 1853 when he burned down Castel Gandolfo and committed suicide.

Amis's rewriting of history involves a continuous aesthetic subtext. Some artists have compromised, placed their considerable skills in the service of the Church and paid the price by sacrificing imaginative range and freedom for dogma. Others have been silenced. It was not that Amis was conducting a selective exercise in character assassination, judging these figures according to how he imagined they would have responded to an oppressive orthodoxy. (Shakespeare Good, Mozart Bad would hardly be consistent with his frequently professed view of them as the two greatest artists of all time.) His selection is random. His use of art as a kind of oblique index to the evil that permeates society is intended to give sharper definition to Hubert's dilemma. If he is castrated he will surrender a key element of his condition as a human being for the absolute of high art, and Amis is here suggesting a necessary correlation between an individual's ability to be and do exactly as they wish and the value, irrespective of the quality, of their aesthetic product.

Amis suggests parallels between the doctrinaire obsession with pure aesthetics which permeates his created world and its intrinsic state of evil. Along with Monsignor Sartre, we encounter Monsignor's Henricus and Laurentius. Before ordination each had been known in their native 'Almaigne' and 'Muscovy' by their family names, Himmler and Beria.

Hubert's escape bid through London sends him into the world of Jacob and his assistant Jack. Jacob inhabits the setting and language of Dickens's Fagin. At one point he quotes Shylock – 'Have we not eyes. . .' – but Hubert has never heard of the banned Shakespeare and, significantly, nor is he aware that practising Jews are forced to live mostly in hiding and in public to display the Star of David on their clothing.

His enlightenment continues when he reaches the New England embassy where the liberal Protestant Pastor Reverend Williams explains to him the status of his servant Abraham, a native American. 'His mind is less capable to be developed than yours or mine, because his brain is smaller, as our scientists have proved. To mingle with him truly is impossible, and no good can come of trying to. That's why, under God's guidance, we in New England have a design we call separateness' (Chapter 5).

When Amis and Jane visited the United States in the late 1960s they found that a version of neo-Nazi racism was alive and well in the American South, the so-called Bible Belt, and it appears that in Amis's conflation of religious dogmatism with cruel inhumanity Protestants can be just as foul as Catholics.

Unlike many writers and intellectuals who rejected Christianity, Amis did not feel angered or threatened by organized religion. He had no reason to, since it had never interfered with his life. It therefore seems slightly odd that Amis's most horrific, terrifying version of the human potential for systemized inhumanity should focus upon the Church. In 1973 Amis had listened to a scratchy 1909 recording of the last known castrato, Alexandro Moreschi. He recognized that the performance was 'very fine'; Moreschi, then aged forty-six, had retained the unique skills of the prepubescent vocalist. But for other reasons Amis found that its quality was 'intolerable'; it caused him to endure for several days a state of 'jittery depression'. There was something horrific about a culture, in this instance, the Roman Church, which could persuade a man to exchange his manhood for an effect.

'[Moreschi's] decision brings out everything of importance in human life. Your arguments for and against, your duty to God, to sing his music. Your duty to art, sex. Love. Marriage. Children. Fame. Money. Security' (*New Review*, Vol. 1, No. 4, 1974, pp. 21–8). The consiliences between these units of lived experience were what made the whole experience worth while; with the exception, in Amis's case, of 'duty to God'. The alteration for Moreschi, and potentially for Hubert, destroyed even the possibility of there being a relationship between the components because it had caused the removal of their fulcrum – sex.

When he planned and wrote this novel Amis was not facing anything so drastic and, as he saw it, dehumanizing as Moreschi's and Hubert's alteration, but elements of his life were beginning to alter in ways that were unprecedented and disorientating. His sexual relationship with Jane continued but was in a state of perhaps irreversible decline. The fact that his original feelings for her were now becoming a memory was supplemented by a more general disinclination towards sexual desire. Whether this was due to the onset of later middle age, the effects of alcohol or some obscure psychophysical ailment were questions that he would not seriously address until his condition worsened. But whatever the cause he was beginning to experience the effect, which involved the imagined prospect of living and writing in the absence of the element that had been their central generating feature.

The novel involved the projection of his feelings of uncertainty on to its central character, with a number of typically ironic distortions. For Hubert, sex, let alone the ways in which sex influences other parts of life, is a hypothesis. It is an activity confined exclusively to language and the operations of the mind. It is something that potentially he will never experience, and one can imagine Amis considering the bizarre possibility that he might someday undergo a version of Hubert's state in reverse; that sex might become a remembrance, a disembodied memory recorded in his novels. This also throws some light upon his almost obsessive recreation of the known world as something which is unnervingly familiar yet at the same time disjointed and reconfigured, with iconic presences from the arts and history caused to be and live as distorted images of themselves. Moreover, the ideology that permeates every part of the novel's social, political and cultural landscape is sanctioned and enforced by men who have chosen to live without sex. For them, sex is a necessary but debased feature of the human condition; it ensures the continuation of God's created species, yet it involves degrees of temptation and pleasure that should remind us of our fallen state. To give it up will bring us closer to God. For them, therefore, Hubert's surgical displacement from this state is not a deprivation; rather, it will enable him to contribute to one of the few human activities which honours the deity: art.

It is intriguing to compare Amis's horrified account of the 'jittery depression' which followed his hearing of the Moreschi recording with that of two elderly clerics seated in the balcony at the conclusion of one of Hubert's performances. This occurs in the closing pages of the novel when Hubert is now an adult castrato.

Neither moved so much as a finger until the voice had ceased and the great auditory was filled with applause that quite blotted out the orchestral postlude. Then they turned to each other. Tears covered the face of the older of the two, who nodded his head slowly.

'Deo gratia,' said Viaventosa.

'Amen,' said Mirabilis.

In a subsequent interview Amis told of how ideas for the novel had gradually formed in his mind (*Illustrated London News*, No. 266, September 1978, pp. 54–5). He did not of course refer to its autobiographical element, but one can read between the lines. He had thought about the kind of book which would be at once relevant to the contemporary reader but be even further removed from mainstream fiction than the ghost story of *The Green Man*. Perhaps an eighteenth-century historical novel? He knew the period quite well from his taste for Richardson and Fielding and his academic teaching, but the necessary in-depth research would be 'too boring'. Maybe a study of isolation and its supernatural-psychological supplements, rather like John Fowles's *The Magus*? He had spent quite a few periods on Mediterranean islands, had even thought about turning himself into a version of Fowles's Nicholas D'Urfe on Majorca a couple of years before Fowles had come up with the idea. Too easy: 'the coward's way out'. 'Then it dawned on me': science fiction. He had always enjoyed it, had indeed written a book about it and edited volumes of it. The problem here was that one could not simply treat this genre as an exercise in the unusual. 'You have to have a reason. And here was the reason. Because in SF you have a sub-genre called . . . Alternative World. And by using Alternative World, I could have the castrato living here and now.'

This is a deliciously intriguing avoidance of his own question. The sub-genre of Alternative World was just as abstract and theoretical as the generalized notion of science fiction. Amis's puzzling *volte face* was in fact a disclosure that Alternative World was more than an idea. It was, in 1978, when he did the interview, a reasonably accurate description of his state. For him, then, the alteration had occurred.

18

Decline and Introversion

W ERE Amis and Jane compatible? At first it seemed that they were. When they met she was the kind of woman whom Amis's alter egos had fantasized about in his 1950s' novels – sexy, sophisticated, alluringly experienced – and her actual presence had caused him to transform fantasy into realization in the 1960s' novels in which she featured. Behind the novels there were, of course, less tractable problems. Before they actually moved in together the illicit nature of the affair had effectively sidelined the potential difficulties of the pairing of two forty-somethings, each with long-established habits and idiosyncrasies, and during the later 1960s and 1970s protocols were agreed to cope with these. But, after the move to Lemmons particularly, the day-to-day routines of cohabitation seemed to become for Amis emblematic of a more intrinsic state of unease and dissatisfaction. In the real world this simply made him more difficult to live with, but in its fictional counterpart it would eventually inform the curious fabric of *Jake's Thing* (1978) where Jake and his narrator treat their surroundings, people included, with a mixture of indifference and contempt.

Once Amis had formed an opinion on someone, however immediate or impressionistic, he rarely changed it. There might be no obvious basis for conflict – temperamental, cultural or political – but for reasons known only to himself he would decide that some individuals did not deserve his continued attention. During their early years he sometimes tried to moderate this habit, yet at the same time Jane found herself having to continuously reschedule meetings with a number of her friends for whom, as he made clear, his level of tolerance was low. Jane went along with this, even agreeing that her close acquaintance Dolly Burns could provide the model for the loathsomely snobbish Lady Baldock in *I Want It Now*. She also had to put up with Amis's tendency to be hostile to writers in whose work he had no interest or with whom he had not already made friends. Jane had been on sociable terms with John Osborne since the late 1950s, but Amis refused to speak to him: he seemed to blame Osborne personally for the invention of the Angry Young Men. Laurie Lee had been a friend of Jane's for two decades, but, because Amis regarded *Cider with Rosie* as a monument to self-indulgent mythologizing, he displayed an active dislike for its author.

Jane, however, was expected and was indeed willing to play hostess to Amis's circle of acquaintances, irrespective of what she thought of them. Most, such as Conquest, Gale, Montgomery and Szamuely, she found agreeable, and she had enjoyed the company of Betjeman for as long as Amis. She tried to get on with Larkin, who would often stay with them when down from Hull, but she found this more difficult. He was, as she put it, 'snarled up about women' in a way that made Amis's views on the intellectual and social status of the other gender seem liberal by comparison. During Larkin's visits she would 'leave them alone to play their games'.

Throughout the 1960s Jane was willing to tolerate this somewhat unbalanced state of social and behavioural conventions, because there were compensations. They spent as much time as possible exclusively in one another's company. She knew that since *Lucky Jim* Amis had never discussed his ongoing work with anyone before he sent the draft to the publisher, except with her. He genuinely valued her opinion as a critic and fellow novelist, and their sense of humour was similarly attuned to the dry and sardonic. He would test the comedic episodes on her, and her enjoyment of them would become infectious. Often they would find themselves in a state of mutual and uncontrollable laughter. On the surface, their lives, particularly his, had improved; Lemmons was spacious enough to allow its permanent residents and regular visitors a degree of privacy. The assembly of Jane, Sargy Mann, Monkey and, during vacations, Martin ensured that Amis would never be alone in the house, while the exclusive use of his study enabled him to get on with his work without interruptions. His shift from Cape to Hutchinson after *The Alteration* secured him a better deal with advances and royalties: money was not a problem. Jane had taken on Hilly's role and more. She had endured Philip's and Martin's early feelings of bitterness and resentment and become an effective step-mother – without her encouragement Martin would probably never have retaken his O levels, sat his A levels and secured a place at Oxford. She, assisted by Mrs Uniacke, had taken charge of the time-consuming practicalities of Lemmons – buying the food, preparing it, supervising the day-to-day upkeep of what was in effect a country house with grounds. She had become her husband's chauffeur, taking him to the station when he was to spend the day in central London and on longer excursions. As a consequence, her own work suffered; during her marriage to Amis she produced only two novels. But she had not complained. This was her contribution to her third marriage, which she wanted to work.

Yet, after about two years in Lemmons, around 1970, things began to go wrong. Periodically and habitually Amis would become possessed by an enthusiasm for something new, a change of place and circumstances. With Hilly his wish to stay on in Princeton, his eventual move to Cambridge and his plans for Majorca had been motivated by a combination of the somewhat naïve belief that a different area and lifestyle would improve marital relations and the hope that alterations in the real world would open up new fictional counterparts. The most predictable consequence of these uprootings, when they came about, was that his initial enthusiasm would rapidly be dispersed by a blend of disinterest and disappointment. Something similar happened with Lemmons.

The idea of moving out of central London, beyond the suburbs, had been a collective one, but once it had been mooted and Lemmons viewed as the potential location Amis was visited by an almost adolescent excitement. As usual, the image of something unprecedented and untried, in this case playing lord of the manor, displaced considerations of its practical consequences, which would be more problematical for Amis than for the others.

During the 1960s he had, virtually every week, met up with a group of close friends and other acquaintances for lunch, often in Bertorelli's in Charlotte Street, and these would be frequently extended to day-long drinking sessions. Robert Conquest, Tibor Szamuely, Anthony Powell and Bernard Levin were regular attenders. They were not, despite Amis's self-mocking description of them as 'Fascist lunches', serious political gatherings, but there was a feeling of collective dislocation from a political and cultural milieu which seemed to demand left-of-centre sympathies. Nicholas Ridley MP, later to be Mrs Thatcher's aide-de-camp, sometimes called in. Amis and Conquest often attended similar gatherings in the Marlborough Arms in Torrington Place, the so-called '*Spectator* pub'. The *Spectator* has always been a magazine with conservative associations but which has prided itself on its political independence; and in the 1960s and 1970s this involved practically any state of mind that was not left-leaning. Amis was a regular contributor and reviewer.

It obviously did not occur to him that aspects of his 1960s' life that he took for granted would be seriously affected by the move to Lemmons, but they certainly were. The station was a mile and a half away, followed by a tube journey of up to an hour. Routine and impromptu activities such as going to a pub for a drink, visiting the shop for cigarettes, a typewriter ribbon or a loaf of bread required the use of the car and the cooperation of Jane. Soon Amis's enthusiasm for the move began to be replaced by disillusionment and a litany of complaints. In order for him to exercise his independence, particularly regarding his circle of friends and acquaintances in London, he was dependent upon Jane.

Jane recalls that in 1975 Amis, after a couple of drinks, had slipped on the stairs and injured his shoulder but not seriously enough to require immediate medical assistance. Next morning, however, the pain had increased. He wondered if something might be broken, and they arranged an appointment with the local GP for later that day, when Jane was due to be in Broadcasting House discussing material for a radio play. Amis was enraged because, in Jane's view, he was obliged to confront a number of what were for him incompatible yet equally irritating sets of circumstances. He was reminded of how much he relied upon her, which in itself embittered him, while at the same time he was faced with the fact that the woman on whom he depended but no longer loved had a career and a life that were independent of his.

In late 1975 Lemmons was put on the market, and Amis and Jane began looking for somewhere closer to central London. By the end of the year they had found a detached eighteenth-century property called Gardnor House in Flask Walk, Hampstead, and a buyer who was seriously interested in Lemmons. Amis wanted to move back towards the centre of town, but just as significantly they were, at his instigation, engaging in a familiar ritual of desperation: a change of place might encourage a change of mood and state. They moved to Gardnor House with Monkey and Sargy in May 1976, but the condition of their marriage did not improve.

In Hampstead Amis finished *Jake's Thing* (1978). This novel, far more than any assembly of verifiable facts, tells us why his relationship with Jane had gradually, through the mid-1970s, entered an irreversible spiral of decline: sex. The specifics of their life – shared and unshared inclinations and friends, the practicalities of location and day-to-day existence, temperamental affiliations and antipathies – all of these comprised the standard, orbital features of a shared existence, a marriage, and involved resolvable problems. Supplement these with one partner's lost sex drive and in most cases there would still be room for optimism, given the catalogue of cures made available by modern medicine and psychology. Amis did lose his sex drive, but this became far more than a supplement to other issues. For him, sex had always been the feature of a relationship that both cemented and energized its other elements. Consequently he now faced a conundrum. Logically, a restored sex drive would improve the other ailing features of the relationship, but in Amis's case the absence of sexual attraction removed the desire to repair everything else.

Jake Richardson's 'thing' is his lack of desire to have sex with women. He is still, physically, able to, but he does not want to and he cannot remember why he ever did. For Jake, this condition is made worse by the fact that his prolific libidinous career was always a substantial part of everything else: his interest in sex was coterminous with his interest in life. By the time they moved to Hampstead Amis was going through an experience not unlike Jake's. There was a slight difference in that while Jake's physical capabilities are overruled by a general and unexplained disinclination Amis's ability to have sex and his desire for it seemed equally dormant. Amis altered things slightly for the novel, because by making Jake's problem more a mental than a physical one he could better target those individuals for whom with Jake he shared a comprehensive loathing: psychologists and psychoanalysts. In his *Memoirs* Amis refers obliquely to having during the 1970s consulted two therapists; one, a Dr Cobb, 'called himself a psychologist', and another, unnamed, was an upmarket marriage guidance counsellor. In truth, the Amises, mostly at Jane's instigation, had involved themselves in a more extensive schedule of consultation and group therapy than disclosed in the *Memoirs*. Amis, owing to his periodic bouts of depression and panic attacks, had consulted experts in mental-physical imbalances on a number of occasions before this, and he had debunked their pretensions in *The Anti-Death League*, but the two individuals who claimed to be able to provide remedies for his lack of interest in sex and the state of his marriage were almost beyond parody. None of them told Amis and Jane any more than they already knew, and their solutions seemed more like exercises in humiliation.

All of this is reworked in *Jake's Thing* and, while it is intriguing enough to find Amis writing a novel about his own sexual problems, he supplements this with an even more curious autobiographical parallel. Jake Richardson is about ten years older than Amis, but he is also Jim Dixon thirty-five years after *Lucky Jim*. There are plenty of intertextual clues. Jake's given name is James, and Richard is of course the formal version of Dick: Richardson? Dickson? Dixon? Jim left the academic profession. Jake has stayed in it, but he testifies to the three decades of cynicism which would have attended Jim's career had he not abandoned it. Jake's specialization, classics, is, appropriately, more ancient than Jim's, and his interest in it has become, as Jim's already was in his, little more than a dutiful habit.

Jim, or rather the legend of Jim, was interwoven with Amis's memories of his career as a successful sexual predator, and by the late 1970s that was all they were: memories. With Jane, Amis had significantly reduced, if not entirely given up, his extra-marital inclinations, but now the notion even of monogamous sex had become little more than an abstraction. Jake, like Amis, has an impressive record of sexual excursions – more than two hundred as far as he can recollect. He has a night of sex with Eve, one of his past conquests. He can do it, but it no longer involves pleasure. Jake Richardson is a living, functioning version of his previous self, but something is missing. Amis was considering a hypothesis. What would Jim be like in late middle age without the desire for and enjoyment of sex?

The opening of the novel is characteristically, almost self-consciously, Amisian, taking us back to his first use of the gradual orientation technique – the apparent beginning of Jim's lecture blending into his ape imitation in his bedroom being the most famous. But there is a difference. *Jake's Thing* begins with Jake talking to someone about when he first noticed that 'something was wrong' and whether 'it' might be connected with the 'other trouble'. Before the narrator tells us who the speakers are they might well be discussing international politics or a car engine. Even after these figures are introduced as Jake and his GP, Dr Curnow, their topic, Jake's sexual problem, remains undisclosed until Chapter 2. But despite these coat-trailing allusions to the world of Jim the intervening passage, involving Jake's journey home to his wife Brenda, shows us just what effect his yet-to-be-specified problem has had upon him.

The plenitude of detail is obsessive, randomized and chaotic. We consider the practical and financial differences between taking a 127 bus or a taxi to Warren Street. We encounter pedestrian lights, the Orris Park National Westminster Bank, double-parked cars with CD plates, a person who Jake thinks could well be the chap who played the superintendent in 'that police series' and roadworks with no one working on them. Jake is enticed by the cut-price offers of Winesteads Ltd and is delayed at the check-out by a man in 'dirty whitish overalls smoking a cigar and chatting to the senior of the two shopmen'. The exchange is relayed in meticulous detail, with the customer revealing himself to be a verbose bore who will not stop going on about his recently acquired expertise in very expensive malt whiskies.

It is as though Amis is inviting us to compare what happens here with what would have happened if a younger Jake – or rather Jim – had found himself in similar circumstances. Then the alliance between character and narrator would have got to work on the drab mundanities of London street life and have taken crisply sardonic vengeance upon the whisky bore. But the alliance has been broken.

We know that Jake witnesses all of this, but we are not told of what he thinks. He endures it, but he evidently no longer has either the energy or the inclination to make fun of it. 'Jake paid, picked up his goods and left, remembering he should have said Cheers as the exit door shut after him. Out on the street he noticed that away from the sunlight the air was chilly.' Only the brief reference to 'Cheers', used by the bore and the shopman as part of their exchange of fashionable, late-1970s demotic, indicates on Jake's part a slight residue of satirical angst.

As the story unfolds it becomes clear that Jake is as much the hapless victim of the darkly comic mood of this novel as he is a contributor to it. Jake's encounters with the psycho-sexual specialists Professor Trefusis and Dr Rosenburg involve some of the most brilliant comedy that Amis ever produced, but it is also the blackest. In Chapter 4 Jake is referred to Proinsias Rosenburg, MD MA (Dip.Psych.), of 878 Harley Street.

Jake found himself closeted with a person he took to be a boy of about seventeen, most likely a servant of some kind, in a stooped position doing something with an electric fire. 'I'm looking for Dr Rosenburg,' he said.

It was never to cut the least ice with him that the other did not reply, 'Ah now me tharlun man, de thop a de mornun thoo yiz' – he might fully as well have done by the effect ('Good morning' was what he did say).

The following ten pages are crowded with references to Rosenburg's Irishness. After Rosenburg asks him when he last masturbated, the narrator tells us that 'It took Jake a little while to get the final participle because the Irishman had stressed it on the third syllable.' Rosenburg explains the Germanic origin of his surname and fails to understand Jake's reference to Austria as a more appropriate location. The narrator discloses Jake's unease at 'being asked to believe in a student of the mind who didn't know where Freud had come from'.

Rosenburg's most bizarre characteristic is his habit of switching idioms and frames of reference without warning. He shifts seamlessly from his explanation of his surname to his rate of £17.50 a session and from an apparent interest in Jake's profession to the weight of his wife. Worst of all, he does this without any awareness of its darkly comic effect. At the end of their session he introduces Jake to the nocturnal mensurator which, he explains, will measure the frequency, duration and size of Jake's night-time erections. He tells him how to fit the plastic loop to his penis, how an erection is registered on the disc and circuit breaker and that he should not forget to turn off *both* switches when he gets out of bed. All this is delivered by someone who, as the narrator reminds us, 'didn't really talk like an O'Casey peasant, his articulation was too precise for that, but he did talk like a real Irishman with a largely unreconstructed accent'.

The creeping sensation of Rosenburg as a figure beyond parody is given a crisp finale when he hands Jake his visiting card.

'Proinsias. Is that a German name?'
'Irish. It's pronounced Francis. The correct Gaelic spelling. I take it you've no objections to exposing your genitals in public.'

The last sentence refers to Jake's forthcoming appointment with Dr Trefusis, but read it with a particular emphasis on 'your' and its potential as the punchline to the running Irish joke becomes apparent. The speech acquires a degree of continuity, with an implied subclause: 'as I do, habitually, being Irish and given to talking bollocks'.

The comedic fabric of this passage is tinged with a feeling of hostility never before apparent in Amis's work. Jake has been reduced to the condition of the participant in a farce which, for him, is humiliating and over which he seems to have no control. His mildly racist reflections, deftly orchestrated by the narrator, indicate a blend of malice and hopelessness, and the whole passage reflects Amis's feelings about what he had to go through with the likes of Dr Cobb.

Things get even worse when in Chapter 8 Jake undergoes an 'experimental session' at the hands of Professor Rowena Trefusis, attended by Dr Rosenburg, assisted by the appropriately named Miss Newman and a Ghanaian whose function is not explained. The event is witnessed by eight medical students. Jake is seated on a straight-backed chair, formally dressed in grey suit jacket, regimental tie, grey socks and polished black shoes but without his trousers and underpants. This mildly surreal juxtaposition of public and intimate presentation is echoed throughout the episode.

Jake is asked to read passages from the flattest and most abstract philosophical tracts, alternated with photographs of naked women undergoing a variety of bizarre and physically strenuous sexual acts. One assumes that this polarity of extreme sexual and non-sexual registers is administered as a means of returning Jake to the position, somewhere between the two, that he had occupied before his 'thing'. But its purpose is continuously parodied and undermined by the manner in which Jake and his specialists are obliged to communicate with each other. Professor Trefusis opens the session by running through their respective curricula vitae: Jake is sixty, married, employed by Oxford University, has a house in Orris Park; she is thirty-six, married to a photographer, has two teenage children and a house up the road in Tooting. This exercise is presumably designed to disperse the prevailing atmosphere of clinical formality. Instead, it becomes a double echo of a lonely hearts column and the kind of modestly suggestive exchange between a male and a female at a dinner party. With grim and unintended irony, Professor Trefusis moves on without comment to an explanation of how Jake's sexual responses will be measured, via an instrument attached to his penis, on an impressively elaborate set of dials.

All through the session Trefusis and Newman ask Jake polite questions about his sexual responses to the material, whether he is concentrating properly and the state of his erection. Again, these exchanges carry twisted but very recognizable parallels with a conversation between sexual partners in bed.

The crescendo of this bizarre double-parody of a real and a clinically engineered sexual encounter occurs when Professor Trefusis offers to conclude the session with an instrument called the 'artificial stimulator'. Their exchange shifts brilliantly between an implied memory of Jake's previous experience of intimate contact and the standardized and innocently ambiguous mannerisms of an air stewardess.

> Professor Trefusis came and muttered in his ear, 'Would you like a climax? We can give you one, not out here of course, or we can arrange for you to give yourself one in private.'
>
> 'I don't think I will, thanks very much all the same.'
>
> When they parted a few minutes later she said to him, 'I hope to see you again soon.'
>
> 'Again? Soon?'
>
> 'After the successful completion of Dr Rosenburg's treatment.'

Martin gives an account of how after reading *Jake's Thing* he asked his father if it was true, 'that genital focusing stuff and going to bed with a ring around your cock?' 'Yes,' he answered, 'some of it'; adding that 'in a case like this you have to show willing'. Martin commented enigmatically that 'the *novel* didn't show willing, did it?' (*Experience*, p. 230), suggesting that its style evinced an uncharacteristic mood of detachment, as if the events described did not merit comment. Indeed, Jake does not, via his narrator, reflect on the episode with Professor Trefusis.

The reader, if he or she is so inclined, is left to assemble an exercise in black comedy from the components of a largely objective report. In the majority of Amis's other third-person novels there is a cooperative alliance between the heterosexual character and the narrator. Sexuality, predominantly male sexuality, is always there, and the text will provide routes between this instinct and practically all other idioms and experiences. Jake's own condition, in which sex is something simultaneously remembered and absent, insinuates itself into the structure of the novel. If any of Amis's other male characters had been substituted for Jake the parallels between the experimental session and the real world of mild flirtation, suggestive discourse and sexual intimacy would have become a running joke shared, implicitly, by character, narrator and reader. Jake's loss of sexual desire detaches him from four decades of familiar emotional, intellectual and verbal operations, and it has a concomitant effect upon the relationship between character, narrator and reader that in Amis's novels had lasted almost as long as Jake's sexual career.

Amis is forcing a middle-aged version of Jim Dixon to undergo a kind of humiliating, penitential exercise. The writing is sharp, beautifully timed, but it has also, deliberately, lost something. Jim Dixon and his many reinventions formed an axis between their books' parodic atmosphere and an equally pervasive sense of tolerance: situations and people might be irritating, but if they could be made funny they were also endurable. But not now.

At the end of the novel there is an exchange between Jake and his wife, Brenda, which is a distillation of those which took place between Amis and Jane. Brenda:

> 'Take away love or sex and the impression ought to be clearer, not distorted by emotions and wishful thinking and so on. But it's the other way round. You used to see as most men see, now you don't. Or it's more like . . . What's that stuff they put in ships to keep them from going all over the place?'
>
> 'What? Oh . . . ballast?'
>
> 'That's right. People's sex drives are like ballast, they keep them steady. It sounds wrong but they do.'

This is a shrewd analysis of Jake's condition. Before his 'thing' all aspects of his life were tinged with sexuality. It was not that he was disagreeable to women he found attractive, but practically every woman he met, irrespective of the context, raised the question of whether he would or would not wish to have sex with her. The ever-present notion of sex – speculative, probable, undesired, or unlikely – was his 'ballast'. It attended and frequently determined the direction of his thoughts and acts. Now, without the ballast, his world had become unsynchronized, its familiar patterns distorted – an experience which Amis ingeniously reproduced by reviving Jim as a man who has become detached from the fabric of his fictional world.

The Alteration and *Jake's Thing*, published within eighteen months of each other, offer intriguing insights into the relationship between Amis's life and his writing. Both focus on the disabling, disorientating consequences of life without sex. Throughout *The Alteration* he presents us with a society governed by an asexual ideology: it is a bizarre, surreal reshaping of a world we recognize. Jake's world is similar, in that for him it is comprised of experiences and phenomena that are familiar but changed. In the 1974 article, Moreschi, the castrato, is perceived by Amis as someone who witnesses existence as an assembly of non-sequiturs: everything is there, but there is no activating force, no informing mechanism. Amis recreates a version of Moreschi's experience in the fabric of both novels, and in turn each reflects his own sense of a world altered by the absence of sex. According to Jane, there were discernible similarities between Amis and Jake, both as husbands and more comprehensively. His attitudes to women in general, and not just her, seemed to change. In Jane's opinion Amis had previously embodied many of the more tolerable characteristics of post-war, middle-class English maleness. He maintained a balance between the socially prescribed protocols of politeness and tolerance regarding all women and a more selective preference for women who were variously attractive, intelligent, amusing and agreeable company. During the 1970s, however, he began to take on his version of, in her view, Larkin's attitude of unease and nervous hostility regarding the opposite sex. He started to treat women not just as a separate gender but as a separate species, to observe them from a distance. And, again, there is the sense that once the keystone of sexual attraction had been removed the edifice that it once supported began to crumble.

Amis's perceptions of women writers offer an intriguing index to his broader attitudes to gender. He respected Jane's writing, he enjoyed the poems of Elizabeth Jennings and the earlier fiction of Iris Murdoch, but in general he felt that women writers were encumbered by a genetic characteristic which caused them to treat the emotional or psychological pretext of writing as more important than matters such as style or an obligation to entertain the reader. He regarded this tendency as particularly evident in women poets because this was the genre in which the dense precision of the writing was at least as important as its subject. Women were more concerned with the communication of emotional states than with the act of communication, or as he had put it in 'A Bookshop Idyll',

> We men have got love well weighed up; our stuff
>> Can get by without it
> Women don't seem to think that's good enough;
>> They write about it,

> And the awful way their poems lay them open
>> Just doesn't strike them.

Of the pre-twentieth-century women poets, he gave a respectful nod towards Katherine Philips, Ann Finch and Christina Rossetti, but that was about it. Amis's eccentric perception of the canon is refashioned in *Jake's Thing* as a far more misogynistic, clinical diatribe by Smith, an English don in Jake's college. Amis, as if witnessing a cruelly honest version of his new self, has Jake fully approve of it. Smith is a homosexual, and it is implied that, as a consequence, he can evaluate women's writing more objectively than those who have also to cope with the hindrance of being sexually attracted to women. And it is clear that, because of his similarly detached condition, Jake is better able to appreciate Smith's thesis.

In short, it was only the excitement of sexuality that had caused Jake to treat the other half of humanity with something resembling respect and tolerance. At the end of the novel Jake is informed by Dr Curnow that his thing is probably curable with carefully selected drugs. Jake reflects on this and ponders all of the features of women which sex had obliged him to marginalize but which now he is able to perceive with dispassionate clarity: their tendency to talk about nothing in particular, their extravagant concern with objects and appearances, their automatic assumption of the role of injured party in debates and disagreements, their fondness for the major share of feeling in crises, their use of misunderstanding and misrepresentation as weapons of debate. His response to Curnow's offer of a cure is the closing sentence of the novel, 'So it was quite easy. "No thanks," he said.'

There was no immediate cure available for Amis's condition, and this reworking of the autobiographical core of the novel raises an intriguing question about Amis's state of mind when he completed it. A year later he wrote a short poem called 'Senex' which offers an alternative to Jake's choice. The first stanza transposes Jake with Sophocles.

> To find his sexual drives had ceased
>   For Sophocles was no disaster
> He said he felt like one released
>   From service with a cruel master.

But the second involves the voice of Amis.

> I envy him – I miss the lash
>   At which I used to snort and snivel;
> Oh that its unremitted slash
>   Were still what makes me drone and drivel!

Jake and Sophocles treat their new condition with a mixture of stoicism and embittered relief while the speaker of the poem cannot quite accept his loss, and this assembly of unsettled, antithetical attitudes is a fair reflection of Amis's state of mind.

For Amis, the involvement of other people in what was essentially a very private physical and emotional problem was almost as bad as the problem itself. In 1978 he wrote to Robert Conquest of how Jane was giving a great deal of attention to 'her recently bereaved analyst and the worthless persons in her "group"' (1 December 1978). The group referred to had been part of their lives for two years and was composed of analysts and persons with problems, a non-hierarchical arrangement in which disclosure and open exchange were necessary for a cure. Amis had taken part in this on a number of occasions, and in *Jake's Thing* a savagely hilarious account of what it involved is offered in Chapter 15, 'At Mr Shysters'. Ed, the coordinator, introduces Jake and Brenda to the rest of the participants: 'he can't get it up any more, and what's with Brenda is she thinks it's her fault for having gotten middle-aged and fat, so she feels bad' (Jane Howard, too, was concerned about her size, and ironically it was from one of her frequent visits to a health farm that she dispatched the letter to Amis informing him that their marriage was over). In the 1978 letter to Conquest Amis states that 'Tonight the "group" comes here for a party' and that he intends to go out with friends. To Larkin (29 September 1979) he writes of his 'self-pity themes, don't tempt me, son'. It is a long list and scrupulously ordered, beginning with his hay fever, moving on to high blood pressure and the irritating side-effects of his 'anti-blood-p pills', plus his 'increasing phobias that stop me travelling almost anywhere . . . and make me dread and hate being alone'. But these are mere distractions compared with the torments that conclude the list: 'a wife who puts herself first and the rest nowhere and constantly goes out to GROUPS and WORKSHOPS and crappy "new friends", and total loss of sex drive; I haven't had a fuck for more than a year and a wank for over a month'. A couple of months later, masturbation briefly returns. 'Had a wank this morning, which makes it a light-grey-letter day. Consequence of encountering a v. depraved looking female last night. NO, MEETING HER SOCIALLY NOT SCREWING HER.' He finishes his account of how half-formed desire and sex without a partner are neither depressing nor exciting with a reflection. 'Funny how different life is when you lose your stand. But funny how much it stays the same.' These two sentences catch the mood of *Jake's Thing* perfectly, particularly the way in which Jake's perception of everything is rather like a black-and-white continuance of what had once been a colour film: the same but different. Martin Amis remembers this period in his father's marriage to Jane as being very much like Jake's sceptical but biddable attendance to Brenda's pursuit of a cure. Frequently 'the house was filled with psychotherapists and other appalling people', and when Martin asked his father how he could stand all this he answered that 'One has to show willing.' As did Jake.

Uncertainty and Mrs Thatcher

IN July 1981 the *Sunday Times* published a lengthy article by Amis in which he describes a two-week cruise holiday taken the previous summer by himself, Jane, Violet and Anthony Powell and Paul and Betty Fussell. The MTS *Orpheus* set sail from Southampton and called at Nantes, La Rochelle, Lisbon, Granada, Barcelona and, finally, Nice, where the Amises and Fussells disembarked. After that they spent some time with friends of Jane in the Dordogne and travelled home through France.

The article is intriguing in that it reflects Amis's prejudices and sympathies yet for a number of reasons grossly exaggerates them. His encounters with art, architecture and food occasion bouts of calculated nastiness. A visit to the Museo Picasso in Barcelona causes Amis to dismiss the artist as an untalented, opportunistic fraud. Pictures of faces 'with both eyes on the same side of the nose' were shrewd contributions to a fashion, modernism, that would make him rich. Also in Barcelona he has a look at the famous Church of the Holy Family, a flamboyant compendium of ancient and modern styles, begun in 1885, still unfinished and supposedly a token of the city's cultural radicalism. Amis regards it as 'self-aggrandizing and self-indulgent'. He praises the Gulbenkian Museum of Lisbon mainly because its exhibits seem to reflect its founder's distaste for modernism. Although he quite liked the older buildings – mostly churches – and artworks encountered in these places, he felt that they were devalued and limited by the dogma of their patron, the Church.

The food on the liner is horrible, and on land things are even worse, prompting Amis to ponder an inverse correlation between nationality and cuisine. Spain: 'like English, nice people, nasty food'. In France the food is better but spoilt by the necessity of consuming it in the presence of so many loathsome people.

It was not unusual for Amis deliberately to cultivate some of the worst aspects of his public image. It was a useful self-regenerating procedure which, particularly with articles such as this, generated a healthy readership, even if many of them knew in advance that they would be variously angered and unsettled by what they read. His comments on food were not so much evaluations as incitements, designed to offend those readers for whom European cuisine was the badge of cosmopolitan sophistication. His virulently anti-modernist and generally dismissive appraisal of European culture *per se* was similarly overstated and calculatedly provocative. It was as though he had sorted through and made appropriate selections from his wardrobe of personae and then combined his post-*I Like It Here* reputation as a xenophobic little-Englander with the cynicism of restaurateur Allington, who despised the pretensions of his foreign-food-loving clientele.

The article might seem to be of slight value as part of Amis's literary output, but considered in relation to its private subtext it discloses a number of fascinating clues to the mindset of Amis the novelist. On several occasions he reflects, somewhat enigmatically, on the relationship between writing that attends to real people, places and events and that which uses these as the basis for invention. For example,

> I suppose I am used to doing descriptions in novels, which are not
> really descriptions but extensions of mood and drama by other

means. If your travel-piece, unlike this one, is full of mood and drama, then the kind of set-piece description I am thinking of would probably work. Well, anyway.

When Amis claims very emphatically that what he has written is not based upon reality it usually indicates that it is. The real cruise involved a good deal of 'mood and drama', but Amis employed his talents to systematically excise both.

For one thing, Amis had a very enjoyable time. He told Conquest that 'all in all the cruise was quite fun' (Jacobs, p. 323). He and Fussell engaged in exchanges of jokes and banter that often had both of them convulsed with laughter. The change of pace between relaxing all day, with drink, on the liner and excursions ashore he found most agreeable and far better than the conventional and, in his opinion, tedious holiday in one place. The article, however, conveys an almost uninterrupted feeling of disappointment, disenchantment and impatience.

It might be argued that he refashioned things simply as part of his bait-trailing exercise for cosmopolitan *Sunday Times* readers, but his motive was far more personal and complicated than that.

It was his last holiday with Jane; she would leave him for good in December 1980, and she remembers the cruise as the occasion for some of their worst exchanges. At the beginning of the piece he describes how the timetable had been misinterpreted, causing them to arrive in Southampton shortly before the *Orpheus* departed. Ostensibly, this is the pretext for a digression on the potential hazards of foreign travel, but soon afterwards he notes his 'self-approval for not bollocking Jane – she it was who had screwed the time-table'. According to Jane, this involves two untruths. She was not responsible for misreading the timetable, but he did indeed blame and 'bollock' her for doing so, without apology. Amis terminates his account of the journey at Nice, as well he might. Jane recalls that he spent much of his time on the liner and ashore drunk and that this sequence reached its nadir in the Dordogne where he was consistently rude and insulting to their host, her friend. Soon afterwards he lost his notes and early drafts for the article and accused Jane of stealing them. She had not, and eventually he found them, but he did not bother to apologize.

Amis closes the article with a lengthy reflection on the difference between travel writing and novel writing. In his view, the principal advantage of the latter is that it makes usable the less agreeable aspects of experience. Boring anecdotes, flat dialogue, funny remarks that turn out to be unfunny can become elements of characterization; people who in the real world we might wish to avoid can, in the novel, be turned into interesting specimens. But with travel writing the awfulness of life is 'quite beyond being passed off as anything but what it is' and, as a consequence, the writing must be commensurately good. Amis is preparing a case for an admission of guilt. Given the difficulties of travel writing:

> we can hardly wonder if a travel writer improves upon reality. But he must do so only with extreme care and self-restraint; one obvious fabrication and the reader's confidence is destroyed . . . [W]hatever insight we may gain, or seem to have gained in this place or that people, his only real subject is himself. So he is a bit of a fraud at best . . .

Amis, ever addicted to the amusing trick of the light, leaves the ordinary reader wondering what aspects of the preceding piece of apparently dry, documentary realism are in fact fabrications or improvements upon reality. One person, Jane, would already know, and his conclusion would strike a very personal note. In many of his novels of the previous two decades fiction had been underwritten by a private, autobiographical message available only to the two of them, and his almost obsessive concern throughout the article with the blurred distinction between invention and truth-telling invokes this history. His account of the timetable mix-up adheres to his questionable affirmation of blame, but in a manner that is relaxed, affectionate. Also, of course, he had excised from the article those features of the cruise that for Jane and him were most significant: it was a contribution to the imminent collapse of their marriage. But in a characteristically Amisian manner he had turned it into a note of apology. He had enjoyed the holiday, albeit selfishly, while in the article it becomes a litany of barely endurable punishments. *Mea Culpa*, he seems to be saying. He deliberately reinvents the cruise and, as he discloses, 'his only real subject is himself'. Perhaps by rewriting pleasure as disappointment he thought he was, in a perverse manner, apologizing.

The article, by its very nature as a hybrid of various genres and techniques, tells us much about the way in which Amis produced his novels. His digressions on the relation between travel writing and fiction involve some of his most subtle literary-critical observations, but it is the aspect of the piece that is kept from the ordinary reader that reveals most about his writing. It was reprinted in *The Amis Collection* (1990), but it could have been placed just as appropriately in *Collected Short Stories* (1987). He does not make up any actual events, but he reschedules the effect upon himself of what did happen to such an extent that it qualifies as fiction, and the fact that the central figure and narrator is Kingsley Amis is the supplement which confirms its status as one of his most honest, self-referential disclosures regarding the character of his novels. It is intriguing to compare it with the article he wrote for the *Times Literary Supplement* in 1973 called 'Real and Made Up People'. As the title indicates, its principal subject is his method of inventing fictional characters and circumstances, and it is largely a pack of lies. He states that only once did he 'try to put real people on paper [including himself] and produced what is by common consent my worst novel, *I Like It Here*'. There is a degree of truth in this, given that the novel draws exclusively upon the events, chronology and a number of the people of his Portugal trip, but what he should have added was that a large number of his other novels, indeed in 1973 all of them, are cunningly rewritten contributions to a multi-volume autobiography. In fact, the most ironic feature of the *I Like It Here* exercise is that it involves fewer of the most passionate, troubled, embittered and affectionate aspects of his life than the novels in which he disguises himself; and one wonders if the article was prompted by the previous decade in which at the core of, sometimes the inspiration for, his fiction was his relationship with Jane. In 1973 things were beginning to go wrong, and maybe the article was as much an act of self-denial as denial.

In 1981 he was on his own, and he wanted Jane back. The article about the cruise would not be what it is without this factor – even its title 'Amis Abroad' conveys an ironic sense of loss and dislocation - and the same scenario of life imitating, configuring, art applies to his novels. The first novel that he would produce after their break-up, *Stanley and the Women* (1984), would, similarly, not be what it is without that event, and it is his most shamelessly unpleasant, contemptuous and contemptible piece of work.

The novel that precedes it, *Russian Hide and Seek* (1980), was written approximately a year before the break-up and it has fewer autobiographical resonances, at least regarding his private life, than anything he had previously published. However, his opinions, particularly regarding politics and culture, feature prominently enough.

The story is set in England in 2030, half a century after Britain's occupation by the Soviet Union, but Communism had effectively died out about ten years before. This rather unexpected development might be seen as a shrewd and prescient analysis of international politics, although Amis's prediction of the timing of events was somewhat pessimistic: European Communism had in fact little more than a decade left. More significantly, the consequences of its disappearance, particularly in Russia, and in some of its more economically backward satellite states is unnervingly foreseen. Britain, and practically everywhere else still under Russian control, has become less a totalitarian nightmare and more a distorted echo, a depressing parody of the past. The class systems that existed before the so-called 'pacification' have re-emerged as a kind of anarchic feudalism. The ex-Communist rulers still hold positions of power and influence but as a hapless, directionless aristocracy. Their lives and day-to-day privations are not far removed from those of the English peasantry. Economic collapse has caused rulers and ruled to become united in a state of bucolic tedium, and the technological ambitions of the Soviet monolith are a darkly comic memory; transport takes place mainly by horse and mule. It could be Romania.

Amis had done a good deal of research into these matters, although not originally for the novel. In 1969–70 he had proposed a television series for the BBC to be called 'General Tomski's Army', in which the eponymous Red Army officer and a number of similarly inclined colleagues plot a counter-revolution that will destroy Communism from within. In the end the series was not commissioned, but the proposal includes an impressive list of academic and political writings which Amis advises his potential producers to consult as evidence of the plausibility of his dramatic thesis and, by implication, of his own expertise. These include Conquest's Soviet Studies Series, along with Miller's *Life in Russia Today*, Mehnet's *The Anatomy of Soviet Man* and *The Penkovsky Papers* detailing the activities and state of mind of the Russian diplomat turned Western spy. All point to intrinsic flaws in the Soviet system as an ever-present incitement to dissent, but none goes quite so far as Amis does in the planned series and more so in the novel to propose that change would begin at the top: another impressively accurate foretelling of what would be initiated by Gorbachev and carried forward by Yeltsin. For the names of all his Russian characters in the novel Amis used the index of Conquest's study of Stalinism, *The Great Terror*, but this was more an eccentric nod of thanks to his friend than a suggestion of direct parallels.

The hero of the novel is Alexander Petrovsky, a young cavalry officer who is drawn, more by boredom than idealism, into the so-called Group 31, a collection of subversives who intend to accelerate the demise of Communism with counter-revolution and return Europe to an imagined ideal which they are all too young to remember and which has been variously rewritten or eradicated in official histories. Their plot fails, causes no reverberations and the novel ends with Petrovsky's funeral.

Russian Hide and Seek might seem to belong in the tradition of Orwell's *Nineteen Eighty-Four* and Huxley's *Brave New World*, but in truth it is as closely related to the Victorian 'Condition of England' novel, diagnostic of the collective moods and countercurrents of contemporary society. Amis himself said so in an interview shortly after publication. 'I'd hate it to be thought of as a novel about the Russian menace. It's more about the destruction of beliefs. It is a warning not about what the Russians may do to us; it is a warning about what we may do to ourselves' (interview with Dale Salwak, 1980; reprinted in Salwak, 1992).

One suspects that Amis's interweaving of Russian and English sensibilities is as much a literary allusion as a political prophecy. Ivan Turgenev spent many years in England, and his novel *Fathers and Sons* (1862), which was planned here, is credited with the invention of Nihilism. Bazarov, its hero, reacts to the 'special odour of corruption', which permeates Russia, by repudiating all of the high ideals and principles that had already been defiled by his contemporaries. Petrovsky is a modern version of Bazarov, a complex individual for whom the moral and emotional dimensions of love, commitment and death have become abstractions.

England almost became Turgenev's adopted country. He was passionately enthused by the work of contemporary poets and novelists and admired Shakespeare inordinately. He regarded the literary traditions of this country as the token of a durable civilization, a personal antidote to his experience of Russia's decline, and there is an ironic parallel between this and an initiative launched by the Russians in Amis's novel. Their 'New Cultural Programme' is an attempt to revive England's indigenous artistic heritage, suppressed by Communism, and reintroduce it to the population. This enterprise is founded upon the tendentious premise that an appreciation of art involves a concomitant respect for ethics and responsibility: Turgenev's ideal in practice.

When Amis was completing the novel, in October 1979, he gave a lecture at the Conservative Party Conference held that year in Blackpool. He explained that his title 'An Arts Policy?' carried a question mark not because he wished to consider whether a particular political policy involving the arts was good or bad but because he regarded the fundamental notion of government involvement in the arts as extremely questionable. The lecture is a redrafted version of key elements of the novel. He referred to what he regarded as a sinister proposal made in a Labour Party pamphlet (*The Arts and the People*, October 1977) ('a vile document') that 'a policy-making National Conference for the Arts and Entertainment will be set up' by the next Labour government. This was to be comprised of government ministers, civil servants, Arts Council representatives, persons from 'interest groups' such as 'Regional Arts Associations' and, almost as a footnoted concession, a few 'individual artists'. The Russians' 'New Cultural Programme' was obviously born out of Amis's distressing encounter with the Labour Party's 'National Programme for the Arts and Entertainment'.

In the lecture he makes a number of his opinions clear. The quality of literature, music and painting should be determined by market forces, in the sense that artists, like others who earn a living by selling their product, can only survive if what they make is attractive enough to guarantee sales. This would not, he argues, encourage a consumer-oriented decline in standards. Populist art has always existed comfortably in its own area of the market, but people with advanced aesthetic sensibilities would as consumers ensure that artists with higher cultural aspirations produced good work. If they did not it would not sell. Government sponsorship, however, encourages and sustains bad artists and bad art. He quotes from the Labour Party pamphlet:

> 'A socialist policy . . . requires more books, and a wider range and higher quality of books to be published, written by authors of every sort of social background.' Naturally, but why aren't people writing these high-quality books already? . . . a clear example of the Socialists' habit of giving the public not what it wants but what they think it ought to want . . . Happily, the public won't take what it doesn't want. It goes somewhere else. (*The Amis Collection*, p. 246)

The people who run the Arts Council and would control Labour's projected 'National Programme' are, he claims, elitists (in that without their patronage modernism would have died a natural death through lack of demand) and condescending.

> It's a traditional lefty view, the belief that anybody can enjoy art, real art, in the same way that everybody is creative. In the words of that old idiot and bad artist Eric Gill, 'the artist is not a special kind of man; every man is a special kind of artist'. That's only possible if making mud pies counts as art, which admittedly is beginning to happen. (p. 246)

Practically all of the ideas and sentiments that Amis savages in the lecture are voiced in the novel by Commissioner Mets, the senior Russian bureaucrat in charge of implementing the New Cultural Programme. In Chapter 4 Mets explains that, with the recently unbanned *Romeo and Juliet*, 'our instructors have had to explain every other word' to the English actors who are rehearsing for a performance, audience attendance for which will, by various means, be made compulsory. The performance is a horrible projection of Amis's notion of enforced culture, with the audience, having been informed in advance as to what parts are funny and what parts tragic, responding inappropriately. The comic elements are greeted with a mixture of glum silence and muttering while the deaths of the lovers generate laughter. An earlier performance of *Look Back in Anger* is more successful. Having been instructed by the Russian experts that it is a slapstick comedy, the audience agrees. 'Only very rarely in the past could the theatre have rung with so much happy, hearty laughter' (Chapter 17). The music recital involves works by a number of composers deemed to be of equally high quality. 'Dowland, Purcell, Sullivan, Elgar, the composer of "Ta-ra-ra-boom-de-ay", Noël Coward, Duke Ellington (taken to have been an English nobleman of some sort), Britten and John Lennon.'

As well as providing Amis with the opportunity to ridicule Osborne, his presentation of the New Cultural Programme reflects his view that while culture, particularly literature, should be part of the education system it can only be taught to those with the intellectual capacity, and the inclination, to appreciate it. Moreover, it emphasizes his opinion that the educators – prompted by a socialist-inspired trend towards valuing disposable entertainment as equal to the bourgeois notion of high art – are contributing to the general decline in artistic standards. He refers in the lecture to his claim of almost two decades earlier that with the expansion of universities 'more will mean worse', and in a letter to *The Times* in 1981 (3 August) he questions the validity of 'university departments of drama', no doubt privately recalling what happened when the Russian instructors tried to teach people to appreciate Shakespeare.

In Chapter 2 two Russian bureaucrats greet one another with '*Good evening, my dear chap*' and '*Fine to see you, old customer*'. The dialogue is italicized because it is English, an inaccurate (*old customer*, for example) but fashionable revival of the language of the lost culture of pre-occupation Britain. The English characters use the old language with only a little more confidence and authenticity, and the effect of this device upon the reader is bizarre. The third-person account, including dialogue originally in Russian, is rendered in convincingly modern English but largely without Amis's usual locutionary range or his characteristic interplay between the idiomatic individualism of speech and the sardonic dryness of description. It is almost as though he is doing a translation of his own work and, as he made clear in his account of his discussion of translation with the Russian poet Yevtushenko, 'an interest in the paraphrasable content of literature [is] an anti-literary interest' (*What Became of Jane Austen?*, p. 170). His translation of his own novel is a good one, but it loses much of the original.

Why did he do this? In 1980 he published an essay called 'Getting It Wrong' (in *The State of the Language*, ed. L. Michaels and C. Ricks, University of California Press). Its principal subject is malapropisms, the misuse of particular words, but it is effectively a distillation of a series of broadcasts he did for BBC Radio during the mid-1970s on the general decline of standards in spoken English. He is convinced that since about 1960 linguistic usage has become increasingly shoddy and careless. Worst of all, he is able to give examples from language in print of the more frequent and self-sustaining malapropisms, indicating that the 'supposedly educated', particularly journalists and people who write letters to quality newspapers, are causing the deterioration in standards. People who use language in public seemed no longer to concern themselves with how individual words had acquired their meaning, and while Amis is familiar with the thesis that if languages do not change they die, 'it seems to be often forgotten that death is a very important form of change' (p. 304). The novel offers an exaggerated version of this. For the intellectual elite, those who run society, English is, literally, a foreign language, and as a consequence it has for everyone become almost a dead language. Its complexities, its ability to enliven perception and thought, are largely a memory.

The election of a Conservative government in May 1979 was greeted by Amis with a mixture of satisfaction and optimism. The post-war Labour government had transformed completely the economic and social fabric of Britain by nationalizing all of the major utilities along with the production and natural resource industries, creating a National Health Service and inventing the modern welfare state. All subsequent administrations, with the Conservatives spending slightly more time in office than Labour, had involved a blend of consensus and compromise. The Tories had made no serious attempts to dismantle Labour's creation of 1945, and in dealings with the immensely powerful trade-union movement both parties exchanged ideology for pragmatism. Mrs Thatcher's election manifesto of 1979 promised to implement the true principles of Conservatism: the free market would replace government control, privatization was mooted, if not too clearly specified, and entrepreneurialism would unweave the culture of dependency.

In 1968 with *Lucky Jim's Politics* Amis had publicly and officially renounced his previous commitment to the Labour Party, and the tone of the piece suggested that he was no longer really interested in politics at all, given that the policies of two major parties had become largely indistinguishable and the legacy of leftism was now the status quo. His drift even further rightward during the 1970s was mainly a private exercise: it was reflected in his writing, but he could not be bothered with active involvement. Mrs Thatcher changed things. Robert Conquest, while staying with Amis in Hampstead in January 1979, suggested that he should join him at a forthcoming dinner party at the Thatcher house in Flood Street, just north of Chelsea. Amis said yes, Conquest phoned Mrs Thatcher and she enthusiastically extended the invitation – the support of a popular and respected writer would be a useful addition to her forthcoming election campaign. Amis, like many of Thatcher's male Cabinet ministers, was mildly besotted with her: middle-aged but in her manner of dress, speech and dealings with men exuding a blend of power and aggressive flirtation. Males of Amis's generation rarely encountered women who were as self-confidently tough as men. He joined the Conservative Party. His invitation to give a lecture at the 1979 post-election conference was from Mrs Thatcher, and his promotion of market forces is consistent with her doctrine. Indeed he chides the Conservatives for not, in their own party document on the arts, having fully detached themselves from the socialist principle of sponsorship. He even proposes a policy initiative. Grants, loans and tax exemptions should be offered not to self-indulgent writers but to people who want to open bookshops. There are, he claims, only five hundred 'chartered bookshops' in England, a classification which excludes shops that also sell such things as pop records, toilet requisites and lampshades. In Germany, apparently, there are six thousand. His proposal is consistently Thatcherite; books should be sold, not sponsored.

In August 1980 he was invited to a reception in 10 Downing Street. By fortuitous coincidence this was also the day on which *Russian Hide and Seek* was published, and he took with him a copy of the novel. 'The inscription mentioned things like respect rather than undying passion, etc.' Mrs Thatcher thanked him and asked him what it was about. He began to explain that it was a vision of Britain under Russian occupation, but before he could expand on this and inform her of its relevance to contemporary society she interrupted him. 'Huh!' she cried. 'Can't you do better than that? Get yourself another crystal ball!' She moved on, and he amused himself thereafter by watching Larkin, another recruit to the new Tory fold, apparently being rendered silent by a version of his own technique of boring people at parties. 'Denis Thatcher was telling Philip Larkin about the current test series without the possibility of interruption' (*Memoirs*, p. 318).

Amis continued to admire, indeed revere, Mrs Thatcher. She merits a chapter in his *Memoirs* in which he becomes a 69-year-old adolescent; she even, apparently, featured in a modestly erotic dream of his. The only issue on which Amis disagreed with the Thatcher government was education. He was happy enough with their advocacy of traditional doctrines, such as vocational training in schools and their repudiation of left-leaning, customer-friendly disciplines such as media studies, but he was personally affronted by their underfunding of 'education as education, definable as the free pursuit of knowledge and truth for their own sake' (*Memoirs*, p. 319), a coded reference to the fact that even the more prestigious universities had been made to suffer. He supported the decision of Oxford not to award her an honorary doctorate.

PART 4

RETROSPECTION AND HILLY

20

Stanley and the Women

JANE left Amis in November 1980. She arranged to spend ten days at a health farm and while there she got her solicitors to deliver a letter to Gardnor House informing Amis that she did not intend to return and that divorce proceedings would follow. He wrote to Larkin in early December informing him of what had happened and of how he felt about it. In his view, she had gone partly because of his lack of interest in sex with her and partly because he did not like her any more. In truth, she left him because she could no longer tolerate the effects of his drinking. In September they had gone to the Edinburgh Festival. Amis, with gleefully masochistic expectations, attended a performance-art exercise and a play by Lillian Hellman. 'Frightful piss,' he told Conquest. He did not go to anything else, drank a lot and, according to Jane, spent an evening being incessantly abusive and insulting to the conductor Claudio Abbado.

The effect of Jane's departure upon Amis can only be described as shock. Throughout his life he had dealt with his various fears, weaknesses and unangelic predispositions by preparing himself for their likely consequences. This was different, in that while he was fully aware that continued life with Jane would be far from easy he had not envisioned its sudden termination. The letters he wrote to several of his close friends in the months after Jane left him are intriguing. To Larkin (5 December 1980) he states that she 'just buggered off . . . partly to punish me for stopping wanting to fuck her and partly because she realized I didn't like her much'. At the same time, however, 'not having her around and trying to take in the fact that she never will be around is immeasurably more crappy than having her around'. A similar mood of vacillation informs his account to Brian Aldiss (15 December). 'No word from the old bitch. By God she was hard to live with but living without her seems altogether pointless. I had no idea she meant that much to me.' Following this period, in late December, he resumed regular communication with Jane, and they began to make a number of tentative attempts to repair the break-up. Jane eventually agreed to return to him but only on the condition that he gave up drink, completely. He attempted to negotiate a number of compromises – wine only with meals, a modest intake of spirits just at weekends, occasional and regular days of total abstinence and so on – but Jane's terms were final and absolute. He turned her down. During January he confided in his friend Anthony Powell, and when it looked as though an accommodation with Jane was unlikely he stated that 'a final parting of ways . . . arouses in me, among many other things, a profound sense of relief' (5 January 1981). More than a month later he wrote to Powell again, thanking him for 'being so sympathetic to my tale of woe' and indicating that Jane had in the end been implacable. '[S]he was quite sure I wouldn't be able to cut down drink and my only chance was to give it up entirely. How did she know that?' He would be giving her grounds for divorce: '"unreasonable behaviour" on my part. Things like trying to stop her getting away with murder and bestial stuff like that. You know, I've a bloody good mind to defend it. It wouldn't half feed her up' (12 February 1981).

The letters indicate a number of Amis's personal traits. Uncertainty, an ambiguous blend of reproach, loss and dislocation, was gradually transformed into a more focused sense of bitterness and potentially vengeful resentment, and the lever in this process was drink. Drinking in general and alcoholism in particular merit parallels with the equally tendentious issue of religious belief: with both a perception of what exactly is the truth will depend upon the extent to which the perceiver is possessed of or witness to a particular state of mind. Amis drank quite a lot, he always had, but he never regarded himself as an alcoholic. Alcoholism is an addiction, a surrender to something beyond your control; if acknowledged it is an admission that aspects of your life and behaviour are variously unplanned, unremembered and perversely related to your perceived self. For a literary writer, whose faculties and perceptual regimen are the foundation for his work, the acknowledgement of alcoholism would be comparable to the priest who confesses to agnosticism.

So when the final, decisive moment of their relationship hinged upon her demand that he should give up drink completely and his that a moderate intake was a fair compromise we encounter something more than a domestic dispute: Jane was telling him that she knew him as a man and a writer better than he knew himself. (Ironically, a few months after his rejection of Jane's conditional offer he secured a contract, with the *Daily Express* via his friend George Gale, to write columns on drink which would eventually feature in collections called *Everyday Drinking* (1983) and *How's Your Glass?* (1984).)

Only once, with Allington in *The Green Man*, had Amis presented drink as as much an affliction as a habit. He claimed that he turned Allington into an alcoholic to guarantee that his encounters with ghosts, demons and God would be treated by his family as symptomatic of his condition. He did not refer to the fact that when he wrote the novel his own intake had increased sufficiently to worsen the state of his marriage, as indeed it does with Allington and Joyce. Allington, the narrator, is telling two stories or, rather, he very convincingly tells one story to the reader while acknowledging that the people closest to him, particularly his wife, do not believe it. More significantly, Allington is presented as a drunk who, despite his addiction, is in control. He does his job dutifully and competently, his sexual career and his social life are undamaged by his boozing and his remarkable, almost obsessive, attention to detail in his telling of the story show us that his mental condition is unaffected by drink. It is almost as though Amis is predicting his experiences of the forthcoming decade and beyond. His *Memoirs* chapter on 'Booze' is consistent with Allington's account of things. But Jane and Joyce saw things rather differently.

The four-year gap between *Russian Hide and Seek* (1980) and *Stanley and the Women* (1984) was the longest in Amis's career as a novelist. He did not give up writing – his articles on drink and the subsequent book, along with regular reviews for the *Observer*, the *Spectator* and other organs testify to that – and during the first eighteen months of his separation from Jane he worked on a novel. This and *The Legacy* were Amis's only substantial projects that would not go into print, and for similar reasons.

For much of his life Amis had depended upon, sometimes enjoyed, the predictability of a routine. His childhood at home and at school, Oxford, the army, academia and eventually the exclusive profession of writing had provided him with a timetable of objectives and obligations. These organized the components of his life and they also licensed various degrees of rebellion, excursion and imaginative reinvention. In practically all of his fiction there is a tension between two states of mind. One involves performance, responsibility and a foreseeable future, while the other incorporates factors which might threaten or seem preferable to these.

Since he had married Hilly in 1947 he had never been without a permanent partner, an anchor, and frequently, with Hilly, a counterpoint for whatever he did in his spare time; adultery included. When Jane left him he was fifty-eight; hardly the age to go out in search of a replacement, especially since he was no longer interested in sex. For the best part of a year and a half he was, apart from Ms Uniacke, on his own in Gardnor House, which was sold in

1982. He was visited by his friends, his sons and daughter, and he spent many afternoons in the Garrick and elsewhere, but his day-to-day home life carried an air of impermanence and dislocation; there was not even a regular presence with whom he might have arguments or could upset.

The only time in which he had experienced anything similar to this was when he returned to Oxford after the war. This, too, was like finding himself in a familiar but empty house. Larkin and his other close friends from the pre-army period had all gone. He got his first and began a research degree, but he was neither completely committed to an academic career nor certain that a job would be available – a state of mind he could only feel confident enough to turn into comedy, with Jim Dixon, when it had become part of the comfortably distant past. He met Hilly, but she became a permanent feature of his life only after her pregnancy.

It was during this period that he produced *The Legacy* and his poetry collection *Bright November*, the first unpublishable and the second published with a mixture of desperation and retrospective regret. Both were second-rate because Amis addressed them as much to himself as to the reader, and something similar happened with the unfinished novel of three decades later.

Much of *The Legacy* concerns itself with the unceasing struggle of a character called Kingsley Amis to turn his confused and pessimistic state of mind into a novel. He fails to do so, and the notion of a novel which is an intense and sympathetic exploration of not being able to write a novel goes someway to explain the real Amis's failure to find a publisher. Exclusive self-examination and consequent inattention to the audience resulted in bad writing. Similarly the 130-page typescript produced after Jane's departure was, like its predecessor, self-indulgent, more a letter to himself than a performance for the reader. Its central character is a homosexual and, the period being circa 1962, he keeps his sexual inclination to himself. Even the wife of his closest friend presumes that he is heterosexual. She wants an affair with him, takes his rejection of her advances as an insult and seeks revenge by accusing him of interfering with her children. This might not sound like an account of Amis's recent experience, but boil down my summary into its most powerful constituents and the parallels are clear enough. There is a man who does not wish to have sex with women. There is a woman who wants him to have sex with her and, because of his disinclination to do so, seeks a malicious, ruinous form of revenge. This is of course a rather prejudiced, perverse version of his break-up with Jane, but it was written immediately after their attempts to achieve some kind of reconciliation had failed, in Amis's view because of her unreasonable demands and conditions. His early feelings of loss were being overtaken by a compensatory sense of loathing.

Eric Jacobs suggests that Amis abandoned the book because he feared that the hardcore of reactionary homophobes at the Garrick and elsewhere might have responded with more than a raised eyebrow to a novel that was not only sympathetic to homosexuality but which also appeared to reflect an intimate understanding of it. Perhaps they might, but I would argue that he gave it up because it involved a spiral of insularity and retribution that caused him both to disregard the reader and for related reasons made the novel impossible for him to complete. The main character's forthcoming trial would find him caught between the disclosure of his real inclinations, themselves illegal, or some other defence against heterosexual paedophilia. What had begun as a purgation of Amis's unsettled feelings now appeared to demand an intense exploration of sexuality, law, prejudice and perversion. His first inclinations had run out of control.

Its provisional title, *Difficulties with Girls*, was appended, with characteristic Amisian irony, to a later novel which addresses the shortcomings of manic heterosexuality. Its motive, however – his act of vengeance against Jane – did not disappear and after abandoning the first attempt in 1982 he turned it into readable copy for what would be his most controversial, provocative novel, *Stanley and the Women* (1984).

Amis abandoned his first attempt to fictionalize his break with Jane because he knew that anger had displaced the modulating prescriptions of writing. But it was as much a change in environment as a self-critical instinct that enabled him to redress the balance. In early 1982 he was joined in Gardnor House by two people with whom he would share his domestic life for the rest of his natural one, Hilly and her third husband Alastair Boyd, Lord Kilmarnock. This somewhat unusual threesome sounds, as Amis would later reflect, like something from an Iris Murdoch novel, but it was the very real and pragmatic idea of Amis's sons Philip and Martin. In late 1981 Philip took on the role of principal negotiator and spelt out the benefits of the plan to the three potential participants. Hilly and Boyd were short of cash, and a home close to central London would help out with Boyd's regular attendance at the House of Lords. They had a teenaged son Jaime. At the time they were living in a modest cottage in Buckinghamshire, and the Lords provided a minor source of income. The arrangement would remedy Amis's fear of being alone at night, and Hilly would take charge of day-to-day domestic practicalities. Moreover, Amis would have a housekeeper he knew very well indeed and one who had a comprehensive knowledge of his largely unchanged habits and preferences. He and Boyd had never met, but during their first encounters to discuss the set-up they seemed to get on well enough.

Apart from practical and terse exchanges during the 1960s, involving their divorce and their children's future, Hilly and Amis had remained largely out of contact since he left her for Jane. Indeed she had spent most of this time outside England. In 1967 she married David Roy Shackleton Bailey, whom she had first met during Amis's period in Cambridge. He was Senior Bursar at Gonville and Caius. Less than a year after their marriage Bailey became Professor of Latin at the University of Michigan and he, Hilly and Sally

moved to the United States. It was not an entirely disastrous relationship, but they seemed from the beginning to be incompatible.
In 1967 Hilly, in her late thirties, was still the vivacious, amusing,
slightly irresponsible individual to whom Amis was attracted in
1946. Bailey was the archetypal Oxbridge don, ten years older than
Hilly and in terms of temperament and habits her complete opposite. He had never been married nor, it was rumoured, had any kind
of relationship with a woman. Gonville and Caius, and classics,
were his life, and although Michigan was very different from Cambridge Bailey did not change. Perhaps the fact that he was so completely unlike Amis was what prompted Hilly to marry him. Apart
from anything else he seemed safe and dependable. In 1970 he and
Hilly spent part of the summer touring the Mediterranean coast,
and at the end of the holiday Hilly simply refused to go back to
America. She and Sally stayed in Spain, and in the autumn of that
year she met Alastair Boyd.

If Bailey might have appeared in a novel as the stereotypical
don, Boyd could have joined him as his down-at-heel aristocratic
counterpart. All that was left of an impressive ancestry was the title.
The barony had once been an earldom. This had been suspended
completely in 1745, following the Earl of Kilmarnock's participation in the Jacobite rebellion and subsequent execution for
treason. It was revived in 1831, and Boyd would become seventh
baron of the demoted line. When Hilly met him in 1970 he was
running a language school in Ronda, southern Spain. They began a
relationship, lived together in Spain and married in 1977. Boyd's
father died that same year. He inherited the title and they moved to
England so that Boyd could take his seat in the House of Lords. In
1985 he became deputy leader of the Upper House branch of the
newly formed Social Democratic Party.

The first meeting of the eventual threesome was arranged by
Philip and took place in a west London restaurant, and it must have
been unsettling for all involved. Amis, once his relationship with

Jane had started to go wrong, had begun to recall his years with Hilly with a mixture of fondness and regret. Now they were discussing a most unconventional reunion, along with their two sons and her husband. The scenario was too implausible for fiction, even in a reworked form, and it would be twelve years before Amis fully recreated Hilly in a novel, *You Can't Do Both*, published in 1994, a year before his death.

After the sale of Gardnor House in 1982 they moved first to a flat in Hampstead and then to a house in Leighton Road, Kentish Town. This proved to be too small to accommodate regular visitors, mostly Amis's friends, and in 1984 they purchased a more spacious Edwardian house, 194 Regent's Park Road, Primrose Hill, which would be Amis's home for the rest of his life. Boyd and Hilly stayed on until 1998.

The house had four storeys. Boyd and Hilly lived in a virtually self-contained basement flat; Amis occupied a study, bedroom and bathroom on the ground floor; the first floor was a communal collection of sitting-room, dining-room and kitchen, and upstairs there were bedrooms and a bathroom for guests. The arrangement was perfect for Amis. He could spend the morning writing, undisturbed, but when he was not out at the club or elsewhere he was never on his own. A more cramped version of this had operated in Leighton Road, and it was during the two years there that he wrote *Stanley and the Women*.

This novel was his goodbye note to Jane, far more perspicuous and calculated than his first attempt but just as savage. The abandoned *Difficulties with Girls* was, despite its refashionings of circumstance and character, too driven, too intensely personal to make it a good read. Amis's new domestic arrangement restored to his life a degree of order and stability; it returned him to a dependable routine, and he regained the ability to more astutely interweave autobiography and fiction.

By 1984 the women's movement had become a significant feature of the literary-critical world. Works such as Kate Millett's *Sexual Politics* (1970) reflected the burgeoning influence of feminism within the intellectual fabric of Britain and America. In this book Millett argues that male authors, particularly Lawrence, Miller, Mailer and Genet, had in their representation of male and female characters reproduced the normative values and expectations of a patriarchal, male-dominated culture. Amis had probably not read Millett's book, but he was certainly aware that its premise was becoming more and more influential in literary circles.

Amis was a shrewd diagnostician of contemporary moods and trends, a talent he discovered with *Lucky Jim*. That novel was a success partly because of its capacity to both enrage and amuse. It offended the keepers of an outdated educational and cultural hierarchy, and in doing so it delighted a generation for whom disrespectful unorthodoxy was a welcome alternative to the drab rigidity of post-war Britain. *Stanley and the Women* would be seen by many as the complete opposite of the anti-establishment, mildly anarchic mood of *Lucky Jim*. It is indeed a compendium of reactionary opinions, last-stand defences of chauvinism and presentations of women, practically all women, as calculating and malicious. Misogynistic is something of an understatement. However, like *Lucky Jim* it sold and for similar reasons. Both books guaranteed complaint and controversy.

Soon after it was published in Britain the *Times Literary Supplement*'s American correspondent Christopher Hitchens (a close friend of Martin's from their teens) reported that it was effectively being blacklisted by US publishing houses, where, he implied, feminists were in control. 'I shall state the obvious and say that there are influential feminists who believe that the reading public should be spared certain fictions . . . three [of the potential publishers] candidly excused the rescinding of offers [to publish] by reference to objections from feminists on the editorial board' (*Times Literary Supplement*, 'American Notes', 16 November 1984). Amis's usual

American publisher, Harcourt Brace Jovanovich, refused to comment on whether or not the novel would appear under their imprint. Rumours spread and articles about the book and the suspicion of censorship appeared in *Newsweek*, *Time* and the *New York Times Book Review*. No direct comparisons were made, but the spectre of a 1980s' brand of McCarthyism was abroad, which in turn caused other American publishers who were approached by journalists on the matter to stay tight-lipped. In London Jonathan Clowes, Amis's agent, later confirmed, without naming the publishers involved, that there had been difficulties. 'It took a while to find out, but when I pressed them on it, I was told that certain women on their boards were unhappy with the book. And I saw that as a form of censorship' ('Kingsley and the Women', *Saturday Review*, May/June 1985).

Eventually, in May 1985, Summit, a division of Simon and Schuster, agreed to take on the book. One of their editors, Ileene Smith, commented that it was 'not so much a matter of courage . . . as sound literary judgement', a politely understated disclosure that it did indeed involve some courage. She added, proudly, that 'I've had to take a little bit of heat . . . but nothing I can't defend' (interview with Dale Salwak, in Salwak, 1992).

Amis was not so shrewd as to have anticipated quite the degree of controversy and publicity that his book would generate, but as with *Lucky Jim* he knew what he was doing. The parallels are striking. Many reviewers of his first novel were aware that it would upset people and implicitly took on the role of advocates, acknowledging that it was radical, provocative satire but all the more welcome for that and executed with commendable skill. Similarly, the majority of reviews of *Stanley and the Women* were at once defensive and celebratory. The reviewers who praised the book, and most of them did, seemed to feel the need to excuse and explain their admiration for it. Russell Davies in the *Listener* spends a long time distancing himself from anything like sympathy for Stanley's behaviour and opinions before confessing that he can't help liking him: 'he is, well, strikingly unrepulsive' (24 May 1984). Philip Oakes in *New Society* states that it is 'offensive, infuriating and intolerable' and, having paid his dues to the feminist cabal, admits that it is 'exceedingly well written . . . utterly hilarious' (21 May 1984). John Carey in the *Sunday Times* begins with a very elaborate hypothesis:

> If you are a middle-aged chauvinist alcoholic you will enjoy this novel, and its narrator Stanley Duke will strike you as a perfectly normal and reliable chap. If you are any other kind of reader, you will be assailed by doubts. Does Kingsley Amis mean you to notice what a deadly specimen of humankind Stanley is? Does he notice it himself? If so, how can he expect you to swallow Stanley's version of events, as the novel seems to count on you doing? (20 May 1984)

Carey cautiously detaches himself from the kind of reader who might actually identify with Stanley, a wise preparation for his subsequent disclosure of how despite himself he likes the book. One might note also that virtually all of the British reviewers of the novel were men and that Anthony Burgess, Bernard Levin, Melvyn Bragg, John Osborne, Anthony Quinton and George Melly wrote appraisals that involved 'nasty character–good book' swerves and evasions similar to those cited above. The one exception to this all-male regiment of apologists was Harriet Waugh, chosen presumably because of her non-feminist affiliations. She, too, enjoyed the book. The selection of reviewers could cause one either to admire or pity the astuteness of British literary editors. Amis wrote to Larkin, with an air of self-mocking surprise, that 'Stanley seems to have *pleased* a lot of people. I tried to be offensive but the essential niceness of my nature must have got in the way' (18 June 1984).

A couple of weeks later in a letter to Conquest: 'Bloody funny that I've had no unfavourable "feedback" from females about

Stanley, on the contrary. Ones I have never met write to me, others I know only say as wives of acquaintances seek me out, all saying too bloody true and about time somebody said it. Suggests perhaps that the pendulum has started to swing back?' (2 July 1984).

The away-swung pendulum was of course the consensus of feminist dogma and, while he seems to have raised sympathetic responses from a number of British women, the feminist heartland was still in 1984 the United States, where the novel was reviewed by several women a year later – the delay being caused by the publication difficulties.

Mary Mackey in the *San Francisco Examiner-Chronicle* saw it as 'hate mail, aimed not just at feminists but at women of all kinds' (8 September 1985), and for Rhoda Koenig in the *New York Times Magazine* it was an 'ugly, constipated book' (23 September 1985). On receiving copies of these and other reviews by women in the United States Amis wrote to Larkin that, 'Boy they really believe lit. makes statements. Its self-expression you see. All this sort of thing is a marvellous abject confession of FEMALE INFERIORITY COMPLEX and perfectly expresses the point made in the novel' (24 September 1985).

Amis was delighted. It was 1954 relived. Mackey and Koenig echo figures such as Maugham and Weightman; the latter pair read through *Lucky Jim* to an author who was obviously a dangerous cultural vandal, and the former saw *Stanley and the Women* as a personal, transparent polemic against womankind.

He had succeeded in two objectives. The book's calculatedly provocative element had caused the biggest debate on what should or should not be made available to the intelligent reader since the unbanning of *Lady Chatterley's Lover*. And this guaranteed sales. The novel became the fulcrum of diverse opinions on feminism and sexuality; people wanted to know why, and they bought it. Also the controversy it generated successfully sidelined the question of whether any of it was autobiographical. If it did indeed involve a strand of misogynistic loathing this was assumed to be directed at women in general, given that the females of Stanley's account seemed to be too exaggeratedly horrible to be based on particular human beings. In fact it was inventively, maliciously autobiographical.

The principal characters are Stanley Duke and his wife Susan. By the time the novel went into print Amis's and Jane's break-up was public knowledge, and while Amis makes enough changes to deflect the attention of parallel-hunters he interweaves these with resounding echoes of his marriage – or at least his perception of it.

Stanley tells us the story, but he is the least literary, the most culturally indifferent of all Amis's first-person narrators. He is intelligent and verbally accomplished, but he continually gives the impression that being in charge of a novel runs against his temperament, let alone his ambitions. He seems distracted, not entirely happy with his role. He neither enjoys what happens in the tale nor, it appears, the telling of it.

Writing in the first person is arguably the most intriguing and demanding of techniques. The anonymous narrator can deploy all manner of tones, devices and disclosures from a safely uninvolved distance, but someone who tells a story that he or she has been part of cannot claim objectivity. They are one of the characters and can themselves expect to be judged according to the way they portray the events and their co-participants. Stanley is one of the most ingenious first-person presences of modern fiction, but it might be argued that his literary value is diminished somewhat by the fact that his unusualness, his originality, was born out of vengeance.

The opening pages comprise a description of Susan – late thirties, attractive, sophisticated and the literary editor of a Sunday broadsheet – and the house in which a dinner party is taking place. It is only after about a thousand words that we realize the person telling the story is also part of it, and this sense of anxious reticence, almost self-abnegation, sets the tone for the rest of the book. More significantly, it introduces Stanley as someone still in a state of shock from the effects of what he is about to disclose. The delightful, attractive, amusing figure of Susan is first presented to us from a distance because, as we will eventually learn and Stanley already knows, she is a horribly malevolent, evil person. It is as though he cannot quite reconcile his initial perception, his love for her, with her very unpleasant actuality, so he reports things as if he is not quite there.

The Susan who Stanley thought he knew, but discovered he did not, is Jane. Amis compresses eighteen years into about three months. His falling out of love with Jane was gradual, occasionally retrievable but effectively irreversible. Stanley's experience with Susan is much worse, far more accelerated, but involves a bizarre pattern of similarities and, for Jane at least, recognizable distortions.

When Amis began his relationship with Jane there were comments by some of his friends, and a few by the press, that, apart from being beautiful, intelligent and a fellow writer, her class was an element of her attraction. Her background, her previous marriages and her ongoing social network placed her at the opposite end of the middle-class spectrum from Amis, who during the 1950s had cultivated in his writing an image of himself as not quite working class but not far off. Noticeably, the principal male characters of his 1960s and 1970s novels seemed to have moved up the social scale, an elevation that reflected aspects of his own lifestyle – Lemmons, Gardnor House and the Garrick all bespoke status. Amis would still often present himself as an ordinary bloke from the suburbs, mainly when he wished to distance himself from the friends of Jane he did not like.

Stanley's background – south of the river, suburban, lower middle class – is the same as Amis's. He is the advertisements editor for a broadsheet and his general indifference, albeit without hostility, to high cultural matters might seem to detach him from his creator, but in fact he embodies many of Amis's characteristics. By the early 1980s Amis was a devoted fan of *Coronation Street* and *The Bill*. He regarded these as far superior to anything available in the theatre, which, in any event, he never attended. True, he wrote novels that were respected by the literary establishment and frequently he reviewed serious fictional and non-fictional works, but for personal enjoyment he read only science fiction, thrillers and related similarly 'low-brow' material. Stanley, like Amis, can more than hold his own against the cultural sophisticates of the world he shares with Susan. He is clever and articulate, but rather than using language as the vehicle for high-minded pretension and display he gets to the point, again like his creator.

Amis complained, after their break-up, that one of Jane's more irritating habits was her tendency to complicate apparently straightforward verbal exchanges. She would, according to him, turn ordinary factual statements into elaborate disquisitions and rather than answer a question directly she would speculate and enquire about why it had been asked in the first place. Evidence that Jane's linguistic idiosyncrasies were certainly in Amis's thoughts as he planned *Stanley* can be found in a letter to Larkin (22 March 1982), where he imagines and recreates an exchange between Jane and 'her-girl-chum' on how she had recently sent him the proofs of her forthcoming novel. His version of Jane responds to her friend's question on whether Amis had taken an interest in her work with '"Oh yes" – a lot of work with eyes and hands here, "things could be . . . quite good even . . . late on. He isn't the most . . . outgoing of men but he . . . really cares about . . . art. That's one of the things I've always respected about him," eyelids batting fast here – "and I hope he knows it. Because if he doesn't it's too late to . . ."' This digressive, thoughtfully hesitant style of address first surfaced in Amis's fiction with Diana in *The Green Man* (an unflattering version of Jane), but with Susan it becomes more polished and, particularly in her exchanges with Stanley, an indication of a slightly sinister aspect of her personality. At the beginning of the novel, following the departure of their dinner guests, the conversation between Stanley and Susan is a masterpiece of verbal shadow-box-ing, engineered with seamless charm and subtlety by Susan. Everything Stanley says becomes for her not quite what it appears to be. Stanley half suspects that his wife does this kind of thing to remind him of her social and linguistic superiority, but he dismisses such thoughts as unjust – it is not personal, just an idiosyncrasy. At the end of the book, when she leaves him, his charitable assumptions are overturned. She drops her cosmopolitan, classless façade and tells him what she really thinks. 'You little bastard. Swine. Filth.' To emphasize the class of filth to which in her view he belongs she shifts into a subcultural London accent and then elaborates.

> . . . you lower class turd . . . with your gross table manners and your bloody little car and your frightful *mates* and your whole ghastly south-of-the-river man's world. You've no breeding and you've no respect for women. They're there to cook your breakfast and be fucked and that's it. So of course nothing they say's worth taking seriously. (pp. 268–9)

Given that Jane never said anything like this to Amis it is intriguing that he meticulously reinvented her as Susan so that she could.

Throughout the novel Amis conducts a curious exercise in profiling, detailing aspects of Susan's character and personal history that Jane would recognize as her own, while paradoxically causing a number of these to remain recognizable by becoming their exact opposites. For example, Susan refuses to drive a car while Stanley is an avid motoring enthusiast. He owns an exotic and expensive vehicle called the Apfelsine and frequently provides his wife with transport. Amis's and Jane's roles are reversed. Similarly, Stanley has not been to university but Susan has: Oxford. The effect of this, for Jane particularly, would have been like seeing her *curriculum vitae* in a mirror; everything is back to front, but the details of her life can still be recognized. Alongside the reversals Amis inserts largely unaltered elements of Jane's background, very private ones of which few people would know. Before Oxford, Susan was taken out of school and educated at home by a private tutor, an arrangement that was the totality of Jane's formal education. Susan's first husband had been obsessed with book illustration, as a practitioner and collector, so much so that he lost interest in people, including Susan. This is an almost exact description of what happened with Jane and her first husband, Peter Scott, whose obsession was with the natural world, specifically the painting and conservation of birds. Jane's mother, Katherine, was the only one of her parents whom Amis met – she lived with them at Lemmons for two years – and her habits and mannerisms reminded him that he had married into a different class. Susan's mother, a regular visitor to their home, has a title: Lady Daly.

On 3 August 1982 Amis had written to Larkin from Leighton Road and reported that he had finally 'junked my old new novel . . . about a queer'.

> The new one is about a chap with a nasty wife. At the beginning he thinks she's a nice wife, but then he finds out she's really a nasty wife all the time. She's a writer but *he's not* you see. Ha ha ha ha ha ha. Of course it's not thinking of the characters but thinking of what they do in their lives, as you said.

No record of what Larkin did say about characterization exists in his letters to Amis but, given the context, we can assume that Amis is referring to his ongoing plan to recreate Jane from a recipe of circumstantial detail. In the end Susan is not, like Jane, 'a writer' – that would have been a little too close to fact – yet Amis certainly carries forward into the novel the original notion of her cultural sophistication as symptomatic of her nastiness.

Stanley is generally aware of the details of Susan's background, but it is only during a conversation towards the end of the book, with a contemporary of hers at Oxford, Lindsay Lucas, that the more disturbing aspects of her personality are disclosed to him. At Oxford Susan's behaviour was driven by a combination of deranged egotism and loathing for those who seemed to do better than her, socially and academically. She was apparently given to theatrical, almost violent gestures, such as arriving at a party to which she had not been invited and hurling a bottle of champagne through the window into the street.

All of this causes Stanley to re-examine a recent and very worrying event. At the beginning of the novel, immediately after the dinner party and their conversation, Stanley and Susan are visited by Steve, Stanley's son from his previous marriage. It becomes rapidly evident that Steve is mentally ill, and a considerable amount of the novel involves his visits, accompanied by Stanley, to a number of variously incompetent and fanatical psychoanalysts – a rerun of *Jake's Thing* but with the counterbalance of black comedy removed. Susan plays the role of tolerant, helpful wife and stepmother. Steve during a period of derangement stabs her in the arm, but even then she is understanding. It is Stanley who insists on him being committed to a mental hospital. Prior to Lucas's disclosures, Stanley has chided himself for even suspecting that Susan had in some way engineered this sequence of events, perhaps even stabbed herself – she and Steve were alone when the incident occurred – as a means of removing Steve from their lives. Now this becomes more than a guilty suspicion. Her manic egotism has been unsettled by the presence of someone else to whom Stanley directs his love and attention. It becomes evident to him that she might indeed have wounded herself.

Nothing like this ever happened during Amis's relationship with Jane, but at the same time it is built upon circumstantial details that carry private echoes. During the 1960s Jane had taken on, very effectively, the demanding role of caring stepmother. Amis's sons, Martin and Philip, were not mad, but they indulged themselves in irresponsible, potentially self-destructive lifestyles. Jane, particularly with Martin, did her best to improve matters, largely without the assistance of Amis.

Amis's sons came to his rescue after Jane left him in 1980, providing company and support while he tried to make the best of things in the vast, empty rooms of Gardnor House. Philip received special praise in a letter to Larkin written soon after the break-up. 'Your godson is providentially around, having left his intolerable wife and being sacked from his job. I think he's the nicest fellow I've ever met' (5 December 1980). It was Philip who had detached himself from Jane's stabilizing presence and one wonders if Amis, as part of his systematic excision of his best memories of Jane, had recreated Philip as Steve. In the novel it is the father–son bond between Stanley and Steve that discloses for the latter the horrible actuality beneath Susan's decent, caring persona. In reality, the cocktail of loss, confusion and resentment that attended Jane's sudden departure was sidelined by the presence of someone who, despite Philip's unsettled lifestyle, Amis could now rely upon.

It is as though Amis is reinventing Jane as someone who is, for both of them, recognizably herself while at the same time exaggerating and distorting features of her personality, so that she becomes a monster capable of virtually unlimited and calculated acts of malice. It is here that the extent to which this novel is inspired by the same feelings as the abandoned *Difficulties with Girls* becomes evident. In the latter the thwarted suitor seeks horrible revenge; in the former the egomaniac wife shows her true and vicious potential.

Amis's own potential for vengeance in the creation of Susan is, within the mainstream of English fiction, unprecedented. In the nineteenth century, particularly, many novelists modelled characters upon people they knew well and sometimes overemphasized their least attractive or disagreeable features. With Flora Finching in *Little Dorrit* and Dora Spenlow in *David Copperfield* Dickens presents us with none-too-flattering versions of his own wife, Kate, but, compared with Amis's recreation of Jane as a grotesque,

Dickens's distortions seem almost affectionate. Jane did not and would not deliver to Amis the tirade of savage abuse that Susan vented upon Stanley, but two years after she left him she had become in his mind sufficiently loathsome for him to imagine her doing so. Their class differences, amusing and peripheral during their relationship, were refashioned in Amis's presentation of Susan as a hateful and hating snob. And he sews into her speech just enough allusions to their actual backgrounds to guarantee that his invention could only be based upon one person. Similarly, by turning Jane into the Susan who with hideous cunning attempts to detach him from his son, he reconstructs her as her demonic alter ego which, perhaps in his blurred and prejudiced memory of things, she had become.

As the title indicates, there is more than one woman in Stanley's tale. Nowell, his ex-wife and Steve's mother, joins him in his ultimately hopeless search for a cure for their son. Nowell is an actress and, as Stanley implies, she shares with many people in that profession a tendency to be always, perhaps even unwittingly, playing roles. Also she exhibits a more extreme version of Susan's conversational tendencies. Nowell, rather as if she is improvising on stage, will make things up and creatively misinterpret other people's statements, Stanley's in particular. Her presence is to an extent a further exaggeration of Amis's already distorted image of Jane, a private recollection perhaps of an incident in the late 1960s when at a party Victor Gollancz mistook her for an actress. Amis later reflected that Gollancz's error was probably caused because he thought Jane 'affected' (Jacobs, p. 318). Nowell's more important function is that she enables Amis to invent Bert Hutchinson, her husband. Stanley has to wait until the end of the novel, when he discovers the real Susan, to vent his feelings of betrayal and loathing, but Bert provides Amis with the vehicle for a pre-emptive strike against Jane. About half-way through the novel we find Stanley and Bert in a pub, and the latter begins to disclose his feelings about Nowell, and their marriage. At this stage Stanley is still deeply in love with Susan, tolerant of her mild idiosyncrasies and with no preconception of what she will prove capable of doing. It is as though Amis is introducing himself, circa 1980, as Bert, to his earlier, more naïvely optimistic presence from about the late 1960s. It is rather like Scrooge's dream but without the happy consequences.

Bert begins by informing Stanley that 'It's not much fun . . . living with somebody you don't like much.' Not only does he dislike Nowell; he no longer wishes to have sex with her. 'If you don't like 'em you don't want to fuck 'em.' He cannot of course tell her that he thinks 'she's such a bloody horrible creature' because her reaction and its consequences, divorce, which he's been through once before, are too nasty to contemplate. He is in his mid-fifties (Amis's age in the late-1970s, while Stanley, significantly, is ten years younger) and feels too tired to deal with such experiences. Instead he takes refuge in drink and even when he is not drunk he frequently pretends that he is, a desperate but effective means of avoiding sex. This is an account of the closing years of Amis's marriage to Jane, and it contains a number of defensive elaborations. Stanley recognizes in Bert a man, not unlike himself, who when drunk 'had the power of drinking more, perhaps much more, without collapsing . . . Also without losing hold of the conversation.' Bert reads his thoughts: 'It's a protection in a way that probably hasn't occurred to you, sonny . . . ' and, as he might have added, 'not yet'. 'She thinks I'm pissed all the time, right? . . . But I'm not . . . A piss artist couldn't do my job.' This could be Amis answering Jane's claims that all too often alcohol reduced him to various forms of dementia. 'It's a protection . . . She thinks I'm pissed . . . but I'm not.'

The third very horrible woman of the novel is Dr Trish Collings, one of the psychologists who treat Steve. Collings is not based upon a particular individual, but she enables Amis to extend his feelings about Susan/Nowell/Jane to characteristics shared, it seems, by women in general. For Collings, Steve's madness is less a clinical condition and more the effect of living in a society populated by such people as his father. She appears to be a feminist devotee of R.D. Laing, and she insists that Steve's 'cure' must involve him in a regressive confrontation with the worst aspects of his past. What she also wants is the humiliation of Stanley: he must accept that he has ruined Steve, that he didn't really want the child, that his insistence that the teenage Steve should pass examinations, succeed and get a job was a projection of his own dependence upon male aggression. This thesis is propounded by Collings to Stanley and Nowell, and at the beginning of their meeting Stanley detects ominous signs: '. . . they made it clear enough that they got on famously together. They both turned and looked at me. I knew that look, I would have known it even if I had never seen it before – it was the look of two women getting together to sort a man out.' To complicate matters, Collings sometimes peppers her private exchanges with Stanley with indications that she might actually be attracted to him, and after their meeting Nowell suggests to him that Collings hates him because she fancies him.

The alternative to Collings, regarding Steve's treatment, is Dr Nash of New Harley Street, a man who holds views on madness and many other things very similar to those of Amis. Stanley and Bert heroically endure the sly malevolence of Susan and Nowell, and Collings joins the two women as a kind of conspiratorial authority on such matters as gender. Nash enters the frame as Collings's opponent, the theoretician and defender of savagely abused maleness.

Nash regards madness, especially schizophrenia, as an illness and not, as Collings argues, as symptomatic of some collective state of disorder caused mainly by men. Schizophrenia 'tells us nothing about what they [schizophrenics] do in the rest of their lives, gives no insights into the human condition and has no lesson for some people except how sane they are' (Chapter 2). Nash's thesis could be an extension of an Amis essay, published a decade earlier on the presentation of madness in Chesterton's fiction. 'Chesterton is not anticipating, would on the contrary have found devilish, current

357

trendy notions that sanity is a relativist or quasi-political label, that there are insane societies but no insane individuals etc' ('Four Fluent Fellows', p. 37). Nash takes this thesis a little further than Amis and Chesterton. In his view women are, for reasons that he does not bother to explain, much less prone to madness than men.

> Would . . . that . . . they . . . . *were* . . . . mmmmad . . . If only . . . they *were* . . . off their *heads*. We could treat-'em, lock-'em up, bung-'em-in-a-straitjacket, cut-'em-off-from-society. But they're not. They're not . . .
>
> Mad people are hopelessly muddled with their thoughts, their feelings, their behaviour, their talk at variance with one another and all over the place. Does that sound like a description of a woman? Mad people are confused, adrift, troubled, even frightened. What woman is? – really is. I mean.
>
> No. They're not mad. They're all too monstrously, sickeningly *terrifyingly* sane. That's the *whole trouble*. That's the whole trouble. (Chapter 4)

Stanley, being of a more genial, tolerant disposition than Nash, treats this argument with a mixture of sympathy and liberal scepticism, but immediately after leaving Nash's office he joins his friend Cliff Wainwright for a drink. Wainwright is the family doctor and, having examined Susan, informs Stanley that there is an abundance of circumstantial evidence – depth of cut, initial tentative nicks alongside the main wound – to confirm at least for him that her injury was self-inflicted. The remaining three or four pages of the novel involve Stanley and Cliff getting drunk and exchanging opinions on the endemic features of womanhood which becomes a kind of Socratic dialogue, with Stanley, initially unconvinced, becoming converted to Cliff's view that women are, by their very nature, evil.

The passage is arguably the most detailed, calculated recommendation of misogyny to be found in literature. By comparison

Pope's *Epistle to a Lady* reads like an anticipation of New Mannism. Stanley, as a convert to the Nash–Wainwright school of thought, now feels able to confront his previously repressed state of mind.

> 'The root of the trouble', I said, 'is we want to fuck them, the pretty ones, women I mean . . . In fact women only want one thing, for men to want to fuck them. If they do, it means that they can fuck them up. Am I drunk? What was I trying to say, if you want to fuck a woman she can fuck you up. And if you don't want to she fucks you up anyway for not wanting to . . . that's what's Women's Lib is for.'

Stanley and the Women is a brilliant and horrible piece of writing. Stanley is without doubt a victim, the kind who demands the sympathy of the reader – easy-going, tolerant, without a shred of malice. Amis builds into the novel, if not entirely a justification, then an explanation of Stanley's closing outburst. A triumvirate of women, variously deranged, malevolent and compulsively vindictive, have attempted with a degree of success to dismantle his life. The diatribe is an assembly of the opinions, sometimes with verbatim borrowings, from Nash, Bert, Cliff and, ironically, Nowell. It is as though Stanley does not quite believe what he is saying, but throughout the novel he has gradually discovered that there is little point in believing in anything or anyone, particularly women; so being in a state of despair and confusion and drink he might as well join in with the men. The male reviewers, with their combinations of apologetic unease and sympathetic identification, became in a curious way versions of Stanley. They would not of course have agreed with his abusive diatribe, nor even with a cleaned-up, rationalized version in which the women's movement is presented as a conspiracy, a vehicle for the collective loathing of men. Of course not – but then Stanley is no longer in control of his thoughts and feelings, and his reviewers, being men, could appreciate and perhaps empathize with the cause of his distress.

Amis, with a lifetime's experience of how people respond to novels, planned this one with Machiavellian shrewdness. At the beginning Stanley describes Susan as if she is someone he has only just met – 'She looked clever, nervous, humorous, something like devoted or loyal, when she gave a person her full attention, and gullible and beautiful' – and by the end of the story each of these epithets, with the exceptions of clever and beautiful, has been replaced by its opposite. What we should remember is that Stanley is telling his own story and that when he presents us with his initial state of naïveté he is already acquainted with the monstrous actuality of Susan beneath the delightful surface.

There seemed no particular reason why Amis should have chosen to use the first-person mode. Perhaps he was just exercising his repertoire of styles – he had not used the first person since 1971. One suspects, however, a more specific motive. By speaking directly to the reader about events that had happened to him, and by cautiously, almost nervously, delaying the disclosure of the worst of them and his distressed reaction to them, Stanley reminds one of a defendant in a court case. Yes, he has committed the crime, but for the more sensitive members of the jury his unsettled manner of describing the events becomes a kind of mitigating factor. (And one wonders if the problematical scenario of the falsely accused in the original unpublished 'Difficulties with Girls' has found a more subtle and effective manifestation.) Amis in an interview shortly after the publication of the novel in Britain discloses that when writing *Stanley and the Women* he had imagined an unnamed woman acquaintance of his, perhaps an heroic representation of her sex, taking him to court for his libelling of womanhood.

> 'You're suggesting that the character Nowell is based on you?'
> 'Yes, M'Lud.'
> 'But you also claim that the character Susan is based on you?'
> 'Yes, M'Lud.'

'And you also claim . . .' (*Observer Review*, 13 May 1984,
p. 26)

And so on. Amis knew of course that on the one hand this nightmarish whimsy would further incite a feeling of offence in a large
number of women readers. The subtext of his defence is that the
very different female characters are surely individuals and not some
sort of collective archetype, and anyone who thinks otherwise is
obviously a prejudiced and less than discerning reader. Even further
beneath the surface is his awareness that a particular woman would
know that Nowell and Susan are based on her but that if she publicly announced such a recognition she might well appear to be suffering from self-possessed paranoia.

21

The Old Devil

ERIC Jacobs, Amis's authorized biographer, deals with the
closing twelve years of his subject's life in twenty-eight pages,
and one might wonder if such brevity reflects a degree of negligence
or discretion on Jacobs's part. In truth, it was neither. There was
very little to write about.

After the move to Primrose Hill with Hilly and Boyd, Amis settled into a daily routine which remained largely unchanged for the
rest of his life. If not pre-empted by insomnia, his alarm clock
would wake him at about 7.45. Following a shave and a shower, he
would go upstairs to the communal part of the house and take a
modest breakfast provided by Hilly, usually consisting of grapefruit
juice, cereal and fruit. He would read *The Times* and the *Daily Mail*
and by 9.30 at the latest be back downstairs in his study, writing. In
the late 1960s he had bought an Adler typewriter which he never
exchanged for a more sophisticated machine. Sentimental attachment perhaps, but one suspects that a word-processor, with its
temptations seriously to alter and revise, went against his self-
imposed regime. What went on to the page would, with the occasional addition of Tippex, stay there. If in the end it turned out to be
unsatisfactory he would start again.

Around noon he would consider a reward for his morning's
work, and by 12.30 have accepted it, a generous glass or two of

Macallan Malt Whisky. Early afternoon would sometimes be spent in the Queen's pub, a short walk from the house. If he was not promoting a book or being interviewed he would next take a taxi to the Garrick Club for a late lunch, followed by more drinks, mainly whisky, and exchanges with fellow members of similar age and disposition. On 18 December 1984 he closed a letter to Larkin with 'OFF to the Garrick shortly for my Christmas drunk there. If nothing else kept me in London that place would. Somewhere to get pissed in jovial not very literary bright *all male* company. You haven't got a place like that, have you? Don't need one? Balls man you're dreaming.' A taxi would return him to Primrose Hill by early evening for supper, again prepared by Hilly. She might join him and so occasionally might Philip or Sally, both of whom lived nearby. By 7.30 on Mondays and Wednesdays he would be in front of the television set for *Coronation Street*. He might take in whatever was available thereafter, certainly *The Bill*. In a letter to Larkin (14 October 1985) Amis reflects on how self-evident intellectualism must involve all sorts of enthusiasms, mainly for European culture and postmodern indulgence, and only one exclusion: 'we haven't got a television set'. He had, and he listed his preferences for Larkin. Apart from the soaps he liked the 'Rons' and 'B. Hill' along with a little 'wild life and crime'; 'cricket and snooker' he preferred to 'filthy soccer'; and, as for history, these programmes seemed to have two themes: 'How the British killed all the Irish' and 'How the British killed all the Indians.' He even joined a local video library to fill in those evenings when he was not going out, when no one else was in and there was nothing on the set. He would be in bed, most nights, by midnight, preceded by a few more drinks, beer and whisky and perhaps a sleeping-pill.

A version of this formula had become well enough established during his later years with Jane, but then it had provided a bulwark against the less predictable features of his life, predominantly the shambolic, unsettled condition of their marriage. Also their world had involved regular trips abroad, excursions to events such as the Edinburgh Festival, dinner parties involving her friends and his and generally a more active social life. After the move to Primrose Hill Amis hardly ever left London. The annual exception to this was the three-week period in late summer when the Garrick closed and when he would travel to Swansea to stay with his friends Eve and Stuart Thomas.

But he continued to write. During the Primrose Hill years he produced seven novels, almost a third of his overall output. Indeed these works constitute the third stage of his literary career. The first from *Lucky Jim* (1954) to *One Fat Englishman* (1963) reflected Amis's life as a married family man working in a provincial university but with aspirations beyond his job and a tendency towards recreational excursions from monogamy. The principal male characters of the novels confront a variety of similar tensions. This stage concluded with his departure from Swansea and his break-up with Hilly. The second stage ran from *The Anti-Death League* (1966) to *Stanley and the Women* (1984), the duration of his relationship with Jane. Throughout this period Amis alternated one novel which maintained the realist devices and the contemporary focus of his 1950s writing with another in which he would play intriguing games with time, context and plausibility. His marriage to a woman who satisfied his whimsical inclinations – a beautiful, sophisticated fellow writer – yet with whom he was in the end incompatible provided an appropriate enough background for these alternations between the fantastic and the actual.

One Fat Englishman and *Stanley and the Women* were transitional pieces. The first terminated his habit of reinventing Jim Dixon and the second was a malicious and unrepeatable account of his feelings about Jane.

The third stage involves an authorial outlook not unlike that of his 1950s' writing but with key differences. Most of the Primrose Hill novels are set in the Britain of the 1980s and 1990s, but they are all informed by a mood of retrospection. Even those which offer a shrewd, sceptical picture of the present day counterpose this with the sense of a particular life already lived. In these we encounter a presence, a state of mind or a voice that is pivotal, observing the present and existing in it, yet always contrasting it with the past.

Up to and including *Stanley and the Women* Amis's fiction carried an edge of uncertainty which reflected the similarly dynamic state of its author's life – monogamy versus promiscuity, mundaneness versus excitement, stability versus disorder, the plausible versus the invented. At Primrose Hill these tensions were now largely memories. Amis spent much of his time in the presence of the one woman whom, as he stated in his last published poem, he loved more than any other, but their arrangement no longer involved the tensions and potential pitfalls of marriage. Sex for Amis was now an inclination to be remembered or contemplated; his opinions on politics and the human condition, his tastes and diversions, would not be altered by the passage of time.

His last novels included some figures who were uncertain, anxious, ambitious and for whom the future was a blend of possibilities, but they were the observed and never quite the observer. *The Old Devils* (1986) is a novel comprised mainly of characters of Amis's age, one of whom attempts to live as though he is still in his thirties. As a token of the novel's status as the beginning of the third stage Amis kills him. The novel is set in Wales where Amis had lived for fourteen years. Jane was unenthusiastic about her husband's Welsh connections, partly because she found Swansea dull, ugly and provincial and, understandably, because the region and the people were exclusively associated with Amis's life before he met her. Consequently, his visits during the late 1960s and 1970s were infrequent. After he moved in with Hilly and Boyd he made an arrangement with Eve and Stuart Thomas that every year in late August–early September he would spend three to four weeks with them in their bungalow on the outskirts of Swansea. During this period the Garrick was closed, a severe disruption of his daily routine, and as an alternative he transported some of his London habits to Swansea. He would do a small amount of work in the morning, a less rigorous ordination than the London one – he was, after all, on holiday. Then he would go with Stuart to the Bristol Channel Yacht Club, the Swansea equivalent of the Garrick. This routine was maintained until 1993 when Stuart fell out with the club committee and was expelled.

It was during the first of these Swansea excursions in 1984 that the idea for *The Old Devils* occurred to him. His nightmarish vision of old age in *Ending Up* had been created when he was fifty. Twelve years later he was finding that things were not quite as bad as he had imagined they might be.

The Old Devils carries us into the lives of four married couples. They are all about the same age as Amis, retired or semi-retired, have known each other since their university days and are spending their declining years in the town where most of them grew up. The town is unnamed but it is undoubtedly Swansea. There is Malcolm Cellan-Davies, ex-teacher and unsung local writer, who spends his spare time translating *Heledd Cariad*, a fourteenth-century Welsh epic. Malcolm gets on well enough with his wife Gwen, but their exchanges reflect a kind of loveless endurance, particularly on her part. They are, however, too old and tired to voice their true feelings or have a proper argument. Charlie Norris owns a local restaurant but leaves the running of it to a manager. Charlie is permanently, albeit to varying degrees, drunk. He has an impressive intellectual command of practically all topics, but most of these bore him and he has long since lost the inclination to impress other people. Sophie, his wife, puts up with him with a kind of grudging affection; 'I never realized how much he drank till the night he came home sober. A revelation, it was.' Peter Thomas is a semi-retired chemical engineer. In his twenties he briefly taught the subject at the local university, and he married Muriel because her father owned the company which enabled him to exchange academia for a better-paid life in industry. Peter and Muriel have not touched each other for ten years; 'separate rooms, no hugs, no endearments'. Their mutual loathing is evident, but, like the rest, they observe the rituals of enforced cohabitation. On the margins are Garth and Angherad Pumphrey, observed from the outside by the others probably because they are too horrible for closer inspection. Garth, ex-veterinary surgeon, is so mean that on inviting the male devils home for drinks he offers the first round free and charges them for the rest. Angherad is indescribably malicious; she is an ugly wraith-like figure who reminds Charlie of the angel of death.

The world of *The Old Devils* might sound like *Ending Up* revisited, but for each of them their ailments, discontents and disappointments are matched by an enduring sense of life being still, for various reasons, worth living. Chapter 1, entitled 'Malcolm, Charlie, Peter and Others', introduces us to the devils in residence. Their exchanges and states of mind are attended by a kind of muted excitement, a shared feeling of anticipation. Chapter 2 is called 'Rhiannon, Alun', the fourth couple and the cause of the others' sense of imminent disruption.

Alun and Rhiannon Weaver had been friends with the rest during their youth and at university but have spent the previous three decades or so in London. Alun, who was once Alan, is a media Welshman; a television front man and writer whose professional success has been based upon his ruthless exploitation of other people's, particularly English people's, image of Wales. He has written about, made programmes on and publicly idolized the poet with no Christian name, Brydan, a thinly disguised version of Dylan Thomas. Indeed his planned novel, about Wales, his other writings and his media performances betray a calculated dependency upon Brydan's bardic persona and linguistic habits.

The Weavers are coming home, and the frisson of anxiety and aroused expectation which runs through the first chapter proves to be fully justified. The presence of Alun involves for the rest an almost compulsory revisitation of their pasts. He and Rhiannon are the same age as the others, but they are better preserved; they still have sex, they get on well together and, despite Rhiannon's awareness of his adulterous inclinations, they still seem to be in love.

Alun enters the lives of the other characters as rejuvenation personified. He arouses a mixture of feelings ranging through lust, jealousy, contempt, admiration and friendship, which before his arrival had been submerged beneath a weary catalogue of mutually agreed protocols. He even reintroduces the wives of the others to sex. He has had affairs with most of them before, contributing of course to their husbands' unease at his return, and he picks up where he had left off.

The novel is in the third person, but the alliance between narrator and character shifts subtly in each subsection of the chapters from one figure to another and provides a darkly amusing kaleidoscope of perspectives, mainly involving the effect of Alun. In Chapter 3 the controlling hand is Charlie's, and he shows how Alun has, albeit more obliquely, excited the men as much as the women. Charlie looks on with grim admiration as Alun mocks, jokes and humiliates his way through a series of social encounters. Alun has been asked to unveil a monument to Brydan and Charlie observes how he deals with one Llywelyn Caswollen Pugh, 'an official of the Cymric Companionship of the USA', by playing off Pugh's tedious discourses on Pennsylvanian Welshness with slyly ironic rejoinders and a final promise to visit him, perhaps in 1995, a decade hence. Charlie reflects:

The fluid, seamless way Alun converted his unthinking glance towards the waiting car into an urgent request for assistance for somebody to accompany his Mr Pugh, was something Charlie was quite sure he would never forget . . . At the moment before he ducked his head under the car roof Charlie caught a last glimpse of

Pugh, looking not totally unlike an inflated rubber figure out of whose base the stopper had been drawn an instant earlier. Charlie might have felt some pity if he had not been lost in admiration for Alun.

'Bloody marvellous bit of timing,' he told him when they were settled in the back seats. (Chapter 3, Section 1)

Charlie, too, used to have a taste for linguistic devilry, one of the more active features of his personality that age, booze and tired cynicism had subdued, and it is as though Alun is reminding him of how enjoyable it still can be. Alun's presence has a similar effect upon the rest of the men; he takes them back, causes memories to become, almost, enthusiasms.

Significantly, Amis prefaces *The Old Devils* with an 'author's note' conceding that, while the novel is set in Wales, the specific places named or described are pure inventions, that they 'have no more actual existence than any of the characters portrayed'. This is odd given that all of his novels had involved variously romanticized, guilty or vengeful reinventions of himself and people he knew, and he had never before felt it necessary to insert such a disclaimer. None of the old devils are all that bad, and no one was likely to sue. Perhaps he felt slightly embarrassed because at its centre the novel is his most affectionate, almost sentimental piece of writing. He disguises things with characteristic efficiency, but in truth it is about himself and Hilly – now, in an unconventional way, back together – and his memories of their life in Wales before their break-up.

Rhiannon, pretty, witty and tolerant, is a sixty-something version of the women characters of the 1950s who were based on Hilly, but where, one wonders, is Amis? He distributes aspects of himself and his habits among several of the male characters. Charlie's alcoholism is an exaggerated version of Amis's addiction; both are heavy drinkers who can maintain an impressive command of their linguistic and intellectual faculties. Malcolm is a writer who has long since detached himself from the egocentric ambitions of a younger scribbler. He writes because he wants to. Moreover, he disciplines himself to spending several hours a day with his translation, despite the fact that age has relieved him of obligation and a drink with the other devils in the local pub often seems a more agreeable prospect. Amis, with his morning routine and his afternoon reward in the Garrick, is clearly present here. But Charlie and Malcolm are peripheral. More fundamental aspects of Amis surface in the figures of Alun and Peter.

For people who had known Amis for most of his adult life, Hilly in particular, Alun would be at once recognizable and, in a peculiar sense, unreal. He combines the most amusing, agreeable and regrettable features of practically all of the principal men of Amis's novels of the 1950s and early 1960s. Garnet Bowen and John Lewis had rebuked others, and occasionally themselves, for exploiting or mythologizing notions of Welshness. But so apparently had Alun when he was their age. Only when he moved to London did he recognize the potential for self-advancement in playing the role of the Welshman. Indeed, in one of his few moments of genuine honesty he confesses to Charlie that he knows that it has all been an act, although he does so without anything resembling guilt or regret. Just as significantly, Bowen and Lewis involved Amis in albeit moderated acts of confession, given their shared tendency towards adulterous philandering. With Alun this tendency is more candidly disclosed as an addiction. And here of course Patrick Standish comes to mind as a man who wants and commits himself to one woman but who we know will never cease to stray.

As an individual Alun energizes the lives of the other characters. He is a hyperactive embodiment of their pasts, and in various ways he causes them briefly to act as he does, as if they were still in their twenties or thirties; a kind of demonic rejuvenation. Amis had considered a hypothesis. What would happen if a version of his 1950s'

men, now in his sixties but in most respects unaltered, were reintro-
duced to his companions, friends and mistresses of those years?
One of the effects of this is that the narrative accelerates; the fabric
of the novel is, like the lives of those who occupy it, altered. After
Alun arrives the novel itself becomes a throwback to the mixture of
irreverent mischief and calculated wit that characterized much of
Amis's 1950s' writing.

Amis himself was, through Alun, revisiting his past. His annual
trips to Swansea, an area he described in his *Memoirs* as 'the piece
of earth I know best . . . feel most at home in', reminded him of the
novels he had written in the 1950s and the lifestyle that had
inspired them.

Chapter 2, 'Rhiannon, Alun', is a brilliant example of how autobiography can become fiction. It begins, 'A train, a particular train,
the 15.15 out of Paddington . . . emerged from the Severn Tunnel
into Wales.' On it are the Weavers, and Rhiannon's is the dominant
perspective. She looks out of the carriage window and an
unAmisian blend of romanticism and sentimentality informs her
view of things. The landscape and buildings seem similar to those
on the other side of the Severn,

> but something was there, an extra greenness in the grass, a softness
> in the light, something that was very like England and yet not like
> England at all, more a matter of feeling than seeing but not just feel-
> ing, something run-down and sad but simpler and freer than Eng-
> land all the same. Ten minutes to Newport, another hour on the
> train after that and ten or fifteen minutes more by road.

The eyes are Rhiannon's, but the feelings and the language are
Amis's. He, too, in August 1984 had taken a 'particular train' from
Paddington, and as he made clear in his *Memoirs* it was like going
home. The closing sentence effectively ridicules his 'author's note'.
In the novel Swansea is never referred to by name nor even offered

a pseudonym, but an hour after Newport could mean only one station, and it would have taken ten or fifteen minutes after that for Stuart Thomas to have driven him to his bungalow in the Mumbles.

The fact that Amis introduces us to the Weavers via Rhiannon in this chapter is intriguing. Alun is certainly present. His self-promoting witticisms and his generally egotistical inclinations are evident, but we see him from the outside through her eyes and with the sense of tolerant affection that reflects her feelings about him. Hilly did not accompany Amis on his 1984 trip, but in a sense she was with him. They were back together, albeit in a different way, and his return to Swansea would consequently have caused him in his mind to return to his life there with her, when he was not unlike Alun.

Amis started the novel in 1984, but an event the following year contributed significantly to its presentation of Wales and Welshness, most specifically their uneven, hypocritical embodiment in Alun Weaver. In 1985 Amis pre-empted his late summer visit to Swansea with one in June to be made an Honorary Fellow of the University. He was, as he wrote to Larkin, 'pleased to get it, as I dare say you felt over the first half dozen of your hon. degrees' (the Fellowship was the first acknowledgement by academia of Amis's status as a writer and would be the last). This was the first time he had been back to the University since he resigned his lectureship twenty-three years before, and what struck him most was the new bilingualism of signposts, documents and ceremonies, 'an unexpectedly large spok fok spoonful of Welsh bullshit, ie considerable parts of that language, which as you know nobody speaks in S. Wales except on purpose' (letter to Larkin, 20 July 1985). After Alun and Rhiannon get off the train from London, the narrator discloses Alun's thoughts regarding the bilingual sign for Taxi/*Tacsi*; 'for the benefit of Welsh people who had never seen the letter X before'. Apart from Malcolm, who treats Welsh as a scholarly preoccupation much as an Englishman would with Anglo-Saxon, Alun's cynical estimation of its new Celtic fashionableness is reflected in the attitudes of the other devils. Amis wrote to Conquest that Anthony Powell was 'awestruck' by his award of the Fellowship; '"what a terrific honour for a non-Welsh speaker". Even he overestimates the importance of the lang in *S*. Wales. Except as bullshit of course, which is hard to overestimate' (letter to Conquest, 24 July 1985).

This could have been written by Alun, and it is clear that he is a remixing of Amis's various relationships with Wales both as a country and as correlative for particular experiences. During his visit to Swansea for the Fellowship Amis also looked in on the BBC Wales crew who were doing a version of *That Uncertain Feeling*, involving a meticulous recreation of the 1950s; cars, dress, hairstyles, décor. Amis experienced something like time travel in that the novel he had spun out of his own perceptions of Swansea in the mid-1950s had returned to it in the mid-1980s. 'Shot conscientiously in period, which among other things reminded me of how much I used to want to fuck girls who looked like the actress playing Elizabeth Gruffydd-Williams. Her shoes and gloves. Her hat. Her . . .' (letter to Larkin, 20 July 1985). Alun Weaver was born out of this. He would be John Lewis in late middle age, coming home to the place he knew so well, the situational equivalent of Viagra. Also, however, Amis is taking with him a hypothetical notion of what might have happened. What if he had stayed with Hilly just as Alun and Rhiannon had stayed together?

Rhiannon puts up with Alun, her grudging tolerance maintained by a genuine affection for him. But after their return to Wales she suddenly discovers that he is a much worse figure than the one she previously thought she knew. Alun has a half-finished typescript of a novel which he believes will promote him to the status of a real writer, beyond his image as media man and commentator. His egotistical ambitions are undimmed by age. His novel is about Wales, and he shows it to Charlie, whose critical acumen he still respects. Charlie tells him the truth: it is a self-indulgent, calculatedly romanticized account of Welshness with stylistic borrowings from Brydan.

Alun takes revenge in a particularly malicious manner by causing Charlie to spend part of a night alone on a lonely and forbidding part of the West Wales coast: as Alun knows, Charlie is afraid of the dark. Rhiannon learns of this and is shocked by the extent to which the man she thought she loved could be so unpleasant, particularly to a man who was supposedly his friend.

The autobiographical underpinnings of the Alun/Brydan theme are puzzling and intriguing. Alun carries into the novel some of the best and worst aspects of Amis himself, at least when Amis was younger; respectively his talents as a wit and entertainer and his skills as an unfaithful seducer. So by causing Alun also to model his literary ambitions upon a thinly disguised version of Dylan Thomas, whom Amis had for four decades rebuked as an overindulged literary charlatan, was Amis conducting a kind of penitential rite? Amis wrote to Larkin (17 November 1985) and asked him to 'run me up half a dozen lines of sub-Thomas' for his ongoing novel. Amis had already done this thirty years earlier with Gareth Probert's verse in *That Uncertain Feeling*, but he tells Larkin that he wants something different from that, something that blurs the line between parody and imitation so that the reader would 'wonder whether it was genius or piss'. Larkin had little more than a month to live. Amis knew he was seriously ill, but his request was more than an act of deathbed praise for his old friend's talents. He genuinely wanted Larkin to catch Thomas's blend of attractive flamboyance and stylistic excess, to offer an example of work by a potentially brilliant writer who had overindulged his talents. It wasn't that Amis had changed his mind about Dylan Thomas's work; not quite: more that life had overlapped with his fictionalization of it. Just before he wrote to Larkin, Stuart Thomas, Amis's host in Swansea, had asked him to become one of the trustees of Dylan Thomas's literary estate. The coincidence was amazing and darkly comic. The only thing that Alun did not share with his creator was his hypocritical commitment to the myth of

Brydan/Dylan Thomas, and now Amis was being asked to become the one part of Alun that he most certainly was not (in a letter to Larkin of 18 June 1985 he had referred to Thomas's verse as 'Piss with froth on'). What did he do? He accepted Stuart's offer and, despite the fact that his appointment was opposed by practically everyone in Swansea involved with the Thomas estate, he was elected. The novel seemed to be writing itself.

When he wrote to Larkin he informed him that the novel was 'entering its climacteric', as indeed it was. The parallels between himself and Alun had got beyond his control. At the same time that he accepted the trusteeship he killed him.

The men are taking drinks in the sitting-room of Garth Pumphrey, the nastiest, least agreeable member of this elderly crew of boozers, and Alun has a heart attack. The most relevant eulogy comes to Charlie as he and the rest of the devils stand, glasses filled, around Alun's rapidly cooling presence.

> '. . . Of course it was only those few seconds. But they don't usually go off just like that, not with heart, not as a rule.' Charlie missed Alun's being able to say, I suppose you mean sheep and bloody bullocks don't. Not as a rule. (Chapter 8)

Charlie misses the snappy and socially disruptive response to something like death which has now been denied to them with ironic finality.

After this, the stylistic energy which Alun had injected into the fabric of the novel via the minds of its characters gradually diminishes, yet his visit in the end turns out to have had a strangely beneficial effect. The chapter following his departure, the closing chapter of the novel, begins not with a funeral but a wedding. The bride and groom are Rhiannon's daughter and Peter's son. It is several months after Alun's death, and the young couple had met as a consequence of the Weavers' return to Wales.

Peter and Rhiannon are alone in the garden, and it is the first time they have had a proper opportunity to talk. Throughout the novel the reader has become gradually aware of the mildly unsettling subtext for this exchange, via allusions and politely oblique references. Back in the 1950s, before she had begun her relationship with Alun, they were a couple. She got pregnant, had an abortion and they drifted apart. The mood of reunification generated by the marriage of their respective offspring prompts Peter to abandon his usually sardonic, evasive style of address.

> 'Though you might not think so,' he said with care, 'and there was certainly a time when I forgot it myself, I've always loved you and I do to this day. I'm sorry it sounds so ridiculous because I'm so fat and horrible, and not at all nice or even any fun, but I mean it. I only wish it was worth more.'

She asks him to telephone her after the wedding. The autobiographical parallels are at once oblique yet emotionally charged. Alun was a projection of the young Amis. Both have departed; the former recently and suddenly, the latter more gradually but with similar finality. Peter is a version of Amis now. When he was writing the novel Amis had attempted to give up smoking and drinking, albeit temporarily and on medical advice. As a compensation for his lifelong habits he indulged in a form of bulimia, involving the daily consumption of vast amounts of chocolate. He wrote to Larkin that 'I have cut back . . . enough to eat like a horse . . . so my weight goes up by about 50% a month' (24 September 1985). He found himself having to purchase his clothes from an outsize shop. His shirts had seventeen-inch collars. Peter is undoubtedly the fattest of the old devils. Age and indulgence have caused him to become a painfully absurd parody of the memories which so frequently occupy the thoughts of these characters – prompted mainly by Alun who has refused to grow or look old.

As he is aware, Peter had the chance to spend his life with the woman he really loved, and the opportunity had presented itself in Wales. Instead he had married an Englishwoman, Muriel, the only one of the devils who is not Welsh. One wonders if Amis's return to England and his exchange of the Swansea-based happiness of his life with Hilly for a very different relationship with an English woman was in Amis's mind as he constructed this part of the story.

The novel ends where it had begun, in the house of Malcolm and Gwen. Their conversation still ostensibly involves the routine concerns of retirement and cohabitation, but it has lost that blend of anxiety and subdued excitement which had informed the opening exchange. Alun has been and gone. But, almost incidentally, they refer to something else that has recently occurred. Muriel has returned to England, and it seems that Peter will not be joining her. He is currently sharing a house with Rhiannon. Not that they are having an affair, you understand, nothing so youthful as that; more that they enjoy each other's presence much as they had decades before. This was not quite the same as the Primrose Hill arrangement – Hilly was, after all, married to someone else – but not entirely unlike it either. Amis completed the final draft of the novel at the end of 1985, and it is intriguing to note that during the previous two months, when he was writing the last chapter, he found himself spending time with Hilly as they once had been, as a couple. Boyd was away for a few weeks in October, and in early November Amis travelled to the West Country to conduct an interview with Anthony Powell for the *Sunday Times*. It was Powell's eightieth birthday, and Hilly went with him. As he wrote to Powell, 'the four of us [could] make a not-very-long day of it' (16 October 1985). In December he took the train to Hull for Larkin's funeral, sharing a carriage with Charles Monteith, Andrew Motion, Blake Morrison 'and Hilly, natch' (letter to Conquest, 1 January 1986). As he was writing the chapter which evokes, obliquely and indirectly, the reunion of Peter and Rhiannon, the past almost revisited, he was experiencing something very similar.

Through Peter, Amis provokes a number of footnotish references that secure him as autobiographical. Only once would he use the same Christian name for two major characters in different novels, and the adolescent Peter of *The Riverside Villas Murder* was without doubt a version of Amis. The elderly Peter had once enjoyed an occasional drink in a pub called the General Picton and so had John Lewis, and Peter had shared Lewis's mild addiction to *Astounding Science Fiction*. Lewis's novel *That Uncertain Feeling* – which Amis witnessed being meticulously recreated on film as he planned *The Old Devils* – had in the 1950s been Amis's personal message of apology to and love for Hilly.

The Old Devils won Amis the Booker Prize. That year, 1986, the chairman of the selection committee was Anthony Thwaite, only seven years younger than Amis and whose verse of the 1950s and 1960s has been compared with Larkin's (Thwaite had edited Larkin's *Collected Poems* and *Selected Letters*). One might suspect partiality but given that all the other members of the committee were women – Edna Healey, Isobel Quigley, Gillian Reynolds and Bernice Reubens – one might not. After *Stanley and the Women* Amis had become for many the embodiment of cynical misogyny, but *The Old Devils* was very different. The discussions of the Booker committee remain confidential, but they cannot have been all too different from the collective opinions of his reviewers, who agreed that this was his most humane, least vitriolic novel for many years. The *New York Times* thought that it combined 'sardonic gloom with lyric tenderness', and the *Observer* found it 'both consoling and stimulating'.

Amis's competitors for the Booker Prize, Margaret Atwood, Paul Bailey, Robertson Davies, Kazuo Ishiguro and Timothy Mo, had offered a variety of unusual, idiosyncratic contributions to what some people call postmodernism. Amis's novel was a throwback to his 1950s' combination of realism and irreverence. But also there was something else, an engaging sense of sympathy for its participants, that made it in an old-fashioned sense a living novel. The

Booker committee and the reviewers fell for it. By 1986 the event at which the Booker winner is announced had become a public occasion attended by contestants and friends, in evening dress, televised live by the BBC and involving pre-announcement speculations by other writers and critics that closely resembled the preamble to the FA Cup Final. Amis, appropriately enough, began his winner's speech with 'How do I feel? Sick as a parrot.' He continued, 'I used to say to myself and others that the Booker Prize was a bit artificial, but I have changed my mind in the last fifteen minutes. Now I feel it is a wonderful indication of literary merit.'

Despite his light, slightly mocking tone Amis felt very happy, even honoured by his victory. He had been awarded the CBE in 1981, inspired, he knew, by his support for Mrs Thatcher, and in 1985 Swansea University had given him an Honorary Fellowship. But apart from these, official and public acclaim was slight. No university had offered him an honorary degree. Larkin had five, but Larkin was a serious poet, and Amis wondered if popularity plus his tendency to mix comedy with virtually everything had caused the establishment to regard him as low-brow.

He was particularly pleased that this novel had earned him official recognition (plus £15,000, tax-free). He had written in his notes for the novel that one of his objectives would be to 'keep the reader guessing – which [is] the Amis character' and that this was his own 'Ivy Day in the Committee Room', Joyce's delicate blending of disfigured autobiography with a vivid account of contemporary life (Amis Collection, Huntington Library). A very small number of people would have been able to recognize Amis past and present in, respectively, Alun and Peter, and one of them greeted him on his return from the Booker evening at the front door in Regent's Park Road; 'Hello, you old devil,' said Hilly.

In many ways *The Old Devils* typifies Amis's fiction of the last twelve years or so of his life, in that its evocation of the present is always conditional upon something else, another place and time, emotions and events that are remembered, transfigured or projected. Martin Amis considers it his father's best novel, or at least the one he feels closest to. One suspects that his estimation is partly conceived out of admiration of his father's impressive juggling act with states of mind and their temporal registers (Martin Amis's *Time's Arrow* comes to mind), but only partly. In it Amis is remembering, most specifically he is remembering Swansea, and Martin recalls his childhood there with a good deal of affection. The particulars of Amis's life in Swansea and what happened after that do not feature in the novel, but a remembrance of them informs its mood. Two of the old devils, Peter and Rhiannon, are happy and their children have played a very important part in this.

22

Difficulties with Girls

IN 1986 Amis told Conquest that his accountant had recently asked him why, since he was now quite wealthy, he felt the need to go on working. Some writers might have cited their art and their duty to it, but for Amis writing was more an addiction than an aesthetic vocation. He said to Jacobs a few years later that writing 'gives me something to do in the mornings', a characteristic blend of self-mockery and candour. It provided him with a routine out of which would emerge another book, a reminder to the world that he was still there, and the world or at least its reviewers would tell him what they thought of that. What he feared most was running out of things to write about. Stylistically he was as impressive as he ever had been. No one could orchestrate narrative and reported speech in such a way as Amis. The comedian, the ventriloquist and the disciplined portrait painter were still cooperating very effectively, but style required material. His problem was that nothing new ever happened to him. *The Old Devils*, an ingenious exploration of how the remembered and the immediate intersect, could not be rewritten.

He compromised. The original 'Difficulties with Girls', his justly abandoned, vengeful response to his break-up with Jane, was present in typescript. He began to consider how some of its original themes might be returned to and reworked; not those relating to himself and Jane – that was an element of his past he had no wish to revisit – but rather the broader topic of homosexuality. Significantly, he decided to set the new novel in 1967 just prior to the passage through Parliament of the Sexual Offences Act, sponsored by the then Labour Home Secretary Roy Jenkins, which would legalize homosexuality. People were then talking openly about a sexual propensity that previously had been treated with either subdued sympathy or private loathing. Homosexuals feature in the novel prominently enough but not as central figures, more as vehicles for Amis's exploration of the ways in which society had changed irreversibly during the 1960s. For his principal characters Amis for the first time chose to do a sequel to a published novel.

Take a Girl Like You (1960) left the reader wondering if anything resembling a relationship could be sustained between Patrick Standish, the archetypal lecher, and Jenny Bunn, the reborn Clarissa. Seven years later we find them married, in a state of relative happiness, and living in central London. Patrick has given up teaching and now works in publishing, and Jenny disposes compassion as a part-time teacher in a children's hospital. But things are not quite as they seem.

Patrick is, as he had declared in 1960, genuinely in love with Jenny but, as Amis has caused us to suspect, he would not give up his infidelities. To some degree the couple are an extension of *The Old Devils*, in which Alun and Rhiannon were elderly, present-day versions of Patrick and Jenny, and of course projections of what Amis's and Hilly's relationship would have been like had it endured.

The Patrick of 1967 has not significantly altered his previous Lovelace-like persona, but Jenny has become a stronger individual, more sanguine yet more confident, and as a consequence their earlier roles in *Take a Girl Like You* are reversed. Then her alliance with the narrator offered us an intelligent, idealistic yet naïve perspective, while his, as the man and predator, was dominant. Patrick in 1967, while still the wit and charmer, seems also to be trapped and diminished by sexual habits and inclinations he cannot control. Now it is Jenny who is able to operate as the dispassionate, laconic observer; another tribute to Hilly.

In Chapter 16 Jenny simultaneously reduces Patrick to a condition of shameful humility and delivers a remarkably well-informed attack on the earlier lifestyle of the author who created them both.

Patrick has been playing an elaborate game of infidelity, remorse and manipulative self-exculpation – in this case attempting to expunge his adulterous guilt by leading Jenny into an affair with a friend of his. It would make him feel better if she did it too. But Jenny knows him better now. She responds with a confident, savage decoding of the sexual mores on which he seems to rely, and the attack reaches its culmination with her at their bookshelves. First, she considers Amis's old enemy Somerset Maugham: '. . . just one of the literary conventions we used to hear about in the sixth form. Love without going to bed. What an idea.' This is a wonderfully concise return to that moment in the 1950s when *Lucky Jim* had won Amis the prize sponsored by the man who regarded him as an immoral opportunist. Maugham had based his opinions about Amis on a reading of his book; Hilly, from personal experience, knew how shrewd he had been.

After that Jenny picks up an edition of Fielding's *Tom Jones*, a novel which during the 1950s Amis had read frequently and which was the progenitor for his representations of licensed – male – misbehaviour. She quotes a section where Fielding functions as the apologetic advocate for his hero's lifestyle.

'. . . I bet you imagined old Henry Fielding winking when he said that. But now for the clincher. It looks as though you've underlined it heavier than the others, but there's probably nothing in that.

'"Though he did not always act rightly, yet he never did otherwise without feeling and suffering for it?"

'So that's all right, isn't it, Patrick?'

By reinventing Hilly as Jenny, Amis was again exploring his sense of regret and offering another long-delayed note of apology.

I Want It Now (1967) and *Girl, 20* (1971) reflected Amis's disapproving reactionary views on contemporary mores and the ideologies that underpinned them, but in both books these were secondary to his private conjectures on his own state of mind and his relationship with Jane. Twenty years later he could assess this period with the reflective familiarity of the modern historian.

Patrick particularly is aware of an unsettling tendency in practically everyone he meets to either extend and complicate their sex lives or to talk about them with unembarrassed candour. Graham McClintoch, Patrick's shy, principled friend from the 1960 novel, now carries around an unflattering photograph of his wife so that he can remind himself and inform others of how much he dislikes her. Oswald Hart, another friend of Patrick's, tells of how he has recently left his wife because he had got to know her too well, she was no longer intriguing and he had thus 'used her up'. A chauffeur informs his passenger, whom he has just met, of his wedding night sixteen years earlier when his wife had told him, 'Fred, don't you ever do that to me again.'

All of these characters exercise Patrick's cynical, dismissive thoughts on contemporary life, but an episode about half-way through the novel involves a far more personal and disagreeable experience. Patrick has planned an afternoon off work involving adultery with the wife of a colleague, Wendy Porter-King, with whom he has previously only flirted. They are due to meet in a house borrowed from a friend of his, and Patrick arrives first. Amis describes Patrick's journey and arrival with an air of practised familiarity. He has never used the house before, but the procedure seems routine enough. He checks his notebook to make sure he has the correct street, rings the doorbell before admitting himself with a latchkey, considers what drinks are available to offer Wendy on her arrival and makes sure that 'upstairs' is in good order.

None of the book's reviewers or subsequent commentators have recognized this episode as an allusion, but it is almost beyond question that one of Amis's best-known poems, 'Nothing to Fear', was in his mind and very likely on the desk as he typed the chapter.

> All fixed: early arrival at the flat
> Lent by a friend . . .
> Drinks on the tray; the cover story pat
> And quite uncheckable . . .

The poem is a compressed short story. It is autobiographical, based on those occasions in the 1950s and early 1960s when Conquest would arrange locations for Amis's frequent adulterous activities in London. It was written around the same time as *Take a Girl Like You* and was later reprinted in a collection of Amis's verse, ironically in 1967. Its speaking presence is Amis but could just as well be Patrick Standish.

Patrick's habits have not changed, and over the years he seems to have acquired the veteran's ability to suspend his older anxieties. As the speaker of the poem awaits the woman's arrival, he ponders 'guilt, compunction and all that stuff', tries to dismiss these and yet still feels uneasy.

> . . . sitting here a bag of glands
> Tuned up to concert pitch, I seem to sense
> A different style of caller at my back,
> As cold as ice, but just as set on me.

In the novel Patrick settles down to wait with a drink and a book. 'He felt nothing either way, good or bad', but the old tensions have not quite been displaced. 'He felt something, good and bad, when the doorbell rang, tremendously, many times louder than it had sounded outside, like an alarm at a jewellers . . .'

If a sensation close to the blend of excitement and fear which the poem captured so effectively is still part of Patrick's mindset, it is about to be supplemented by something worse. As he entered the house he had noted that its décor bespoke the 'awful' nature of contemporary life: 'unshaped bits of wood mounted or left lying about on shelves . . . tiered cubes in glass and ebony that might have been puzzles or works of art or neither . . .' Domesticated modernism; very fashionable and very 1960s. This setting becomes horribly appropriate because Wendy also turns out to be symptomatic of her milieu. The following are extracts from her half of their exchange before they go to bed.

'Then let it be the moment,' she cried. 'The one and only unrepeatable moment . . . Oh, the moments in our sad little lives that make us real. Frighteningly few, those golden moments . . . then, Patrick, do you feel it too? You do feel . . . something? Promise me you'll always treat me as a person.'

And so on. Patrick, who simply wants sex, puts up with this but only just.

'The sky is blue and I feel gay.'
   She never knew how close she came to losing her front teeth for that. Taken off guard again, Patrick spoke too quickly. 'Are you American?'

Amis via Patrick is both revisiting his 1950s' lifestyle and transposing it with images of the Britain of a decade later. Wendy could be a version of *Lucky Jim*'s Margaret Peel, who has found in 1960s' locutions a perfect medium for her brand of egotistical pretension. Patrick restrains himself, just as Jim had done when he wanted to ram a necklace bead up Margaret's nose.

For Jim, people such as Margaret were avoidable, but Patrick is becoming aware that Wendy is part of an epidemic of loquacious self-obsession, and there is a subtle irony here. Much like the poem's speaker, Patrick had thrived upon the tension between his life as a successful rake and a concomitant blend of guilt and subterfuge, and the restraining social conventions of the 1950s had provided him with the ideal environment for this. Monogamy, commitment and family life were the norms which caused infidelity to be attended by a state of wicked excitement. Amis presents the late 1960s as a period in which promiscuity was becoming licensed by fashionable ideas about society and behaviour. Wendy's ludicrous utterances make Patrick feel as though he is taking part in a civil rights demonstration or listening to a lecture on transcendental meditation.

Seven years earlier Jenny had been the embodiment of conventional morality. This as much as her physical attraction had caused Patrick to pursue her so obsessively. She was the ultimate challenge in that her ideals of virginity, marriage and fidelity, although slightly outdated even in 1960, were the paradigms which fuelled Patrick's addiction to pleasure as iniquity.

In *Difficulties with Girls* Jenny has not changed, but practically everything else has. In the earlier novel her qualities and principles were presented as anachronistic and doomed, but now they appear to protect her from the directionless, self-destructive vicissitudes of the contemporary world. Gradually Patrick begins to perceive her less as the stable counterpoint to his other life and more as the only person who can rescue him from his sense of hopelessness.

Amis wrote the novel twenty years after the period in which it is set. In 1967 he and Hilly had been separated for four years, and the fact that they were now back together in a way caused him to hypothesize. What would have happened if they had not broken up? His marriage to Hilly had been attended by his addiction to infidelity, and many years later this must have seemed paradoxical, given that he was now certain that she was the only woman that he had ever really loved. Would his distaste for the 1960s' mood of self-obsessive licentiousness affect him in the way that it does Patrick? And, more significantly, would Hilly, like Jenny, become by her continued presence a reforming influence?

At the close, Jenny tells him that she is pregnant, and throughout the novel the prospect of children is alluded to as perhaps the only means of cementing their relationship – she has already had a miscarriage. The last paragraph tells us of Jenny's feelings. 'Jenny was happy. She was going to have him all to herself for at least three years, probably more like five, and a part of him forever, and now she could put it all out of her mind.'

In his usual manner Amis was redistributing the chronology of his remembrances, while preserving their emotive essentials. If she had not become pregnant in 1947 Hilly and Amis would probably have broken up, but thereafter their shared sense of responsibility and love for their children had at least steadied the potentially disastrous condition of their marriage. And who had been the principal negotiator during the arrangement which would bring them back together? Philip, their first child.

The most peculiar, ambivalent feature of the novel is the one it carries forward from the original 'Difficulties with Girls'. Homosexuals are everywhere, and the topic of homosexuality insinuates itself into the fabric of the book in the same way that the prospect of a Third World War had done in *The Anti-Death League*. Everyone talks about it in a way that is at once oblique yet obsessive. The book begins with Patrick witnessing the landlord of his local pub ejecting a customer.

'Right, on your way, brother. Out. I'm not having you in my house. Go on, hop it.'

'What for? What do you mean? I haven't done anything.'

'I don't know what you've done, darling, and cross my heart I don't want to know. And don't let me guess. Go on. There's noth-

ing says I got to have one of you in here, okay? Not yet there isn't.
Any moment now but not yet. So out.'

Apart from the collective pronoun 'them', nothing specific is
said during the landlord's subsequent exchange with Patrick about
the group to which the 'one of you' allegedly belongs, but there are
enough cautiously allusive clues to confirm that the unfortunate
man has been ejected not because of his race or his political opinions.

Similarly, in Chapter 4 Patrick overhears an argument between
his two neighbours, Eric and Stevie. Stevie is referred to as 'she',
'her', 'silly cow', 'old bag' and 'half-witted tart', but it is some time
before we learn that Stevie 'was generally known under his professional name of Steve Bairstow'.

Another neighbour, Tim Valentine, presents himself as an
enthusiastic homosexual. It is gradually disclosed that after twelve
years of married life he had suddenly left home and begun 'attacking [seducing] every female in sight'. Disturbed by this, he had consulted a quack psychiatrist, Dr Perlmutter – a continuation of the
Amis tradition of dangerously incompetent psychotherapists – who
informs him that his heterosexuality is symptomatic and unreal, the
result of his 'subservience to custom and family pressure'. He is
apparently a repressed homosexual. Eventually he realizes that
Perlmutter was wrong, and he tells Patrick of his experiences in the
homosexual subculture of clubs and discreet liaisons. 'I can't think
what can ever have possessed me to . . . it was worse than anything
you could possibly imagine . . . They're not like ordinary people at
all . . .'

In Amis's earlier novels, including those written after his
espousal of Toryism, homosexuals had been presented as individuals. Max Hunter's stoicism, Manton's mandarin superiority and
Bernard Bastable's limitless capacity for hate are not the results of
their sexual orientation. What they did share was an experience of

prejudice and isolation, which was consistent with Amis's listing of the legalization of homosexuality in *Socialism and the Intellectuals* (1957) as equal in importance to anti-racist laws and the abolition of capital punishment.

It was not that Amis's shift to the right had now been supplemented by homophobia; not quite. In *Stanley and the Women* he had deliberately provoked the collective orthodoxies of feminism. Now he was turning his sceptical eye towards the generally accepted maxim that the 1960s had been a period of transition and improvement. The Jenkins Act is referred to only once, by Eric.

> 'This law's going to make a lot of difference, you know. Not straight away, but when it's sunk in. I'd like us to stay in touch if you would. Because Patrick, I'm going to need blokes like you more then than I've ever needed you in the past. We all are. Yeah, you're not much but you're all we've got.'

Eric seems to fear that once homosexuals can publicly disclose their orientation without fear of prosecution they will open themselves to an even worse state of prejudice than before. Amis presents this unusual hypothesis as not without cause when, a few pages later, he returns Patrick to the presence of Cyril the horrible pub landlord whose bout of homophobic rage had opened the novel. The pub itself has been transformed to accommodate contemporary tastes. The screens and snugs that had once guaranteed privacy to those individuals and couples who wanted it have been replaced by an open-plan format and a décor that is outspokenly bright and loud. This is a reasonably accurate account of what happened to many traditional pubs during this period, and more subtly it appears to reflect a widespread contemporary inclination towards unfettered disclosure. Cyril, who at the beginning had resembled a docker and now sports a beard, wears a wig and a tan suede jacket, explains: 'I'm bending, mate. I'll go along with all this

... as long as I consider it expedient. Survival ... As long as all these glorious new ideas are in the ascendant I'll stick with 'em. But no longer than that.'

Cyril is obviously the sort of person Eric had in mind when he offered Patrick his pessimistic view of the future, because he goes on to predict that in five or ten years' time 'people will speak out', capital punishment will be restored and those 'disgusting people' – he still can't bring himself to refer directly to homosexuals – will get what they always deserved.

The Jenkins Act did not and could not have outlawed homophobia, but Amis's inference that to legalize a sexual orientation will inevitably create dangers and hazards for its practitioners, or, for that matter, that the promotion of the subject of sex from private to public discourse diminished it both as a topic and an activity, is to say the least partial and some might argue ludicrous.

23

The Last Novels

THE four novels produced by Amis in the 1990s, his last, operate like differently ground lenses, each refracting his life in a different manner. Two of them are conspicuously autobiographical. *The Folks That Live on the Hill* (1990) is about his world in Primrose Hill and the ménage of acquaintances and family with whom he shared it. He wrote it alongside his *Memoirs* (1991). The novel combines the honesty of a letter to a friend with the blend of thoughtful omission and creative indulgence that such letters frequently involve, while the *Memoirs* are simply selective. *You Can't Do Both* (1994) covers the four decades from his childhood years of the 1930s to his break-up with Hilly in the 1960s. It is his most transparent piece of life-based fiction, candid and apologetic. The other two, *The Russian Girl* (1992) and his final novel, *The Biographer's Moustache* (1995), offer much more oblique perspectives upon his experiences, but feelings of remembrance and completion resonate through both.

Harry Caldecote, the central figure of *The Folks That Live on the Hill*, is retired, twice married and spends a good deal of his time in the King's public house and in the Irving, a decent London club. The Queen's was Amis's local pub and the Garrick, founded as a place where 'actors and men of refinement might meet on equal terms', had been regularly attended by Henry Irving. Autobiographical parallels such as these are continuous and generally innocuous. The specific details and personnel of the novel tell us little more about his life than could be found in interviews or book-launch profiles. The most significant and intriguing autobiographical features of the novel are effected by its style. Harry is the central figure, but the third-person narrator also carries us into the lives of his niece Fiona, 'his ex-stepdaughter' Bunty, his sister Clare and his brother Freddie. There are no exact parallels between these characters and the people who make up Amis's assembly of friends and relatives. But Harry's network is like the Primrose Hill set-up in that both involve a slightly eccentric, often shambolic interweaving of memories, lifestyles and states of mind somehow infused and balanced by feelings of mutual affection.

Harry is, as Amis thought himself to be, at the fulcrum of things. This status is guaranteed in the novel by a third version of the technique which orchestrated the life and times of Jim Dixon. Jim and his narrator created a fabric which enabled him to behave badly but remain endearing, while Jake Richardson inverted this relationship to disclose his far less agreeable perceptions and characteristics. Harry is Jim in old age, more composed and avuncular but still prone to a naughty wink at the reader.

Although Harry and his confrère narrator do not control the lives of the other characters, they are never really absent. Even when Harry is not personally involved in accounts of the experiences of the others we feel that he is showing them to us through his eyes. More significantly we feel that his is a caring, protective presence.

There is a wonderfully evocative episode at the beginning of Chapter 13 which involves Henry having his hair cut. For about five hundred words there is no dialogue. We follow the random, largely disinterested thoughts of Harry on age and hair (he, like Amis, has proudly retained a fair amount of the latter) and things he has recently read about the influence of Mrs Thatcher upon the hairdressing unions. Suddenly he sees in the mirror a double image of his own face. This is not a symptom of unfocused regressive senility – Freddie, his brother, is sitting behind him – but Harry visits upon his brother the experience he has almost had and causes him to think that he is watching a version of himself that has taken on a separate life of its own.

The joke recalls the kind of thing that Jim would have done and indeed the manner in which his creator would have reported it, but now this mildly disruptive presence is attended by a kind of thoughtful charity. The amusing introduction of Freddie carries us into a mini-narrative where Harry rescues his brother from the repressive, post-menopausal presence of his wife Desiree. He encourages Freddie to write poetry. It is bad poetry but Amis, with a glance at contemporary trends and tastes, makes sure that it finds an enthusiastic publisher and an equally gullish readership. Freddie earns some money of his own and secures a bit of freedom from the dreadful Desiree.

Amis, of course, was an only child, but his creation in Freddie of a man who is slightly hopeless and unhappily dependent upon his partner, yet whose stronger, more confident dimension rescues him from this state, involves autobiographical permutations a decade hence.

With the niece Fiona, Amis creates for Harry a similar role as sage and helper. Fiona is an alcoholic. Throughout Amis's fiction booze is treated as an almost compulsory indulgence. True, it tests the mettle of some of his characters, but even the bottle-a-day men such as Charlie in *The Old Devils* and Allington in *The Green Man* seem able to cope with its unpleasant side-effects. Fiona is the first of his characters for whom alcohol addiction is a serious problem. She faces a daily spiral of remembering the horrible events of the day before and the inevitability of more alcohol as a mental anti-dote to this. She even suspects that her condition is an irreversible genetic inheritance, her cousin when drunk having killed herself in a car crash and her Aunt Annie, dead at forty-one of liver disease, featuring as continuous spectral presences. (Amis probably borrowed this from his memory of how his mother had feared that she might be prone to a family tendency – two of her aunts had died of alcohol-induced illnesses.) Harry pays for her hospitalization and convinces her that she can make alcohol lose its sinister, destructive power. More than anything, it is Harry's sensible yet sensitive presence which provides her with the strength to sober up.

Fiona is based upon Amis's daughter Sally. Shortly after Jane left him, Sally moved into Gardnor House with her father. He wrote to Conquest stating that 'Having broken up with her very decent boyfriend Sally is staying here, or will be till this afternoon, when I take her to the doc and try to get her into a drying out place. It must be worse to live her life than to be with her and cope with her, but that's not much consolation' (2 February 1981). The last sentence is significant in that it is reflected in Harry's perception of Fiona. Like his creator Harry drinks but both of them seem to have experienced the frightening, disintegrating consequences of alcoholism only from the outside. Fiona's state bears an uncanny resemblance to Jane's version of Amis's in the late 1970s and curiously, after describing Sally's condition to Conquest in the 1981 letter, Amis provides his version of Jane's presentation of him. 'Her [Jane's] scenario, you see, is that my drinking was what fucked up the marriage. And so it did in a way, in that when I'd had a few I would sometimes lose my prudence and tell her a little about her monstrous behaviour.' There is a subtext here in which Amis, albeit implicitly, compares his perception of Sally with Jane's perception of him: Sally's alcoholism is a genuine illness, requiring thoughtful care, while Jane's diagnosis of him as an alcoholic was tactical. According to Martin Amis, his father 'cared more about Sally than the rest of us'. She seemed more vulnerable. 'He would wake up worrying about her.'

Harry Caldecote is not quite a saintly figure; he has his flaws and less than admirable predispositions. He comes close to being Amis's modern version of Prospero, the wise protector, but one should not suspect Amis of self-directed flattery. Harry's existence is very similar to his author's but at Primrose Hill Amis was as much the recipient of generous, charitable fellowship as its initiator.

There is a photograph, a beautifully evocative one reproduced in Jacobs's biography, of Amis in the Queen's, glass in hand, smiling with unconfined glee at the camera. He is seated at the centre of an assembly of eight other people, friends and family, Hilly at his right shoulder, Sally his left. Everyone else seems to be glancing elsewhere, some at Amis, some sheepishly in the general direction of the photographer. They seem happy, Amis happiest of all. It is one of the most accurate visual equivalents of a novel in existence.

In *The Folks That Live on the Hill* Amis was not really reinventing himself as the figure upon whom everyone else depends. There is a subtext. Without the characters for whom Harry provides a degree of stability, Harry himself would have no purpose, no sense of belonging. He needs them as much as they benefit from him.

The Russian Girl (1992) presents us with Dr Richard Vaisey, a lecturer in Slavonic Studies, and Anna, a visiting Russian poet. When planning the novel Amis must have had in mind an incident that had occurred three decades before and which he records in the essay 'Kipling Good'. In 1962, while still a Fellow of Peterhouse, Cambridge, Amis hosted a visit and reading by the Russian poet Yevtushenko. Amis's record of their conversation centres upon Yevtushenko asking him what he thinks of *Dr Zhivago*. As we have seen earlier (p. 328), Amis states that he has not read it because 'an interest in the paraphrasable content of literature [is] an anti-literary interest'. *The Russian Girl* begins with a rerun of the same conversation. This time Richard's head of department, Hallett, is trying to persuade him that it would be better for students to read Dostoyevsky's *Crime and Punishment* in English than not at all. Richard will not be moved. 'You know as well as I do that every word Dostoyevsky writes is written in a way only he can write it. A translation, even the best imaginable, has got to leave all that out.' This theme of the relationship between literary language, indeed all language, and its paraphrasable content, is the enduring subtext of the novel.

Richard falls in love with Anna Danilova completely. His attraction to her parallels his commitment to literature. He knows Russian almost as well as he knows English, and his appreciation of the literary forms that feed on both languages allows him a kind of literary adultery: two separate lives, contacts and intimate acts of communication. Anna is the sexual and emotional personification of everything that has involved his intellect: he can talk to her in Russian and English, she is beautiful and she writes poetry.

Described as such, the novel sounds like the kind of middle-brow love story with which one would not expect Amis, the hardened cynic, to be associated. The book is rescued from the cosy satisfactions of this subgenre by its cunning, almost self-referential, use of disclosures and blind spots. For one thing the topic of translation becomes a somewhat puzzling feature of the novel itself. The private exchanges between Anna and Richard are almost exclusively in Russian, but Amis makes it difficult for the reader to appreciate the difference between these and the ones between others that take place in English. Richard's locutionary habits do not change, and Anna's 'translated' speech involves all the familiar informalities of the native speaker. At the same time, as Richard has pointed out, we have lost the essence of the original. We overhear the most intimate moments between two people in love, but what they have really said will remain private. At Anna's first public reading Richard is reduced to tears. 'He wept that all that honesty of feeling, which he could not doubt it was, all that seriousness of purpose, all that sincerity . . . should have come to nothing.' What she says is, for him at least, immensely moving, but stylistically she is a failure. We have to take this evaluation on trust, because even when we encounter one of her poems it is of course in translation and as Richard states at the beginning of the book someone who reads a Russian text in its English version has only 'A what? A pale – distorted – shrivelled ghost of the reality.'

It is an impressively multi-layered novel and offers some intriguing ruminations on the nature of translation. The latter reflect Amis's long-held belief that translation *per se* is a pragmatic necessity but that translated literature is a contradiction in terms, effectively a sympathetic synopsis, the equivalent of an elegant verbal description of a painting. Does Amis carry into it anything more than his opinions on language and literature? Eric Jacobs evidently regarded the book as completely unrelated to Amis's life in that he does not even acknowledge its existence.

Nothing of any great significance happened to Amis during the writing of the novel, but he chose to do something unusual, unprecedented. He began the novel as he was completing his *Memoirs*, which concludes with 'Instead of an Epilogue', Amis's last published poems. There are three, dedicated 'To H', Hilly, and the third, addressed specifically to his relationship with her, is the most transparent, candid piece of literary writing he ever produced.

> In '46 when I was twenty-four
> I met someone harmless, someone defenceless,
> But till then whole, unadapted within;
> Awkward, gentle, healthy, straight-backed,
> Who spoke to say something, laughed when amused;
> If things went wrong, feared she might be at fault,
> Whose eye I could have met for ever then,
> Oh yes, and who was also beautiful.
> Well, that was much as women were meant to be,
> I thought, and set about looking further.
> How can we tell, with nothing to compare?

The only quoted piece of Anna's verse runs as follows:

> man of all men in Shakespeare's island,
> eyes that shine through the rain in my heart,
> where I came as a stranger,
> finding a hand grasping as firmly as time,
> knowledge that burns like fire
> and makes my heart round and red again,
> music in unity in my snowflake veins,
> thanks, all thanks be in my eyes clear for seeing,
> and I
> can face
> the dawn mounted on our love
> which is you and my love and I and your love,
> quickcatchitbeforeitdisappearslikethenight
> over the river never let go,
> spreading through the world like a boy's tear,
> to turn all the blackest dogs away,
> and you
> have spoken
> and I have listened,
> until like a spring the world runs down,
> and never fear the dark.

The poems would seem to exist at different ends of the stylistic spectrum. Amis, as Amis, abjures conceits in favour of open simplicity and employs, quite beautifully, the kind of free verse line that invokes the ease and control of Wordsworth's blank verse but which cannot be reduced to an abstract formula. Anna's poem seems almost addictively figurative and recalls the studied incoherence of Pound's *Cantos*. But, despite this, both poems are inspired by, indeed address, exactly the same emotional registers, both obviously are written to one person and both involve unalloyed sincerity. When Amis wrote Anna's poem to Richard he was thinking of his own to Hilly.

Anna's poem reduces Richard to tears, partly because he knows that she is speaking directly to him and partly because it reminds him that he has been deceiving her, pretending to admire her verse while privately regarding it as stylistically self-indulgent and substandard. Anna pre-empts his confession and tells him that she always knew that he was lying 'But that lie told me how much you loved me, and it means I'll always love you.' And she adds that 'I don't think I could put that into a poem, but I'll probably have a shot at it one day.' The poem she might write would be equivalent of the one that Amis has already written.

When he wrote his last poem and began *The Russian Girl* Amis had been living with Boyd and Hilly for almost a decade. During this period an admirable state of civility and mature solicitude had been maintained between a man, his ex-wife whom he still loved and her husband. He had also written two novels, *The Old Devils* and *Difficulties with Girls*, in which he explored his feelings for Hilly in a way that was far more intimate than anything that might occur during their daily encounters. He had done so by employing his method of recreating his private world in fiction so that perhaps only one person could unravel the code. Richard and Anna communicate their feelings to each other in Russian. The reader has a translation but, as Richard affirms, translation loses the effect of the original text. *The Russian Girl* is about translation but not in the most obvious sense. It is about Amis's long-established use of literature as two media. His customers will appreciate, understand, be amused by what they have bought, but someone else, someone in particular, will read through the words on the page to a very private mood or experience. We know that Richard and Anna are in love, but we do not really know how they feel because that is communicated to us in translation.

Amis's last published poem inspired the novel, paradoxically, because it was his only piece of literary writing that did not need to be decoded. It was the poem that Anna would 'have a shot at one day'. It would not need to be translated for anyone.

You Can't Do Both (1994) was begun in 1992 at about the same time that Amis agreed to engage Eric Jacobs as his official biographer. No one is certain of which provided the idea for the other, but the two books were written in parallel. Jacobs, when planning his volume, spent roughly two days a week in Amis's company, recovering memories. As a Fleet Street journalist and broadcaster he was well practised in the arts of relatively painless extraction. Both were members of the Garrick.

Most of Amis's novels are obliquely autobiographical, but none has involved such a comprehensive return to his early and middle years as *You Can't Do Both*. The novel covers the same period as the first fourteen chapters of Jacobs's biography, Norbury to Cambridge. Amis alters names and locations, invents a few characters and reshuffles slightly the chronology of events, but at the core of the novel are himself, his parents, Hilly and Larkin. Without doubt, his conversations with Jacobs, involving detailed revisitations of people, places and their emotional registers, provided the foundation for the book.

Amis is Robin Davies, and the first part of the novel takes us to the modest suburban house in somewhere not unlike Norbury where Robin aged about fourteen lives with his parents, Peggy and Tom. He has a brother and sister, but they are much older and they left home years ago. On the bookcase are some detective novels and middle-brow love stories, respectively the preferred reading matter of Robin's, and Amis's, father and mother. At the breakfast table Robin's parents engage in an exchange regarding Peggy's sister's pregnancy, its lateness and her visit to a gynaecologist without referring specifically to any of these things, an amusing version of what had sometimes happened in the Amis household where Kingsley's mother and father also pretended, at least when speaking of it in his presence, that sexual intercourse did not exist. Amis, on page 12 of his *Memoirs*, recalls an almost identical incident.

Robin spends much of his time with his schoolmates discussing sex, while Tom, like William, only ever addresses his son on the dangerous practice of masturbation, which apparently thins the blood and can lead to madness. And, again like William, Tom is something of a snob, discouraging Robin from mixing with a boy called Wade whose accent is not quite what it ought to be.

Amis folds all of this into the novel in an affectionate, tolerant manner, without malice or condemnation, but the detail tells us little if anything more than we can learn from Jacobs or the *Memoirs*. Ironically, the more revealing, personal features of the book become evident when Amis begins to alter facts.

First of all, Robin's father dies before his mother, to whom Amis gives his own mother's name, Peggy. Tom, on his deathbed, completes the sentence that Captain Furneaux had begun at the conclusion of *The Riverside Villas Murder*. Furneaux was about to tell his son for the first time of how he really feels about their relationship. Tom does so. 'You've been a good son to me, better than I've deserved, but I can't help feeling I haven't been much of a father to you. I feel I've let you down in all sorts of ways', which he describes. He had subjected Robin to 'all manner of out of date guff', tried to impose on his son a version of Christian morality without the Christianity. In many ways he had 'restrained' the 'youngster's freedom'. It was not that Amis, now in his early seventies, was condemning his late father, accurate as Tom's confession is. Rather he was providing himself with the opportunity to tell a version of William that there was nothing to forgive, as Robin does. Robin leaves the hospital room and in the corridor bursts into tears. 'It seemed to him that what made him cry was regret, or regrets . . .' Robin regrets that while he knew his father he never allowed his father to get to know him, and when Amis wrote this he would have been thinking of those years in the late 1950s when he was usually too busy to spend time with William, who was then widowed and living with them in Swansea. William returned to London where he would die a couple of years later. The exchange, which allowed Robin a rare moment of emotional attachment to his father, was denied to Amis, perhaps by himself. Regrets indeed.

Two pages later, just before his father's funeral, Robin discovers that his girlfriend, the eighteen-year-old Nancy, is pregnant. Nancy is Hilly, and Amis's removal of Tom/William prior to this spared him the necessity of having to revisit the unpleasant few weeks in which his father had refused even to speak to him following his disclosure of Hilly's pregnancy.

More significantly, the reshuffling of chronology enabled Amis to give more attention to his mother, the co-nominal Peggy. After he told them of Hilly's pregnancy Peggy had persuaded William that, whatever happened, Kingsley was still his son and that if he loved him he should keep quiet and attend the hastily arranged marriage ceremony in Oxford Registry Office. She also seized the initiative and persuaded Hilly's parents that, while they might not approve of the situation, they could not change it. They, too, went to the wedding. The fictional Peggy does this with the Bennetts, Nancy's parents.

Throughout the first part of the novel Peggy exists largely in the background, sometimes emerging to steady Robin's fractious relationship with his father, as did her real counterpart. After Tom's death she becomes a character in her own right, understanding and tolerant regarding the pregnancy and low-key marriage. Amis admits in his *Memoirs* that he never really appreciated his mother, and it seems that Amis the novelist is repaying a debt.

At the time of his father's death Robin is reading Classics at Oxford, which Amis was advised to do and thought about before choosing English. The Oxford chapter is dominated by Robin's meeting and subsequent relationship with Nancy, but before this there is an episode, again based on fact, which involves him losing his virginity. Robin uses the University Classical Society mostly as a means of impressing his peers from women-only colleges, and Amis's spurious attachment to the Labour Club served a similar purpose. At one meeting Patsy Cartland informs Robin that her friend Barbara Bates would be interested in rather more than a discussion of Euripides, and Barbara eventually introduces him to sex. Amis achieved a very similar encounter via two women he met at the Labour Club, and one wonders what we are supposed to infer from his renaming of their fictional counterparts. Exchange their Christian names and surnames and one finds Barbara Cartland, whose romantic fantasies need no introduction, and Patsy Bates, a trisyllabic echo of a much less picturesque activity involving only one person. A joke perhaps but a very Amisian joke at his own expense. The entire novel is a blend of confession and apology directed partly to the memory of his parents but, more specifically, to Hilly. Robin's first sexual encounter is, unlike those created by the other Ms Cartland, without much romance, but it sets the standard for a long career of successful lechery, a series of liaisons involving, at least in terms of their uncomplicated satisfaction of desire, one person.

Robin's closest friend at Oxford is Embleton, whose nearest actual counterpart was George Blunden, later to become Sir George Blunden, Deputy Governor of the Bank of England – it hardly seems necessary to comment on the nominal echoes. Like Robin and Embleton, Amis and Blunden had been friends at school and gone up to Oxford the same year, to different colleges. Blunden was asked by the inexperienced Amis to accompany him to the chemist and assist in the purchase of condoms in preparation for his liaison with a real version of Barbara Bates. This does not happen in the novel, but perhaps the incident was in Amis's mind when he drafted Robin's first meeting with Nancy. They meet purely by accident in Embleton's rooms only a few days after Robin's brief encounter with Barbara. Amis lost his virginity in 1941, and he first met Hilly in the post-war Oxford of 1946. Amis telescopes these two events into one week because they initiate 'both' of the things that first his father and later Nancy tell Robin he 'can't do' – maintain a career of casual, uninvolved sex alongside a relationship with the woman to whom he commits himself.

Real-life chronology is returned to when Amis resumes his relationship with Nancy after war service and she, like Hilly, becomes pregnant. A few days after he learns of her pregnancy he meets Embleton again. With no knowledge of Nancy's condition Embleton advises his friend on the matter of unplanned pregnancies and their consequent responsibilities and commitments, and here perhaps Amis's memory of his trip to the chemists with Blunden became resonant. Robin does not reply but instead thinks about a note in his pocket, given to him by another woman and promising his first act of infidelity. That Robin's first encounter with Nancy should have occurred via Embleton and that he should return at this point when selfish pleasure overrules commitment causes him to appear as the spirit of reflective decency, a role not played by Blunden but a function of Amis's guilty recollections.

But what has happened to Larkin? Surely a novel which incorporates Oxford as the site for Amis's most enduring emotional relationship, with Hilly, would include some reference to the man who had probably been his closest friend. Larkin does appear but as a more disguised, more spectral presence than Blunden.

Larkin died, of cancer, in December 1985. During his last couple of years he and Amis regularly exchanged letters that closely resembled the manner and tone of their irreverent, mildly obscene pieces of the 1940s and early 1950s, Larkin's closing dedication to his friend always involving the word 'bum'. Amis attended his funeral, with Hilly, and Larkin would no doubt have appreciated the dark irony of this being Amis's only ever visit to Hull. They were very different men, Larkin the withdrawn, pessimistic outsider and Amis the ebullient centre of things. But when writing to each other and in each other's company Larkin became both a version of Amis and, to a degree, his foil. Inevitably, all of this would have filled Amis's thoughts as he planned his fictional reinvention of him for *You Can't Do Both*. No doubt as a gesture of respect to their friendship he surrounded the character of Andrew Carpenter with enough evidential detail to distance him from Larkin (neither Jacobs nor any of Amis's reviewers noticed similarities), but all this is accompanied by private, resonant linkages.

Carpenter is the son of Robin's neighbours, his senior by a couple of years and an undergraduate at Cambridge. He becomes Robin's mentor, and this is a reasonably accurate version of how Amis felt about Larkin during his first period in Oxford. Carpenter takes Robin to his room in his parents' house, plays him some jazz records that he has never heard before and talks to him about literature. Robin notes on the bookshelves a copy of Huxley's *Point Counterpoint*. Larkin and Amis had shared an admiration for Huxley, but, more significantly, Carpenter introduces Robin to a piece by a poet, unnamed, whose style carries some echoes of Auden, again someone they both respected, and which is effectively a catalogue of Larkin's intellectual and literary heroes.

'You might anyway see different things in them from what I see. No, your immediate spontaneous reaction is what counts. But I'll be fascinated to hear. We'd better go down in a minute. God knows what your parents think we've been getting up to.'

Lawrence, Blake and Homer Lane,
      once healers in our English land,
These are dead as iron for ever;
      these can never hold our hand.
Lawrence was brought down by smut-hounds,
      Blake went dotty as he sang,
Homer Lane was killed in action by
      the Twickenham Baptist gang.

Then and at later points in their friendship Carpenter explains to Robin the attractions of Homer Lane and Lawrence. (And one should note also that Robin remarks that his very conventional parents would not have allowed Lawrence's 'obscene' works in the house, while Carpenter's father, like Larkin's, encouraged his son's admiration for him.) Lane was briefly Auden's lover, and his thesis that desire and instinct are the unacknowledged foundations for the intellect influenced Layard who, in the early 1940s, gave lectures at Oxford and for whom Larkin became an advocate. Lawrence, whom Larkin also admired, advanced similar theses in his literary and non-literary writings.

At the beginning Robin is fascinated by a man who has read so much radical, unorthodox material, but gradually respect is replaced by tolerance. Amis, too, moved beyond the feeling of awe and inferiority that had initially attended his friendship with Larkin to the extent that he forbade from their exchanges any mention of Lawrence, whose work he loathed because it broke his rule that literature should not be the vehicle for ideas.

At the same time Carpenter is a memorial to the closeness and sense of fun that Amis had shared with Larkin, particularly in their early years. Carpenter entertains Robin with imitations. 'He turned out to be a wonderful mimic, at least the voices and faces he did were hilarious in themselves.' This is generous, given that Amis had held centre stage as the imitator-in-chief at St John's. Carpenter's imitation of a Cambridge don is actually a version of Amis's parody of Lord David Cecil: 'I want all to wemembah . . . you owe a duty to your college . . . not only to ush, your pahstorsh and mahshtorsh . . . not only to this great univershity . . .' Robin is particularly impressed by 'something with no words to it, a killing upper-class-moron face with a lot of blinking and as many as possible of the lower teeth showing'. This, too, is an account of Amis himself, not his friend, but in an oblique manner it involves a note of gratitude. Jim Dixon could not have been invented without the blend of absurdity, wit and anti-intellectualism that flavoured their exchanges. Larkin was the junior partner, but by reversing their roles, via Robin and Carpenter, Amis was acknowledging a debt; the irreverent dynamics of their times together and their letters were the foundation for Dixon's similarly energetic double-act with his narrator. Robin reflects that Carpenter 'was just about the most marvellous and amusing companion anyone could ever have wished for'.

Late in the novel Carpenter offers Robin his opinions on women. 'I mean surely one of the great things about women is they're rather thick and *don't mind*. At least I've not come across a nice one or even an attractive one who seemed to mind. So a chap hasn't got to be on his best behaviour all the time.'

Read through Larkin's *Selected Letters*, particularly those of the late 1940s and early 1950s, and you will find similar sentiments – even Carpenter's style is an accurate reproduction of Larkin's jagged, emphatic manner. Carpenter is a homosexual, who had 'tried them a couple of times, girls, years ago on a making sure basis'. Larkin, particularly during the 1940s, frequently felt uncertain about his sexual orientation. He had had 'a few messy encounters . . . Nothing much' (Motion, p. 65) with Philip Brown, his Oxford roommate, and in a letter to Amis in 1943 he writes of how the actress Wendy Hiller reminds him of 'a boy I was in love with in rather a . . . physical way' (Thwaite, p. 68). Much of his unpublished fiction of that period involves homosexuality as the anchor for complex investigations of isolation, frustration and bitterness. Amis regarded Larkin's early enthusiasms for figures such as Layard and Lawrence more as attempts to explain or even compensate for his frequently disastrous sex life, particularly his brief and uneasy encounters with women, than as serious intellectual commitments. As Larkin grew older, these enthusiasms began to fade, and Amis with a degree of satisfaction presents Carpenter, now in his forties, as someone who has become sensibly cynical. On Homer Lane,

Carpenter states that 'all that sacredness-of-desire stuff was just queer propaganda . . . that was in the days when I wanted moral support for wandering off the straight and narrow'. And, 'I've never come across any kind of Lawrence-disciple, queer or not who wasn't in a proper pickle about sex.'

Following the publication of Amis's *Letters*, two reviewers, John Carey in the *Sunday Times* and Julie Burchill in the *Guardian*, more than inferred that Amis and Larkin had been conducting a repressed, non-sexual homosexual relationship. Burchill diagnoses Amis as 'at heart, a bit of a bender', compares the 'private baby talk' of his letters to Larkin with listening to a couple having sex in the next room and concludes that 'heterosexuality was something of a curse to him'.

It is certainly the case that in many of the 1950s' letters Amis involves Larkin in an intimate, frequently obscene exchange and sometimes addresses him as 'dear' and 'sweet', but this was not evidence of repression, more a laddish excursion into then illegal territory. The real reason for Amis's presentation of Carpenter as a homosexual involved an extension of his rather selfish, possessive attitude to Larkin. In his *Memoirs* he recalls with regret that 'He was my best friend and I never saw enough of him or *knew him* as well as I wanted to' (p. 64, my italics), but with more honesty, after learning more of his friend's life from the letters that Thwaite was compiling, he wrote to Conquest that 'He didn't half keep his life in compartments' (17 November 1986). He did, and Amis to his surprise and perhaps his chagrin found that he had been in one of them. Carpenter enabled Amis to re-establish control, to recreate his friend as a preferred version of his real self, one who would in the end come to share Amis's contempt for Lane and Lawrence.

The novel's treatment of Wales is its most oblique, eccentric autobiographical feature. The location for most of the story is England, but Wales and Welshness are never really absent. Tom Davies is Welsh. He spent his childhood there but has purposely Anglicized himself. He has lost his accent and rarely communicates with his relatives across the border. However, he encourages Robin to spend regular holidays there with his uncle and cousins, and Wales becomes a curious subtext to other elements of Robin's and Tom's uncertain, shifting relationship. As Amis states in his *Memoirs*, his father was 'glaringly at a loose end' (p. 22) for much of his time in Swansea. He did not dislike the area, and he got on well with Hilly and the children, but he felt somehow out of place, and one might find parallels between Tom's deliberate distancing of himself from Wales, his tolerance of his son's attraction to it and a sense of the place as in some way indicative of Amis's and Williams' continued state of distance.

The most obvious difference between Nancy and Hilly is that the former's parents are Welsh, the only connection being that for reasons known only to himself Leonard Bardwell learned the language. The Bennetts' Welshness plays no significant part in the story; it seems to be a gratuitous coincidence, and there are many more. After discovering her pregnancy Nancy and Robin decide, without really knowing how, to terminate it. Following some tragi-comic episodes with gin and 'things' borrowed from a nurse, they find that Nancy's Oxford landlady, Mrs Pendry, can put them in touch with a respectable doctor who, for a large fee, will do safe abortions. Mrs Pendry has previously been presented as the arche-type of lower-middle-class respectability, and her improbable role as an agent for illegal terminations is half explained by Robin's rec-ollection that her late husband had been a chemist in Pontypridd. Dr Beck, the abortionist, practises in Cardiff, and it is there at the last minute that they decide they want the child and discover the depth of their love for each other.

Amis and Hilly in 1948 had planned an abortion, and their experience of what this would involve, almost two decades before it was legalized, was much worse than Rob's and Nancy's. In one of the longest letters he ever wrote to Larkin (12 January 1948) Amis gave a detailed account of their experiences in London. One doctor, a 'Central European', had assured them that it 'was not a serious matter', but another, contacted by Amis's army friend Frank Coles with whom they stayed in London, stated that there was at least a one in twenty chance that Hilly 'would have a haemorrhage afterwards and die of it'. They decided, like Robin and Nancy, that the prospect of married life and a family was preferable to the alternative, and Amis confessed to Larkin about how the whole experience had made him feel: 'as if I had committed an outrage on a schoolgirl and then murdered her, leaving my identity card near the body . . .' In the novel Amis alters some of the details, and, most significantly, he changes the location in which they were to have the operation but then decide on a life together from London to Wales. The Amises went to and left Wales as a couple; it was where their relationship endured, albeit precipitately and despite Amis's inclination, like Robin, to 'do both'.

Amis's last novel, *The Biographer's Moustache* (1995), is an intriguing blend of mirrors, false clues and blind alleys. It was published in the same year, 1995, that Eric Jacobs published his biography of Amis. Over the previous two and a half years Jacobs had spent several days a week drinking, dining and talking with Amis. In the diary that Jacobs published in the *Sunday Times* soon after Amis's death, their relationship, at least in Jacobs's view, resembled a modern version of Boswell and Johnson. During the same period Amis had published *You Can't Do Both*, his most candid, although fictionalized, account of his own life. His last novel, involving the relationship between a journalist and his biographical subject, an elderly novelist, would seem to be founded upon immediate experience. Yet these tantalizing similarities between the fictional and the actual are superficial. The novel is effectively an act of expurgation. Amis systematically excises any connections between our knowledge of his world and the story of the biographer and the novelist. The fact that he supplies the former, Gordon Scott Thompson, with an intrusive middle name and the latter, J. R. P. Fane, with the familiar title of 'Jimmie' is probably his last false trail for truffle-hunting scholars. Jacobs is indeed a 'Scot'; and 'Jim' Dixon was part of the Amis mythology that he was never 'fain' to disregard.

Fane is a Bloomsbury Group throwback, in love with the pure aesthetics and psychological intensities of literary creation and even more closely attached to the habits and prejudices of the English aristocracy. He is everything that Amis is not. Gordon hates his novels, which seem to have attained a minor cult status among devotees of self-indulgent inaccessibility, and he eventually comes to detest their author. Jacobs praised Amis's novels because they are nothing like this, and his biography involved an inexhaustible admiration for Amis.

Fane has agreed to participate in the biography, but he turns each interview into a mixture of avoidance and incitement. Gordon's enquiries regarding his opinions are subtly transformed by Fane into investigations of Gordon's own ambitions, social class, temperament and intentions regarding Fane's wife Joanna. The reader is left with the impression that the only good novel that Fane might have written is the one that he has strenuously avoided, in which the manipulative verbal skills, the opportunistic nastiness of J.R.P. Fane are offered to the central character.

When discussing the biography with his publisher, Gordon concedes that it will sell not because Fane is a literary cult figure but because his life intersects with the fantastic indulgences of the English upper classes. He knows that its claim to be a 'literary life' is a token gesture, a fraudulent concession to respectability. At the end of the book Gordon abandons the biography. He tells both his publisher and Fane that he cannot involve himself in a text whose subject he finds so repulsive. We know that he is lying. He has had an affair with Fane's wife Joanna, and his attraction to her is more than physical. His real reason for abandoning his Life of Fane is that it has become part of his own.

Amis's last novel is a beautifully crafted exercise in the ironies of fabrication. The novel about Fane tells us more than the biography ever could, and the biographer does not need to produce a fascinating insight into his mysterious subject because, by existing in the novel, he has already done so. The other presence who leads us confidently through this maze of real lives and written lives, fiction and non-fiction, is of course the narrator. And who is he? He is the Kingsley Amis that most of us know but have never met. He is the figure who, since *Lucky Jim*, has constructed, orchestrated and introduced us to worlds that soon become as familiar as our own. As a person, he is a shadowy presence; as an experience, he is a fitting memorial to the man who cast the shadow.

Amis died on Sunday 22 October 1995. In late August, in Wales, he had a fall and a suspected stroke. He spent some time in the Chelsea and Westminster Hospital but recovered sufficiently to return home to Regent's Park Road. But his condition worsened. He was admitted to University College Hospital on 6 September and, after contracting pneumonia, he died there two weeks later. He was cremated on 31 October after a funeral service at St Mark's Church near his home. For an account of Amis's last days read 'One Little More Hug' in Martin Amis's *Experience*. Kingsley Amis – wit, grammarian and genius with the personal nuances of speech – is now 'lost for words', terminally brain-damaged. His son, the other novelist, is witnessing this, and Martin's refining of his own addiction to verbal performance into pure feeling creates one of the most moving passages ever written.

Eric Jacobs reported the funeral in the *Sunday Times*, which was a lie because he was not there; it was family only. The paper's use of it caused Martin Amis to resign as their book reviews editor. Jacobs had stated that Sally only had cried. A year later, at the Memorial Service at St Martin in the Fields, Jacobs cried.

The Biographer's Moustache had been sent to HarperCollins in the spring, and Amis's remaining months involved a constant struggle to maintain the routines of his life against his worsening disabilities. That August he spent his usual three weeks in Wales, but during his stay he was visited by a good deal of pain. His speech had begun to slur, and he had frequently found it difficult to keep his balance. He continued to write virtually until the last few weeks, most of which were spent in hospital. According to Jacobs, he had produced a hundred or so pages of another novel (provisionally entitled 'Black and White' and in the Huntington Library, California), although its subject seems undecided. Over the summer he completed what would be his last book; *The King's English: A Guide to Modern Usage* was published posthumously in 1997. It is a somewhat eccentric counterpart to Fowler's *Modern English Usage*, and its general mood is indicated by the title, implying, one assumes, that the language used by most of *Her* Majesty's subjects had deteriorated so much as to no longer merit the title of English. The cover photograph, supplied by Hilly, shows Amis circa 1953, the Coronation year.

The book reflects two complementary dimensions of Amis. There is the old-fashioned grammarian, ever alert to misuse and corruption and attentive to the mutations of history. He does not cite the removal of Latin and Greek from the curriculum of most schools as the only cause of the unfixed, anarchic state of our language, but for him the effects of it are evident enough. The contrast between dialecticisms, provincialisms, slang of all sorts and older usages is, he affirms, the condition of a living language, but without a knowledge of the 'dead languages' as 'a kind of trainer' we lose an informed awareness of how our particular medium operates as it does. Alongside this presence is Amis the entertainer, continually supplementing his lament for correctness and learned awareness with personal anecdotes. Apparently, in 1955 Victor Gollancz had telephoned to warn him that John Lewis's use of 'poor bugger' would lose him the sale of at least 2,000 copies of *That Uncertain Feeling*; Boots Booklovers' Library would not tolerate the term. Amis suggested 'bloody fool' as an alternative, which Gollancz judged to be 'Perfectly acceptable' (p. 72). Amis comments that 'bugger' was in South Wales, the setting of the novel, a friendly and acceptable synonym for 'chap' or 'customer': sociolinguistics with a smile and without the jargon.

When he wrote *The King's English* Amis was confident that he could survive his encroaching illnesses, at one point informing Jacobs that he intended to see in the new millennium. He did not know that it would be his last book, but it carries that air of reflective candour often found in fiction and film when a character suspects that there is not too much time left.

As he points out, it is not 'complete and exhaustive', and many of the entries become a kind of prompter for digressive recollections. Read from A to Z, it is rather like an informal supplement to his *Memoirs*. The entry on 'Four-letter words' tells us of how Jim Dixon's lecherous inclinations were 'virtually limited to his imagination', unlike his author who 'was conscious of no unnatural restriction at the time or later'. Amis has, he admits, used 'fuck' in print but sparingly and only in his later novels, while Martin in *Dead Babies* 'used the word several dozen times in one page'. Larkin, he recalls, used it frequently in his letters as a means of being mildly subversive and to encourage the recipient to 'feel he was a member of the same secret army as the sender'.

Under 'Shibboleth' he cites the case of a Moroccan who insists that his name should be pronounced 'Sam-EER' rather than 'Sham-EER', the S as SH pronunciation being favoured by the Israelis. Sameer, Amis informs us, is a character in *Coronation Street*.

Wales, and Amis's unpatronizing affection for it, features in several entries, Leonard Bardwell's interest in Romanish is mentioned in the 'Dialect or language' piece, and Amis's fond recollections of the 1958–9 visit to Princeton opens the section on 'Americanisms'. The more disagreeable year in Nashville is not referred to.

The unusual entry on 'Typewriter vs word-processor' is the

occasion for an account of how Amis writes his books, including an exchange between himself and an energetic advertising agent who wants to cite Amis as a convert to the new technology. Amis informs him that his typewriter involves a self-imposed disciplinary regime and that the 'typewriter or something even more primitive, like a human hand holding a pen' maintains a kind of material link between the user of the words and their eventual recipient.

A brief and curious piece called 'From year to year' examines the various written conventions by which a period of time is specified, such as 'He served in the Royal Pikestaffs from 1965 to 1980.' Surely this evocation of the hardships and endurances of army service has no connection with the no doubt randomly selected dates, the first being the year he married Jane, the second the year she left him.

Amis's constant interweaving of dry humour and personal anecdote with entries that reflect his authoritative command of language is a reasonably accurate extension of his life and work. He would compensate for the various setbacks, calamities and frustrations of his existence, many self-inflicted, in two ways. He never stopped writing, and his meticulous attention to linguistic correctness indicated that whatever else happened there was something durable and certain in which he could involve himself. His sense of humour, although sometimes less than charitable to others, never left him. He used comedy in a way that has since the eighteenth century been relegated to the second division in the league of literary endeavour. When we are laughing with Amis or at his literary world, or even if we refuse to do so and substitute offence for amusement, there is a sense of immediacy which draws his presence out beyond his fictive creation. Moreover he is serious *because* he is funny. To locate similar, respected writers for whom 'comic incident' is subtly interwoven with an accessible and challenging echo of their contemporary world we must turn back to the age of Pope, Swift and Fielding. Amis did not write parables or submit disguised solutions to personal, intellectual or political problems, because to have done so would have been in one sense boring and in another pointless, since literature, as Auden put it, 'makes nothing happen'. I'll close with a quotation I have already cited. The words are uttered by Nash, the cynical psychiatrist of *Stanley and the Women*, but the real speaker is Amis. It crystallizes the close relationship between the man, his life and his writings and is his essential literary and personal precept.

> The rewards for being sane are not many but knowing what's funny is one of them. And that's an end of the matter.

Select Bibliography
Including works cited in the text

WORKS BY KINGSLEY AMIS

Novels
Lucky Jim (London: Victor Gollancz, 1954)
That Uncertain Feeling (London: Victor Gollancz, 1955)
I Like It Here (London: Victor Gollancz, 1958)
Take a Girl Like You (London: Victor Gollancz, 1960)
One Fat Englishman (London: Victor Gollancz, 1963)
The Egyptologists, with Robert Conquest (London: Jonathan Cape, 1965)
The Anti-Death League (London: Victor Gollancz, 1966)
Colonel Sun, as Robert Markham (London: Jonathan Cape, 1968)
I Want It Now (London: Jonathan Cape, 1968)
The Green Man (London: Jonathan Cape, 1969)
Girl, 20 (London: Jonathan Cape, 1971)
The Riverside Villas Murder (London: Jonathan Cape, 1973)
Ending Up (London: Jonathan Cape, 1974)
The Alteration (London: Jonathan Cape, 1976)
Jake's Thing (London: Hutchinson, 1978)
Russian Hide and Seek (London: Hutchinson, 1980)
Stanley and the Women (London: Hutchinson, 1984)
The Old Devils (London: Hutchinson, 1986)
The Crime of the Century (London: J.M. Dent, 1987)
Difficulties with Girls (London: Hutchinson, 1988)
The Folks That Live on the Hill (London: Hutchinson, 1990)
The Russian Girl (London: Hutchinson, 1992)
You Can't Do Both (London: Hutchinson, 1994)
The Biographer's Moustache (London: HarperCollins, 1995)

Poetry

Bright November (London: Fortune Press, 1947)
A Frame of Mind (Reading: School of Art, University of Reading, 1953)
Kingsley Amis: No. 22, The Fantasy Poets (Oxford: Fantasy Press, 1954)
A Case of Samples: Poems 1946–1956 (London: Victor Gollancz, 1956)
The Evans Country (Oxford: Fantasy Press, 1962)
A Look Round the Estate: Poems 1957–1967 (London: Jonathan Cape, 1967)
Collected Poems 1944–1979 (London: Hutchinson, 1979)

Short stories

My Enemy's Enemy (London: Victor Gollancz, 1962)
Dear Illusion (London: Covent Garden Press, 1972)
The Darkwater Hall Mystery (Edinburgh: Tragara Press, 1978)
Collected Short Stories (London: Hutchinson, 1980; 1987, including 'Investing in Futures' and 'Affairs of Death')

Criticism

New Maps of Hell: A Survey of Science Fiction (London: Victor Gollancz, 1961)
What Became of Jane Austen? and Other Questions (London: Jonathan Cape, 1970)
'Four Fluent Fellows: An Essay on Chesterton's Fiction', in *G.K. Chesterton: A Centenary Appraisal*, ed. J. Sullivan (London: Paul Elek, 1973)

Works edited or with contributions by Amis

Oxford Poetry 1949, with James Michie (Oxford: Basil Blackwell, 1949)
G.K. Chesterton: Selected Stories (London: Faber and Faber, 1972)
Tennyson, Poet to Poet series (Harmondsworth: Penguin, 1973)
Introduction to G.K. Chesterton, *The Man Who Was Thursday* (Harmondsworth: Penguin, 1986)

Miscellaneous writings

Socialism and the Intellectuals (London: Fabian Society, 1957)
Lucky Jim's Politics (London: Conservative Political Centre, 1968)
An Arts Policy? (London: Centre for Policy Studies, 1979)
The Amis Collection (London: Hutchinson, 1990)
Memoirs (London: Hutchinson, 1991)
The King's English: A Guide to Modern Usage (London: HarperCollins, 1997)
The Letters of Kingsley Amis, ed. Zachary Leader (London: HarperCollins, 2000)

BOOKS AND ESSAYS ON AMIS

Amis, Martin, *Experience* (London: Jonathan Cape, 2000)

Bradford, Richard, *Kingsley Amis* (London: Edward Arnold, 1989)

Fussell, Paul, *The Anti-Egotist: Kingsley Amis, Man of Letters* (Oxford: Oxford University Press, 1994)

Gardner, Philip, *Kingsley Amis* (Boston: Twayne, 1981)

Jacobs, Eric, *Kingsley Amis: A Biography* (London: Hodder and Stoughton, 1995)

McDermott, John, *Kingsley Amis: An English Moralist* (London: Macmillan, 1989)

Moseley, Merritt, *Understanding Kingsley Amis* (Charleston: South Carolina University Press, 1993)

Salwak, Dale, *Kingsley Amis: Modern Novelist* (London: Harvester, 1992)

OTHER WORKS CITED IN THE TEXT

Fowler, Roger, *Linguistics and the Novel* (London: Methuen, 1977)

Josipovici, Gabriel, *The World and the Book* (London: Macmillan, 1971)

Larkin, Philip, *Collected Poems*, ed. A. Thwaite (London: Faber and Faber, 1988)

Larkin, Philip, *Required Writing: Miscellaneous Pieces 1955–1982* (London: Faber and Faber, 1983)

Lodge, David, 'The Modern, the Contemporary and the Importance of Being Amis', in *The Language of Fiction* (London: Routledge and Kegan Paul, 1966)

Lodge, David, *The Modes of Modern Writing: Metaphor, Metonymy and the Typology of Modern Fiction* (London: Routledge and Kegan Paul, 1977)

Motion, Andrew, *Philip Larkin: A Writer's Life* (London: Faber and Faber, 1993)

Paulin, Tom, 'The Cruelty That Is Natural', an article on *Jake's Thing*, reprinted in *Ireland and the English Crisis* (Newcastle upon Tyne: Bloodaxe Books, 1984)

Phelps, Gilbert, 'The Novel Today', in *The Penguin Guide to English Literature*, Vol. 7, *The Modern Age* (Harmondsworth: Penguin, 1973)

Thwaite, Anthony (ed.), *Selected Letters of Philip Larkin, 1940–85* (London: Faber and Faber, 1992)

Index